Chengadu and Scheepers have edited an important and innovative book, bringing to life the often unheard voices of female leaders in emerging markets and challenging the dominant narrative of Western and Euro-centric leadership paradigms. Through this framework, the editors skill-fully illuminate the resilience of these pioneers and the trends they are setting.

Debora Spar, *President, Barnard College, USA*

From this book, I learned that the notion 'glass ceiling' often has no relevance, particularly in environments where people are happy to have any 'ceiling' above them. The book confirms that gender balance is a success factor in business and society, particularly in emerging markets. It is full of examples of how visionary, entrepreneurial, and courageous women can be agents of change in their organisations and societies.

Danica Purg, *President of IEDC-Bled School of Management, President of CEEMAN, Slovenia*

Women Leadership in Emerging Markets

This book focuses on the increase in female leadership over the last fifty years, and the concrete benefits and challenges this leads to in organizations. It moves beyond the typical focus on developed, Western contexts and answers the call for research on how women in emerging markets rise above the proverbial "glass ceiling".

The authors integrate two underdeveloped topics that are highly relevant to modern business: women in leadership roles, and women in emerging markets. They examine how women leaders in a range of professional services—including accounting, consulting, law, engineering and medicine—have managed to navigate their careers while considering the role emerging markets play in their work. Based on cutting-edge research, the topics are brought to life through examples and profiles of leading women across Africa, the Middle East, and the Far East. These narratives, told in the leaders' own words, are key to understanding women's achievements and the barriers they face.

Students of leadership, diversity, gender studies, and human resource management will learn much from this insightful book.

Shireen Chengadu is an adjunct faculty member at the Gordon Institute of Business Science, University of Pretoria, and Founding Director of Chengadu Advisory, both in South Africa. Her advisory business and lecturing expertise lie in unlocking full leadership value through the intersectionality of gender, race and class, and business, government, and society.

Caren Scheepers is Senior Lecturer on Contextual Leadership and Organizational Development and Change at the Gordon Institute of Business Science, University of Pretoria, South Africa. She holds a PhD in Psychology and is an accredited professional coach with the International Coaching Federation.

Women Leadership in Emerging Markets

Featuring 46 Women Leaders

Edited by
Shireen Chengadu and Caren Scheepers

Routledge
Taylor & Francis Group

NEW YORK AND LONDON

First published 2017
by Routledge
711 Third Avenue, New York, NY 10017

and by Routledge
2 Park Square, Milton Park, Abingdon, Oxon OX14 4RN

Routledge is an imprint of the Taylor & Francis Group, an informa business

Library of Congress Cataloging in Publication Data
Names: Chengadu, Shireen, editor. | Scheepers, Caren B. (Caren Brenda), editor.
Title: Women leadership in emerging markets : featuring 50 women leaders / edited by Shireen Chengadu and Caren Scheepers.
Description: 1 Edition. | New York : Routledge, 2017. | Includes bibliographical references and index.
Identifiers: LCCN 2016057005| ISBN 9781138188952 (hardback) | ISBN 9781138188969 (pbk.) | ISBN 9781315641959 (ebook)
Subjects: LCSH: Leadership in women–Developing countries.
Classification: LCC HQ1233 .W5967 2017 | DDC 305.42–dc23
LC record available at https://lccn.loc.gov/2016057005

ISBN: 978-1-138-18895-2 (hbk)
ISBN: 978-1-138-18896-9 (pbk)
ISBN: 978-1-315-64195-9 (ebk)

Typeset in Times New Roman
by Taylor & Francis Books

The editors would like to thank the peer reviewers at Routledge and Prof Albert Wöcke; Prof Karl Hofmeyr and Dr Charlene Lew for their reviews.

Contents

Illustrations

Figures

Tables

Contributors

Kelly Alexander presently holds the position of Research Associate (Business Intelligence) at African Management Services Company (AMSCO). She has been responsible for the development and implementation of AMSCO's enterprise-wide strategic mapping framework and facilitating company and divisional strategy development through the provision of strategic insight and data on industry trends.

Cecily Carmona is Associated Director with management consulting firm A.T. Kearney, in their Johannesburg office. Cecily is extremely active in promoting women in business and plays a significant role for A.T. Kearney globally in their Women's Network, including writing and contributing to thought leadership on the topic.

Shireen Chengadu is an Adjunct faculty member at University of Pretoria's Gordon Institute of Business Science (GIBS) and holds an acting director position at the University of Pretoria. She runs Chengadu Advisory, a Leadership and Advisory practice. Over the last decade Shireen has built extensive experience in the areas of business and management education and has gained board-level experience in the education, consulting and NGO sectors.

Desray Clark is employed by Anglo American, where she is a principal specialist at the state-of-the-art Centre for Experiential Learning. As a leadership development specialist, her analytical abilities and conceptual skills combined with her deep theoretical understanding of the issues surrounding leaders in the workplace enable her to design and deliver exceptional programs for developing leaders.

Kerry-Lee Durrant is a research assistant at Gordon Institute of Business Science. Her passion for education and learning and desire to be surrounded by excellence has had a huge influence on her career choice. Her work within GIBS over the last six years has been focused on ensuring excellence in program execution and logistics, working closely with business leaders, society leaders, government leaders and international professors from across the world on a variety of specialized programs.

Verity Hawarden has over twenty years' experience in both corporate and small businesses in South Africa. Verity is a director and partner in Abbellard Business Innovation, a gender balance consultancy. She is involved in client engagement and the design and delivery of both facilitated workshops centred on gender diversity and women's leadership development programs.

Maxine Jaffit consults widely in the field of organization development, specializing in the impact of corporate culture on individual, group and organizational performance. She started Maxine Jaffit & Associates in 1999 and works in South Africa and the USA, facilitating leadership development, strategy, corporate culture research and the implementation of various organizational change initiatives.

Jasmien Khattab is a PhD candidate in organizational behavior at the Rotterdam School of Management, Erasmus University Rotterdam. Other keywords that describe Jasmien's research interests are team diversity, diversity management and inclusion, leader group prototypicality and authentic leadership.

Pravina Makan-Lakha is a development specialist with multifaceted experience in executive leadership and management in the development sector. Pravina is currently General Manager of Business Development and a member of the executive committee at ACCORD (African Center for the Constructive Resolution of Disputes).

Renuka Methil is Editor of *Forbes Woman Africa*, a bi-monthly pan-African women's interest magazine brought out by the Africa Business News Group in Johannesburg, which profiles powerful, influential and inspirational women on the continent.

Yogavelli (Yogi) Nambiar is Director of the Enterprise Development Academy at the Gordon Institute of Business Science (GIBS), the business school of the University of Pretoria. She started the Academy in 2014 to offer scholarship-based education and support to entrepreneurs of start-up, micro- and small enterprises who were previously marginalised or underserved.

Mpho Nkeli is currently Director of Search Partners International (SPi). She trained as an environmental scientist and moved into marketing, communications, social investment and enterprise development.

Hema Parbhoo is founder and Director of independent consulting practice Umbo Human Potential Solutions. Hema Parbhoo's passion is in creating direction, alignment and commitment across organizations and individuals, thereby "Igniting their Potential".

Ashleigh Shelby Rosette is a tenured associate professor of Management and Organizations and a Center of Leadership and Ethics scholar at the

Fuqua School of Business at Duke University. She was ranked as one of the Fifty Most Influential Business Professors by mbarankings.net and one of the Forty Best Business School Professors Under Forty by Poets & Quants.

Caren Scheepers is a registered counseling psychologist with the Health Professions Council of South Africa and has Professional Coach certification with the International Coaching Federation (ICF). She is currently a senior lecturer at the Gordon Institute of Business Science (GIBS), University of Pretoria, lecturing on the Organisational Development and Transformation MBA program, an MBA elective titled Contextual Leadership Intelligence and various company-specific programs.

Sunny Stout-Rostron coaches at senior executive and board level and has a wide range of experience in leadership development and business strategy. Sunny has played a leading role in building the emerging profession of coaching and her passion is developing the knowledge base for coaching through research and the critical reflective practice of dedicated practitioners.

Sonja Swart has been an independent change consultant, running her own change-management practice, Sonja Swart Change Consulting, since 2000. She consults on a variety of areas, namely executive coaching, design and implementation of change processes, design and implementation of people performance and development strategies, team effectiveness workshops and conflict resolution workshops.

Shirley Zinn is currently Group Head of Human Resources at Woolworths Holdings Limited. She also registered her own company, Shirley Zinn Consulting, which provides consulting and advisory services in HR, transformation, leadership and education.

List of interviewees

Aneshree Naidoo is currently CFO at Deloitte Consulting Africa. Finance standardisation and automation are her primary focus. She prides herself on being a "millennial" and uses traditional practices like connecting with teams and strong work ethic to enhance results through systems "connectivity".

Barbara Dale-Jones is the CEO of BRIDGE, an educational NPO. She has experience in organizational leadership and management, strategic planning and execution, project management, knowledge management, e-learning and publishing.

Barbara Creecy belongs to Gauteng Finance MEC. Ms Creecy was elected to the Gauteng Provincial Legislature in 1994. She has served the legislature for ten years in a number of capacities, including Deputy Chief Whip and Chairperson of the Social Development and Education committees.

Barçın Yinanç is currently opinion editor of the English-language *Hürriyet Daily News*, where her columns are also published. She also conducts the paper's weekly interviews. She is invited to provide her comments to various international media outlets such as BBC Radio, Al Jazeera English and France 24.

Betty Bigombe, a Ugandan national, has played a key role in conflict resolution in Africa. Her career has included a development focus in previous positions at the African Development Bank and at the World Bank, where she was a senior social scientist focusing on gender and conflict, disarmament and child soldiers.

Brand Pretorius joined McCarthy Motor Holdings as Chairman and CEO and was promoted to CEO of the holding company, McCarthy Retail Limited, in October 1999. Brand has received numerous national marketing, motor industry and leadership awards, including Marketing Person of the Year, Automobile Man of the Year and Boss of the Year.

Cheryl de la Rey has been Vice-Chancellor and Principal of the University of Pretoria since November 2009. Her previous executive positions include Chief Executive Officer of the Council on Higher Education, Deputy Vice-Chancellor at the University of Cape Town and Executive Director at the National Research Foundation.

Daniela Chikova presently holds the position of Partner Financial Services at A.T. Kearney. With over fifteen years of consulting and industry experience, Daniela is a leading expert in banking, with a focus on topline growth strategies.

Deepa Vallabh is a director at Cliffe Dekker Hofmeyr within the Corporate and Commercial practice and is Head of Cross-Border M&A for Africa & Asia. Deepa specialises in a number of legal areas, including mergers and acquisitions (both domestic and cross-border), corporate reorganizations and restructurings.

Deirdre Venter is an equity partner in the Employment and Employee Benefits Practice of Webber Wentzel. Deirdre, in addition to practising law, is an accomplished conciliator and arbitrator of disputes in her role as a part-time commissioner of the CCMA.

Dion Shango was appointed as Southern Africa CEO of PWC on 1 July 2015, the first black African to be appointed to the role. In addition to his experience in the mining industry, Dion has also enjoyed exposure to other sectors and industries throughout his career, by virtue of being involved in the audits of companies and organizations such as the South African Reserve Bank, Vodacom and MonteCasino.

Dolly Mokgatle is an executive director at Peotona Group Holdings. Prior to serving as CEO of Spoornet, she was MD of the Transmission Group in Eskom where she was the first woman, first black person and first non-technical person to be appointed to that position.

Edith Kikonyogo is an engineering professional with solid managerial experience in both business development and operational roles. She currently holds a general management role, heading up the Power Generation Service business of a global power and automation technology company in Africa.

Edward Kieswetter retired recently from Alexander Forbes, as Group Chief Executive 2010–2016. Edward is a life-long scholar with a keen interest in leadership, as well as a committed servant leader actively involved in community and social projects.

Ekaterina Sheremet presently holds the position of Principal at A.T. Kearney, the leading global management consulting firm. She joined A.T. Kearney in 2008 and held various positions at the company (Manager, Associate and Senior Business Analyst).

Elena Escagedo is presently Senior Advisor to Executive Education at IE Business School. As an executive coach Elena has participated in more than eighty different coaching processes. Prior to being Director of Open Enrolment Programs at the IE Business School, Elena was a controller for three business units (Management College, IT College and College of Law).

Francie Shonhiwa's professional experience spans more than forty years in agro-industry, engineering and diversified manufacturing, with extensive experience in social entrepreneurial development. Francie retired from the corporate world and in March 2016 set up the Francie Shonhiwa

Foundation, which focuses on the empowerment of women and the youth of Zimbabwe.

Geraldine Joslyn Fraser-Molekti is a special envoy on Gender at the African Development Bank, where she leads a strategy to mainstream gender in the bank's policies and operations, making the bank a reference institution on gender equality in Africa.

Gert Schoonbee was appointed Managing Director of T-Systems in South Africa in 2012. Gert has more than twenty years' experience in the ICT industry, spanning all the key sectors and playing different roles in areas such as Solution Crafting, Business Development and Sales.

GG Alcock, fluent in Zulu and conversant in most South African ethnic languages, is founder, CEO and creative and strategy guru of Minanawe Marketing. Minanawe Marketing develops and runs marketing campaigns built on strong consumer insights and understanding.

Gil Oved is an astute businessman and serial entrepreneur. Gil is co-CEO of The Creative Counsel (TCC), which he co-founded with Ran Neu-Ner in 2001. Carefree yet serious, Gil pays more than mere lip service to being innovative and bold; he injects creativity and fun into his daily working environment.

Gill Marcus was appointed Governor of the South African Reserve Bank 2009–2014, the first woman to hold such a position, and in this capacity represented South Africa at meetings of various international bodies such as the Bank for International Settlements and the G20.

Isabel Neiva is a principal with A.T. Kearney, focusing on the Communications, Media and Technology practice for the Middle East and Africa. Isabel has built solid expertise in the communications industry, with a special focus on strategy and cost optimization.

Johan Aurik is A.T. Kearney's managing partner and Chairman of the Board, a position he assumed in January 2013. Johan has been a partner with A.T. Kearney since 1997 and has more than 25 years of consulting experience with the firm in the consumer and retail, transportation and chemicals industries.

Joyce Banda, former President of the Republic of Malawi, is an entrepreneur and activist, a politician and philanthropist. Her Excellency was voted Africa's most powerful woman by Forbes Magazine for two years running and also voted one of the most powerful women in the world.

Lerato Mosiah is a founding director of Lerato Group (Pty) Ltd, a woman-owned black economic empowerment (BEE) company formed in 2015. Its main aim is to harness and build business partnerships with strategic partners in the healthcare and energy sectors in order to participate in BEE opportunities.

Marianne Roux is a partner in Silverstone Edge Consulting, a leading strategy, transformation, executive leadership development, coaching and organizational development consulting firm operating across Australia, New Zealand and Asia.

Martha Cecilia Bernal Uribe runs her own management development advisory company, with a wide expert network from around the world. During her time at the UniAndes School of Management in Colombia she built the Executive Education Unit into what it is today.

Martly Rademeyer currently holds the position of T-Systems International (TSI) Diversity Manager at TSI Human Resources. This includes increasing the inclusiveness, gender equality and internationalization of TSI. Working in nine different countries across four continents has given her wide experience.

Melanie Botha is an international business executive with an insatiable appetite for igniting new businesses and unleashing untapped potential. A key focus area during her tenure at Microsoft was to establish the Women in Leadership Academy to grow and expand the skills of middle-management females.

Mónica Sacristán has been Dean of Executive Development and University Extension at ITAM since 1999. Monica has been responsible for all Executive Development operations, and has designed, coordinated and lectured in several open enrolment and custom executive education programs for the Mexican branches of international companies.

Nicky Newton-King has been Chief Executive of the Johannesburg Stock Exchange since January 2012. Nicky was a World Economic Forum Global Leader of Tomorrow and subsequently a WEF Young Global Leader. She was South Africa's 2003 Businesswoman of the Year.

Nicola Kleyn has held the position of Dean of the University of Pretoria's Gordon Institute of Business Science (GIBS) since April 2015. In addition to her executive management responsibilities at GIBS, she is an active researcher and teacher.

Ntombi Langa-Royds has thirty years' experience in the human resources environment. She has worked in financial services, manufacturing, electronic and print media industries. Ntombi has been a part-time faculty member at USB-ED (Executive Development Ltd, University of Stellenbosch Business School) and is a member of its international advisory board; she is involved in the MAT program at Wits Business School and has contributed to the INSETA programs at Wits and the University of Cape Town (UCT).

Phatho Zondi is a sports and exercise medicine (SEM) physician experienced in clinical sports medicine, medical strategy and leadership. She is passionate about developing and mentoring young women and future leaders of South Africa.

Phumzile Mlambo-Ngcuka is United Nations Under-Secretary-General and Executive Director of UN Women. She is the founder of the Umlambo Foundation, which supports leadership and education. A long-time champion of women's rights, she is affiliated with several organizations devoted to education, women's empowerment and gender equality.

Phuthi Mahanyele is Executive Chairperson of Sigma Capital. Phuthi mentors young professionals, supports students and is involved with the

"Dignity Day" program. She is a patron of NEET (National Education Empowerment Trust), an honorary member of the Golden Key International Honour Society and a patron of the Bosele Foundation.

Polo Leteka is co-founder and CEO of IDF Managers, an entrepreneurial SME financier which she established in 2007. IDF Managers manages multiple funds for institutional and corporate investors and received the "ABSIP Emerging Women-owned Company Award 2015".

Priscilla Seki, a partner at A.T. Kearney, is leader of Strategy, Marketing and Sales in Brazil. She has fourteen years' experience in management consulting with local and international corporate clients.

Ramyani Basu is a senior principal with A.T. Kearney, responsible for driving technology and digital transformation across industries within the UK and Irish markets. Within A.T. Kearney she has passionately championed the Women Career Progression initiative at EMEA level to drive gender parity.

Rania Habiby Anderson is a leading expert on the career advancement of women in emerging economies, an international speaker and an executive coach. The founder of the global women's platform, The Way Women Work, Rania speaks to, advises, trains and writes for women and men at corporations, universities and conferences.

Renuka Methil is Editor of *Forbes Woman Africa*, a bi-monthly Pan-African women's interest magazine brought out by the Africa Business News Group in Johannesburg, which profiles powerful, influential and inspirational women on the continent.

Roelof Petrus (Roelf) Meyer is a director of In Transformation Initiative (ITI), a South African-based institution that focuses on sharing the South African experience in order to contribute to the peaceful resolution of conflict situations worldwide. Until recently he was chair of the South African Defence Review Committee, appointed by the Minister of Defence to recommend on defence policy and strategy.

Rosette Chantal Rugamba is the founder and Managing Director of Songa Africa, one of the leading tour companies in East Africa specializing in luxury tours, consultancies and lodges. She is President of the Women in Tourism Chamber and a board member of the Women's Chamber in the Private Sector Federation.

Sheba Maini is an experienced corporate coach, change management consultant and trainer, addressing the management of change, leadership and business strategy and coaching top management. She is founder and Director of Spirit of Leadership (SOL Management Consultants), a specialized leadership development coaching and consulting firm.

Silvana Machado is a partner at A.T. Kearney in Brazil, where she leads on financial services practice. She has worked extensively in banking, insurance and cards and payments segments, covering such areas as growth strategy design, segmentation and customer management, channel management, organization and transformation and operational efficiency.

Sindi Mabaso-Koyana is currently Chairperson of the African Women Chartered Accountants Investment Holding Company. She is a founder member and former President of African Women Chartered Accountants. Sindi is a renowned leader in and champion of the growth and development of young women.

Stacey Brewer is the co-founder and CEO of SPARK School, eAdvance. She has received numerous awards and media coverage and was recently profiled in a book brought out by the Gordon Institute of Business Science, *The Disruptors: Social Entrepreneurs Reinventing Business and Society*. Stacey believes that improving the state and status of education in South Africa will guarantee the global success of this country and create a prosperous future for all South Africans.

Stella M. Nkomo is Deputy Dean for Research and Postgraduate Studies in the Faculty of Economic and Management Sciences at the University of Pretoria. Professor Nkomo is a sought-after consultant for both profit and not-for-profit organizations addressing issues of diversity management and leadership development and leading change and managing human resources in South Africa, the USA and Europe.

Susan McNerney lives just north of Toronto, Canada, where she pursues entrepreneurial interests alongside her European Bank for Reconstruction and Development (EBRD) contracts in Eastern Europe and Central Asia. As a senior industry advisor for the EBRD Susan has worked with many remarkable women in management in Albania, Kazakhstan, Romania, Bosnia and Herzegovina, and Mongolia.

Thandi Lujabe-Rankoe was South African High Commissioner to Mozambique. She is a pioneer in many respects, having started the first South African High Commission in Tanzania and being one of the first women to document the experience of being exiled from South Africa.

Wendy Ackerman has been a director of Pick 'n Pay since 1981. She joined her husband, Raymond Ackerman, in the business and has been involved in the group's development, employee benefits and welfare. In August 2008 she received an award in recognition of her achievement in the consumer business sector from *CEO Magazine*, which named her as one of SA's most influential women in business and government.

Wendy Appelbaum chairs DeMorgenzon Estate, a wine farm and agricultural business in Stellenbosch. Through the Wendy Appelbaum Foundation her company initiates, selects and drives programs addressing the health and education interests and concerns of South African women.

Wendy Lucas Bull co-founded Peotona Group Holdings in 2005 with Cheryl Carolus, Dolly Mokgatle and Thandi Orleyn. The company has both a for-profit and a non-profit developmental side.

Acknowledgments

A journey like the one we have undertaken to get us to this momentous point of the book would not have been possible without the passionate, instantaneous, persistent and patient support of many individuals. We, the two editors, are hugely indebted to our families, colleagues, friends, sponsors and patrons and we acknowledge the following people in order of how the book project took off and landed. To every individual named: we could not have done this without you, and the success and pride of publishing this book is as much yours as it is ours.

We would like to acknowledge the supreme powers that prevailed to bring all the pieces of the puzzle together to make this magic happen. It is nothing short of a miracle.

To Professor de la Rey, vice-chancellor of the University of Pretoria, we are indebted to you for your financial commitment, expert guidance and leadership support from beginning to end, which extended even to affirming post-publication commitments. Your endorsement of the project and the personal support shown to us made us still more resolved to produce a final product of substance, scalability and longitudinal impact. We hope we have done you proud!

We wish to extend heartfelt gratitude to the following for their various levels of support and their contribution to bringing the book to fruition.

Routledge, for their scholarly reviews, and the academic review panel from the Gordon Institute of Business Science, University of Pretoria, Professor Karl Hofmeyr, Professor Albert Wöcke and Dr Charlene Lew, for their unwavering support and rigor.

Professor Helena Barnard, for getting the book into gear by acting as our academic sounding board and helping us craft the proposal that won the confidence of Routledge.

Professors Nick Binedell, founding dean of the Gordon Institute of Business Science (GIBS), and Kathryn Kolbert, Constance Hess Williams Director of the Athena Center for Leadership Studies, Barnard College, New York—we are grateful to you for the insightful forewords that capture the essence of why our book matters.

Professor Nicola Kleyn, dean of GIBS, we are very thankful to you for your ongoing support, for acting as our sounding board and for your interview.

The 46 women and seven men leaders (whose names appear earlier in the book): we are deeply appreciative of your generosity of spirit, time, knowledge, vigor, energy and passion. You invited us into your homes and offices, across the digital divides, and made it easy for us to engage with you despite your grueling schedules and priorities as leaders. It is your authentic voices that have enabled us to produce a book that is credible.

The chapter leads and co-chapter authors (whose names appear in each chapter): without you, your commitment and your incisive minds we would have struggled to land this book on time and to the required high academic standard. And the fact that you undertook this challenge with no promise of a financial reward, quietly absorbing individual expenses that were incurred, makes you the heroes and winners. You epitomize authenticity.

Kerry-Lee Durrant, Kelly Alexander and Kim Forbes: you became our voices of reason—our backbones—and we loved how you kept us honest and accountable every step of the way. The quiet manner in which you undertook the research and delivered on time enabled the chapter leads to maintain academic rigor.

It is apt at this point that we acknowledge the GIBS Information Centre members, who went beyond the call of duty in sourcing the best literature and academic articles for us. Thank you, ladies.

Kerry-Lee and Kovashni Gordhan: your excellent project management skills and your ability to keep us sane and our heads above water in the trickiest and most harrowing of times is testament to the strength and resilience of women. The fact that you undertook this as a labor of love with, respectively, no and little pay makes us forever indebted to you.

Kelly Young: you are one of the finest young editors we have ever worked with. You took on the project quite late on in the process and without the clearest of guidelines or firm timelines and you made the magic happen. Thank you, Kelly.

We also thank the transcribers, Pegasus Transcription Services: Ellen Kriel and various individual editors who were contracted independently by individual chapter leads.

And without the guidance and ongoing support of Sharon Golan (Acquisitions Editor) and Erin Arata (Editorial Assistant), US Business and Management, Routledge/Taylor & Francis Group, we would not have got to this glorious point.

We would like to wholeheartedly thank the artist Andre Swanepoel (Swany) for the photograph of the artwork in his possession of the "Corset" series.

In advance, we also wish to acknowledge the overwhelming commitments we have received to host book launch events in South Africa and Mauritius. We are deeply appreciative of the generosity of the University of Pretoria, GIBS and the many corporate entities and individuals who have pledged support. We can't wait to get the show on the road!

While we have previously acknowledged Kerry-Lee Durrant for specific roles she played throughout the process, we wish to make special mention of this young woman's dedication, commitment, passion and abundant optimism from the word go! Kerry-Lee's calm demeanor, compassion and thirst for knowledge made our admiration for her grow from day to day. Even when our steam and patience waned she managed to keep us in check. Thank you, dearest Kerry-Lee—you have won the hearts of all who worked with you throughout this journey. We foresee a bright future for you!

We wish to acknowledge our dearest and nearest: our families! Without your inspiration, your endless tolerance and intellectual guidance, the endless cups of coffee, meals, shoulder rubs, high tolerance thresholds and the sacrifice of many, many weekends and long working nights we would not have reached this ecstatic point of conclusion.

This beautiful end result is as much mine as it is yours, my treasured and loving family. To my husband Raj, son Kreeson, daughter Nicole and my precious puppies Scooby and Doo, you kept me inspired and energized through the journey. You are my abundant source of all that is good and beautiful in life. I am indebted to my dearest siblings, whose constant support and love kept me true to my north star. And finally, I acknowledge my late mum and gran; they are the giants on whose shoulders I stand and they continue to be the wind beneath my wings. The women in my family epitomize what women of substance can achieve even in the most adverse of times. And it is the loving and generous men in our family who allow us to be disruptive—often! It is the constant love, contentment and real peace I feel, surrounded by my family, that enables me to take on the big, hairy, audacious goals.

May our passions and purposeful lives be the catalyst for bigger flames and greater agency and urgency. (Shireen Chengadu)

It was a privilege to be part of this momentous research project and the pure grace involved in finishing this book. I am grateful to my source, Jesus Christ. I acknowledge my husband Marius for consistently encouraging me to fulfill my potential; my children Clarisse and Darius for their support; my in-laws, colleagues and friends for their interest. I am grateful for my mother's role model of dedication and perseverance. Sadly, due to Alzheimer's she will not be celebrating this milestone with us. My parents' financial contribution to my education was invaluable. I would like to thank the various institutions—the University of the Free State; the University of Cape Town, Centre for Creative Leadership (Brussels); and the University of Pretoria—for creating my learning space. The Gordon Institute of Business Science has offered me the opportunity of a lifetime—thank you for your support!

May this book make a significant difference to current and future "Women leaders in emerging markets"! (Caren Scheepers).

Overview and orientation

The journey of this book has been an interesting and rich one, starting off in a meandering fashion, then adopting a firm, strong path as collaborations and synergies unfurled and flowed. The book concept initially germinated in the minds of the editors, but the initial gentle humming turned into insistent and raging sounds in their heads and cascaded when they worked alongside each other in another book project on leadership. Catalyzed by that collaboration and hastened by first-hand experiences and their roles as lecturers at the University of Pretoria's Gordon Institute of Business Science (GIBS), as supervisors of GIBS MBA students' dissertations and as researchers and business consultants, their sense of agency and urgency became greater as they heard more of the dominant rhetoric on gender debates and gender inclusion discourses that were happening in and out of their classrooms.

Layered on that was their own history and journeys as women leaders, both South African women yet as diverse as could be, one coming from a middle-class white, Afrikaner family and the other an Indian woman, an intimate product of the apartheid legacy, wizened by first-hand experiences of "othering" or of being the "out-group" and raised by a single working-class mother and grandmother. There was not what might be described as a natural attraction, but what drew them together was their deep and passionate interest in leadership, women's leadership in particular, and the relevance of leadership diversity in a highly complex and uncertain world. Through a series of ongoing engagements they began to appreciate how gender, complicated by the simultaneity of race, class, traditions, culture, religion, socio-economic narratives and where women were geographically located, shaped their leadership narratives.

Compelled by a desire to make further contributions to the existing literature describing or accounting for barriers to or opportunities for women to reach their full potential as leaders, the editors wanted to challenge the dominant narratives located particularly in Western or Euro-centric paradigms of leadership. This is where the concept of writing a peer-reviewed book on women's leadership in emerging markets became the loudest in our heads. As we pondered who we should interview for the book, we knew that we primarily wanted the voices of women leaders in emerging markets from a diverse range of sectors—but it also dawned on us that the narratives could not and should not only be by women, about women and for women, so we decided to talk to a handful of male leaders to hear their perspectives on female leaders in emerging markets, given the fact that it is still men overwhelmingly at the helm of institutions.

Then another gnawing thought took hold! Why not bring in other women from our networks—academics and practitioners, local and global—to contribute as chapter leads! The rationale for this became more compelling: instead of having two authors' narratives dominate the book, in the interest of true inclusion and diversity of thinking and practice and in the interest of "debunking" the myth that women (especially A-type personalities) can't work effectively together, we decided to embrace the challenge to disprove the notion. And we did! Of course, the flow of the tide was not always easy, plain sailing or one-directional, but that is precisely what we wanted in order to bring you the best and richest version of the book. We believed the diversity would make for a more compelling read.

As we pondered and debated pitches for expression of interest to potential publishers, a miracle happened. An angel in the form of Professor Helena Barnard, a well-respected researcher and scholar, a frequent conference participant and presenter, was heading off to an Academy of Management gig in the US and she brightly suggested that we craft a concept paper for presentation to publishers who gather at such events. So Helena, another amazing woman, got involved. Her involvement shattered another gender stereotype: that women don't help other women to get to higher levels of success. Helena weighed in, pushed and prodded our concept note into shape and off she went armed with our paper, absolute goodwill and a genuine interest in landing us the best publisher. And here we are some twenty-two months later, in a very exciting phase.

Finally, another miracle brought this book to fruition. We had no financial support to make the book a reality. How on earth were we going to pay chapter contributors and a project team, cover travel costs and incidentals? We were either overly optimistic or naively stupid but we just thought if we landed the deal with a reputable publisher, the rest would fall into place. And by the grace of God and the goodwill of many, many individuals who gave most generously of their time and expertise, the book is here.

We hope you will enjoy reading and extracting value from *Women Leadership in Emerging Markets* as much as we loved the journey of researching and writing it for you.

Emerging markets are generally patriarchal societies with large-scale poverty and severe inequality. Although there are pockets of excellence, the basic human needs of the majority of citizens are not fulfilled. The few women in powerful leadership positions are isolated cases of resilient pioneers in a male-dominated work and entrepreneurial environment. The 46 women leaders profiled in this book epitomize these extraordinary women.

We acknowledge those women within emerging markets who do not even have access to clean drinking water, safety, healthcare or education, let alone a decent job with career prospects. We also acknowledge those women who leaked through the leadership pipeline, whom we did not interview. Future projects might include them.

This research project focused on a sample of women leaders in the context of emerging markets who rose above the proverbial "glass ceiling". We were curious about what enabled them to achieve this and were interested in their perspective on the barriers for others. From a contextual leadership perspective, as described in Chapter 2, we investigated how women, despite obviously not fitting the leadership prototype of the time or the emerging markets context, overcame the barriers. Most current research has been conducted in more developed Western contexts. This book answers the call of a number of leadership scholars for academic studies within other environments and it contributes to the body of knowledge on women's leadership in emerging markets. We investigate whether women leaders in emerging markets had similar experiences to those in developed markets. Chapter 3, for example, concentrates on nine emerging market countries and shares perspectives on the evolution of women's issues in these unique contexts.

Another contribution is the deep-delve into a number of different work environments. Scholarly and popular press publications on women's issues frequently describe corporate environments (discussed in Chapters 9 and 10 of our book), whereas educational institutions (Chapter 4), political leadership (Chapter 1), entrepreneurial (Chapter 7) and professional services (Chapter 8) receive limited attention. We found that these contexts offer unique challenges that require focused attention. Our chapters are therefore centered on these distinctive landscapes and our discussion on the corporate environment is balanced with discussions about the entrepreneurial, educational and professional services landscapes.

Women leaders from a range of contexts were interviewed for this volume, through which we hope ultimately to contribute to workplace gender equity. The book offers persuasive learning material for academics and trainers in women's management education, in response to the UN Women's seven Principles for Responsible Management Education. While statistical evidence on the lack of representation of women at top management levels in emerging markets is valuable, the personal accounts of women leaders are essential to shed light on the numbers. This book fulfils that requirement by quoting numerous interviewees' actual experiences of real life and unique work environments.

The logical flow between chapters tells the story of women's leadership in emerging markets based on Von Bertalanffy's classic general systems

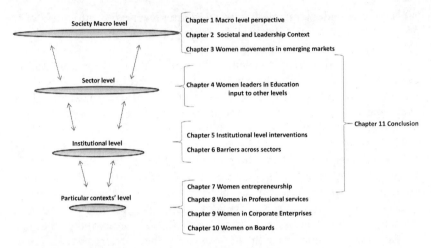

Figure 0.1 Levels of system as framework for chapters

theory (Von Bertalanffy 1973), as discussed in Chapter 11. His hierarchical system levels form the framework for the chapter sequence. The first chapters offer larger perspectives, while the chapters that follow are more specific to particular contexts. See an illustration of these levels in the figure above.

Table 0.1 Overview of chapters representing societal; sector and institutional levels

Macro-societal level		
1	Macro-level perspective on women's leadership	(Shireen Chengadu and Pravina Makan-Lakha)
2	Women's leadership in context	(Caren Scheepers)
3	Women's movements in emerging markets	(Caren Scheepers, Hema Parbhoo, Sonja Swart and Kelly Alexander)
Sector level		
4	Women leaders in education	(Sunny Stout-Rostron)
Institutional level		
5	Institution-level interventions in women's leadership	(Desray Clark and Verity Hawarden)
6	Workplace barriers faced by women leaders in emerging markets	(Ashleigh Shelby Rosette and Jasmien Khattab

We then delve deeper into particular contexts:

Table 0.2 Overview of chapters representing particular contexts' level

Particular contexts level		
7	Women's leadership in entrepreneurial contexts	(Yogavelli Nambiar and Renuka Methil)
8	Women's leadership in professional services	(Cecily Carmona)
9	Women's leadership in corporate enterprises	(Maxine Jaffit and Kelly Alexander)
10	Women on boards	(Shirley Zinn, Mpho Nkeli, Cecily Carmona and Hema Parbhoo)
11	Conclusion	(Caren Scheepers, Shireen Chengadu and Kerry-Lee Durant)

Chapter 1: Macro-level perspective on women's leadership

In this introductory chapter the authors demonstrate, with evidence, why this book is relevant for the present time and why women's leadership of corporations is important in emerging markets. The authors discuss the dominant arguments for why women matter in leadership and how they can improve company and public service performance. They delve into the role of women's leadership in promoting the competiveness of companies, particularly in emerging markets. Through dialogue with a diverse range of women in leadership roles in emerging markets and by incorporating the views of a small sample of men with leadership experience, the authors provide a framework for a range of perspectives for attracting, developing and retaining top female talent as a mechanism to help improve the financial performance of companies, especially in emerging markets. The authors deliberate on the prevalence and impact of quotas for women's representation.

Chapter 2: Women's leadership in context

This chapter also offers a larger perspective. Where the previous chapter focused on the economic reality around women's leadership, this chapter pays attention to the discourse in current leadership literature. Chapter 2 unpacks the current zeitgeist, or spirit, of our time with regard to women's leadership. The author offers a sociocultural perspective with hindsight and insight into current trends in leadership studies and women's leadership in particular. A broader societal context is thus highlighted, specifically around the social construction of masculinity and femininity. The work landscape as hegemonic masculine context is described, as are women's responses to these challenges. This book explores a variety of environments to obtain a more comprehensive view of the unique experiences of leaders, largely through the accounts of the women leaders interviewed. This chapter is therefore centered around the contextual view on leadership as an introduction to the chapters that follow. An extensive integrative literature review is offered, in the form of a matrix and summary table of arguments, to lay the foundation for succeeding chapters. Themes from a number of interviews of women leaders in various emerging markets are drawn, based on in-depth analysis, coding and frequency counts, as well as a conceptual map of the interrelationships of the identified categories.

This volume gives women leaders in emerging markets a voice for their experiences of leadership, without comparing them to male leaders; instead, the uniqueness of the range of contexts requires unique leadership practices illuminated in succeeding chapters.

Chapter 3: Women's movements in emerging markets

Chapter 3 describes the societal background against which the revelations of the chapters that follow can be understood. The authors dispel myths about women in emerging markets. This chapter also builds on the "leadership in context" thesis of Chapter 2; in particular, patriarchy as a contextual variable with which women have to contend. It examines the evolution of economic and political realities in emerging markets, which form the background for the position of women in these countries.

The authors focus their investigation on the major emerging markets and therefore include the BRIC (Brazil, Russia, China and India) countries. Nine countries are discussed in this chapter, which is structured around the four regions they represent, namely Eastern Europe, featuring Russia and Poland; Southeast Asia, featuring India, Malaysia and China; South America, featuring Brazil and Colombia; and Africa and the Middle East, featuring South Africa and the United Arab Emirates (UAE). The countries are discussed in terms of their histories and dominant ideologies, key milestones and future challenges for women's movements. The authors challenge the claim of a uniform women's experience, arguing that "woman", or gender, is a historical condition rather than a natural fact. The role of women's movements in these regions is compared with Western women's movements. The chapter concludes by integrating the themes revealed in the four regions.

Chapter 4: Women leaders in education

The previous chapters highlighted the importance of education in developing the leadership pipeline and this chapter is dedicated to women leaders in the context of education. The author expresses concern about the shortage of women leaders in higher education; internationally, women continue to be under-represented in prominent academic or managerial positions in the sector.

The author shares the stories of 10 remarkable women from six different regions who play powerful leadership roles at extremely senior levels in education. Every story has its own unique voice and powerful dynamic. These accounts offer in-depth disclosure of their social construction of leadership—and that of others.

The research for this chapter followed a social constructivist approach in which meanings are constructed by the participants from their own stories and new meanings are created. The chapter explores contemporary research into leadership development, noting the emergence of a new leadership paradigm—strongly influenced by women's global contribution to the workplace.

Distributed leadership in educational literature is well recognised and therefore provides a valuable lens for understanding educational leadership specific to women. The 10 women leaders from Colombia, Mexico, Spain, Zimbabwe, South Africa and India have varied and wide-ranging experience in the field of education, and interesting themes are revealed by their stories.

Chapter 5: Institution-level interventions on women's leadership

The next chapter moves on to the institutional system level. The authors contribute cases of institutions working towards a more gender-balanced working environment, culminating in recommendations for organizations. The chapter highlights the responses of organizations faced with the dilemma of choosing an appropriate reaction to the question of how to advance women into leadership positions to create a gender-balanced workplace. Two contrasting approaches are focusing on women's leadership development or focusing on gender-diverse development. This chapter offers a case study for each of these approaches, looking at service firms and an organization in the ICT industry. The authors also present the findings from interviews with champions of gender-balanced working environments within these two industries.

Chapter 6: Workplace barriers faced by women leaders in emerging markets

While Chapter 5 explores two institution-level interventions in two industries, Chapter 6 investigates barriers to women's ascent to the top of organizations across a number of industries and serves as a reality check. The authors investigated 22 interviews with women from a number of emerging markets to ascertain whether women in emerging markets who have successfully worked their way to the top of their organizations experience comparable or distinct barriers compared to women in developed countries.

Chapter 7: Women's entrepreneurship

The authors explain that entrepreneurs are the engines powering the economy and that small business is really big business, citing the contribution of small and medium-sized industries (SMEs) to national economies in emerging markets such as India. They point out that the number of female entrepreneurs across the world is rising. This chapter discusses the historical socio-economic landmarks that have driven women entrepreneurship. The authors quote from a number of studies, including the Forbes Women 2015 research and a study conducted across eight townships in South Africa. The chapter concludes with recommendations for women in entrepreneurial contexts.

Chapter 8: Women's leadership in professional services

The author examines how women leaders in a range of professional services, including accounting, consulting, law, engineering and medicine, have managed to navigate their careers. This chapter investigates the dynamics of particular professional services organizations in relation to women leaders. The author identifies common factors to which women who have been successful attribute their success. Practical actions are suggested for professional service firms to enable women to follow the path to partnership. The author interviewed a number of women in professional services from different emerging markets, including Brazil, Bulgaria, India, Middle East, Russia, South Africa and Uganda, in all the professions mentioned above. The author explains that the medical profession requires serious commitment, with several years of training plus extensive hours of on-call duty, community service and emergency room practice. This chapter contributes to our understanding of the unique challenges faced by women in professional services and offers recommendations to these firms on gender equity.

Chapter 9: Women's leadership in corporate enterprises

In emerging markets, women in corporate enterprises face a unique set of challenges and opportunities—namely, dealing with patriarchal societal norms. This chapter addresses the traditionally male-centric corporate enterprises head on. The authors report how 10 current female leaders were able to develop—personally and professionally—and attain their current positions despite existing gender stereotypes. This chapter provides advice for women in corporate enterprises—specifically women transitioning into senior positions in these organizations.

Chapter 10: Women on boards

This chapter introduces the roles, skills required and selection processes for board members. The authors offer a perspective on gender diversity on boards in emerging markets and share themes from the experiences of the women interviewed. They go on to discuss the challenges of gender parity on boards as well as the existence and effect of quotas and policies.

Chapter 11: Conclusion

This overview highlights seven trends that emerge in this book and considers whether they are consistent with or different from the themes in the literature about women's leadership in the developed world. A number of new concepts, such as "emerging markets threshold" and "access to finance", are suggested and contrasted with the Western notion of the "glass ceiling".

Realities in emerging markets, such as informal relations and mass unemployment are presented. An interesting finding from the research reveals the internal psychological processes of the women interviewed—paralleling their observable leadership journeys. A conceptual framework for this phenomenon, as well as the influencing factors, is offered. The chapter also discusses limitations of the research for the book and provides suggestions for further research. It concludes with suggested actions on the macro-, meso- and individual levels.

As you set out to read this book ...

We invite you to journey with us through the landscape of emerging markets and, in particular, the women leaders in these environments.

May this book open up possibilities for you. May the accounts of the 46 women inspire you to advocate opportunities:

- for women to realize their dreams and destinies
- for realising potential
- for economic growth
- for fulfilment.

The banquet is laid. We invite you to partake of it!

Shireen Chengadu and Caren Scheepers

Foreword
Women's leadership in emerging markets

Women's advancement to leadership in the last half-century has been quite remarkable.[1] Today, women can be found among heads of state, cabinet ministers, executives and board members of multinational companies, as well as military leaders. They are successful entrepreneurs, astronauts, doctors, scientists, religious leaders and more. Worldwide, women comprise nearly 40% of the workforce and in the 34 OECD nations, mostly in Europe and the Americas, that number rises to 72%—with increasing numbers in management positions. Although in many countries women still face barriers to education, across large swatches of the globe women are obtaining knowledge and educational credentials that will help them advance to leadership across a range of professions.

Perhaps even more important to women's future progress than these raw facts, however, is the strong evidence—and growing recognition—that including more women in key positions of influence produces concrete benefits. Gender-diversified enterprises are more profitable, more innovative and more responsive to their customers or clients' needs. And these benefits accrue across a wide range of companies and organizations, from business to politics, in the arts and media, and within social movements fighting for peace and human rights.

Significantly, the benefits of diversified leadership accrue not just to the women themselves or the organizations they lead. Women leaders improve the economic conditions of their families, their communities and, as we are increasingly seeing, the economies of nations, particularly in emerging markets.

As this book details, there are multiple explanations for the value women bring as leaders. It only makes sense that, recruiting from a larger pool of talent, we ensure a smarter, more innovative workforce. And the *particular* skills and talents that many women often bring to the table—collaboration, flexibility, social responsibility, sensitivity to others, the ability to multi-task—are particularly valuable in today's economy. Whatever the forces propelling the benefits of expanded female participation, the bottom line is clear: an increasingly competitive, varied society requires the holistic and balanced pool of leadership talents, views and assets that can only come when both genders are strongly represented.

But despite this progress, the advancement of women to leadership roles remains far behind what one might expect given women's impressive achievements. At the current rate of advancement, reaching parity will take another 200 years.

The explanation for this persistently slow progress is complex and multifaceted and may vary in different parts of the world. There appears to be broad agreement, however, that because women have not been the principal holders of top positions for most of recorded history, people are less likely to associate women with competence, power and leadership. In addition, there remain widely held prejudices about how women "should" behave and a depth of resistance and censure when they appear to break out of that mold. For many women, advancement is stalled because they are the primary caretakers for children, older parents and spouses. And many of the organizational structures set in place to advance people to leadership—experience in differing corporate environments in different parts of the world, long, inflexible hours and daily travel—disadvantage women, who need to be rooted in one locale in order to provide for and take care of their families.

Whatever the particular combination of barriers standing in the way of increased female participation at the world's decision-making tables, it is clear that the barriers that women face run deep; it will take concerted and consistent individual and collective efforts to eradicate them. Organizations will need to promote the assets that women bring to leadership practice, recognize the value women offer internally and within a larger world and build systems that support women's rise to leadership.

Nonetheless, as today's bold new generation of women continue sharpening their skills and developing their leadership approaches, they will inevitably change both the face of leadership and the terms of its practice. And they will, thereby, create the balanced, innovative diversity of leadership that our modern world requires.

This book does a wonderful job detailing the facts about women's leadership in emerging markets. But equally, if not more importantly, it provides us with the sometimes dramatic, sometimes heart-breaking stories of women who have broken through to the top. These narratives of women, told in their own words, are key: for us to truly understand the achievements and barriers women face, we need to understand their trail-blazing journeys. Children's rights advocate Marian Wright Edelman reminded us years ago that children "cannot be what they cannot see". This is also true for adult women.

Recent studies demonstrate starkly that when women ascend to power, particularly when they reach a critical mass of approximately 30%, they are able to change agendas, frequently responding to the needs of their constituencies.

MIT Professor Esther Duflo and her colleagues studied what happened when, in 1992, India mandated that one third of village council seats and one third of the pradha (council leaders) were reserved for women. Among other things, Duflo found that the leader's gender influenced the council's agenda. Not only were women villagers more likely to speak at council meetings about issues traditionally of interest to them, there were fewer words spoken by the leadership and more by the villagers, and this resulted in a greater investment in drinking water infrastructure and public works. In villages where women were leaders twice in a row, the second female leader was able to increase spending on public works, and when men took over from a woman pradhan, they tended to continue their predecessors' policies.

But even more striking is that Duflo found the aspirations of young women and their families changed once they were able to see women in leadership roles. In particular, when women led the village councils two terms in a row, villagers found it easier to associate women with politics and the aspirations of young women changed:

> Girls were more likely to say they wanted a career and that they wanted to serve as a pradhan. Their parents, also surveyed, gave similar answers when asked about their aspirations for their children. Overall, in places that had been led by a woman pradhan, villagers said they would be more likely to vote for a woman in the future.
>
> (Bolder Policies for Women at the Top: A research symposium report, Dec. 10, 2010. See www8.gsb.columbia.edu/ leadership/research/dec2010/report)

By chronicling the stories of courageous women who are breaking glass ceilings and challenging stereotypes, this book provides role models for women to become leaders in all aspects of business and be agents of change in their families and communities.

Kathryn Kolbert
Constance Hess Williams Director
Athena Center for Leadership Studies
Barnard College, New York

***

Having grown significantly in assertion and contribution, women around the world are defining their leadership role in society, business and politics. This remarkable evolution over the last fifty years has changed almost every aspect of social and economic life. The establishment in 1994 of South Africa's democracy came at a time when women's rights and contributions were increasingly being recognized. For many, South Africa has been an important and constructive model, opening doors and creating an environment in which women have been able to assert themselves. In this sense, it may be at least a good case study if not role model.

The truth of a modernizing economy like South Africa is that it is based not on natural resources but on knowledge-intensive institutions. If we track the nature of work over the last 200 years in significant enterprises employing thousands of people, working life has moved from the physical to the cerebral. If we go back fifty years to the peak of Fordism, the majority of work was manual and required more brawn than brain.

The past thirty years have seen a massive evolution, if not revolution, as we have entered the information and knowledge age, which is now the core of modern economies. The centrality of brawn meant that men dominated economic, military and other spheres of life. During World War II, in the US, Europe and Japan, millions of men went to war. In many factories, they were replaced by women. That simple fact, along with the politics of gender that gained momentum from the 1960s—particularly led by the US—has led to a new era at the center of economic life.

The dynamic goes beyond equality. In an age when brainpower dominates, the focus is not only on equality but also on the advantage of ways of working that may be particular to women.

Without overgeneralizing or simplifying, it may be that relationship-building, good communication skills and the complexity of managing personal, family and professional life, not to mention intuition, are all advantages in this information economy and world.

In South Africa, our political settlement introduced a significant acceleration in government, business and civil society of leadership roles filled by women.

I recall facilitating, in 1993, a dialogue and planning retreat of the ANC Women's League (ANCWL) in which it dawned on us all that the Women's League itself would have to change its objective from supporting men in the struggle to playing a strategic and creative role, which later led to a progressive constitution and the appointment of women, certainly in government.

Although in business this has been a slower progress and we still lag behind what is right and what is possible, there has also been significant progress in most countries, including South Africa.

Who knows what is to come? As women increasingly initiate, imagine and create, it may be in this complex networked world that they bring a new energy and creativity and, in fact, advantage to the institutions that so dominate our life from birth to the other end.

I hope this comes to pass because, undoubtedly, it will make life more complex, more interesting and probably more creative.

As we enter the great acceleration of the Anthropecene geological epoch in which the behavior of humans will determine the fate of our planet, the active and rewarding participation of women may mark an era in the human story that goes beyond the boundaries of how we have got to where we are.

It is particularly in the area of leadership that women are asserting themselves and will continue to do so ... as uncomfortable as that may be for the men. It is precisely because institutions are so important that those who make decisions that matter most and allocate scarce resources should be creatively informed by a strong leadership presence of women.

South Africa is a non-racial democracy in a multiracial society and not all communities regard the ascent of women with an equal eye. However, along with the great levelling of becoming an increasingly integrated society, in the decades ahead many will have to learn to accept the basic constitutional right of equal access, participation, leadership and rewards.

For most South Africans, the understanding of "otherness" is something we sometimes embrace with reluctance, but it is something that inevitably enriches us. Whether we refer to race, ethnicity, age or gender, all of us are made potentially richer by "otherness" in South Africa.

Since I grew up in a male-dominated household in a patriarchal society, being open to "otherness" has been a good curriculum for me—at times hard to manage and at other times liberating.

Many years ago, I was privileged to be in Ahmedabad on the banks of the Sabarmati River, from where Gandhi led the rejection of British rule and witnessed the dawn of India's independence. In his tiny cottage is to be found a quotation that has always inspired me and which we may borrow for the purposes of encouraging openness about the content of this book:

> I do not want my house to be a house walled in on all sides and my windows to be stuffed. I want the cultures of all lands to be blown about my house as freely as possible. But I refuse to be blown off my feet by any.
>
> Mahatma Gandhi[2]

Let more winds blow.

Nick Binedell
Former Dean
Gordon Institute of Business Science
University of Pretoria

Notes

1 See *The Athena CORE10: Leadership Reimagined*, published by the Athena Center for Leadership Studies at Barnard College, for a more in-depth review and underlying data to support the ideas expressed in this foreword.
2 Goodreads quote by Mahatma Ghandi, www.goodreads.com/quotes/575759-i-do-not-want-my-house-to-be-walled-in, accessed November 3, 2016.

1 Macro-level perspective on women's leadership

Shireen Chengadu and Pravina Makan-Lakha

Introduction

Globally, women constitute about 50% of the population, while in some countries—for example, South Africa, Japan, Russia, Canada, Argentina, Kazakhstan, Mozambique, Namibia and Nepal—they count for just over 50% (World Bank 2015). At the same time, women now make up 40% of the labor force. These two variables are significant in and of themselves and make this citizenry highly relevant politically, economically and socially. Regarding business, not only do women comprise half of the consumer market, they also make up not much under half of the constituency that labor is drawn from. Concomitantly, gender equality remains an unrealized aspiration for almost half the world population.

Why does the inclusion of women matter for leadership? What is the business case for women in leadership? These questions are increasingly being posed in the wake of shifts towards empowering women in business.

Women in leadership roles deliver better financial results for business corporations. Studies on the correlation between women's leadership and bottom line in companies indicate that "Companies with top-quartile representation of women in executive committees perform significantly better than companies with no women at the top" (Carter and Wagner 2011). These studies indicate that there is a 47% increase in return on equity and a 55% increase in average earning before interest and tax. Despite these findings, globally, women's leadership in business, while improving, remains low, averaging at 24%, with a staggering 33% of businesses revealing a complete absence of women in their leadership structure (McKinsey & Company 2010).

As the greater significance of the potential of women in business is realized and understood, a number of studies and research, coupled with shifting trends towards investing in women's participation, are becoming observable, even in developmental agendas.

Equally significant is the global gender equality gap and the failure of any country worldwide to achieve gender equality to date (World Economic Forum 2016). Given these findings, why are businesses slow to appoint women to leadership roles? To what extent can women's leadership and gender equality, in emerging markets, contribute to the competitiveness of companies and, in turn, the prosperity of these countries? What range of perspectives can women who have risen to leadership roles share, not only with aspiring leaders but also regarding the complexity and ambiguity of the macro environment of women's leadership? These are the questions that will be explored and discussed in this chapter.

Why women matter in leadership

Today, gender diversity is widely embraced as a starting place for diversity of thought and perspective on boards and for senior management (Brunswick 2016). Having women fairly represented in decision-making roles brings the right mix of skills and perspectives necessary to successfully tackle the business and national challenges that increasingly characterize the dynamic landscape in which we live and work.

Later in this chapter we sketch the uninspiring performance of corporations and society in their response to achieve gender parity in leadership. While the gender equality gap exists in both developed and developing markets, it is more prevalent in the labor markets, in political representation and in households of emerging markets.

Several arguments, together with a growing body of evidence to illustrate why women matter in the business sector, will be presented in this chapter and throughout this book. The empirical evidence is drawn from previous research in this field and is corroborated by the data we have gathered through interviews, conducted primarily with women leaders from emerging markets. Through dialogue with a diverse range of women in leadership roles in emerging markets and by incorporating the views of a small sample of men with leadership experience in developed and emerging markets, we analyze a range of perspectives on attracting, developing and retaining top women talent as a means to increase the financial business performance of companies, particularly those in emerging markets.

These arguments continue to gain strength and contribute to hastening the slow progress we witness across the business sector, but also importantly in the political sector. While it is our aim to draw particular attention to women's leadership in business, if we did not also reflect on women in leadership in politics we may communicate the incorrect view that women's leadership and equality is a matter peculiar to the business sector, when in fact the issue is clearly a cross-sectoral challenge. The slow progress is systemic to our core sectors of society—politics, business and civil society. This chapter explores the importance of overall progress in the political sphere and its meaning for the business sector. We focus on three dominant arguments for why women's leadership matters.

The economic argument: the bottom line

The first argument is purely an economic one: does women's leadership have a direct impact on the bottom line of corporations by boosting economic results? Research carried out by Catalyst, McKinsey and the Credit Suisse Research Institute has dominated the discourse on the economic value of women in leadership. The research comprised year-on-year studies on women's representation on boards, at directorship and management levels. The outcome was improved financial performance of companies. The study by Carter and Wagner (2011) of Fortune 500 companies illustrated that companies with the highest representation of women at the level of board of directors demonstrated a higher than average financial performance. The basis of these claims is constructed on three important financial measures of performance—Return on Equity (ROE), Return on Sales (ROS) and Return on Invested Capital (ROIC) (Carter and Wagner 2011). Increases in women's leadership lead to improvements across all measures: 42% in ROS, 53% in ROE and 66% in ROIC.

McKinsey's "Women Matter" studies have underscored these earlier claims with several subsequent studies. Their longitudinal studies (2009, 2010, 2012 and 2013), which included the BRICS emerging markets, attest that companies with the highest share of women on boards reported a 41% higher return on equity compared to companies with no women on their boards. Also, companies scoring in the top quartile of organizational performance had more women in top management. While follow-up studies went on to explain the reason behind these varied results, the McKinsey studies demonstrated a definite correlation between the performance of companies and the proportion of women serving in their leadership.

The Credit Suisse Gender 3000 study, which has tracked 28,000 executives at 3,000 companies in 40 countries, has shown that "the average ROE of companies with at least one woman on the board over the past six years is 16%, four percentage points higher than the average ROE of companies with no female board representation" (Credit Suisse Research Institute 2016). While exploring their studies through the lens of gender diversity and corporate performance, they emphasize the core of their study by declaring that "While much of the focus continues to center on the equality or fairness argument, we believe that the question should be whether diversity is to the benefit of not just women themselves, but also to the benefit of other stakeholders, corporates, investors and the wider economic environment."

Justus O'Brien of research firm Russell Reynolds, who works with organizations around the world on succession planning and recruitment of board directors, suggests that a primary issue inhibiting the gender composition of boards is that the talent pool is too limited (Brunswick 2016). It is typically a cohort of retired or active CEOs—primarily men given, the historical legacy of leadership of corporates. The "old boys' club" mentality is strongly entrenched and this grouping is often seen as the only talent pool to draw from. Similarly, in emerging markets where there are women being appointed to boards, they too are drawn from a small pool, which leads to the phenomenon of many women occupying multiple board positions. The talent pools have to be widened and the networks of "old boys' clubs" and the small, tight group of women already occupying board positions must shift to sponsorship of more women into board and leadership positions. This habit of "soft recruiting", as O'Brien calls it, is the habit of introducing potential candidates to other directors at social gatherings. Boards now have the duty of care to plan ahead and expand their networks to include eminently qualified women to the seats of power. In order to address this issue, governments from a number of developed countries such as Norway, Spain, France and Finland have taken steps to introduce quotas, targets and recommendations regarding the percentages of women on corporate boards in publicly listed organizations (Sealy et al. 2010). But the very idea of quotas and targets challenges women being appointed to positions of power based on targets rather than on merit. How women get there is another matter for investigation, but for the purpose of this argument, that they actually get there is important because of the growing body of evidence that points to the business benefits of diverse boards and senior leadership roles.

While the economic arguments mostly focus on the difference women's leadership offers in corporations, in countries such as Norway and Denmark more empirical studies are being commissioned at a country-specific level to test the correlation between gender representatively in political and economic participation and country competitiveness. For example, in the African region alone, "the total annual economic losses due to gender gaps in effective labour could be as high as US$255 billion. Results confirm that Africa is missing its full growth potential because a sizeable portion of its growth reserve—women—is not fully utilized" (Bandara 2015).

In later chapters we demonstrate that there is certainly no scarcity of critical skills and merit, so there must be variables in play that keep the numbers of women lower in the top positions. We therefore ask whether the economic argument alone is sufficient to turn the tide for women in leadership.

The equality and equity argument: a moral obligation

Women's rights are human rights. Rights, justice and fair treatment are moral obligations. In 1945 the founding charter establishing the United Nations (UN) emphatically declared "equal rights for men and women". In 1979, the UN adopted "The Convention on the Elimination of Discrimination of Women" (CEDAW), which is considered the bill of rights for women. CEDAW defines discrimination and provides guidance on how to address it.

Towards the end of the 20th century, several legislative initiatives, policy frameworks and action plans resulted from the efforts of the global women's movement for gender equality and women's empowerment. With less than half of the labor force comprising women, gender equality in the business sector remains evasive. Women continue to suffer discrimination in the types of job they are offered and able to hold, their access to power and decision-making in these jobs, and their pay scales. While this inequality shows up most prominently in the business environment, it does not stem from within the business sector. A primary cause is the cultural norms that determine gender roles and their resultant impact on the female labour supply. The 2005 World Development Report as cited by Hiller (2014) has emphasized that economic and cultural inequalities might feed on each other, leading to such gender inequality traps.

A wide spectrum of research has recorded the inequitable treatment of women in the business environment. This dearth of leadership has its origins and perpetuation at various points in the journey of women from birth into adulthood. Consider the norms dictating the manner in which each gender is nurtured; the social discrimination inherent in the performance of household chores; the skewed availability of primary and secondary education; the unequal access to tertiary education and, later, positions in the job market. Hiller (2014) agrees that initial cultural norms entrench gender inequalities from the time an investment in education is made in boys rather than in girls; such discriminatory practices are not easily overcome by legislation and institutional practices to create greater equity. Advocates and champions for gender equality, rights, fairness and justice have enabled the establishment of normative frameworks to advance gender equality, but the results have been poor and most evident in women's under-representation in leadership roles. Even though women have a right to equality and fairness to assume leadership positions, the statistics of women occupying leadership positions at board and CEO levels and as heads of states in emerging markets show the obvious lack.

Smart economics is the developmental approach of investing in women and girls for economic competitiveness and growth. Chant and Sweetman's (2012) research into this strategy points to the ambiguity of the approach that aims to "fix women or fix the world". In it, they allude to the linearity and simplicity of this reductionist approach: the very problem we are trying to fix might become more burdensome because it discounts strategies which aim to ensure women are seen as equal to men; instead the approach of investing in women to fix the world is advocated. This research also points to the lack of attention paid to the role of other critical stakeholders in women's lives, such as men and societal actors who have influence on women's ability to reach their full human potential. They argue that "smart economics is concerned with building women's capacities in the interests of development rather than promoting women's rights for their own sake" (Chant and Sweetman 2012).

While we recognize and support the need to place particular focus on the developmental needs of women and the inclusion of women in all levels of decision-making roles, we also acknowledge that this approach cannot be adopted solely for economic or business imperatives; it must be embraced for women's own sake as well. The gender inequality trap cannot be eliminated by women or by development agendas alone; it also requires the shifting of deeply entrenched cultural norms and mindsets of other significant role-players in women's lives.

The diversity argument: moving from gender diversity to leadership diversity

Gender diversity has various definitions, but perhaps most common and relevant to this argument is "the mixture of attributes within a workforce that in significant ways affects how people think, feel and behave at work and their acceptance, work performance satisfaction, or progress in an organization" as a concept has several meanings. While diversity and inclusion have been two concepts advocated extensively for responding to complex issues like race, gender, religious orientation, culture, and so on, they are criticized for being simple solutions to a complex problem (Bendick 2007; Hays-Thomas and Bendick 2013).

The gender diversity argument has been easier to advance for the inclusion of women in corporations and when dealing with the larger gender inequality in corporations and companies for two primary reasons. First, business explores new approaches to improving profit on a daily basis. Second, the human resource factor in business is critical. The argument of diversity speaks directly to a more effective use of the workforce and harnessing human capital to its full potential; this makes business sense. However, effecting these strategies has several new challenges that present themselves to both women and the institutions.

In addition to these studies on gender representation in corporations, the global executive advisory firm Brunswick has reinforced the argument that while the demand for more female board directors may be growing due to legislative requirements, the limited pool of female executives in senior leadership positions from which to draw continues to be a barrier (Brunswick 2016). In this regard, there was agreement from those we interviewed for this book that growing the pipeline of female talent in executive leadership positions is more important than filling quotas.

But creating a more inclusive work environment that is supportive of gender diversity and women's empowerment and embraces feminine leadership traits and values is important for a third and equally powerful reason; and this reason is an often less frequently articulated argument for gender equality. How women lead, their character traits, their roles as mothers, wives, partners, daughters and societal champions, and their leadership relevance for these times that are characterized by greater volatility, uncertainty, complexity and ambiguity, may well translate into an advantageous way of working, one more appropriate to our current business context.

The economic and social challenges that are facing global leaders and leaders of corporations today create the impetus for an argument that challenges traditional leadership and calls for more diverse leadership in response to the changing dynamics of the world order.

It is widely accepted that effective leadership in business or political arenas must result in improved operational and financial performance (competitiveness of institutions and nations), an increase in innovation, better problem-solving through group performance and enhanced company or country reputation. With increasing complexity and volatility in the strategic landscape of emerging markets, there is the awareness that calls for a new way of leading, one that is less hierarchical and traditional, characterized by a collaborative and inclusive approach. A recent study undertaken by Gerzema and D'Antonio (2013) posits that the leadership traits and characteristics of women and men more attuned to this way of thinking and being are more relevant for the times. In their book, *The Athena Doctrine*, they surveyed 64,000 people in 13 countries in both developed and emerging markets. Their data reveals the preference for leadership styles, values and leadership characteristics that require fresh ways of leading, more precisely, a paradigm that favors the adoption of women's influences and feminine values in leadership roles in business, government and society. We are witnessing some seismic shifts in our world order currently—in developed markets such as the US, Democrat presidential candidate, Hillary Rodham Clinton, battles for arguably the biggest and most powerful presidential race against Donald Trump, the Republican front-runner; and in the UK Britain's exit from the EU (Brexit), Theresa May has become the second female prime minister in a challenging time to lead the UK forward and upwards through its challenges. In Syria and Greece there is growing political and economic instability; in emerging markets such as South Africa, university students have challenged the ruling government to hold it to its promises and political and service delivery protests are more frequent across the nation. In Turkey a coup, failed or not, voices the disillusionment of the people— these occurrences represent challenges to the traditional leadership norms. Macro- and meso-level leadership in developed and emerging markets is at a crossroads. Does this not beg the question: if our countries and institutions, still largely led by men and therefore by extension driven overwhelmingly by traditional hierarchical leadership styles and mindsets, are experiencing challenges of this sort, is the current leadership paradigm effective? Is it not time for this system to be replaced or, at the very least, complemented by women leadership styles? Eagly (2013) suggests that "Transformational leadership is a hybrid and androgynous approach to leadership, given that it employs both masculine and feminine behaviours." Research shows that "female managers are somewhat more transformational than male managers. In particular, they exceed men in their attention to human relationships" (Eagly 2013). Research by McKinsey (2012) agrees that some leadership behaviors, which are more frequently applied by women than men in management teams, prove to enhance corporate performance and will be a key factor in meeting tomorrow's business challenges.

Just as politics and economics are inextricably linked, so too are the private and public sector in advancing gender equality and leadership diversity. Women holding formal political leadership positions can play advocacy and activist roles to promote women's empowerment agendas and women's rights. Were women absent from such ranks, their perspectives would be silenced in important issues affecting the holistic well-being of women and, in turn, that of communities. But what are the experiences of women politicians? How well are they represented in decision-making roles, and, once in the roles, how effective are they in advocating for change to benefit women and create more equitable societies?

Women in emerging markets, as in developed markets, struggle to attain leadership positions and gain support as heads of states or in executive roles within political parties. Change at this level in both developed and emerging markets is painfully slow. In her interview Phumzile Mlambo-Ngcuka, South African politician and executive director of UN Women, stated:

> Twenty years on from the UN conference in Beijing 1995, a girl child born today will have to be 81 before she stands the same chance of being a CEO of a company and she will have to wait 50 years to have an equal chance of leading a country.
>
> (*The Guardian* 2015)

Men still hold most positions of power and decision-making in business and politics. According to the UN's World's Women 2015 report:

> Women continue to be underrepresented in national parliaments. They are seldom leaders of major political parties, participate as candidates in elections in small numbers and, during electoral processes, face multiple obstacles deeply rooted in inequality in gender norms and expectations. Once elected, few women reach the higher echelons of parliamentary hierarchies.
>
> (United Nations 2015)

It would appear that women shifting into positions of influence is a painfully slow process and there are too few examples of women breaking the mold and occupying these pivotal decision-making roles.

Angela Merkel became the first woman chancellor of Germany and at the time of writing Hillary Clinton has a 50% chance of becoming the first woman president of the most powerful nation in the world. Other firsts for women occupying political leadership roles are Nkosazana Dlamini-Zuma, the first female chair of the African Union, and four past and present presidents of African or South American countries—Dilmah Roussef (Brazil), Joyce Banda (Malawi), Ellen Johnson Sirleaf (Liberia) and Bibi Ameenah Firdaus Gurib-Fakim (Mauritius). While we celebrate these achievements, there are simply too few such role models for there to be sustainable impact. Women have historically played strong leadership roles in their communities, especially in politically and socially challenging times, and now they are increasingly being represented at all levels in emerging market governments. Yet Rosser-Mims (2005) says, "access to a range of political leadership positions remain an elusive dream for a vast majority of women in the world".

Despite the lower levels of participation and representation than men in political leadership, there has been steady progress since 2003. Interestingly, as highlighted in United Nations (2015), the record for women's representation in a national parliament is no longer held by any of the Nordic countries, as was the case for decades. Instead, Rwanda is currently ranked as number one (64%), Bolivia (53%), Andorra (50%) and Cuba (49%). In Ecuador, Finland, Iceland, Mozambique, Namibia, Norway, Senegal, Seychelles, South Africa, Spain and Sweden, women's representation ranges between 40% and 44%. All these countries have reached and surpassed the international target of 30% of women in leadership positions originally set by the United Nations Economic and Social Council (ECOSOC) in 1990 and reaffirmed in the Beijing Platform for Action in 1995. In 2015, a total of 43 out of 190 countries reached or surpassed this target (United Nations 2015).

It is true that quotas are in place in some countries to enable more women to enter the political arena, but they decrease significantly in relation to powerful positions in executive roles and heads of state. Even when women do make it to executive positions in parliament, they are more often appointed to portfolios that may be perceived as less important than to the most powerful cabinet and portfolio posts (World Economic Forum 2016).

There is progress, but the rate of change is slow and women continue to be under-represented in public and private sector leadership positions. The gender composition of executive boards of private companies and the proportion of women in executive positions in parliaments and as heads of state point to deeply entrenched gender inequality issues that keep most women out of influential roles. However, when comparing women's participation in leadership roles in politics to that in the private sector, the glass ceiling appears to be far more intact in the latter, particularly at CEO level.

State of representation of women in leadership

As women's leadership commands more attention, the number of studies conducted by international corporate consulting companies, intergovernmental organizations, governments and academics to gain a clearer understanding of what the representation is has been increasing. This has led to more data and analysis on the state of women's leadership.

Globally, there are noticeably fewer women in leadership at the level of board of directors, in chief executive officer and chief financial officer positions, and in senior management. This is a conclusive finding from data collected by MSCI, which is a stock market index of 1,643 "world" stocks covering over 1,500 companies worldwide: Grant Thompson's focuses on mid-market businesses globally, McKinsey's focuses on Fortune 500 companies, and African Development Bank focuses on regional African stock exchanges. The data confirms that the percentages of women in leadership remains well below 30% and far from any progress towards gender parity. In fact, at the current levels of representation, global scenario projections estimate that a 30% global representation of women on boards will only be achieved by 2027. What does this mean for gender-balanced leadership of corporates or gender parity at this level?

Data on women's leadership is expanding and improving since the more targeted attempts to monitor women's leadership in corporates instituted just over a decade ago; nevertheless, there are criticisms of the validity of the data. The data is sometimes criticized because of the limitations of its validity for use for comparison purposes. Each of the sets of data to measure women in leadership is based on a unique set of definitions, indices and measures adopted. Despite the limitations, the range of information collected across nations and across the sizes of corporates does provide us with some assessment of the status of women's leadership regionally and globally.

The state of women in leadership has been changing in recent years, but not fast enough to achieve gender parity. The increased research effort in data collection, more academic studies of causality and correlation and attempts at disaggregating data for global corporates, medium cap companies and across the regions are no doubt giving us a clearer picture of the state of women's leadership. This has benefits for identifying enablers, barriers and trends and, more importantly, adds to the understanding needed for designing strategies to dissolve the limitations and barriers to achieving, at a minimum level, gender parity in women's leadership.

Women's representation at board of director level

The numbers illustrate that the proportion of women in leadership at the level of board of directors in blue chip companies is 18% in the EU, 16% in US Fortune 500 companies and 14.4% in Africa's large cap companies;

while the average percentage of female directors in listed companies is 9.8% in the Asia-Pacific region, 5.6% in Latin America and 1% in the Middle East (see Figure 1.1). While Africa was not far behind the EU and US, it was significantly higher than continents such as Latin America that comprise a significant number of emerging economies.

The proportion of senior management roles held by women averages 24% globally. This is 2% more than in 2015. More than 35% of businesses have no women in leadership. While Japan, Germany and India are amongst the poor performing countries, Russia tops the list at 45%, with Eastern European countries in general displaying the higher proportion. Chapter 10 explores fully the impact of creating more diverse boards.

In Russia and former Eastern European countries where the percentages are glaringly higher than in the rest of the world, the gender demographic of 120 women to 100 men and the emphasis of communist rule enforcing equity (and specifically gender equity) have been identified as the reasons for the differences.

A comparative assessment of women's leadership levels

The leaking leadership pipeline

In new evidence from Credit Suisse Research, which reflects on women's leadership positions by function and region, a more comprehensive picture emerges of the dearth of women's leadership as one progresses through the hierarchy (see Figure 1.3). While women are only achieving around 30% at the level of senior management positions, we begin to see how the percentage continues to decrease as we get to CEO positions. As we look purely at the global indicator, it is evident that less than 5% of women reach the CEO level. This is in spite of the pool being at a 30% level in senior management. What is causing the leak in the leadership pipeline?

A macro-assessment of the extent of women in leadership roles

At a macro-level, the World Economic Forum (WEF), which has been surveying the gender equality terrain vigorously from 2009, sketches the results and progress of gender parity by region and across the four sectors: economy, education, health and politics. The latest results and trends (2015) reflected in Figure 1.4 indicate that much work is still to be done.

Although there is a large gap to close to achieve gender equality in the economic sector, its progress over the last year has been a mere 2%. At the same time, the gender parity gap in sub-Saharan Africa, Asia and Latin America is in excess of 30% and closing at a rate of 4% per year. However, it is the trend in the economic participation and opportunity index for the period 2009–2015 that demonstrates the most worrying position for women's leadership. The statistic shows a downward trend over the past three

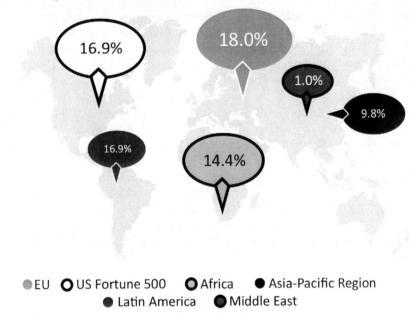

Figure 1.1 Women's representation in boardrooms
Source: African Development Bank (2015).

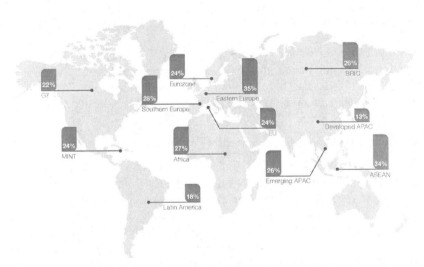

Figure 1.2 Women's representation in management
Source: Grant Thornton (2015).

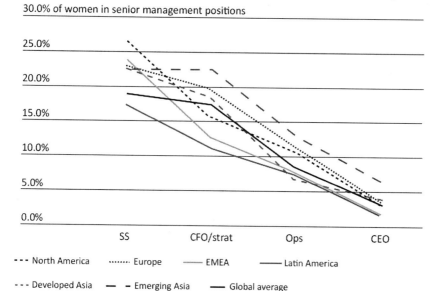

Figure 1.3 Women in senior management positions by function and by region
Source: Credit Suisse Research Institute (2016).

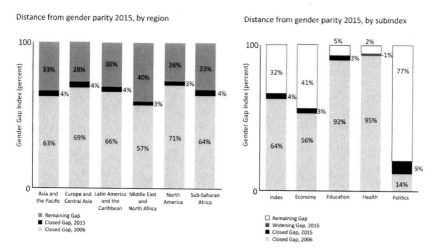

Figure 1.4 Gender parity by region and across sectors
Source: World Economic Forum (2016).

years since 2013 in economic participation and opportunity for women, and the economic sector, business and corporations are facing a dilemma.

Examining a comparison of the four sectors over the 2009–2016 period (see Figure 1.5), we observe that the Economic Participation and Opportunity index showed steady growth until 2010, dropped in 2011 and then increased over the next three years, peaking during 2013 and dropping in 2014 and 2015. The curve at this stage shows a downward trajectory. What happened in 2013 to realize the progress recorded has not been studied as yet, but could the "gender diversity campaign" with increased spending through human resources strategies be the possible explanation for this? Did this campaign represent the latest fad and hence a surge in the results? What needs to be repeated to realize this, and similar growth trajectories, is what academic research must focus on to help identify multiplier strategies.

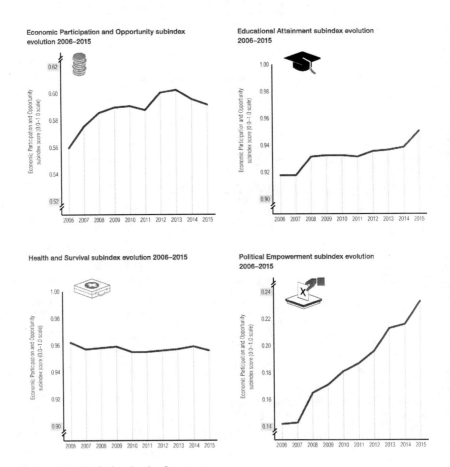

Figure 1.5 Evolution in the four sectors
Source: World Economic Forum (2016).

Perhaps most striking across the four sectors observed by the WEF is the Political Empowerment index. The steady progress in the political area is reflecting visibly across the world.

Why women in leadership roles are critical for markets and especially so for emerging markets

Recent popular press has had much to draw on in support of the notion that women are about to take on the world and some are boldly asking, are there any men out there who still want to lead? Citing the successes of German chancellor Angela Merkel, IMF MD Christine Lagarde, Democratic candidate Hillary Clinton, Scottish first minister Nicola Sturgeon and, more recently, Theresa May sworn in as prime minster of the UK, Khalf (2016) claims the spotlight on women leadership has suddenly brightened. But these women are the exception rather than the rule and, further, the rise of women into leadership roles in emerging markets lags behind what is happening in these developed markets. In an online discussion of the roles of women in leadership roles in the public and private sector, participants from Argentina, Cameroon, India, South Africa, Suriname, Syria and Australia shared their views. Victoria Kenny from Argentina said, "women are still under-represented in Latin America in most sectors. There is a cultural shift that is slowly taking place, allowing a window of opportunity for women to move into leadership positions." In addition, Phelele Tengeni from South Africa said:

> the government has laid a solid foundation in terms of policy putting the public service firmly on the route of transformation. In 1995 the equity target was 30% representation of women in management positions. By October 2006 many government departments achieved that minimum quota.

In Suriname, 25% of parliament consists of women representatives, said Chitra Mohanlal. But more participants from Guinea, India, Pakistan, Tanzania and Zimbabwe said that despite positive gains by a handful of women, the majority of women continued to face barriers to entry into leadership roles. And in countries experiencing socio-political upheavals, there was an additional challenge in reaching gender equality in leadership roles. Seyhan Aydŷnlŷgil from Turkey stated that "in an environment of rising conservatism, there may be backsliding in hard-won achievements made towards gender equality" (Women Watch 2007). The participation of women in the public sector may be getting better in emerging markets but women are still not being given critical government portfolios or occupying the very top leadership roles. There are similar reasons put forward for the under-representation of women holding leadership roles in political life as on the business front. According to Hejnova in Madsen et al.

(2015), women's political representation is low because of "prejudice and discrimination, the demands of housework and childcare, various socio-economic factors and political socialization". Interestingly, as we watch what is transpiring in the political arena in the US, a developed economy, what Hejnova describes as two levels of prejudice and discrimination—one directly in the office itself and another among voters themselves—may account for lower voter confidence in Hillary Clinton and her lack of popularity (Madsen et al. 2015). Another reason for greater representation of women in political leadership being as important as their greater representation in business leadership is that a critical mass in all areas of decision-making will help make it a less hostile environment and enable easier access for aspirant women leaders.

On the business front, emerging markets represent the new business frontiers and the new markets in the world for increasing economic growth and achieving development goals. Today's business context is characterized by a highly globalized world, and dominated by a rapidly changing technology environment. The recent World Economic Forum (2016a) refers to this business environment as the "Fourth Industrial Revolution". There is increasing evidence to suggest that businesses across the spectrum from large conglomerates to multinationals and medium-sized corporates to small and medium-sized enterprises (SMEs) are facing unprecedented disruptions that require revolutionary thinking about the competitiveness of companies and by extension nations. Diversifying leadership beyond men can introduce more revolutionary thinking.

At the center of emerging markets there is a valuable, neglected and underutilized resource—women. For emerging markets, the inclusion of women in strategies to improve growth, performance and competitiveness represents a non-traditional approach but at the same time espouses contemporary thinking and solutions. Emerging markets are considered to be the fertile markets, highly sought after for productivity and growth in this defining moment in history and globalization. According to Hewlitt and Rashad (2011), the economic power has started to tilt away from the previously dominant West to the "rest", and they contend that women in Brazil, Russia, India, China and South Africa (BRICS) and other emerging markets such as Turkey, Mexico, Indonesia and Korea are a large part of the formula for unlocking the new economic power. Because they have been the untapped talent, through education, ambition, diversity of thought and experiences they now have unprecedented advantages to become the economic and social game changers in emerging markets (Hewlitt and Rashad 2011).

As quoted in World Economic Forum (2016b), this argument has been packaged in various forms, including calls for better use of the talent pool—"Get the other half working and participating in the economy" (Melinda Gates 2016)—and expanding the current talent pool—"If you exclude 50% of the talent pool, it's no wonder you find yourself in a war for talent" (Theresa J. Whitmarsh, Executive Director of the Washington State Investment Board, Davos 2016). Hutt (2016) concurs that there is more than enough educated "women talent" in growth economies, yet it is often overlooked and underutilized. Anderson (2014) suggests that women in emerging markets have a trait in common that makes them the most sought-after talent: they are "undeterred". And it is this undeterred spirit that changes the narrative from that of victim and survivor mindset to a winning and excellence mentality. Obstacles are in the lived experiences of these women; they have learnt how to navigate the hilly terrains, to move from uncertainty and ambiguity to stability and success. This is the courageous talent that emerging markets need to alter the balance of power in their favour. The face of talent is changing and companies—both the global ones wanting to embark on global expansion in emerging markets and the local ones wanting to become more prosperous in their own country—have an opportunity to get this right in their talent management systems and processes. Bluen (2012) points out that emerging markets are "susceptible to losing talent to developed markets", and he suggests that "greater engagement leads to greater retention". Therefore, women whose skills and experiences are not valued and embraced through inclusive leadership will be lost to emerging markets because they are highly sought after elsewhere.

The rationale for our choice of emerging markets is developed in a later chapter.

An analysis of women in leadership roles

The question remains: will these imperatives alone drive the pace of change required. This book endeavors to offer both an analysis of the current status quo and recommendations of enablers and strategies that might attract, develop and retain women for leadership positions. To ensure that the analysis is substantive and representative of voices in emerging markets, the authors dialogued with a diverse sample of women in leadership and incorporated the views of a select number of men with leadership experience.

Whatever the underlying motivation—be it improving "the bottom line", meeting the "moral obligation" of fairness or fulfilling the business requirement for leadership diversity, business goals and decisions on how to increase the number of women in leadership must form an important component of the overall business short- and long-term strategy. This matters against the backdrop of various international, regional and national policy commitments to addressing gender inequality in leadership.

Theorizing about these factors is important, but the power of tried-and-tested knowledge derived from women's practical experience in leadership offers a host of invaluable lessons, including surmounting obstacles and capitalizing on enablers, and most importantly transforming the insight into solutions and responses to increase the number of women in leadership roles.

From the macro-assessment of women's leadership globally, it is evident that women's leadership is changing, but the change is too slow to have any significant impact on the arguments in support of it, be it the economic imperative, the matter of principle, or the value of feminization of leadership. Scenario assessments show us that at the current trajectory of efforts and progress it will be several decades before any change of significance is noted. Women's leadership remains at a low level, well under the 30% mark in most sectors, especially the traditionally male-dominated ones, with several obstacles and the glass ceiling seemingly most impenetrable in the business sector.

The assessment of senior management roles held by women by industry (see Figure 1.6) is another important indicator of the challenges faced by those addressing the broader women's leadership dilemma. In these personal accounts by a range of leaders from the private, public and social sectors, we share the highs and lows of their leadership trajectory. We also look at them particularly through the lens of leaders pursuing the vision for gender equality and inclusivity within and amongst the leadership roles they have and continue to be involved in. Why did women and gender equality come to matter for these leaders? Why did it become their purpose and calling? How did they handle women's leadership and gender-equality goals within and beyond their broader leadership roles?

Four features of leadership experience—the personal, the context, the barriers and the enablers (see Figure 1.7)—proved to be fundamental and common across the leaders we dialogued with. In the following section we capture this wisdom, conscious that there are limitations to being able to share all the nuances we gathered. The information remains on a database created as a resource on women's leadership. This database is rich and multifaceted and can be used to trigger further research by academia and practitioners in emerging markets. The stories of the women themselves

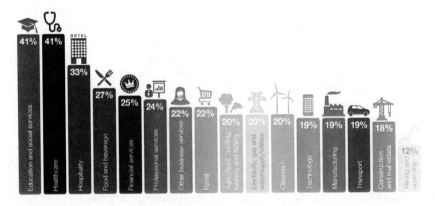

Figure 1.6 Proportion of senior management roles held by women: by industry
Source: African Development Bank. 2015. "Where are the Women? Inclusive Boardrooms in Africa's Top Listed Companies". Abidjan, Côte d'Ivoire.

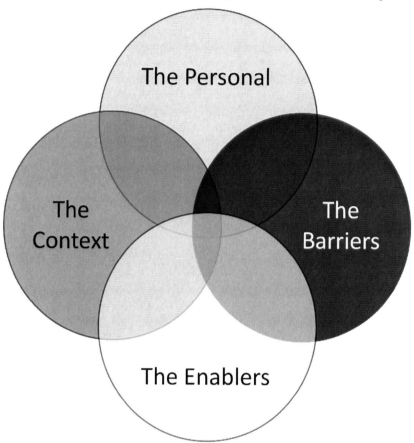

Figure 1.7 Leadership experience: the four-features model

are diverse, rich in contextual appreciation and nuance and could be used to craft teaching cases for management and leadership studies. In emerging markets there has been a scarcity of relevant teaching cases profiling women in leadership roles as role models. This data will change that. It is the hope of the contributors to this book that it will act as a catalyst for more collaborative research among academics and practitioners in developed and emerging markets.

The personal

The personal aspect was a primary factor—that is, the role of family in building gender equality consciousness and leadership characteristics. This was followed by the role of broader social interactions in shaping a purpose and eliciting a commitment and willingness to be engaged in and part of much bigger national and societal agendas than just personal growth and success.

Emphatic about the power of "the prevailing narratives", leaders expressed that their experiences from a young age—in the home, in the community and in the surrounding environment—shaped gender consciousness. The early socialization into roles that can be assumed by both women and men, the differences between men and women and the possibilities of equality were all encountered at an early age. For instance, Phumzile Mlambo-Ngcuka recognized that her gender awareness was rare:

> I think my introduction to issues of public interest, and the fact that it came through a women's organization, created the awareness of the inequality between men and women ... something that I think wasn't always the case with some of my peers.

Comparable views are expressed by Geraldine Fraser-Moleketi and Gill Marcus about being socialized in a context that instilled the importance of "what kind of society we are living in" and "wanting to be a part of making a contribution to change it". Gill shared:

> It wasn't about being somebody or having a leadership role. I was very young, and the goal was always to look at what kind of society we were living in, and I just wanted to be part of making a contribution to changing it. That was my only goal. I never saw myself as a leader.

In both Gill's and Geraldine's comments we see the personal influence coming through strongly.

Dolly Mokgatle said that her childhood world was humble but shaped her character:

> I am not sitting here today because I was plucked from some magnificent world out there, you know. Even with the death of my father when I was seven, even in all of the adversity I experienced, I have something to celebrate. I was first of the eight children to go to university. My mum was a cleaner in a department store but she made sacrifices and borrowed money from her employer to pay my registration fees.

Thandi Lujabe-Rankoe described how her parents were role models that influenced her life. She spoke passionately about the family sacrifices that enabled her to receive education as a child and the powerful role that parents play in shaping moral commitments:

> My father was a teacher, my mother used to sell beans and mealies to ensure we had school fees and clothes and to ensure we had opportunities. I am a strong woman because I learnt a lot from my parents about determination to do the right thing at the right time. And to walk tall even under difficult conditions.

We witness through dialogue with Thandi how the personal aspect in the family extends to broader social interactions:

> Being at the forefront of the liberation struggle, being trained as a freedom fighter alongside men and even in the harshest circumstances, women walked tall and held the secrets; even when men were falling, the women were strong and carried on. They displayed resilience and were not selfish.

Joyce Banda, ex-president of Malawi, reflected on her childhood and how from the age of six her father "would laugh and say 'let me nurture the seed'; he kept reminding me, 'Uncle John said that you are destined to do something great', so the seed was there". Sometimes this socialization is at household level, the way we treat our boys and girls, but what we say to our children also matters.

Isabel Neiva, principal at A.T. Kearney Dubai, reflected that even in traditional homes parents influence choices women make. Talking about her parents' role, Isabel said, "they are traditional, but at the same time they were always very open in a way. I don't remember my parents imposing anything on me. So it was always about what the choices were."

Geraldine Fraser-Moleketi affectionately shared a story her brother told at their mother's eightieth birthday. Her mum was a factory worker and later also supervised the women who cleaned the malls, mainly at night. When her brother dropped off and picked up his mum at the malls it made him see "the invisible people". As a result, when he and other members in her family enter a mall, they always "see" the people who clean, because these are essentially the "invisible people". The impact of childhood impressions and experiences have shaped how women like Geraldine notice all people, both the visible and the "invisible", the voiced and the voiceless, and these deeply embedded personal memories form the basis for women like Geraldine to build stronger and more inclusive societies.

Another interesting personal aspect that had an impact on Geraldine in her formative years was the idea of families sitting together and openly discoursing on a wide range of controversial topics:

> So we played card games or dominoes. And we would have all the 'no holds barred' discussions on political issues, social issues and such. So, when we sat at the table, or under the table, depending where you were sitting as a child, you were exposed to these discussions.

It is these discussions that became the springboard for the battles against injustice.

The context

Evidence of how the macro-environmental context shapes leadership qualities and the purpose behind which leaders chose to rally was overwhelmingly a feature of every interview. While context was acknowledged as shaping leadership qualities such as commitment, skills and expertise, passion and time, it also proved a catalyst for leadership capabilities to evolve. So context appeared to determine the purpose and calling for leadership and act as a catalyst for leadership qualities. This is perhaps captured most succinctly in Roelf Meyer's comment:

> [a] leader is a creature of his paradigm, of the environment in which his leadership or her leadership is being exercised. I think in a certain way a leader is the product of a paradigm that he or she is coming from or in which he or she has operated. The leadership opportunities that I had from an early stage as a student are completely different to what I experienced in my later life because of the paradigm shift.

From those we interviewed it was mostly an *incident* in the prevailing environmental context that provided an impetus for the leadership role to emerge. The prevailing context also played an enabling role to build champions in these leaders.

On the one hand, Nicola Kleyn, in South Africa, talks about being "shaped far more by the occurrences that have happened in my personal life that have then informed my capability at work". Gill Marcus was categorical that "leadership has to be about people looking to you because you add value in a discussion or in a thinking process or in a policy or problem-solving way". Roelf Meyer drew attention to leadership being a "heart and mind exercise" and an "intellectual capability exercise". Speaking more to the qualities that leadership instills, but still reflecting on the importance of the context, Geraldine Fraser-Moleketi said:

> And I think there was one thing that I would say was significant. I thought nothing too menial to do. Nothing was too difficult, or too complex, to do and there was a need for hard work all the time. And that came through. Because, that was the route coming through the "ranks" in exile and later on our return.

Betty Bigombe, originally a minister in Uganda and now at the World Bank in Washington, echoed how her desire to be an agent of change to build nations started by witnessing the drivers of conflict in nations and how through building that confidence, and getting people to start seeing one another as one people, having a shared vision on development, she initiated peace talks. This personal agency and contextual awareness made her pursue the peace talks even when they stalled.

Barçin Yinanç from Turkey added:

> My advantage was that I came from a multicultural background. It was an advantage and disadvantage. I think that's very important as far as my personal story is concerned. That's why sometimes when I see other people who have had, let us say, a less privileged education, doing as much as good as I, I believe their success is bigger than mine, you know. Sometimes it can also be a disadvantage to you, because this multicultural culture taught me that, if you work a lot success will come, and with it you will go up the stairs, you know. But sometimes it doesn't work like that, especially sometimes you have to ask for it.

Isabel Neiva from Dubai shared that women's contextual appreciation is now far richer because women's experiences are no longer localized. "Women's experiences, qualifications and demand for their skills have enabled them to travel extensively. So I have been posted to work in Kuwait, in Qatar, in Saudi Arabia, in Egypt, in Jordan, in Sudan into West Africa, in Ivory Coast, and within the region."

For Phumzile Mlambo-Ngcuka, a South African now executive director of UN Women in New York, the context that honed her political and social activism was her time at university. That was when her political activism became stronger. She said:

> In my formative years pre-university I was thrust into race, class and gender, but I didn't even know that they had a name. It was at the University of Zululand. And we had many issues to grapple with, from the issues of inadequate library services, issues to do with our residences, fees and so on. And such that being at school, at university, at that time when you really grasp that there is a bigger picture than me, and even if I do well as a student, if I continue to live in that society, I will never be the best I can be. So, while I am focused on completing my education, I also had to be focused on bringing about changes in the country. A lot of young people, not just me, were put into those situations and really had to make macro-decisions, which impacted on your own life and could do so in a fundamental way that could change your destiny.

The barriers

What was common to all the leaders we dialogued with was the numerous barriers encountered in their leadership journey. In some instances these barriers related to personal circumstances, but they were more frequently found at institutional level. At the same time, we heard how the barriers served as catalysts for change. According to Phumzile Mlambo-Ngcuka, education was and remains the catalyst for change. She said,

We know for instance that education is important universally, but we also know that for education to be useful for women we need quality. So this is something for women to fight for. Quality education for girl children anywhere and everywhere in the world.

The barriers described ranged from the internal to the external, the most fundamental being that we still live in a patriarchal society. Internal issues ranged from lack of personal confidence to the demands of social responsibility. The impact of the culture of institutions and work environments was extremely significant. Surprisingly, the majority of the women interviewed suggested that the most significant barriers to the advancement of women were personal rather than institutional. Elena Escagedo Suarez De Bustamante from Spain echoed this with:

My *internal* barriers is [sic] what holds me back. I think that is common to many women, that we tend not to communicate what we do, or what we are doing. We never talk about the progress. We talk, we just present the results. Men tend to say, oh, because I am working so hard, because I am doing this and that. And women usually do not say that. I never say that, for example. And I think that is a barrier I have and that I should talk more about.

Isabel Nevia agreed that it is more her internal barriers that prevent her from achieving more. She said, "There are no external barriers to continue the progression. It is an internal one in being, recognizing that what has happened in the past does not necessarily make an impact on the present or on the future."

Roelf Meyer believes that the internal barriers in women arise because:

both women and men under-estimate their capabilities but it is so much more pronounced in women; so much so that it leads to paralysis in women. In addition, these barriers which are around for men and women, are more visible in women probably as result of their cultural background.

Culture and its impact as a barrier was also commonly referred to by various leaders. Barçin Yinanç talked about the complicated role of culture:

Cultures of certain emerging market countries complicate the career progression paths of women. Double bind effects are visible in a country like Turkey with the Muslims, but also, even if you don't include the Muslims, but where family ties are very important, you know, women have an extra burden about running the family and running the children. I think this is one of the issues that is preventing women from taking a more active role, for instance.

She added how intricacies of patriarchy are woven into everyday circumstances:

> But this division of labor in Turkey that, you know, men are sup-
> posed, are responsible for the welfare of the, you know, the financial
> situation, and women, even if they work and contribute equally to the
> financial structure of the household, you know, they should be more
> thinking of the children. Thinking more of, you know, how many of
> the groceries are needed that night, or if there is an evening to be
> organized, you know, what should be done. Therefore, I think, as far
> as Turkey is concerned, we have to try to change this mentality.

She said that women in Turkey are less encouraged to ask for certain positions because of the deeply entrenched mindset of "I have too much, I am not going to ask for a higher position because a higher position means higher responsibility, less time of my family."

Isabel Neiva underscored a similar sentiment on culture and patriarchy:

> Patriarchy is related to religion and the norms. It is not that men don't
> think women should work or whatever. As a woman I never, I never
> felt disrespected or I never felt ignored by the clients, but for a local
> man, and even for a local woman, the weight of the tradition is very
> strong so that sometimes it is much more difficult to accept the ideas
> of women from the same tradition if she is sitting at the table.

Dolly Mokgatle believes that patriarchal mindsets still prevail in business today. The men create and access the boys' clubs easily but women's social responsibilities, their leadership aspirations and "motherhood call for a major balancing act, one in which women are constantly juggling the demands of being a mother, wife and a leader in a corporate".

Locating the barriers in terms of the external, Phumzile Mlambo-Ngcuka said, "We haven't arrived. I think the bottom line is, we haven't arrived. We have made some strides. They have unfortunately not as yet added up to a major breakthrough. But we do have building blocks that provide us with evidence of what works." She cited the building blocks as being economic emancipation, education and the general well-being of women, which allows women to negotiate relationships. For instance, when it comes to violence against women, although violence against women exists in all classes, the better educated a woman is, the more able she is to defend herself and her children and to take herself out of that situation. She added that the legislative landscape of the world since the ground-breaking 1995 UN Conference for Women held in Beijing (which took the vital step of bringing women's equality issues to the global stage by draft-ing an action plan to see women achieve gender equality) has changed dramatically, but the implementation of the legislation in the statute books of most countries is not giving women the relief that we hoped for. In other words, we also have to deal with attitudes, with norms, because good laws survive side by side with cultural practices that are harmful to women.

For Johan Aurik, the barrier can be seen in the numbers:

> The percentage of women partners in the consulting sector is around 10% with, for us and for all our competitors. The intake level at a junior level, it is around 25%, maybe 30% at best, or so. And then those 25% get reduced to 10%. And we have been shouting about it and saying that we are frustrated about it, for years, decades even, and it is only slowly improving or becoming less bad is maybe the word. It is a very frustrating topic because a lot of people have said, yes, that is not right, it should not be. And we all had our women's days and paid lip service to it, but the progress simply has not been there. Not only for us but for everyone else. So, the whole industry actually has failed. Let us call that word, "failed", to deliver on gender parity. There is no gender parity. None.

These are hard-hitting words: clearly, having intent is not good enough and there needs to be a refinement of strategies and measurement of progress. Otherwise we will continue to have these frustrations decades from now.

Another barrier unsurprisingly attracting a lot of research is the failure of women in leadership to advance other women into leadership roles. Thandi Lujabe-Rankoe was explicit:

> We are going through difficult and sad times and we are not supportive of one another. Women are not supporting each other because we don't want to let other women in and see them succeed. Fear if I let you in, you will be better than me rather than thinking if I let you in, and you are doing things better than I do, I can learn from you.

Interestingly, another barrier is women's loss of authenticity as they rise to the top. When women take the gender equality debate too seriously they lose track of their own authenticity. Brand Pretorius described this internal wrestling thus:

> I have also seen instances where women are too aware of the challenge they are facing. They are too determined to break through the glass ceiling and then they overdo it. They become extremely assertive, in some instances even aggressive. And as a result they lose their authenticity. So, I think the challenge is not to take that challenge of breaking through the glass ceiling too seriously. Rather, let your example, the quality of your leadership and the results you deliver, do

the talking. Do not focus on your position or ambition. Focus on the results. Believe in yourself. Be authentic.

The enablers

Discussing what enables women to aspire to and achieve leadership is a complex discussion. We attempt here to bring out, simply from the dialogues, some of the factors that were shared.

Rania Anderson captures poignantly why now is indeed the time for women:

> Throughout history there have been periods of time that were particularly advantageous for specific groups of people. If you are a woman of working age in a growth economy, this is your time! You are in the right place at the right time to capitalize on unprecedented opportunities for women. You have education, talent, and desire to effect change for yourself, your community and the world—and you live in a country where is now possible for you to do so.

In the accounts of the leaders we interviewed we determined that a set of personal characteristics, which included qualities of selflessness, integrity, lack of fear and the need to act responsibly, were often deemed the enablers for women to reach their full leadership potential.

Dolly Mokgatle stated:

> I actually became in a sense a role model to my siblings but my mum and eldest sister were my role models. My sister had a thirst for life and a betterment of her own position despite our circumstances. I also I learnt from that, firstly not to get stuck in the barriers but to start learning the smart ways to enable myself such that I don't have an excuse not to succeed. Learning to optimize little resources to succeed.

Thandi, making reference to strong role models, cited women like Thuli Madonsela, the South African public protector for the last seven years, as her role model. She was particularly attracted to how "Madonsela, in doing her job, she is not afraid to speak her truth. She may have been afraid sometimes but she stood up. Women should take lessons on leadership from Thuli."

The value of education was very much emphasized. Dolly Mokgatle shared what her father said:

> without education you are going to be nothing. Whilst your mother and I are uneducated, we work very hard to make sure that you have something in your hand that will help go and discover the world and conquer whatever your personal aspirations are.

Resilience is another enabling force for women's achievements. Joyce Banda, former president of Malawi, said, "I left Malawi a better place than when I found it. I came into office at a very difficult time. The economy had almost collapsed, but in 24 months I was able to turn it around." She talked of a book she is keen to write in which she will "tell any African woman reading it that [you] can be at the lowest in [your] life and bounce back. Every woman who reads my book will know that when you fall, you get up and run again." Brand Pretorius said this about women's resilience:

> You need to be very resilient. Because, some of the odds are stacked against you, because frankly there is still prejudice. I mean, I am not saying anything new, but merely confirming that there is still prejudice. Regrettably, it is very entrenched.

Resilience was an abundant characteristic of all the women we interviewed. Every woman leader we interviewed for this book saw failure or challenges as opportunities to persevere and to achieve the impossible. Nkosazana Dlamini-Zuma, the first female chairperson of the African Union Commission, strongly suggested that the enablers lie in women themselves: "Women have to invest in Africa ourselves and work towards a more united and strong Africa." In 2015, when the push was for women's empowerment, she devised the perfect solution to restore the dignity of female farmers. The solutions for the future of Africa lie within women themselves.

Another enabler is how leaders, through the adoption of a wider and inclusive approach to engagement, enable individuals to shine. Barçin Yinanç put it thus:

> A leader is one that, when working with the team, understand who has what talent, and work with them according to their skills and talents. I think this is one of the messages I have learnt when I worked, especially on issues that requires teamwork, you know. You shouldn't expect the same thing from everybody, and you should not think everybody is like you. Everyone is different, everyone is precious, everyone has a talent, you know. And you have to see though, whoever has the skill, and, you know, make use of these skills accordingly.

Sometimes the enabler is the simple belief that leadership is not unattainable but rather that it is, as Joyce Banda expressed it:

> "a love affair". You fall in love with the people that you serve and the people must fall in love with you. When you are not benefiting anything from what you are doing, that love affair becomes real and meaningful to them. Something drives you and you can't stop, you

can't accept that you are leading a better life and they are not. You feel it is your responsibility to improve that situation. That is leadership, and most women are servant leaders.

Conclusion

Globally, for women's equality and leadership to progress beyond aspirations expressed by a plethora of policy concessions, a sprinkling of women in leadership positions and a small group of both women and men as champions and advocates, there has to be a concerted effort to move on from a "business as usual" mode.

The evidence is there to show that women in leadership roles are vital for companies in terms of their bottom line; in terms of meeting their moral obligation to more than half the population; and in terms of their diversity and accessing larger pools of talent. At the same time, women and men in leadership positions have told us from their experience that it is hard work in these roles, especially in unhelpful and unsympathetic environments. But they have also provided us with a range of practical strategies they have found useful. Drawing on the experiences of women and men leaders we have developed a leadership model that consists of four key elements—the personal, the context, the barriers and the enablers—which must be considered holistically in designing strategies for businesses and by extension the content of education offerings. Women in leadership positions are vital for the competiveness of companies and, ultimately, of nations.

We have the opportunity to change the state of women's leadership as we find it today. The success of our efforts will depend on our ability to bring about an interconnectedness between the many initiatives taking place. The digital world we now live in offers limitless opportunities to establish an interconnected women's leadership portal. It serves as a "go to" resource on women's leadership, servicing women aspiring for leadership as well as institutions aspiring to build women's leadership.

It is clear that women and men must actively pursue the changes they wish to realize in their home country and, eventually, the world. We must go back to basics and start rebuilding the country, the continent—looking at the challenges in the world right now. What we need is communal and collaborative leadership. But we also need the support of male sponsors and leaders to change the policies, practices and mindsets if we are to make a breakthrough in incorporating women into the economy and on all decision-making platforms. The imperatives have to be wider than smart economics and the moral obligation to include women: one more significant imperative is the kind of leader needed for the complex and volatile world in which we currently live and work. Brand Pretorius from

South Africa suggested some characteristics that might be desirable in leaders for these fractious times:

> Over the years, I met some incredible women in leadership positions. I think in many situations, women acquit themselves in their leadership roles much better than men because of their courage, unquestionable integrity, the absence of ego, a higher level of emotional intelligence, a great emphasis on relationships and a caring, servant leader approach.

Perhaps Gerzema and D'Antonio (2013) latched onto something powerful when they wrote, "women, and the men who think like them, will rule the world".

References

Anderson, R. H. 2014. *Undeterred: The Six Success Habits of Women in Emerging Economies.* New York: The Way Women Work Press.

Bandara, A. 2015. "The Economic Cost of Gender Gaps in Effective Labor: Africa's Missing Growth Reserve". *Feminist Economics* 21(2): 162–186.

Bendick, M. 2007. "Situation Testing for Employment Discrimination In the United States of America". *Horizons stratégiques* 3(5): 17–39.

Bluen, S. 2012. *Talent Management in Emerging Markets.* Bryanston, JHB: Knowledge Resources Publishing.

Brunswick. 2016. "The Boardroom". *Brunswick Review* 10(Spring): 6.

Carter, N. M. and H. M. Wagner. 2011. "The Bottom Line: Corporate Performance and Women's Representation on Boards (2004–2008)". *Catalyst* 1.

Chant, S. and C. Sweetman. 2012. "Fixing Women or Fixing the World? 'Smart Economics', Efficiency Approaches, and Gender Equality in Development". *Gender & Development* 20(3): 517–529.

Credit Suisse Research Institute. 2016. "The CS Gender 3000: Women in Senior Management". Zurich, Switzerland.

Eagly, A. H. 2013. "Why 'Lean In'? Hybrid Style Succeeds, and Women Are Best at It". *nytimes.com.* Accessed July 19, 2016. www.nytimes.com/roomfordebate/2013/03/20/shery-sandberg-says-lean-in-but-is-that-really-the-way-to-lead/why-lean-in-hybrid-style-succeeds-and-women-are-best-at-it.

Gerzema, J. and M. D'Antonio. 2013. *The Athena Doctrine: How Women (and the Men who Think Like Them) will Rule the Future.* Hoboken, NJ: John Wiley & Sons.

Grant Thornton. 2015. "Women in Business: The Path to Leadership", Grant Thornton International Business Report 2015. Retrieved June 10, 2016. www.grantthornton.global/globalassets/1.-member-firms/global/insights/ibr-charts/ibr2015_wib_report_final.pdf.

Hays-Thomas, R. and M. Bendick. 2013. "Professionalizing Diversity and Inclusion Practice: Should Voluntary Standards Be the Chicken or the Egg?" *Industrial and Organizational Psychology* 6(3): 193–205.

Hewlett, S. A. and R. Rashid. 2011. *Winning the War for Talent in Emerging Markets: Why Women are the Solution.* Boston, MA: Harvard Business Review Press.

Hiller, V. 2014. "Gender Inequality, Endogenous Cultural Norms, and Economic Development". *Scandinavian Journal of Economics* 116(2): 455–481.

Hutt, R. 2016. "8 Top Quotes on Gender Parity from Davos 2016". *World Economic Forum*. Retrieved June 28, 2016. www.weforum.org/agenda/2016/01/7-quotes-on-gender-parity-from-davos-2016/.

Khalf, R. 2016. "The March of the Sisterhood". *Sunday Times*, July 17, 18.

Madsen, S. R., F. W. Ngunjiri, K. A. Longman and C. Cherrey. 2015. *Women and Leadership Around the World*. Charlotte, NC: Information Age Publishing.

McKinsey & Company. 2010. "Women at the Top of Corporations: Making it Happen". New York.

McKinsey & Company. 2012a. "Unlocking the Full Potential of Women at Work". New York.

McKinsey & Company. 2012b. "Women Matter: Making the Breakthrough". New York.

McKinsey & Company. 2013. "Women Matter: A Latin American Perspective. Unlocking Women's Potential to Enhance Corporate Performance". New York.

MSCI (Modern Index Strategy Indexes). 2015. "2015 Survey of Women on Boards: Global Trends in Gender Diversity on Corporate Boards". Retrieved June 23, 2016. www.msci.com/documents/10199/04b6f646-d638-4878-9c61-4eb91748a82b.

Rosser-Mims, D. M. 2005. "An Exploration of Black Women's Political Leadership Development". Unpublished doctoral dissertation, University of Georgia, Athens. Accessed February 27, 2017. https://getd.libs.uga.edu/pdfs/rosser-mims_dionne_200508_phd.pdf.

Sealy, R. 2010. "Changing Perceptions of Meritocracy in Senior Women's Careers". *Gender in Management: An International Journal* 25(3): 184–197.

The Guardian. 2015. "Gender Equality Still Decades Away, Says Chief of UN Women". March 6. Accessed June 23, 2016. www.theguardian.com/world/2015/mar/06/gender-equality-still-decades-away-un-women.

United Nations. 2015. "The World's Women 2015: Trends and Statistics". Department of Economic and Social Affairs, Statistics Division, New York.

UN News Centre. 2016. "UN Commission on Status of Women Opens with Calls to 'Seize the Day'; Ensure Gender Equality". March 14. Accessed June/July 2016. www.un.org/apps/news/story.asp?NewsID=53437#.V5rzbfl97IV.

WomenWatch. 2007. "Women in Leadership Roles". November 19. Accessed June 23, 2016. www.un.org/womenwatch/feature/women_leadership/Online_discussion_report_Women_in_Leadeship_Roles.pdf.

World Bank. 2016. "World Development Indicators 2016". Washington, DC. Accessed February 17, 2017. http://dx.doi.org/10.1596/978-1-4648-0683-4, p. 70.

World Economic Forum (WEF). 2016a. "The Global Gender Gap Report". Cologny, Switzerland.

World Economic Forum (WEF). 2016b. "Eight Top Quotes on Gender Parity from Davos 2016". Cologny, Switzerland. Accessed July 2016. www.weforum.org/agenda/2016/01/7-quotes-on-gender-parity-from-davos-2016/.

2 Leadership in context

Caren Scheepers

Introduction

Looking back, we acknowledge the earlier generations of women leaders, paving the way. It is to these women that we dedicate this volume. Looking forward, we leave it as a legacy to those following in our footsteps. We live now in exhilarating and challenging times. Illuminating hindsight, insight and foresight represents a contextual approach to leadership (Kutz 2008). This chapter thus offers a contemporary perspective on the current era to promote insight, and requires hindsight to show how far we have come and foresight in where we are heading. The chapter "Leadership in Context" offers a broader perspective than the discourse in current leadership literature. Studies on leadership to date have been dominated by the viewpoint and accounts of Western white corporate males; there is now a call by a number of scholars to expand and diversify this sample— and this book seeks to answer that call. To obtain a more comprehensive view of the unique experiences of leaders, a variety of environments is explored in this book, largely through the accounts of the women leaders interviewed. In addition, we examine the divergent ways in which women's leadership is defined, given the various contexts—for instance, the corporate, entrepreneurial and educational—in which it is expressed, and the chapters that follow will feature these particular environments.

In advocating a contextual view of leadership, Chapter 2 functions in tandem with Chapter 3, which focuses on particular geographical contexts within emerging economies, underlining the evolution of women's movements in these locations. A broader societal context is highlighted in Chapter 2, specifically around the social construction of masculinity and femininity. Furthermore, Chapter 2 illuminates the evolution of leadership research into contemporary contrasting views on women's leadership. It uncovers societal contextual variables and organizational dynamics responsible for maintaining the gender inequality in organizations. In illustrating "Leadership in Context", Chapter 2 introduces the chapters that follow.

Helgesen (1995) laments that "the challenge today is the same challenge that the suffragists faced in the 1920s", and we must ask if this holds true.

Have we made such limited progress over the last few centuries, and is this reflected particularly in emerging market countries? The women interviewed as part of our research reported some progress; nonetheless, the societies of emerging markets are still perceived as having patriarchal structures. For instance, one interviewee, Ntombi Langa-Royds from South Africa, observed: "The sad part for me is I see too few examples of my peer group having broken the glass ceiling. I would say, no, we haven't moved. So, I am a woman, it's a barrier, let's decide what we are going to do about it. Am I going to go full in there and show those boys what I am capable of, or I am going to shrink back and say—Sorry, I am a girl. You make those decisions."

While we were conducting research for this book, the film *Suffragette* (Gavron 2015), directed by Sarah Gavron and authored by Abi Morgan, was being screened in cinemas all over the world. The film features the 1897 founding in Britain of Millicent Fawcett's National Union of Women's Suffrage—fighting for the right to vote. In Chapter 3, these women's movements and others in emerging markets are highlighted. The extensive public response to the film reveals contemporary interest and relevance of discourse on issues around women's positioning in society. In this regard, Chapter 2 unpacks the current zeitgeist or spirit of our time in relation to women's leadership.

The focus of our research methodology was a number of interviews conducted with a range of women from diverse contexts, a rich source for this leadership study. Included in their personal accounts are the societal structures within which these women play a leadership role. In this chapter we primarily focus on those interviewees whose responses open up discussion in this regard. Chapter 11 offers a thorough analysis of all interviews and describes the patterns that emerged.

While Chapter 1 focused on the economics of women leadership, this chapter deals with the sociocultural realities of women leadership in emerging markets. Given that so much current research on leadership has originated in the US, geographical locations form an important part of the context of our study. In addition, the data collected for this book is derived from interviews with women at a particular level of management—certainly women with substantial standing in their organizations—and this status undoubtedly informs their outlook.

The particular contexts of the women leaders discussed in this chapter include consulting in Russia and Dubai, journalism in Turkey, human resources in a multinational technology company; roles range from a political activist (and later cabinet minister) and board member of blue chip companies in South Africa, a venture capitalist originally from China, an economist originally from the Middle East who lives in the US and consults in emerging markets, and a former South African who consults in Southeast Asia. A number of these women are married, some are single, and their ages vary from late twenties to fifties. For most of the women in our interview sample the emerging markets offer opportunities for gender equality. One interviewee, Martly Rademeyer from South Africa, expressed her views on the emerging markets context in the following way:

> I think culture plays a huge role, for example, how the German culture or the Japanese culture versus how my colleagues from Norway or Denmark or Sweden think about women and the woman's role and equality. So there is the cultural thing. In the emerging markets I think, yes, there is much more opportunity because there is almost a sense of, well, let's see what happens, we don't know. I think, for example, emerging markets like South Africa or Brazil or China have a greater openness and seek innovative solutions for the organization, whether it is through appointing younger leaders or having more females. So there is more space in a way.

The structure of the chapter first provides the reader with a broad view as a starting point for the book's unique offering, then moves on to contemporary work environments and women leaders' responses. We offer an integration of the literature on women leadership in a matrix and summary table of arguments. While quotations from the interviews are cited that relate to a particular section of literature under discussion, the latter part of the chapter concentrates on specific themes that were revealed in the qualitative analysis of the interview transcripts.

New vantage point

Alimo-Metcalfe and Alban-Metcalfe (2005, 52) and James (1998, 67) contend respectively that the most "commonly accepted models of leadership are virtually all based on US studies" of "white males", confirmed by Avolio, Walumbwa and Weber (2009). Elliott and Stead (2008, 159) warn accordingly that conceptions of leadership draw largely on the leadership experiences of a limited population and of those in a restricted range of organizational settings, and that "locations in which studies of leadership take place contain a number of biases". In this regard, Dickson, Den Hartog and Mitchelson (2003) report on the decline in the quest for universal leadership principles and instead, unique ways in which leadership manifests in cultures. House et al.'s (2004) GLOBE study reveals culturally influenced differences in leadership prototypes.

In this study we were particularly interested in how the women leaders we interviewed had been able to lead where they did not have similarity with followers and therefore did not represent the leadership prototype for their time and location. Shamir et al. (2005, 26) emphasize that "the leader's similarity with followers increases the followers' perceptions of the leader's proto-typicality and their acceptance and endorsement of the leader". Some evidence is available on expectations of leaders in the US—for instance, that traits associated with masculine leadership are preferred (Eagly 2007; Sinclair 2012), with limited studies available on these expectations in emerging markets. Most of the emerging market women leaders interviewed for this book have risen within the ranks of their companies and organizations, be they corporate, educational or entrepreneurial. Thus, we are provided with useful touchpoints for comparison, and this book aims to address the bias in leadership studies to date by examining the experiences of women in emerging markets. For instance, our interviewees remarked:

> In Europe they tend to stick to the facts. Here, it is a much broader discussion. Sometimes the most difficult part is not being a woman, but being a man. And sometimes the most difficult part is—you are not a local. Whether you like it or not, these circumstances are pretty much attached to your Western mindset and to very rational processes. And here there is a different perspective. So here you have a much more, how can I put it, constant social responsibility perspective. So sometimes it is the changing of mindsets that is more difficult and not necessarily being a woman.
>
> (Isabel Neiva, UAE)

> Some of the leadership practices like courageous conversations and performance management are very hard in the Asian culture and we need to find other ways people can raise issues that are less threatening to them.
>
> (Marianne Roux, consulting in Asia Pacific)

In Chapter 3 the particular environments in a number of the emerging markets is described; nonetheless, there are unique challenges for women in societies where traditional norms do not support advancement of working women. Note this comment from Barçin Yinanç, one of our interviewees in Turkey: "There are a lot of women journalists, especially at the bottom. But the more you go up, you know, the less you will see them, that's for sure. Yes, there is a glass ceiling."

Contextual view of leadership

Leadership scholars have recently reminded us of contextual variables in leadership studies (Porter and McLaughlin 2006; Tozi 1991; Walter and Buch 2010). In this regard, leadership research is entering "a new era" (Osborn and Marion 2009, 191). Porter and McLaughlin (2006, 559) declare that "leadership in organisations does not take place in a vacuum. It takes place in organisational contexts." Kellerman (2013) warns that we ignore the context of leadership at our peril. Kark (2004) criticizes studies on simple statistical connections, without suggesting why these differences occur by investigating the cultural patterns and structures. He therefore calls for more studies on comprehensive models including contextual characteristics and cultural patterns. While context is often an afterthought in a research project, here it is integral to the study, given the role that it plays in shaping leadership development.

Consistent with this new era, our study considered that patterns over time and history mattered. For example, the multi-layered complexity of the setting is illustrated by an interviewee, Marianne Roux (consulting in Asia Pacific), who mentioned: "You keep on being told not to be a 'tall poppy'—don't be so straight." This quotation exhibits the environment within which this woman leader needs to operate. The spirit of the time or zeitgeist in which leadership is embedded and which subsequently plays a role in leader emergence or endorsement is thus an important focus of the study (Mayo and Nohria 2005).

Leadership as such is more than the influence of an individual leader on his or her subordinates, it is the "collective influence of leaders in and around the system" (Osborn, Hunt and Jauch 2002, 789). Kellerman (2013) contends that the dominant focus in the field of leadership studies is the leader–follower exchange and leaders' characteristics and styles, whereas followers and context would seem to be as important. The promising perspective of contextual leadership is extending the focus of the leader–follower exchange. Kutz (2008, 18) defines contextual intelligence of leaders as "the ability to recognise and diagnose the plethora of contextual factors inherent in an event or circumstance, then intentionally and intuitively adjust behaviour in order to exert influence in that context".

Contextual intelligence requires an intuitive grasp of relevant past events, an acute awareness of present contextual variables and a view of a preferred future. As such, hindsight, insight and foresight are all required. Kellerman (2013) concurs that contextual intelligence is as important as emotional intelligence. In our sample an interviewee, Isabel Neiva from UAE, observed:

> The Middle East is quite different from other mature markets or from Europe, where I had experience. And when in Europe, I am looking at a very rational worksite; it is very unemotional and, in a way, rational and straightforward. The Middle East is not like that, so there are a lot of other factors that are as important.

Scholars such as Osborn et al. (2002, 797) assert: "Change the context and leadership changes." Thus, context dictates expectations of leaders, and what models are acceptable. Mayo and Nohria (2005) define contextual leadership intelligence (CQ) as the ability to understand an evolving environment and to capitalize on those evolving trends. Alimo-Metcalfe and Alban-Metcalfe (2005) describe leaders as sensitive to the impact of their actions on staff, in line with Tichy and Devanna (1986), who identified environmental sensitivity and particularly sensitivity to members' needs. In our sample, it was evident that the women leaders were attuned to their contexts:

I think the lack of authenticity is much easier to catch if you know the person; I watch the body language and watching people, it is clear that there are these different tribes and families … .

(Ekaterina Sheremet, Russia)

I take a systems view: I gather perspectives as broadly as I can through deep listening; I co-create, I coach. This has changed a lot over the years.

(Marianne Roux, consulting in Asia Pacific)

From a contextual view of leadership, we can appreciate the complexity and nuances those women leaders have to deal with in both the societal and organizational environment.

Gender bias is the backdrop

In terms of the context in which women leadership finds itself, there are four main reasons for our argument that gender bias still exists.

First, recent research findings reveal that most women are in jobs associated with their gender stereotype, such as the "softer" disciplines like human resources and marketing, whereas most CEOs are sourced from the "harder" disciplines such as finance or operations (Grant Thornton 2015). Women are most likely to lead education and social services and healthcare businesses. The types of entrepreneurial businesses that women start are frequently in the beauty and cosmetics or food industries that stereotypically serve women. Our distinct perceptions inform our decisions consciously or subconsciously. This reality suggests a serious consideration of the influence of society's gender stereotypes on the destiny of working women. In this regard, Rania Habiby Anderson (formerly from the Middle East) explicitly noted: "If globally, we cannot figure out how to fully engage educated women in the workforce, companies will fail. Also, access to financing is always a challenge for women."

Second, with the still persistent notion that women work within the household and men beyond it, it is no surprise that men dominate organizations. Gherardi and Poggio (2001, 256) contend that "the presence of women in male-dominated jobs breaks down the symbolic gender order". Accordingly, women are almost twice as likely to cite gender bias as their male peers, states Grant Thornton (2015, 11). Stereotypes and gender bias are significant hurdles on the way to leadership, and, as a consequence, women may find that they constantly have to prove themselves better leaders in order to take up roles more readily acquired by their male counterparts. The horizontal and vertical occupational segregation is still very evident and produced by cultural and symbolic practices, Gherardi and Poggio (2001) assert. Olsson (2002, 142) describes leadership as a "masculine archetype—a powerful image which exists in the collective unconscious of groups of people which seem universal to the nature of leaders."

Third, in line with their findings, the International Labour Organization has recently stated that "While there has been progress in elevating more women into management roles, it is slow, and at this pace it will be more than 100 years before parity is achieved" (International Labour Organization 2015). Isabel Neiva remarked: "It [leadership] is very much related to the religion and the norms. It is not that they don't think women should work, women are working, but they stop at middle manager. There are not many in senior management positions."

Several other studies also indicate that women are still experiencing gender bias (Ibarra, Ely and Kolb 2013). Clark and Kleyn (2011, 203) provide evidence of organizational paternalistic cultures as barriers to advancement. Leimon, Moscovici and Goodies declared that they were appalled at the sheer waste of talent in the workplace, referring to the low proportion of women in senior roles and declared that women "have to prove that they did not throw out their brains with the placenta" (2011, 30). Tarr-Whelan concurs by declaring, "We neglect one of our nation's most vital resources" (2009, ix). Women are caught in the dilemma of not being perceived as feminine enough when they are assertive, or too feminine and therefore weak (Catalyst 2007; Rosette and Tost 2010). One of our interviewees, Ekaterina Sheremet from Russia, advised in this regard: "I have observed that many women tend to be shy and are not aggressive enough because of fear—so very often women under-present themselves. Don't be afraid to seem aggressive. Don't be afraid to be looked at negatively."

Fourth, Gherardi and Poggio (2001) consider those economic theories weak that consider gender segregation in professional advancement and achievement a natural outcome of these contexts when there has been a different investment in the education of males and females. This argument is contradicted by the fact that young women who are entering the workplace today are sometimes better educated than men. One of the women in our sample—Rania Habiby Anderson, originally from the Middle East—expressed this dilemma as follows: "We will have a massive talent shortage in fast-growing economies. I will give one extreme example: in Jordan there are 26 universities, 75% of students are women, 56% of the graduates are women. And they comprise 10% of the workforce."

Flanders (1994) emphasizes that women's careers are interrupted by maternity and that most never catch up with their male colleagues. These gender issues have been featuring in leadership studies. The next section is dedicated to the evolution of leadership studies.

The evolution of leadership studies

The history of leadership studies can be traced back seventy years to the 1930s, Alimo-Metcalfe and Alban-Metcalfe (2005) assert. They call for a re-evaluation of leadership models that were developed more than thirty years ago, given the technological, economic, social and political changes over this time span. The new approach to leadership studies focuses on the realities of constant change. Avolio et al. (2009) call these new theories "new era" theories. Examples of such theories include the transformational leadership of Burns (1978) and Bass (1985). This leadership model implies an ability to engage followers' higher needs; also included is House's (1971) charismatic leadership and Hunt's (1996) visionary leadership where strategic leaders empower organizational members to realize leaders' long-term organizational vision. The models of leadership that were designed for the past century may not fully capture the leadership dynamic of organizations operating in today's knowledge-driven economy (Uhl-Bien, Marion and McKelvey 2007).

Likewise, Fletcher (2004) emphasizes that leadership had shifted in response to the environment that changed from the industrial era of demand and control to knowledge-based settings that call for collaborative leadership, distributed throughout the organization. In our sample, leadership was described in these terms:

> an ability to hear people's views, to give others the opportunity to share different opinions and to consider that. You are really flexible and ready to change your mind if you hear some arguments.
>
> (Ekaterina Sheremet, Russia)

> You need to be able to convince someone both to understand and buy in to a particular vision you put on the table.
>
> (Geraldine Fraser-Moleketi, South Africa)

Alimo-Metcalfe and Alban-Metcalfe's (2005, 65) findings suggest the need to be wary of relying exclusively on models that currently dominate the literature: "there is increasing evidence in the western world that there is growing discomfort with the heroic models of visionary-charismatic leadership". They point to the distinct shift in thinking away from extolling these charismatic-inspirational or heroic models of leadership and refer in this regard to Hogan's studies on the damage that can be done by narcissistic leaders (Nelson and Hogan 2009), particularly after corruption scandals like Enron and WorldCom. In his turn, Mintzberg (1999) also challenges the idea of the heroes of American leaders, who so-called "single-handedly" turn around organizations; whereas leadership distributed throughout the organization is required for such success to develop. Fletcher (2004) concurs in describing post-heroic leadership as focusing on the more mutual, less hierarchical leadership practices and skills needed to engage collaborative, collective learning. In this regard, Geraldine Fraser-Moleketi (South Africa), an interviewee in our sample, noted:

> When I was promoted to the position of ..., I first went to see a highly regarded specialist and said, "Look, I need to understand how the

sector operates." I asked her to teach me; we spent two weeks together and I created an advisory team of around 20 people from all over.

Another interviewee, Ekaterina Sheremet (Russia), described her growth as a leader in the following way: "It's changed from the way that I used to be—very authoritarian. I think it stems from the fact of wanting to control and being responsible for everything ... . I now work with my colleagues and I act as a coach; it also required some investment into people ... ."

Alimo-Metcalfe and Alban-Metcalfe (2005, 60) emphasize humility and vulnerability in admitting when making mistakes, and consider whether this factor represented the UK public sector service ethic and thus reflects "an important contextual leadership variable". Researchers such as Osborn and Marion (2009) have lately confirmed earlier studies' findings such as those of Osborn et al. (2002) that leadership is indeed embedded in its context. These findings prompt scholars to assess the influence of context on leaders and represent another milestone in the evolution of leadership theory. In line with this trend, our focus on women's leadership includes a contextual view.

Femininity as the "Other"

One of our earliest feminists, De Beauvoir (1949, 736), states that "there is no reason to conclude that her ovaries condemn her to live forever on her knees". As far back as the time of Aristotle, women have been defined in terms of their insufficiency, rather than their own definitive qualities. De Beauvoir (1949) quotes the ancient philosopher as saying: "We should regard the female nature as afflicted with natural defectiveness. The female is a female by virtue of a certain lack of qualities. Thus humanity is male and man defines woman not in herself, but as relative to him." De Beauvoir also cites Plato thanking God that he was not a woman. She notes the zeitgeist of the 1940s as "Man is the Subject ... the Absolute—she is the Other" (1949, 19). This idea persisted into the 2000s, with Elliot and Stead (2008, 162) emphasizing that "attention to women leaders is framed in relationship to male leaders."

De Beauvoir laments that a woman "is often very well pleased with her role as the Other" (1949, 21). In a more hopeful stance, Leonard states, "If a woman really values herself she is then able really to dialogue with the masculine. Neither is she subservient to the masculine, nor does she imitate it" (1982, 164). Popular psychology books like John Gray's (1993) *Men are from Mars, Women are from Venus*, which sold over 30 million copies, highlight the prevalence of gender stereotyping. The popularity of romantic comedies like *What Women Want*, starring Mel Gibson and Helen Hunt, further emphasizes the binary outlook on gender. Henry Higgins' refrain of 1964 in *My Fair Lady* is renowned in the West. We may find Sir Edmund Hillary's sincere objections to taking women on his expedition in the 1950s to Mount Everest archaic, but such influential voices have certainly shaped current notions of femaleness. Coughlin, Wingard and Hollihan (2005) lists Hillary's three reasons: women did not have the qualities of leadership required, were not strong enough to carry the packs and would become hysterical at high altitudes. These were explicit sentiments, whereas researchers warn us that in our current age, particularly in our work contexts, they are more subtle and insidious. The following section takes up the discussion on masculinity and femininity in the workplace.

South African artist, Andre Swanepoel, sought to capture the constrained gender identity within which women are compelled to conduct themselves in his "Corset" series of works. In another emerging market, Poland, the Women League activists in the 1980s declared that "the corset they once laced us with—continues to disable us" (Fuszara 2005). Figure 2.1 below shows an example of Andre Swanepoel's work: an army boot's leather is the material from which the traditional female corset is constructed:

Charlotte Perkins Gilman, a prominent American sociologist and feminist, who once compared women's labor in the home to those of horses, famously used the corset as metaphor:

Put a corset, even a loose one, on a vigorous man or woman who never wore one, and there is intense discomfort, and a vivid consciousness thereof. The healthy muscles of the trunk resent the pressure, the action of the whole body is checked in the middle, the stomach is choked, the process of digestion is interfered with; and the victim says, "How can you bear such a thing?"

But the person habitually wearing a corset does not feel these evils. They exist, but the nerves have become accustomed to these disagreeable sensations, and no longer respond to them. In fact, the wearer becomes so used to the sensations that when they are removed, – with the corset, – there is a distinct sense of loss and discomfort.

(Edles and Appelrouth 2010, 228)

It is this metaphor that is visually extended and referenced in my "Corset" series of works. My "corset" pieces were intended to reflect this pervading sense of claustrophobia induced by the rigidity of the power structures set in place within institutions and organizations. As their bodies were, quite literally, constricted, contorted and shaped by the corset so our female leaders now endure the corset of what a man's idea of leadership is in our patriarchal society.

("Corset" piece rationale by Andre Swanepoel)

Our societies have a number of images to describe the ideal woman, and in the next section we offer some examples from the work context.

Figure 2.1 Corset from Andre Swanepoel's art series
Source: With permission from artist: Andre Swanepoel (Swany).

Work landscape as hegemonic masculine context

Metaphors such as "glass ceiling", "glass elevator", "glass cliff", "glass hammer" have become familiar in the discussion of bias against women and their empowerment in organizational cultures. Hayward (2005) suggests that women need sharpened stilettos to shatter this glass ceiling. Such imagery has emerged because of the seemingly impenetrable barriers that women encounter in the work landscape. Various studies suggest that organizations are not only dominated by the number of masculine representatives, but perhaps more importantly by a masculine culture in which men are the leaders and dictate the practices by which the organization is run. Kolb, Williams and Frohlinger (2010, 8) observe: "We expect men to take charge and women to take care."

An interviewee, Martly Rademeyer from South Africa, reflected on this in the following way: "In executive meetings, 80% will be male, many of them in the room. So I think, yes, it was definitely a barrier just being in the minority in a very male and [specific nationality] oriented culture."

Elliott and Stead (2008, 162) and Moss-Kanter (1977) note that the image of the archetypical business leader is forceful masculinity. Gherardi and Poggio's (2001) study also highlights the hegemonic masculinity underlying the dominant social practices at the workplace. Here, women are allowed to compete only if they wear the clothing of invisible but hegemonic masculinity. As women in our sample observed:

> We also need to encourage women that they can get higher positions. And this should not be a man's world only, that they should be self-confident. So basically it is mentality.
>
> (Barçin Yinanç, Turkey)

> It is so far a male environment, in the industry I work in, I think it is not an easy thing, overall. You are always the minority and that's kind of a challenge.
>
> (Ekaterina Sheremet, Russia)

> It is very masculine.
>
> (Marianne Roux, consulting in Asia Pacific)

Ruderman and Ohlott (2002) of the Center for Creative Leadership also highlight that modern organizations are based on masculine experiences and ideals and that women subsequently struggle with authenticity. Women realize, though, that they have to work within the culture of the organization, as Martly Rademeyer (South Africa) describes: "We learned that you had to grow and that you have to work inside the culture of the organization."

Perriton (2006) emphasizes in her turn that the deliberate and knowing exclusion of women from important informal networks by men is an explanation for the glass ceiling. To change this cycle, men would need to purposefully sponsor women, as interviewees asserted:

I think that one of the things that a lot of women lack in general is being sponsored … and to men, would be to sponsor the women they have in their team.

(Isabel Neiva, UAE)

Offer to mentor younger women; call [out] behaviors that are sexist or undermine women.

(Marianne Roux, consulting in Asia Pacific)

The next section will pay attention to the responses of women to this context.

Responses of women leaders

The researchers for this book identified two main categories of responses of women leaders.

First, women give up their female identity. Flanders (1994, 72) declares in this regard that "in the past, those women who made it to the top often did so because they submerged their femininity, projecting an image which would fit the stereotyped view of the successful male executive." Fletcher (2004) suggests that because men have dominated the spheres of influence in the work world for so long, women experience subtle pressure to "do masculinity" at work in order to be perceived as competent. For instance, Gherardi and Poggio (2001, 254) state that "the glass ceiling is reproduced through the norms associated with masculinity assumed to be the universal and therefore genderless and invisible, cultural model". An interviewee, Ntombi Langa-Royds from South Africa, mentioned: "she was also very man-like and that is why she didn't survive, because the men didn't like the competition, in my view."

Nonetheless, Gherardi and Poggio (2001, 252) contend that there are "implicit rules that prescribe an image of womanhood closer to the male ideal type"; namely, being determined, taking risks and being aggressive rather than being gentle and passive. Interviewees in our sample remarked in contrast to the literature cited above:

There is the other sentiment that, yes, if you have reached a top position, it is because you act a lot like men. I think that is not true anymore. It might have been maybe a few years back, maybe 10 or 15 or 20 years back. Because more and more we have great examples of women who do not behave like men and don't have the leadership style like men.

(Isabel Neiva, UAE)

It is not to say if you are feminine you are weak.

(Ntombi Langa-Royds, South Africa)

Second, Gherardi and Poggio (2001) describe yet another tactic in contrast to the first one that women adopt to survive in the male-dominated world: they develop relationships with politeness and political astuteness called "one down" strategies. We found some evidence of this strategy in our study. This viewpoint represents a strategy of non-competitiveness, even meekly feigning ignorance so that men do not feel threatened. The difference between men and women is hereby affirmed, but instead of assimilation, women feel compelled to assume a veneer that reinforces female stereotypes. These two strategic choices with their consequences are illustrated in Figure 2.2 below.

As the figure below illustrates, these two strategic choices are limited and have explicit consequences either by reinforcing stereotypes or by negating femininity altogether. In this regard, Perriton (2006, 102) criticizes the "how to" leadership literature that declares the key to overcoming barriers to women's career progression is to identify the barrier and then implement an appropriate winning strategy. She calls this a simplistic approach and emphasizes that the advice usually entails mentors, business cases, fashion or networking, as if the solution to persistent discrimination is for women to grasp and implement. Ely and Meyerson (2000) concur by describing these studies as "fixing the women" and not challenging existing power relationships. Ekaterina Sheremet (Russia) observed how she did not in fact adapt her style:

> I wouldn't say I changed my style to work with the male leaders. It is very important that you continue to act normally—not a male style, but try to be yourself. And that is very important, because after that because you feel relaxed, they accept you as a member of their team.

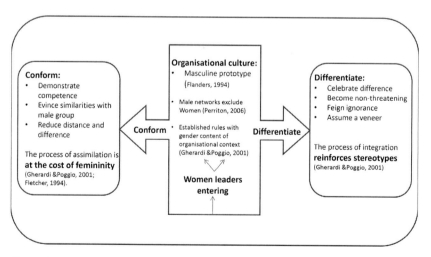

Figure 2.2 Women's responses to hegemonic masculine context
Source; Author's own (2016).

The two main responses of women leaders described above equate to opposing views in the literature on whether gender differences have to be emphasized and even celebrated or whether they actually disadvantage women. Figure 2.3 illustrates these opposing views in quadrant 2 and 3 of the matrix. This study contributes to the literature by offering other options of approaching women's leadership.

Quadrant 1

In the Figure 2.3 matrix, Quadrant 1 represents apathy towards gender issues in the workplace and specifically around leadership studies. Often, gender is not seen as its own conceptual framework to be studied, but rather as simply another demographic variable among other categories in the sample being researched. There is lack of awareness and perhaps also interest in the impact of a patriarchal context on women entering the top managerial echelons.

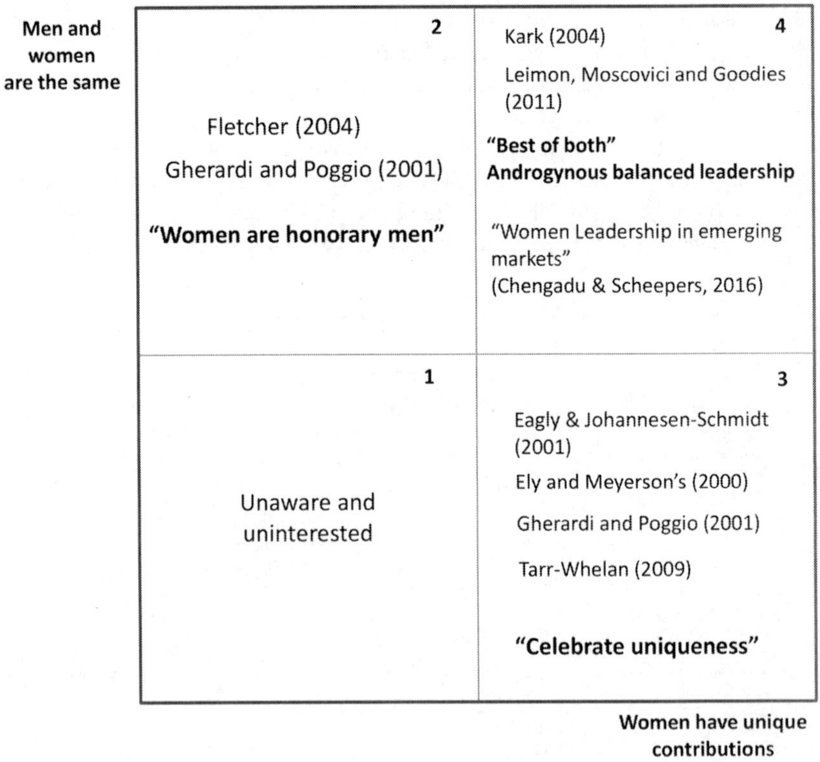

Men and women are the same	**2**	Kark (2004)	**4**
		Leimon, Moscovici and Goodies (2011)	
	Fletcher (2004)	**"Best of both"**	
	Gherardi and Poggio (2001)	**Androgynous balanced leadership**	
	"Women are honorary men"	"Women Leadership in emerging markets" (Chengadu & Scheepers, 2016)	
	1		**3**
		Eagly & Johannesen-Schmidt (2001)	
		Ely and Meyerson's (2000)	
	Unaware and uninterested	Gherardi and Poggio (2001)	
		Tarr-Whelan (2009)	
		"Celebrate uniqueness"	

Women have unique contributions

Figure 2.3 Emphasizing gender differences vs. similarities matrix
Source: Author's own, 2016.

Quadrant 2

Quadrant 2 represents the argument that women equal men. Leadership scholars such as Yukl (2002) contend that there are no overall differences in effectiveness between women and men leaders, but rather gender-related differences for certain behavior and skills in some situations. Accordingly, Fletcher (1994; 2004) found that the hypothesized differences in how women and men enact leadership have not been borne out empirically and it is even counterproductive to restrain women to a narrow set of leadership ideals as it will limit them and hinder their integration into leadership positions.

Quadrant 2's stance promotes equality and warns against the argument that women lead in a different way to men—which could, of course, reinforce gender stereotypes (Olsson 2002). For instance, feminine leadership was found to be communal (cooperative, affectionate, helpful, kind, sympathetic, interpersonally sensitive, nurturing, gentle, inclusive, relational, democratic, participative, adaptive) in contrast to masculine leadership being agentic (assertive, ambitious, aggressive, independent, self-confident, daring, directive and competitive) (Eagly and Carli 2003; Eagly 2007; Nielsen and Huse 2010; Rosette and Tost 2010). In our study the interviewees, contrarily, exhibited bold behavior, as the following quotations demonstrate:

> And I did not ask for permission. I just did it, because I knew if I was going to ask for permission, there was going to be every reason why it could not be done and good reasons as well; I also never hesitated to take on the difficult issues.
>
> (Geraldine Fraser-Moleketi, South Africa)

Fletcher (2004, 653) warns that when women use their relational skills to lead, their behavior is likely to be conflated not only with femininity but also with selfless giving and motherhood, whereas collaborative leadership implies a reciprocity and mutual benefit. Therefore, conflating a collaborative stance with selfless giving and femininity does not serve women and hinders effective leadership practice. Kark (2004) quotes in this regard a theoretical framework of gender reform feminism that contends that biological differences should be ignored and that men and women are similar in their common humanity. Seeing that gender-role socialization produces individual differences in the characteristics of men and women, developing women's skills would equip women to compete with men. He also emphasizes that women can assimilate into the culture of organizations with minimal disruption to the status quo. Our study, in turn, revealed the focus of consultants in Southeast Asia on women's empowerment:

> We assist them to develop business speak and a more business-like demeanor.
>
> (Marianne Roux, consulting to Asia Pacific)

Quadrant 3

Quadrant 3 emphasizes the differences that women bring to the workplace; for instance, Helgesen (1995, 5) argues that the "leader as warrior is a traditional view of leadership", and she promotes instead the uniquely feminine contribution women bring to leadership, using the example of Anita Roddick of The Body Shop, who declared that she ran her company according to the feminine principle of caring. Tarr-Whelan (2009) also asks in this regard whether we would be in the same mess if Lehman Brothers had been Lehman Sisters. She asserts that women's values and visions have a preference for collaboration, for a longer time horizon, for valuing relationships and for preventing crises. The observations of Isabel Neiva (UAE) highlight the unique contribution of women at the boardroom table: "Being the only woman at the table might sometimes help. You bring a different perspective to the table. Whether they like it or not."

Tarr-Whelan (2009, 10) emphasizes that "the values-based, future-orientated leaders are more likely to be women than men." In our interviews, Isabel Neiva (UAE) observed in this regard:

> Women have a different way of thinking and a different perception and that you can bring to the table very easily. So that for me is an advantage. And with clients as well and the teams listen to you because of that, you have a networking advantage, or you acquire relationships. The consequence of that is that usually decisions are very collegial. In a lot of discussions, there are a lot of the different perspectives to make sure that these points are covered and that is very different from Europe.

Bass (1999, 9) and Rosener (1990) quote several studies in which "women leaders tend to be more transformational than their male counterparts", and the manifestation of this is accompanied by greater satisfaction and rated effectiveness according to both genders. An Eagly, Johannesen-Schmidt and van Engen (2001) study also discovered that, owing to the resistance women encounter, they were more transformational. Assumptions of women leadership being preferable for contemporary organizations, as characterized by complex adaptive systems (CAS) (Uhl-Bien 2011), have been getting theoretical scholarly attention; however, limited empirical studies have been conducted to test these assumptions.

In contrast to the reform feminism-oriented studies, represented by quadrant 2 in Figure 2.3, Kark (2004) reveals the gender-resistance feminism orientation (quadrant 3) to women leadership studies, where, as with Ely and Meyerson's (2000) study, differences in experiences and interests should not be eliminated, but rather acknowledged and celebrated, under the existing patriarchal conditions. They resisted the notion of achieving equality by equating women to men. According to this stance,

transformational leadership particularly represents feminine characteristics, such as being sensitive to followers' needs. Therefore, their femininity makes women better leaders and they are not viewed as disadvantaged,
but as having valuable contributions to make as leaders with transformational styles. This celebration approach, while often well-meaning,
may actually channel women into dead-end jobs and reinforce unhelpful
stereotypes—for instance, where organizations institute sensitivity training for male managers to appreciate women's listening and collaborating styles, and assign women to jobs where they market products to
women or head up HR initiatives. As we discussed previously, since
CEOs are regularly sourced from financial disciplines, it can be questioned whether this approach actually ultimately benefits women. We
therefore offer a fourth option in approaching women leadership that we
name quadrant 4.

Quadrant 4

In quadrant 4 we advocate for a more androgynous approach to women
leadership studies by arguing against a binary outlook on gender. A consequence of the dichotomized approach of quadrants 2 and 3 is that it
directs the focus away from deeply entrenched systemic factors. Our premise is that women do not face individual challenges, but rather systemic
challenges within a society where masculinity defines the norm; for
instance, training individual women in assertiveness and even golf does
not address patriarchal social forces. A contextual approach to women's
leadership studies subsequently takes the complexity of the environment into
account, in addition to individual leaders' experiences. Another consequence
of the polarized approaches of quadrants 2 and 3 is radical ideals—for
example, replacing the masculine culture with a feminine culture, rejecting
the Freudian biological determinism of females' Electra complex (in
which women envy the male penis) and promoting a female-centered
psychoanalytical understanding.

Our stance is more in line with Kark (2004), who envisions an androgynous culture in which a biological male or female would be both masculine and
feminine. Accordingly, transformational leaders may employ a more
androgynous style, using the best in both masculine and feminine gender-
typed behavior. In this regard, Leimon, Moscovici and Goodies (2011)
emphasize *balanced* leadership that is visible, resilient, strategic, emotional,
decisive, intellectual and facilitating of meaning, representing characteristics
of both genders. Our argument thus contradicts that of Gherardi and Poggio
(2001), in which male and female are perceived as alternative categories and
belonging to the one necessarily entails a non-belonging to the other.

Kark (2004) summarizes the criticism of a universal category of women
as gender rebellion feminism. It is the direct challenge of the gender order
as being dual, oppositional and fixed. Accordingly, Hackman et al. (1992)

indicate that transformational leadership indeed consisted of both feminine and masculine behaviors. Isabel Neiva (UAE) noted how individual women have unique personalities and styles: "Maybe it was the case a few years back also because women were a whole number and kind of behaved like the others. Women I think, we have our own personality and our own style, whatever that style is."

Fletcher (2004) also emphasizes establishing more fluid, two-directional patterns of influence and power, and using difference, whether on cross-functional teams or difference that comes from gender identity, to challenge assumptions. The consequences of these two-directional patterns of influence are opportunities to grow, learn and ultimately innovate. Two interviewees made the following remarks in this regard:

> But I tried to focus on the person, or the personality of the person in front of me, whether it is a male or female leader, not just gender.
> (Ekaterina Sheremet, Russia)

> Do not restrict yourself to a group in which you feel comfortable. I always built diverse teams, I never pushed out anybody because I disagreed with their views, as I felt one also needs to hear opposing opinions. Unless, of course, that dissenting view was undermining progress.
> (Geraldine Fraser-Moleketi, South Africa)

By studying women leaders' life stories in this study from a contextual approach, we have uncovered cultural meanings of women's leadership and historical developments in its meaning. Narratives about episodes in which the symbolic gender order is challenged throw light on what women experience in male-dominated sectors. With the focus on context, we describe how the origin of gender inequality lies in cultural patterns around social identity entrenched in our mindsets and, consequently, in our organizations as systems. Ekaterina Sheremet (Russia) remarked, for instance: "I am confident that, if you talk about the priorities here, I think that there are some stereotypes, and in some positions or some industries there are naturally more males and it is too early to talk about men and women being equal."

The aforementioned quotation illustrates the view of current women leaders. The next section focuses on a comparison of arguments in women's leadership literature.

In this section, we offer a summary of the main arguments in the literature on women leadership.

As Table 2.1 illustrates, various arguments in the literature on women's leadership exist. The next section hones in on particular themes revealed by our study.

Table 2.1 Comparison of arguments in literature on women leadership

	Argue that women contribute unique attributes	Argue that women and men are equal	Argue that wider than US sample is required	Argue that when women are agentic, they are not liked	Argue that women submerge their femininity	Argue that there is inequality in workplace between genders	Argue that there is stereotyping of women leadership	Argue that fixing the women is not the answer
1	Eagly and Johnson (1990)	Kark (2004)	Alimo-Metcalfe and Alban-Metcalfe (2005)	Kolb, Williams and Frohlinger (2010)	Flanders (1994)	Gherardi and Poggio (2001)	Kolb, Williams and Frohlinger (2010)	Kark (2004)
2	Eagly et al. (2003)	Fletcher (1994)	Mohanty's (1991)	Catalyst (2007)	Gherardi and Poggio (2001)	Tarr-Whelan (2009)	Perriton (2006)	Ely and Meyerson (2000)
3	Eagly, Johannesen-Schmidt and van Engen (2003)	Gherardi and Poggio (2001)	James (1998)	Eagly (2007)	Ruderman and Ohlott (2002)	Leimon, Moscovici and Goodies (2011)	Flanders (1994)	Perriton (2006)
4	Ely and Meyerson (2000)	De Beauvoir (1949)	Dickson, Den Hartog and Mitchelson (2003)	Rosette and Tost (2010)	Acker (1990)	Hayward (2005)	Elliott and Stead (2008)	Gherardi and Poggio (2001)
5	Tarr-Whelan (2009)	Vermeulen (2004)	Anderson (2014)	Leonard (1982)	Bryans and Mavis (2003)	Meyerson and Fletcher (1999)	Sinclair (2012)	White (1992)
6	Uhl-Bien, Marion and McKelvey (2007)	Hackman, Furniss, Hills and Patterson (1992)	Van Zyl (2009)			Ibarra, Ely and Kolb (2013)	Eagly and Carli (2003)	Ryan and Haslam (2007)

#	Argue that women contribute unique attributes	Argue that women and men are equal	Argue that wider than US sample is required	Argue that when women are agentic, they are not liked	Argue that women submerge their femininity	Argue that there is inequality in workplace between genders	Argue that there is stereotyping of women leadership	Argue that fixing the women is not the answer
7	Bass (1999)		House, Hanges, Javidan, Dorfman and Gupta (2004)			Ruderman and Ohlott (2002)	Nielsen and Huse (2010)	
8	Helgesen (1995)					Helgesen (1995)	Heilman (2001)	
9	Uhl-Bien (2011)					Grant Thornton (2015)	Olsson (2002)	
10	Vinnicombe (1988)					Timberlake (2005)	Billing and Alvesson (2000)	

Core themes emerging from women leaders

For this chapter, we note broad themes, transcending particular contexts, in the qualitative analysis of the cases' interview transcripts. During our analysis process, we distilled the central themes of women leadership until there were no other major categories identified and saturation was achieved. In this section, these particular themes will be offered by discussing general ones and then more specifically those with high frequencies that revolved around the context of these women leaders, such as the contribution of the developmental ecosystem. A number of our findings confirmed current studies in the developed markets and, in light of this chapter's limited scope, we offer only those findings that we found to be fresh perspectives. The section thus revolves around three themes: first, the value of leaders' stories, second, a developmental ecosystem and third, contextual leadership intelligence.

Leaders' stories

Most leadership theories rate leaders' characteristics as important; in contrast, Shamir, Dayan-Horesh and Adler (2005) use leaders' life stories as the source of leaders' influence. Like Shamir et al. (2005), we too noticed that leaders' stories had carved a self-concept from which they could lead. In addition, we observed that a leader's biography appeared to be an important source of influence: Geraldine Fraser-Moleketi's impact owing to her involvement in the African National Congress for the last 35 years is a good example:

> And, you know, I did everything in the African National Congress, from licking the stamps if there was a need to sending postal items, to doing the organising, to acquiring the relevant training for specific tasks or missions required at a given point in time. There was no task too mundane or too complex.

We concur with Shamir et al.'s (2005) suggestion that a biographical and narrative approach to leadership studies could complement the currently dominant emphasis on leadership styles. A proudly South African example in former president, Nelson Mandela, illustrates how the stories of self-sacrifice of the leader influence followers. It enhances trust in the leader when followers learn about the leader's dedication to their shared values. Stories about leaders' breakthroughs allow them to accumulate idiosyncratic credits. In turn, this process offers them credibility to challenge the groups' existing norms. French and Raven's (1959) classic work revealed valuable sources of power and referent power as one of them. There is no doubt that, in profiling leaders in this book and citing their stories, those leaders' referent power is reinforced. We propose that what followers know about the leaders' life stories serves as these leaders' referent power, even in these indirect ways, in line with Shamir et al.'s (2005) views. For instance, the interesting notion that expatriates have a far better probability of being promoted creates a power base for those women who had spent time abroad, as Isabel Neiva (UAE) observed:

> some of them are expats, meaning they don't share the same culture. They don't share the same background. The race is the same, but the background, the religion, the culture are not. And they are the ones normally that would reach some of the top positions. Local women because of their religion, culture, norms are behind that track.

Nicola Kleyn, who is profiled in Chapter 4, revealed the hardships she had experienced in her life openly and authentically and the response of women listening to her was a willingness to be vulnerable and share their own experiences.

Developmental ecosystem

We were intrigued that the women leaders in our sample repeatedly mentioned the fact that they had the privilege of being exposed to good schooling. We realized that while it would be taken for granted in the developed countries, in the emerging markets women leaders would appear to acknowledge their access to enabling resources. They mentioned such a large number of resources, in different contexts, that we compiled a conceptual framework to illustrate what we called "a developmental ecosystem". Other researchers, such as Bennis and Thomas (2002), emphasize that leaders experience at least one critical transformational experience or trial. This event illustrates leaders' strong will and their ability to take on significant challenges, their high tolerance for stress and their toughness. In our study, a number of transformational experiences were described—for instance, see in Figure 2.4 the importance of challenging circumstances and these women leaders' sense of responsibility.

The coding process revealed families of codes. Table 2.2 below shows these results. The first column contains the code families and the columns that follow show the frequency with which interviewees mentioned that particular aspect. This indicates how many times that theme was mentioned by interviewees. The graphs and table reveal a number of code families, indicating that our interviewees perceived their academic competency, coaching and mentoring support, and professional and global exposure as important in their development.

The women leaders explicitly mentioned their social ecosystems and support structures as also important formative experiences. Furthermore, the interviewees had internal contexts such as boldness and deliberate self-sponsorship that had an influence on their development as leaders. We

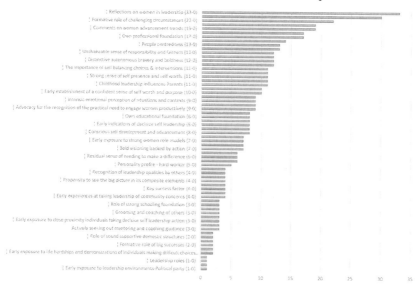

Figure 2.4 List of themes from sample
Source: Author's own through Atlas.ti.

Table 2.2 Code families for analysis of interviews (Chapter 2)

Code families	1	2	3	4	5	6	Total
Academic competency	5	3	2	3	2	0	15
Coaching and mentorship support	14	11	7	1	6	4	43
Global exposure	1	5	3	8	6	4	27
Personality traits, values, boldness, bravery and passion	60	23	9	13	15	19	139
Pointers on the advancement of women	5	25	11	23	13	14	91
Professional exposure and sponsorship	23	12	5	5	6	24	75
Role of high self-awareness, deliberate self-sponsorship	47	17	9	11	11	10	105
Social ecosystems and support structures	11	6	10	6	4	3	40
Influence of formative experiences	25	8	11	10	3	8	65
Totals	191	110	67	80	66	86	600

compared these findings with current research: in our sample, the women leaders exhibited what we called deliberate "self-sponsorship", in which they promoted and believed in themselves. This is contrary to current research, where Flanders' (1994) findings emphasize the culture trap—that is, women's own attitudes and lack of belief in themselves.

An important finding of our research is that these women leaders were exposed to a context in their early years in their homes which was different to that experienced by others; for instance, their parents held views that did not reflect the prevailing cultural values around women's position in society and from an early age offered them an opportunity to express themselves independently and to question cultural assumptions. Nonetheless, in our sample the women leaders witnessed a lack of confidence in women lower in the hierarchy. An interviewee said in this regard, "The women in my executive team do not negotiate promotions or a raise, and sell themselves short." (Name withheld)

Figure 2.5 maps the interrelationships between a number of the elements of the developmental ecosystem and is illustrative of the following:

In analyzing the transcripts, we realized that the women leaders' lives could be divided into a number of episodes or phases that contributed to their development. First, in their early development, they cultivated a confident sense of self-worth and purpose. Several elements contributed in turn towards this development outcome—for instance, the influence of parents, a strong schooling foundation and solid female role models, as well as taking ownership of community concerns. Early in their lives they developed a sense of responsibility towards an entity larger than the family unit. They were allowed, and encouraged, to voice their opinions.

Interestingly, these interviewees had a self-proclaimed source of philosophical distinctiveness:

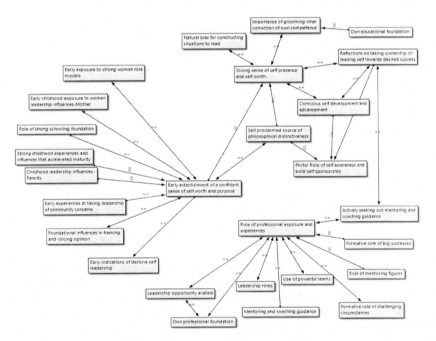

Figure 2.5 Conceptual map of the developmental ecosystem
Notes: = = is associated with; [] is part of; => is cause of
Source: Author's own compiled through Atlas.ti network maps.

I am concerned about giving my children a legacy and that is not only the children I bore, but the girl children of the world.

(Ntombi Langa-Royds, South Africa)

I am driven by a sense of curiosity to learn and grow and a sense of purpose and social justice to make a difference in the world.

(Marianne Roux, consulting in Asia Pacific)

I got angry when we had passed children on our way to school, who were too poor to attend school.

(Rania Habiby Anderson, formerly from Middle East)

I stood up for my rights at the age of 14.

(Geraldine Fraser-Moleketi, South Africa)

This aspect, in turn, played an important role in bold self-sponsorship. They demonstrated a distinct self-awareness and were conscious of their self-development in grooming an inner conviction of their own competence, which in turn led to a strong sense of self-presence and self-worth. This prompted these women very naturally to construct situations in which they led.

Another important chapter in these interviewees' development was their professional exposure and experiences. During this time they availed of opportunities and, due to their professional foundation, took on leadership roles. All of these interviewees had been challenged and they reached out to powerful teams and sympathetic individuals for mentoring and coaching guidance. They also experienced huge successes, which was further valuable experience.

Other researchers have commented on these elements: Alimo-Metcalfe and Alban-Metcalfe (2005) contend that an ability to make the difficult unpopular decisions, and self-confidence, are important for transformational leadership. Shamir et al. (2005, 23) observe that the "stories of political leaders reveal a theme that does not appear in the stories of other leaders"—namely, identification with a cause through developing a political or ideological outlook. Our findings on philosophical distinctiveness relate to Shamir et al.'s (2005). In the next section we share another fresh perspective on women's leadership in our sample.

Contextual leadership intelligence

Scholars have declared that strategic leaders need to have a solid understanding of the environment within which their organizations function and explore long-term changes in the organization's environment (Osborn, Hunt and Jauch 2002). Navigating the challenges of a complex environment is a skill that is sustained over time by remaining contextually aware and relationally responsive (Werhane and Painter-Morland 2011).

In this regard, the women leaders in our sample were in tune with their environment and commented on the masculine culture not being ready for a feminine approach to leadership or how the varied environments of business are different, such as between Europe and the Middle East. Mayo and Nohria (2005) and Kutz (2008) would name these insights "contextual leadership intelligence." The women interviewed indicated how they were changing the context by working with what they had:

> Those that are making a difference are working within the Islamic system; they make incremental progress and do not take on the system upfront.
>
> (Rania Habiby Anderson, formerly from Middle East)

> Either I can say, "How dare you think like that," make a big issue about it, or I work with the person and say, "Well, you know, there are a lot of people like me and I should introduce you to some of them," and then his world opens up. Then leave it. That has been taught to me in later life.
>
> (Ntombi Langa-Royds, South Africa)

> Cultural intelligence is key in building relationships—never assume you know or understand a different culture. For this reason, storytelling is effective in leading others, especially in emerging markets.
>
> (Marianne Roux, consulting in Asia Pacific)

Conclusion

The women from emerging markets that we interviewed described elements of leadership that resemble transformational leadership, such as having a compelling vision. Bass (1997) similarly contends that in all the countries researched, people's ideals or prototypes of leadership are transformational. House et al. (2004) concur, arguing that the transformational leadership style is universally preferred by followers. Many other contextual variables could have been discussed in this chapter; however, in the chapters that follow more variables are examined—for instance, the positional power associated with specific roles. These discussions refer to relevant studies such as Eagly et al. (2003), in which role-congruity is an important variable.

It is unfortunate that there is currently gender and race bias in our context and we echo the opinion of our interviewees, as the following quotation from Ntombi Langa-Royds (South Africa) illustrates:

> My experience is that it is still very real. I still get invited to events because I am a black female and I am educated. Race does play a

part. I think that it is unfortunate that there are not enough places where you just go and it is because you are who you are.

A worldview of feminism, like all "isms", represents one side of a binary view. This book is not about exclusion. When we move away from the tendency to label leadership traits as either masculine or feminine, as we suggest in the discussion of quadrant 4, we open up possibilities of discovering unique leadership practices. We encourage and applaud the participation of male colleagues as partners in the dialogue. Gender is a powerful filter that influences how behavior is interpreted and understood. Sadly, the viewpoint of what constitutes masculine or feminine does not keep abreast of the subtle changes in these constructs over time. Traits attributed to the "good girl" or "good woman" have certainly changed over centuries. We are thus in favor of gender being regarded as merely part of identity and note that other contextual factors, such as cultural, political, historical, societal and even sector or industry environments, are equally important. We advocate for contextual leadership intelligence where "both and" is more important rather than "either or", and therefore the contextual leadership idea is rather "leading in times of". We hereby offer our readers a different conceptual model of how to lead effectively.

In line with Elliot and Stead's (2008) assertion, we also argue for leadership as a social process rather than a particular attribute of an individual. We assert that we are doing women a disservice by attributing either feminine or masculine stereotypical behavior to them, when they are, in fact, operating within a role where the expectation is, for instance, to hold others accountable. The pertinent question is rather how we can create a fair environment for *both* genders.

This book offers women leaders in emerging markets a voice on their experience of leadership without comparing them to masculine leadership; instead, the uniqueness of the range of contexts requires unique leadership practices that the succeeding chapters will illuminate. We set out to develop a model of women leadership to enable us to begin to address the gap in leadership studies. The model emerged from the qualitative analysis and coding of the interviews of a sample that was inclusive of ethnicity and emerging market contexts. In Chapter 11 we will offer this conceptual framework, based on the themes emerging from all the preceding chapters. Why should we care about wedging the door open for women and changing the status quo? Our hope is that this book will offer a clear answer. Another question organizations should consider is: "How can we create the appropriate context for women leadership to be nourished?"

References

Anderson, R. H. 2014. *Undeterred: The Six Success Habits of Women in Emerging Economies.* New York: The Way Women Work Press.

Acker, J. 1990. "Hierarchies, Jobs, Bodies: A Theory of Gendered Organisations". *Gender & Society* 4(2): 139–158.

Adams, R. B. and D. Ferreira. 2009. "Women in the Boardroom and Their Impact on Governance and Performance". *Journal of Financial Economics* 94(2): 291–309.

Alimo-Metcalfe, B. and J. Alban-Metcalfe. 2005. "Leadership: Time for a New Direction?". *Leadership* 1(1): 51–71.

Avolio, B. J., F. O. Walumbwa and T. J. Weber. 2009. "Leadership: Current Theories, Research, and Future Directions". *Annual Review of Psychology* 60(1): 421–449.

Bass, B. M. 1985. *Leadership and Performance Beyond Expectations.* New York: Free Press.

Bass, B. M. 1997. "Does the Transactional-Transformational Leadership Paradigm Transcend Organisational and National Boundaries?" *American Psychologist* 52 (2): 130–139.

Bass, B. M. 1997. *Transformational Leadership: Industrial, Military and Educational Impact.* Mahwah, NJ: Lawrence Erlbaum Associates.

Bass, B. M. 1999. "Two Decades of Research and Development in Transformational Leadership". *European Journal of Work and Organisational Psychology* 8(1): 9–32.

Bass, B. M. and B. J. Avolio. 1990. *Multifactor Leadership Questionnaire.* Palo Alto, CA: Consulting Psychologists Press.

Bennis, W. 2007. "The Challenges of Leadership in the Modern World". *American Psychologist* 62(1): 1–5.

Bennis, W. G. and R. J. Thomas. 2002. *Geeks and Geezers: How Era, Values and Defining Moments Shape Leadership.* Boston, MA: Harvard Business School Press.

Billing, Y. D. and M. Alvesson. 2000. "Questioning the Notion of Feminine Leadership: A Critical Perspective on the Gender Labelling of Leadership". *Gender, Work and Organization* 7(3): 154–157.

Bryans, P. and S. Mavis. 2003. "Women Learning to Become Managers: Learning to Fit in or to Play a Different Game?" *Management Learning* 34(1): 111–134.

Bruner, J. S. 1991. "The Narrative Construction of Reality". *Critical Inquiry* 18(1): 1–21.

Burns, J. M. 1978. *Leadership.* New York: Harper & Row.

Catalyst. 2007. "The Double-Bind Dilemma for Women in Leadership: Damned if You Do, Doomed if You Don't". www.catalyst.org/knowledge/double-bind-dilemma -women-leadership-damned-if-you-do-doomed-if-you-dont-0. Retrieved January 22, 2017.

Clark, D. and N. Kleyn. 2011. "Why do they Leave? Voluntary Turnover of South African Women Executives". In P. H. Werhane and M. Painter-Morland, *Leadership, Gender and Organisation.* New York: Springer, pp. 185–209.

Collins, J. 2001. *Good to Great.* London: Harper Business.

Coughlin, L., E. Wingard and K. Hollihan (eds). 2005. *Enlightened Power: How Women are Transforming the Practice of Leadership.* San Francisco, CA: Jossey-Bass.

De Beauvoir, S. 1949. *The Second Sex.* Translated and edited by H. M. Parsley in 1997. London: Gallimard.

Dickson, M. W., D. N. Den Hartog and J. K. Mitchelson. 2003. "Research on Leadership in a Cross-Cultural Context: Making Progress, and Raising New Questions". *The Leadership Quarterly* 14: 729–768.

Eagly, A. H. 2007. "Female Leadership Advantages and Disadvantage: Resolving the Contradictions". *Psychology of Women Quarterly* 31(1): 1–12.

Eagly, A. H. and L. L. Carli. 2003. "The Female Leadership Advantage: An Evaluation of the Evidence". *The Leadership Quarterly* 14(6): 807–834.

Eagly, A. H. and L. L. Carli. 2007. *Through the Labyrinth: The Truth About How Women Become Leaders*. New York: Harvard Business School Press.

Eagly, A. H. and M. C. Johannesen-Schmidt. 2001. "The Leadership Style of Women and Men". *Journal of Social Studies* 57(4): 781–798.

Eagly, A. H. and B. T. Johnson. 1990. "Gender and Leadership Style: A Meta-Analysis". *Psychological Bulletin* 108: 233–256.

Eagly, A. H., M. C. Johannesen-Schmidt and M. L. van Engen. 2003. "Transformational, Transactional and Laissez-faire Leadership Styles: A Meta-Analysis Comparing Women and Men". *Psychological Bulletin* 129(4): 569–591.

Edles, L. and S. Appelrouth. 2010. *Sociological Theory in the Classical Era: Text and Readings*. California: Pine Forge Press.

Elliot, C. and V. Stead. 2008. "Learning from Leading Women's Experience: Towards a Sociological Understanding". *Leadership* 4(2): 159–180.

Ely, R. J. and D. E. Meyerson. 2000. "Theories of Gender in Organisations: A New Approach to Organisational Analysis and Change". *Research in Organisational Behaviour* 22: 103–151.

Flanders, M. 1994. *Breakthrough: The Career Woman's Guide to Shattering the Glass Ceiling*. London: Paul Chapman Publishing.

Fletcher, J. K. 1994. "Castrating the Female Advantage: Feminist Standpoint Research and Management Science". *Journal of Management Inquiry* 3(1): 74–82.

Fletcher, J. K. 2004. "The Paradox of Postheroic Leadership: An Essay on Gender, Power and Transformational Change". *The Leadership Quarterly* 15(5): 647–661.

French, J. and B. H. Raven. 1959. "The Basis of Social Power". In D. Cartwright (Ed.), *Studies of Social Power*. San Francisco, CA: Jossey-Bass, pp. 150–167.

Fuszara, M. 2005. "Between Feminism and the Catholic Church: The Women's Movement in Poland". *Sociological Review* 41(6): 1057–1075.

Gatrell, C., C. L. Cooper and E. E. Kossek. 2010. *Women and Management*, vol. 1. Cheltenham: Edward Edgar Publishers.

Gavron, S. 2015. *Suffragette*. A Ruby Films production in Great Britain.

Gherardi, S. and B. Poggio. 2001. "Creating and Recreating Gender Order in Organisations". *Journal of World Business* 36(3): 245–259.

Grant Thornton. 2015. "Women in Business: The Path to Leadership". Grant Thornton International Business Report. London.

Gray, J. 1993. *Men Are from Mars, Women Are from Venus*. New York: HarperCollins.

Greenleaf, R. K. 1970. *The Servant as Leader*. San Francisco, CA: Jossey-Bass.

Greenleaf, R. K. 1996. *On Becoming a Servant Leader*. San Francisco, CA: Jossey-Bass.

Hackman, M. Z., A. H. Furniss, M. J. Hills and T. J. Patterson. 1992. "Perceptions of Gender-Role Characteristics and Transformational and Transactional Leadership Behaviours". *Perceptual and Motor Skills* 75(1): 311–319.

Hayward, S. 2005. *Women Leading*. NewYork: Palgrave Macmillan.

Helgesen, S. 1995. *The Female Advantage: Women's Ways of Leadership*. New York: Doubleday.

Heilman, M.E. 2001. "Description and Prescription: How Gender Stereotypes Prevent Women's Ascent up the Organisational Ladder". *Journal of Social Issues* 57(4): 657–664.

Hofstede, G. 2001. *Culture's Consequences: Comparing Values, Behaviours, Institutions and Organisations across Nations* (2nd ed.). Newbury Park, CA: Sage.

House, R. J. 1971. "A Path-Goal Theory of Leadership Effectiveness". *Administrative Science Quarterly* 16(3): 321–328.

House, R. J., P. J. Hanges, M. Javidan, W. Dorfman and V. Gupta. 2004. *Culture, Leadership and Organisations: The GLOBE Study of 62 Societies*. Thousand Oaks, CA: SAGE Publications.

HSBC. 2016. "What are Emerging Markets?". https://investorfunds.us.hsbc.com/investing-in-emerging-markets/map-at-night/default.fs. Retrieved March 3, 2016.

Hunt, J. G. 1996. *Leadership: A New Synthesis*. Newbury Park: SAGE.

Ibarra, H., R. Ely and D. Kolb. 2013. "Women Rising: The Unseen Barriers". *Harvard Business Review* 91(9): 3–8.

International Labour Organization. 2015. "Labor force, female (% of total labor force)." World Bank. Accessed May 3, 2016. http://data.worldbank.org/indicator/SL.TLF.TOTL.FE.ZS.

James, A. 1998. "Mary, Mary Quite Contrary: How do Women Leaders Grow?". *Women in Management Review* 13(2): 67–71.

Kark, R. 2004. "The Transformational Leader: Who is (s)he? A Feminist Perspective". *Journal of Organisational Change Management* 17(2): 160–176.

Kellerman, B. 2013. "Leading Questions: The End of Leadership". *Leadership* 9(1): 135–139.

Kutz, M. 2008. "Towards a Conceptual Model of Contextual Intelligence: A Transferable Leadership Construct". *Leadership Review* 8(2): 18–31.

Kolb, D., J. Williams and C. Frohlinger. 2010. *Her Place at the Table: A Women's Guide to Negotiating Five Key Challenges to Leadership Success*. San Francisco, CA: Jossey-Bass.

Leimon, A., F. Moscovici and H. Goodies. 2011. *Coaching Women to Lead*. London: Routledge.

Leonard, L. S. 1982. *The Wounded Woman: Healing the Father-Daughter Relationship*. Boston, MA: Shambhala Publications.

Maher, K. J. 1997. "Gender-Related Stereotypes of Transformational and Transactional Leadership". *Sex Roles* 37(3/4): 209–225.

Mayo, A. J. and N. Nohria. 2005. "Zeitgeist Leadership". *Harvard Business Review* 83(10): 45–60.

Mayo, A. J. and N. Nohria. 2005. *In Their Time: The Greatest Business Leaders of the Twentieth Century*. Boston, MA: Harvard Business School Press.

Mavin, S. 2008. "Queenbees, Wannabees and Afraid to Bees: No More 'Best Enemies' for Women in Management?". *British Journal of Management* 19(5): 75–84.

Meyerson, D. and J. K. Fletcher. 1999. "A Modest Manifesto for Shattering the Glass Ceiling". *Harvard Business Review* (Jan./Feb.): 127–136.

Mintzberg, H. 1999. "Leader to Leader". *Harvard Business Review* 12(Spring): 24–30.

Mohanty, C. T. A. Russo and L. Torres (eds). 1991. *Third World Women and the Politics of Feminism*. Bloomington, IN: Indiana University Press.

Moss-Kanter, R. 1977. *Men and Women in the Corporation.* New York: Basic Books.

Nelson, E. and R. Hogan. 2009. "Coaching on the Dark Side". *International Coaching Psychology Review* 4(1): 7–19.

Nielsen, S. and M. Huse. 2010. "The Contribution of Women on Boards of Directors: Going Beyond the Surface". *Corporate Governance: An International Review* 18(2): 136–148.

Olsson, S. 2002. "Gendered Heroes: Male and Female Self-Representations of Executive Identity". *Women in Management Review* 17(3/4): 142–150.

Osborn, R. N., J. G. Hunt and L. R. Jauch. 2002. "Toward a Contextual Theory of Leadership". *The Leadership Quarterly* 13(6): 797–837.

Osborn, R. N. and R. Marion. 2009. "Contextual Leadership, Transformational Leadership and the Performance of International Innovation Seeking Alliances". *The Leadership Quarterly* 20(2): 191–206.

Perriton, L. 2006. "Does Women + a Network = Career Progression?". *Leadership* 2(1): 101–113.

Porter, L. W. and G. B. McLaughlin. 2006. "Leadership and the Organizational Context: Like the Weather?". *The Leadership Quarterly* 17(6): 559–576.

Reeves, M. 2010. *Women in Business: Theory, Case Studies and Legal Challenges.* New York: Routledge.

Rosener, J. B. 1990. "Ways Women Lead". *Harvard Business Review* 68(6): 119–125.

Rosette, S. A. and L. P. Tost. 2010. "Agentic Women and Communal Leadership: How Role Prescriptions Confer Advantage to Top Women Leaders". *Journal of Applied Psychology* 95(2): 221–235.

Ruderman, M. N. and P. J. Ohlott. 2002. *Standing at the Crossroads: Next Steps for High-achieving Women.* Center for Creative Leadership. New York: Jossey-Bass.

Ryan, M. K. and S. A. Haslam. 2007. "The Glass Cliff: Exploring the Dynamics Surrounding the Appointment of Women in Precarious Leadership Positions". *The Academy of Management Review* 32(2): 549–572.

Shamir, B., H. Dayan-Horesh and D. Adler. 2005. "Leading by Biography: Towards a Life-story Approach to the Study of Leadership". *Leadership* 1(1): 13–29.

Sinclair, A. 2012. "Not Just 'Adding Women in': Women Re-making Leadership: Seizing the Initiative". In R. Francis, P. Grimshaw and A. Standish (eds), *Australian Women Leaders in Politics, Workplaces and Communities* (conference proceedings). University of Melbourne: eScholarship Research Centre. www.womenaustralia.info/leaders/sti/pdfs/02_Sinclair.pdf.

Tarr-Whelan, L. 2009. *Women Lead the Way. Your Guide to Stepping up to Leadership and Changing the World.* San Francisco, CA: Berret-Koehler Publisher.

Tichy, N. and M. Devanna. 1986. *Transformational Leadership.* New York: Wiley.

Timberlake, S. 2005. "Social Capital and Gender in the Workplace". *Journal of Management Development* 24(1): 34–44.

Tosi, H. L. 1991. "The Organization as a Context for Leadership Theory: A Multilevel Approach". *The Leadership Quarterly* 2(3): 205–228.

Uhl-Bien, M. 2011. "Relational Leadership and Gender: From Hierarchy to Relationality". In P. H. Werhane and M. Painter-Morland, *Leadership, Gender and Organisation.* New York: Springer, pp. 65–75.

Uhl-Bien, M. 2006. "Relational Leadership Theory: Exploring the Social Processes of Leadership and Organizing". *The Leadership Quarterly* 17(6): 654–676.

Uhl-Bien, M., R. Marion and B. McKelvey. 2007. "Complexity Leadership Theory: Shifting Leadership from the Industrial Age to the Knowledge Era". *The Leadership Quarterly* 18(2): 298–318.

Van Zyl, E. (Ed.). 2009. *Leadership in the African Context*. Cape Town: Juta.

Valerio, A. M. 2010. *Developing Women Leaders: A Guide for Men and Women in Organisations*. New York: Wiley-Blackwell.

Vermeulen, S. 2004. *Stitched-up: Who Fashions Women's Lives?* Johannesburg: Jacana Media.

Vinnecombe, S. 1988. "What Exactly are the Differences in Men and Women's Working Styles?". *Women in Management Review* 3(1): 13–21.

Walter, F. and H. Bruch. 2010. "Structural Impacts on the Occurrence and Effectiveness of Transformational Leadership: An Empirical Study at the Organizational Level of Analysis". *The Leadership Quarterly* 21(5): 765–782.

Taljaard, C., M. Ward and C. Muller. 2015. "Board Diversity and Financial Performance: A Graphical Time-series Approach". *South African Journal of Economic and Management Sciences* 18(3): 425–448.

Werhane, P. and M. Painter-Morland. 2011. *Leadership, Gender and Organisations*. London: Springer.

Wheatley, M. J. 2005. *Finding our Way: Leadership for an Uncertain Time*. San Francisco, CA: Berrett-Koehler. Leadership and the New Science Publishers.

White, J. 1992. *A Few Good Women: Breaking the Barriers to Top Management*. New Jersey: Prentice Hall.

Yukl, G. 2002. *Leadership in Organisations* (5th edition). Upper Saddle River, NJ: Prentice Hall.

3 Women's movements in emerging markets

Caren Scheepers, Hema Parbhoo, Sonja Swart and Kelly Alexander

Caren Scheepers was chapter lead, with the following contributors: Hema Parbhoo (women's movements in India, Malaysia and South Africa); Sonja Swart (women's movements in Brazil and UAE); Kelly Alexander (women's movements in Russia and Colombia); Caren Scheepers (women's movements in Western countries, Poland, Egypt and China).

Introduction

The social, economic and political empowerment of women is essential for growth in emerging markets, as is investment in developing all human capital. Women are becoming even more essential in knowledge-intensive industries as emerging market economies transform from their emphasis on agriculture to manufacturing and service-related sectors.

This chapter describes the societal background against which the revelations of the ensuing chapters can be understood. It also builds on the "leadership in context" thesis of Chapter 2; in particular, patriarchy as a contextual variable with which women have to contend. We hone in on the evolution of economic and political realities in emerging markets, which form the background for the position of women in these countries, and illustrate the contextual dependency of expectations and perceptions around women in the workplace.

The chapter commences with a perspective on the diversity of women's experiences, followed by our rationale for choosing nine of the 21 emerging markets, in four regions, for this discussion. We dispel myths about women in emerging markets before going on to discuss the countries in terms of their histories and dominant ideologies, key milestones and future challenges. We conclude by integrating the themes revealed in the four regions, setting the scene for the following chapters.

Approach to "woman" in emerging markets

In alignment with feminist theory, our assumption in this chapter is that "woman" is a valid classification and reflects women's collective experiences. It is therefore a category based not on biological character-istics but on common experiences—particularly around oppression (Sebola 2015). "Woman" is a socially constructed term, implying that although we share experiences of oppression, we do not share the same experiences (Bryans and Mavin 2003). The Chapter 3 authors concur: gender—and particularly "woman"—is socially (and, we would add, culturally) con-structed. We challenge the claim of a uniform women's experience. Instead, we share the approach of Marion (2010, 81), who says, "feminism is not a single, unified perspective because of the cultural traditions and diversity found within lived experiences".

The emerging markets women in our study represent several cultural contexts and reveal a number of different characteristics of, for example, "a good woman". Note, however, that during the centuries the definition of "a good woman" has differed. For example, Russian women during the communist era were expected to be involved in society in addition to their roles in their homes, as were women in China in Mao's time. As discussed in Chapter 2, the spirit of the time, or zeitgeist, is an important contextual variable. Our approach is accordingly more in line with Sebola's (2015) notion that "woman", or gender, is a historical condition rather than a natural fact. High expectations of women over centuries relate to early Western feminist notions that women are controlled partly by men's crea-tion of a series of myths about the ideal woman that she cannot live up to (de Beauvoir 1949). De Beauvoir (1949) also states that for women to change their social positions they must join the workforce—the intellec-tuals. In the emerging market discussion that follows, we show that the participation of women in the workplace did indeed liberate their position in society.

Selecting emerging markets

The term "emerging markets" (see Figure 3.1) was coined by Antoine van Agtmael in the 1980s (Sako 2015) to mean low- to middle-income coun-tries, with high growth potential and characterized by high volatility (HSBC 2016; Lawson, Heacock and Stupnytska 2007; *The Economist* 2014; Sharma 2012). White and Brown (2014) also point to the char-acteristic of institutional voids that include corruption and government bureaucracy in these markets.

In 2015, emerging markets accounted for 37% of world GDP, repre-senting most of the world's economy by population and geography (Grosse 2015; Rayner 2015). The Morgan Stanley Capital International (MSCI) index lists 21 countries in this category. One of the major criti-cisms of the term "emerging markets" is that it has become too broad, as too many countries, at diverse stages of development, are viewed together. Given the limited scope of this chapter, we could not discuss all 21 countries. To choose which countries to include, we utilized three criteria.

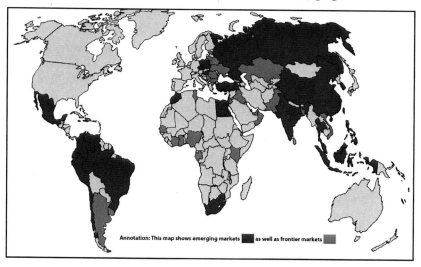

Figure 3.1 Emerging markets
Artist: Andrew Swanepoel; content based on MSCI (Morgan Stanley Capital International) Emerging Markets index, www.msci.com/market-classification.

First, we decided to focus our investigation on the major emerging markets, and therefore included the BRIC (Brazil, Russia, China and India) countries, around which market interest in the emerging countries has mainly revolved (Steen 2012). However, second, we intended to offer a broader focus than the BRIC countries and therefore considered other countries in BRIC continents and regions. South Africa is home to both the researchers and several of our interviewees for this book and we therefore included South Africa in our investigation. Third, in selecting other countries we chose those with similar growth rates to those of South Africa, to aid comparison. The graph in Figure 3.2 shows the gross domestic product (GDP) of the emerging markets chosen for the conversation. It illustrates GDP in terms of purchasing power parity (PPP), which compares income levels of different countries, or the purchasing power of each currency.

The graphic below illustrates Poland, Colombia, Malaysia and the United Arab Emirates (UAE), all within a band similar to South Africa's. As they also represent different continents, we included them in our discussion. The nine countries discussed in this chapter are therefore Brazil, Russia, India, China, South Africa, Poland, Malaysia, Colombia and the UAE.

Dispelling myths about women in emerging markets

Our exposure and experiences were originally mainly informed by a Western mindset but our study reveals a number of commonly held myths about women in emerging markets. This section sets out to dispel these myths.

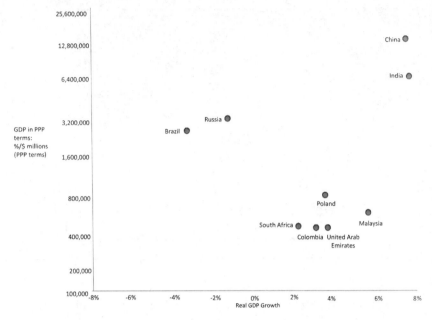

Figure 3.2 Emerging economies in 2016 from Euromonitor International
With permission adapted from "The outlook for major emerging markets in 2016"
by Euromonitor International (National statistics/Eurostat 7 March 2016).

Myth 1: Women in emerging markets do not have civil rights

Contrary to contemporary thought, our study revealed that the rights of
women are protected in the constitutions of many emerging markets,
including India, China, South Africa, Russia, Malaysia and Brazil.
Women have suffrage in all the countries we investigated, except for the
UAE, where both men and women have only limited suffrage, and Saudi
Arabia, where women had to wait until 2015 to vote.

The multi-layered complexity of the evolution of women's positioning in
society is illustrated by the discrepancy in South Africa, where white
women were given suffrage in 1930, whereas Black, Indian and Asian
women only acquired the right to vote in the aftermath of apartheid in
1994, when South Africa became a true democracy.

Gender equity in the workplace today remains a global issue (Sebola
2015). While women make up half the global population, their representation in the workplace varies. In the European Union (EU) the participation rate of women in the labor market was 58.5% in 2012, similar to
that in many emerging markets. For example, the figure is very similar
(53.1%) in Poland. However, globally, as women rise in business, this percentage decreases. In Poland, women's representation at management level
is only 33% and on boards only 12% (European Commission 2012). In

India, women were only represented on 5% of boards and 2% on executive committees in 2010 (McKinsey 2011).

Myth 2: Feminism achieved progress for women

In fact, during certain periods in the history of Russia and Poland, for example, the women's movement was dulled and feminism perceived as obsolete, due to the focus on equality under the communist regime.

External forces and changes in political dispensation have actually made a greater difference to the fate of women than women's movements. In China's Mao era, the premise that economic independence is essential for women's liberation was represented by the slogan "Women hold up half the sky" (Hare 2016). The Second World War (WWII) advanced women's rights in Colombia through the movement against fascism (which was permitted by the Catholic Church, although speaking about sexual and reproductive rights was not). In a number of countries, feminists did create social consciousness about inequalities, however. For example, in Brazil, between 1964 and 1985, resistance to repressive regimes led to the development of perhaps the largest, most diverse, radical and successful women's movement in contemporary Latin America.

But in spite of all the external factors that helped create change for women, patriarchy remains the norm across the world. Many studies on equality on the African continent and in South Africa have focused on how the patriarchal system compromised the development of women, for instance in achieving education (Sebola 2015). In countries like Brazil and Colombia, patriarchy is reinforced by the Church, which exerts significant influence over society. In the UAE (Adam 2009) and Brazil (Pitanguy 2002), strong patriarchal traditions have significantly influenced the way women were treated throughout history.

Myth 3: Inequality has been foremost in the minds of women in emerging markets throughout history

Actually, for many decades, women's quest for equality was on the back-burner as there were more pressing matters to attend to, such as patriotism. For example, in Russia the trajectory of the women's movement was marked by fits and starts, in sync with the rise and fall of the Soviet state; in South Africa, women's movements were aligned to the rise and fall of apartheid. In these examples, the language of democracy and freedom was first required, before gender rights could be championed.

These findings of our study confirm scholarly contentions that identity is multifaceted. As a result, women are not necessarily solely focused on their quest for equality when another facet of their identity is threatened. For example, Elliott and Stead (2008, 167) acknowledge that "gender cannot be regarded as an isolated feature of identity, but interacts with the broader structural, political, historical, cultural and institutional context". Mohanty, Russo and Torres' (1991) classic seminal research also contends that women's experiences can vary according to different identity characteristics such as ethnicity, nationality, class, age, sexual orientation and religion.

Myth 4: Feminism in the West set the scene for the emerging market women's movements

Actually, our research indicated that there is resistance to Western feminist ideas, and a number of feminist activists in emerging markets, including those from Brazil, Malaysia and Colombia, did not want to be associated with Western feminism. We have purposely avoided using the Western term 'feminism' in this chapter because it has such negative associations in many emerging markets, instead using the term 'women's movement'.

Polish scholars explain the hostility towards Western feminists as follows: "the socialist state propaganda planted disdain for western 'bra-burners' and 'men-haters'" (Karpinski 1995), as Marody illustrates in "Why I am not a feminist?" (1993). In Poland, feminists are regarded as radicals and disturbers of social order. Feminism is perceived as an infringement of the social consensus (Gaciarz 2011). Chinese women activists expressed concern that several feminists in China had been open about their sexual orientation and, as a result, experienced resistance to their ideas (Chiu 2013).

In some cases, women's movements in emerging markets are ahead of Western women's movements. The concerns of Western women were not necessarily the same issues facing women in emerging countries. Notably, issues around sexuality and expression for the lesbian, gay, bisexual and transgender (LGBT) community appear less frequently in emerging markets, where enforcement of, and respect for, basic rights around gender equality—although legislated—still need to become the norm.

In the twenty-first century, the agenda of women's movements in the West moved towards implementation of political and economic equality around the world. Reeves (2010) notes the concern of Western women's movements for women factory workers in multinational organizations, for example in Asia and Latin America, where women are subjected to inhuman working conditions.

Our research indicated that the UN Women World conferences play an important role in raising consciousness around women's rights and have immense impact in emerging markets. The UN's Fourth World Conference on Women (Beijing), for example, triggered a number of women's movements in China. In India, there is ongoing support for the UN women's ideals through various initiatives and flagship programs such as "Women's Entrepreneurship for Sustainable Energy", launched in 2015.

A similar theme in the early organization of women's movements was the role of the world wars in pulling women into the labor market and recognizing the importance of their skills, thus boosting women's movements and catapulting women into the public realm.

In Poland, Catholic rules can be interpreted differently and the most conservative interpretation of the Catholic ethic makes it difficult for women (Gaciarz 2011). Similarly, in Brazil and Colombia, the Catholic Church plays a significant role in establishing gender roles and influences the content of discussion permissible by women's movements. For example, reproductive rights, sexuality and abortion are not considered appropriate content.

As happened during the rise of Western women's movements, emerging market women's movements generally commenced with involvement by the upper and middle classes, and later included the working classes. Certain issues, such as suffrage and other human rights, were focus areas prior to moving to women's rights in the work environment. Our investigations revealed that although rights exist in Russia, Colombia and Brazil, these are not always exercised or enforced. Stereotypical behavior thus trumps legal requirements.

Myth 5: The traditional role of women in emerging markets has not changed

In some emerging markets the role of women has not changed much, but there are exceptions. Paradoxically, although there has been significant transformation in many countries at policy level, at grassroots level nothing much has changed.

In China, women's roles have changed dramatically since the Confucian era. Political rhetoric in the Mao era elevated women to the point where it became routine for most urban women to work full time outside of the home (Hare 2016). A traditional view of a "good" woman still exists in Russia: a good wife and mother who looks after the home and respects her husband. Women's movements in Poland are sometimes in conflict with the Catholic Church around family values, which only views women in terms of wives and mothers. Malaysian scholars have observed that there is diversity within diversity and that there is a traditional, conservative interpretation of Islam that perceives women within their traditional roles. Zainah Anwar, together with six other co-founders, created Sisters of Islam to point to other interpretations (Anwar 2007). Regarding women's roles in society, our research revealed that, for example in Poland, women regularly cite the fact that women are more burdened by family commitments than men (Fuszara 2005). In Colombia this is called the "second shift". One of our interviewees observed:

> Especially in Turkey, with a majority Muslim population; but even if you do not factor in the element of Islam, a country where family ties are very important, women have an extra burden about running the family. [Barçin Yinanç, Turkey]

The burden of the "second shift" is probably less for South African women than in other emerging markets where domestic help is less entrenched in the fabric of society. Even within South Africa, however, only the middle and upper classes have access to domestic help. In Brazil, only 18% of children are enrolled in childcare.

In China, members of the extended family assist with childcare and domestic labor. Daycare is widely available and most workplaces have on-site daycare centers. The *Asia News Monitor* (March 12, 2015) reports that 40% of Chinese women have suffered domestic violence. In Brazil, Andrade (2013) reports that every 15 seconds a woman is assaulted; every two hours a woman is murdered; 59% of people know a woman who has been a victim of violence; and 65% of attacks on women happened behind closed doors. Within the past three decades, at least 92,000 women have been killed inside their homes.

Four regions, nine countries: women's movements in our chosen emerging markets

We interviewed women from most of the nine countries chosen for this chapter, and consulted publications in the public domain as secondary data. We discuss our findings in this section. Later, we illustrate the trends we extrapolated as phases on a timeline.

Women's movements are examples of social movements, of collective activity that promotes social change using the active involvement of its members as its main resource (Fuszara 2005). Interestingly, movements aimed at maintaining the status quo lie outside the scope of this definition. A social movement is a protest against existing values and often attacks the structure of power through more than one organization. In the case of women's movements, they share the common aim of changing the status of women in society.

Women's movements in China played an important role in translating individual experiences of oppression into the collective consciousness. They acted as mediators between their members and other social institutions (Korabik 1993). Yiping (2013) emphasizes the creation of opportunities to exchange information, learn about role models and encourage gender studies. An example of mediation between institutions happened in Colombia, where the Catholic Church women's movement was involved in promoting responsible procreation. This expanded into a discussion of women's rights, by providing spaces where rural Colombians, especially women, could "experiment with voice and agency and explore alternative visions of citizenship without fear of reprisal or social ostracism" (Roldán 2014, 27).

Our investigation into emerging markets revealed that the focus of their women's movements has broadened to include the plight of other minority groups and diversity dimensions, namely sexual orientation and disabilities, or women living with HIV/Aids (Yiping 2013). The influence of women's movements on decisions around equality policies, and their ability to mobilize, depend on whether the movements have legitimacy as a nationwide network, which of course amplifies their voices.

In Brazil, under the leadership of Bertha Lutz, peaceful demonstrations brought about change and achieved suffrage. Early women's movements in that country were neither militant nor radical in their goals and provoked little resistance from government. An important method used by women's movements to raise awareness is to organize events. These include peaceful demonstrations, like one in which 20,000 women marched to the Union Buildings in 1956 in South Africa in protest against the passes they had to carry. Women's Day is still celebrated annually on August 9 in that country. In Russia, 40,000 women marched through St. Petersburg in 1917 and were rewarded with the right to vote.

The next section systematically discusses the development and impact of women's movements in specific emerging markets.

Eastern Europe: featuring Russia and Poland

Historical context and dominant ideology

As "the image of the Polish women's movements is not yet particularly extensive" (Fuszara 2005, 1071), the following discussion will in essence revolve around Russian women's movements, with selected references to those in Poland.

Russia's socialist history and communist legacy shaped the structure of society today. A superpower during the Cold War, the authoritarian state with its communist ideology was pervasive and critical in shaping representations of women in society.

Pre-1917 there was tension between the individual focus of feminism and the collectivist focus of socialism in Russia (Aaltio and Peltonen 2009). Following the 1917 Revolution, numerous laws were enacted, allowing women to enter the workforce. These had repercussions for modern times, with it being normal to see Russian women in senior roles (Smedley 2015). Russia's women's movements, and growing awareness of women's rights, were characterized by fits and starts; progress was made and gains won, only to be subsequently lost. Almost at the same time as women's movements became prominent, the First World War (1914–1918) halted their momentum in favor of national interests (Johnson and Saarinen 2013). Thereafter, women's rights were subsumed by the overarching Soviet rhetoric of egalitarianism.

Under Soviet rule, economic activity was the measure by which rights were secured. Thus, free market reforms destabilized Russian women's rights and security (Budrina 2012). State capitalism replaced socialism in 1991, with the disbanding of the Soviet Union. Its demise resulted in counter-reaction against civic participation, creating a feeling of rebellion against overarching structures (Johnson and Saarinen 2013). Perhaps due to the constant rhetoric of egalitarianism, the opportunity for individuation was savored.

Key milestones

The burgeoning women's movement, pre-1917, secured gains for Russian women which were soon eroded. Nonetheless, by 1914, reforms in the areas of inheritance, education and personal rights occurred, and, following 1914, discussions regarding contraception and abortion became common. The Bolshevik party ruling the Soviet regime viewed feminism as "bourgeois" or elitist and saw gender equality as intrinsic to Soviet rule. The Bolshevik regime declared feminism redundant and it is apparent that those within the movement did not, or were unable to, contest this (Edmonson 1977).

Under Soviet rule, the rhetoric of equality belied the reality of gulags, or forced labor camps, which were used to suppress dissent and provide labor to various state-directed projects, and where gender equality was evident only in law (Skiles 2012). White (2005) highlights that under Soviet rule, woman as both mother and worker was the norm. When the Soviet Union ended, ideology around gender norms solidified around the position that a woman's place was in the private realm, relegating women to a traditional, stereotypical role (Johnson and Saarinen 2013). One of our Russian interviewees observed:

> because what I have observed is that many women, they tend to be shy and they are not aggressive enough because of fear—so very often women under-present themselves.
>
> (Ekaterina Sheremet, Russia)

Between 1980 and 1985, Russian women made up 35% of the deputies to the Supreme Soviet of the Soviet Union. By 1990, however, the percentage was down to 8.9% and stereotypes regarding women's roles were conservative and patriarchal (Kanap'ianova 2008). According to Aaltio and Peltonen (2009), only with the advent of Perestroika in 1985 were private businesses allowed to operate, and entrepreneurship is therefore new for many—particularly for women. In Poland, the Helsinki Watch Report, published in 1992, revealed the abuse of equal rights experienced daily by Polish women (Karpinski 1995). Karpinski also warned that women's groups risked head-on confrontation with the Catholic Church by advocating for a separation of church and state.

Russia remains a centralized, powerful state. Women have few opportunities and socio-economic upward mobility is constrained (Skiles 2012). Increased agitation against the authoritarian and paternalistic nature of the state is evident in the actions and support of punk-feminist band

Pussy Riot, for example (Gazeta.ru 2012). Post-Soviet Russia focuses on the idea that rights are gender-neutral and there has thus been an "adoption of a gender-blind approach to equality that ignores the real and pervasive impact that gender and the construction of gendered roles have for women" (Turbine 2012, 1856). PwC (2013) highlights the trend since the end of Soviet rule for younger Russian women to be career-focused, with more than 65% indicating an intention to continue their careers. Almost half (49%) of the respondents, however, indicated that women should not be on company boards (PwC, 2013). Lidia and Feng (2014) note increasing levels of female entrepreneurship as a result of women attaining higher education levels and wanting to avoid the wage gap in organizations. Our investigation into Poland's situation revealed that in 2011 an average of 53.1% of the labor market was made up of women, a very similar situation to that in the EU, where the percentage is 58.5%. In 2009, 24.4% of Polish women had tertiary education and the gender pay gap was 9.8%.

Future challenges

Russia's history informs how women are perceived, how they view themselves and their role in society. Russia has an average 30% pay differential between men and women, and women are under-represented in politics (Gorst 2015). For example, only 9.8% Lower House and 3.4% Upper House parliamentary seats are occupied by women and subsequently, Russia ranks sixteenth out of 80 countries in terms of the Gender Empowerment Measure (Country Watch 2011). Johnson and Saarinen (2013) highlight how many women become entrepreneurs in Russia to escape discrimination in business and politics. A future challenge will be to ensure women can retain their current rights and secure greater rights, freedom and equality. Furthermore, traditional gender roles and the difficult corporate as well as political environment—colored by sexist rhetoric, with, for example, Putin reportedly labelling sailors' wives "whores"—need to be addressed (Johnson and Saarinen 2013).

The challenges that lie ahead for Russian women include expressing themselves outside of traditional gender roles and rising within the corporate world and political structures in opposition to growing entrepreneurial ventures to circumnavigate sexist cultures within these institutions. Furthermore, women need to close the wage gap and receive equal pay for equal work if they are to advance their socio-economic status.

Southeast Asia: featuring India, Malaysia and China

The Southeast Asia region can be viewed as being dichotomous in character. It includes economies such as China and India that are progressing at a fast pace, which contrast with strongly patriarchal cultures like

Cambodia, Indonesia and Vietnam where the progress of women is slower than in Western countries. The Association of South East Asian Nations (ASEAN) plays a key role in addressing social and human rights issues within this region. From its inception in 1967, there has been constant review and alignment to economic, social and people-oriented concerns by this association, with increased focus on issues of gender equality (Koo 2010). The Southeast Asia region encompasses several countries. We have chosen to discuss China, Malaysia and India, with a focus on cultural, religious, racial and gender diversity.

China

Historical context and dominant ideologies

Prevailing ideologies have had a profound impact on the positioning of women in Chinese society. For example, the patriarchal ideology of Confucianism, which was dominant for thousands of years until 1911, deemed women inferior to men. At the time it was a virtue for a woman to have no ability (Lee 2011). The basic characteristic of pre-communist society was that the highly centralized political system and patriarchal system worked together: "for more than 2,000 years, the double chains, footbinding and inhuman ethical codes, confined Chinese women to the domestic sphere" (Zhou 2003, 68).

During the Republic of China period, from 1911 to 1949, China was still a feudal society, isolated from the outside world and characterized by poverty. Although 90% of Chinese women were illiterate, women had property and marriage rights. During the May Fourth Movement of 1919, Chinese women's movements called for women's suffrage, condemning footbinding, arranged marriages and the lack of women's education. However, "Chinese feminists at that time only employed Western feminism and did not establish their own feminism" (Zhou 2003, 68).

The Communist Revolution of 1949 brought Chinese women to a new stage of liberation as the government paid particular attention to women's issues (Zuo and Bian 2001). Women were granted the right to vote in 1953. The second Communist Revolution, around 1978, made a huge contribution to women's liberation in Chinese history. For centuries, Chinese parents displayed a "son preference", which led many families to take extreme measures like selective abortion, abandonment and female infanticide (Korabik 1993; Johnson 1993; *The Economist* 2011).

In the 1970s, the transformation of China's economy from agriculture to manufacturing created employment opportunities for women (Lee 2011). Lee (2011) emphasizes that the one-child policy improved female children's share of intra-household resources and ultimately equality between genders. In 1980, China was one of first countries to endorse the 1979 UN

Convention on the Elimination of All Forms of Discrimination Against Women (CEDAW).

Key milestones

In 1949 the People's Republic of China enshrined the principle of equality between men and women in its constitution—a key milestone for women in China. China's women's movements are aligned through the largest NGO in the country, the All-China Women's Federation (ACWF), established in 1949. This forms the bridge between the Communist Party and the masses of women. It has leverage as a result of its United Nations' ECOSOC consultative status and influence at national, provincial, township and even village level (Yiping 2013).

Zuo and Bian's (2001, 1128) study revealed that, at the start of the twenty-first century in urban China, a "career-orientated" woman was perceived as "non-feminine" and "selfish", rejecting her household responsibility. Hare (2016) notes that contemporary language nearly two decades later reflected the changing times. For example, the original phrase, "family has virtuous wife" (家有贤妻), later had a new character introduced, which changed the meaning to "family has an idle wife" (家有闲妻). This had the same pronunciation, but served to direct negative attention to women who opted out of careers to dedicate themselves to their families.

Ng and Pine (2003) note that over centuries there had been vertical and horizontal inequality as women clustered on the lower levels of management. In more recent years, however, China was perceived as the Asian region's diversity leader (Chaen 2015). Another significant landmark for women in China was the UN's Fourth World Conference on Women, held in Beijing in 1995. This event was a catalyst for the advent of centers for women's studies and several NGOs, such as those for migrant women and others providing legal counsel for victims of domestic violence (Yiping 2013).

Future challenges

Hare (2016) points to the steep decline in women's employment, from 75% in 1988 to 57% in 2009. The gender pay differentials are growing larger, particularly in the upper portion of the wage distribution. One characteristic of the plight of Chinese women is the disparity between rural and urban women. Yiping (2013) highlights the feminization of agriculture and the lack of land rights for rural women. She also states that women make up 65% of the rural labor force yet hold only 1–2% of local decision-making positions.

The dialogue in China has turned away from quotas, as these were ineffective in achieving gender diversity in the upper echelons of management (Chaen 2015). Instead, scholars advocate for cultural change and practical measures, such as embracing flexible working practices and increased board backing for diversity issues. Dongchao (2011) concurs that an analysis of women's political participation should look beyond the numbers.

The president of the People's Republic of China, Xi Jinping, promised during his opening speech on September 27, 2015, at the UN Conference on Women, that Chinese women would play a greater part in the global women's movement and that China would contribute USD 10 million to implement the Beijing Declaration and post-2015 development agenda (UN Women 2015).

Malaysia

Historical context and dominant ideology

According to Amar (2015, 1), the aims of feminist movements in Malaysia have many similarities to those of other developing countries, which "are to establish equality in terms of the economic, education, politics, or social spheres of life". Malaysian women are uncomfortable using the "feminist" label because of its Western association and instead use the term "womanism" (Saleh 2012). Alston and Alamgir (2012, 1) highlight that "the mostly Muslim nation of Malaysia has always walked a fine line between protecting the rights of Malay women and acknowledging the role that Islam plays in the daily lives of its citizens". Our research reveals an ongoing dichotomy between cultural preservation and global change that places the focus on gender empowerment and equality. This is in line with current conflicts worldwide between the role of women viewed from a religious context and the evolving role of women from a shifting societal perspective; the homemaker versus the working woman.

The war and post-war periods served as a catalyst in the mobilization of women against anti-colonialism and the lower status of women in Malaysian society. When Malaysia became independent on August 31, 1957, all citizens, irrespective of gender, were given the right to vote (Anuar 2015). In contrast to Western countries with the strong influence of their suffragette movements, Malaysia's struggle for gender equality was based not on achieving women's voting rights, but on human rights. Independence also resulted in an increase in the female labor workforce due to Malaysia's increased focus on manufacturing (Frank 2012).

Malaysia is an Islamic state and all Muslims have to abide by Sharia law, a system of Islamic laws that supersedes Malaysian constitutional laws (Ufen 2009). Anwar (2007, 2) states that many feminists consider Islam to be a direct contributor to the marginalization of women's rights, and the onslaught of injustices against women is strongly influenced by the patriarchal interpretation of Islam. Both Islam and Confucianism reinforce the glass ceiling that limits the progress of women in senior positions (Abdullah 2014).

Key milestones

Malaysian women's rights organizations played a critical role in raising national awareness around gender equality and social injustices against women. As a result of their persistence, in 1985 the Joint Action Group (JAG) publicly declared that domestic violence was a social concern and efforts were made to pass legislation to address the high levels of abuse (Samah 2010).

In 1995, Malaysia approved the Convention on the Elimination of All Forms of Discrimination against Women (CEDAW). Women leaders were instrumental in creating shifts for the progress of women at national level in the early 2000s, when the country witnessed the appointments of the first female judge and director-general of ministries, as well as several female ambassadors. In 2001, women's organizations were once again instrumental in ensuring the government amendment of Article 8(2) of the Constitution to include gender as a basis for non-discrimination (Saleh 2012).

Future challenges

Grant Thornton's 2016 International Business Report reveals that the number of businesses within Malaysia without any women at senior levels continues to increase, from 21% in 2012 to 31% in 2016. This is a higher figure that in other ASEAN (Association of South East Asian Nations) countries (Grant Thornton 2016). Even though Malaysia has joined the 30% Club, and the prime minister endorses 30% women representation on public boards, the numbers strongly reflect the ongoing embedded barriers that women continue to face within the Malaysian workforce (Abdullah 2014).

According to Samah (2010), many corporates in the private sector do not endorse or support the equal pay principle. She further asserts that women continue to be severely disadvantaged in terms of job placement and career mobility across sectors in comparison to their male counterparts. There are also lower levels of female participation in the labor force in high-income and decision-making roles. Even though the Malaysian government utilizes a quota system to manage equal opportunities for women in various professional sectors, progress continues to be slow. Anuar (2015) points out that even though there are higher numbers of women than men in higher education, the level of women participation in the workforce remains low.

Sexual harassment in the workplace is considered to be a serious growing epidemic (Samah 2010). Malaysian women constantly face the challenge of balancing the role of women from a cultural, religious context versus the evolving role of women as equal citizens from a constitutional perspective. In spite of these challenges, feminism—or, rather, "womanism"— continues to thrive through ongoing cultural dialogue and social awareness.

India

Historical context and dominant ideology

India is strongly influenced by patriarchal traditions. In most of India, males are the heads of households and maintain key decision-making power and authority. As is the case in China, Rahi (2015, 171) asserts that most communities in India have a "son preference" due to strong cultural beliefs about sons being more financially and religiously rewarding. Furthermore, religion plays a critical role within Indian society and reinforces the prevailing gender roles and stereotypes. According to Hinduism, the prevailing religion within India, it is a son's duty to take care of his family and his parents after marriage and to continue the family lineage. As in China, therefore, there is a son preference.

During the nineteenth century, male colonists challenged the Indian practice of "sati" whereby a widow is obliged to show her devotion to her dead husband by burning herself alive (Gangoli 2007). In 1887, the National Social Conference (NSC) was established and placed focus on addressing various social issues. These included widow remarriage, child marriage and the emancipation of women through education. Although there were a small number of matriarchal societies—where women were the key figures of authority—in India, British laws aimed to emancipate and shift the prevailing patriarchal culture of the time. The Hindu Code Bill aimed to formalize various laws to eradicate gender inequality in the 1950s. Although the bill faced resistance from the Indian male population, it was a catalyst in terms of attempting to create equality between males and females from a legal perspective (Singariya 2014).

Patel (2010) highlights that women played a critical and impactful role in the struggle for independence. Gandhi strongly encouraged women to participate in the civil disobedience movement against the British. Women only acquired equal voting rights later in 1935. After independence in 1947, women began to develop a critical consciousness in respect to their rights within broader society. In 1954, a separate women's wing—the National Federation of Indian Women—was created by the Indian Communist Party (Gangoli 2007).

Key milestones

The various women's movements over the years served as catalysts, mobilizing Indian women to raise awareness of the prevalent inequalities and promote overarching gender equality within society. In 1966 Indira Gandhi became the first woman prime minister in the history of India. She was in office for three consecutive terms from 1966 to 1977. In 1980 she served a fourth term until her tragic assassination in 1984 (Green 2013).

The Indian constitution granted freedom from discrimination based on gender and religion in 1976. India's ongoing commitment to gender equality is positively reflected in the constitution, in which Article 14 ensures women the right to equality, Article 15(1) prohibits discrimination on the basis of sex and Article 15(3) provides for affirmative and positive action (Devani 2011).

Through the continued efforts of various female leaders and organizations, the National Policy on Education (NPE) was created in 1986 to address the education gap between genders. The success of the NPE was evident when literate women exceeded 50% of the overall female population in 2001. In recent times India has adopted a quota system to ensure a balance in terms of the underrepresentation of women in the workplace (Beaman et al., 2012).

Future challenges

Saha's (2015) research estimates that it may take up to 81 years before the gender gap within the workforce is closed. She points to a recent study showing that the proportion of women in senior management roles declined from 19% in 2013 to 14% in 2014. McKinsey's Women Matter 2012 survey reveals that the "double burden" syndrome was the key challenge for women within senior management (McKinsey 2012). This refers to the double roles that women undertake in terms of work and home responsibilities.

Vasavada (2012) states that women make up a mere 36% of the labor force; 22.6% are employed by organizations; 6% are in senior management and 4.9% are on boards of directors. Despite rapid urbanization and industrialization, strong embedded religious and patriarchal influences continue to reinforce male superiority and female inferiority. This continues to impact on the progress of women across the Indian workforce and in all spheres of society negatively (Rahi 2015).

As there are limited workplace opportunities, women's education continues to be low priority, thereby perpetuating a cycle of continued economic dependency and high illiteracy (Sen 2001). As a result, the workplace restricts women to lower-paid jobs within the unskilled sector. This also further perpetuates various forms of female exploitation, including trafficking, and their vulnerability to sexual harassment in the workplace and violence.

Women's organizations have played, and continue to play, a critical role in raising awareness of the social injustices that women face. They have been directly responsible for many legislative changes over the years, including the Family Courts Act (1984), Rape Law (1980), Dowry Prohibition Act (1961) and Domestic Violence Bill (2002). Women's movements in India continue to show their commitment to improving the plight of women and are strong advocates and supporters of gender equality.

Our review of the Southeast Asia countries reveals commonalities and distinct differences. The chief commonalities include the importance of women's movements and the need for women to mobilize to raise awareness and effect change at both a social and legislative level. Another commonality is the presence of strong religious influences and the secondary role of women within these patriarchal cultures. The key differences between the countries are the individual leadership and political contexts that served as catalysts for gender equality. For example, Malaysia is the only country in which women were given voting rights post-independence. Suffrage was not achieved through the focused efforts of a suffragette movement, as it was in other countries. Despite the progress and milestones achieved, there appears to be an increase in gender-based crimes within this region. More than ever, there is a strong need for women across the continent to mobilize and collaboratively address embedded cultural and gender mindsets.

South America: featuring Brazil and Colombia

Brazil

Historical context and dominant ideology

In Brazil (and Colombia), colonization was instrumental in creating a machismo culture and adherence to Catholicism was a powerful social force. Historical, theological, cultural and strong patriarchal traditions have significant influence on the way women in Brazil were treated throughout history, how they perceive themselves and how they are perceived by others (Pitanguy 2002). Brazil is the largest Roman Catholic country in the world and the influence of religion on the perceptions of Brazilian women is profound.

The Brazilian women's movement, created in the mid-nineteenth century, was not radical and initially focused on female enfranchisement. The movement gained momentum under Bertha Lutz, who founded the League for Intellectual Emancipation of Women in 1919 and in 1922 the Brazilian Federation for Women's Progress, a political group advocating Brazilian women's rights (Lôbo 2010). Lutz was appointed to draft the first page of Brazil's new constitution in 1933, promoting equal rights and giving women preference in government jobs dealing with home, children and women's working conditions (Snider 2013).

The South American political landscape and history of military dictatorships shaped the women's movements (Maluf 2011). Between 1964 and 1985 Brazil experienced repression and poverty. Most women's organizations in Brazil and Colombia emerged during protests against dictatorship and political instability and Fiedler and Blanco (2006) regard Brazil's women's movement as the most organized and effective in Latin America.

The Brazilian family structure has recently altered—families are smaller and often headed by dual-working parents or a single parent. Generally, women remain responsible for the domestic sphere. This is replicated in Colombia, where the most fragile families are female-headed. Violence against women is widespread in both countries (Merkin 2009).

Key milestones

Brazilian women, given the vote in 1932 (Hahner 1979)—ahead of Colombia, which attained suffrage in 1957—were slow to obtain legal equality. Brazil's 1988 constitution entrenches equality and prohibits all discrimination (Van Klaveren et al., 2009). There are regular national conferences for women's policies and Brazil is committed to respect and implement international agreements such as CEDAW (Convention on the Elimination of All Forms of Discrimination Against Women) (Leones 2014).

Of the four leading 2014 election candidates, three were women (De Paula 2015). In 2011, Dilma Rousseff, who was in the top 10 of Forbes's 2011 list of the World's Most Powerful Women, was appointed the first female Brazilian president (Jalalzai and Dos Santos 2013; Torregrosa 2011). Her emphasis on entrepreneurship inspired multiple woman-headed start-ups, supporting the "Dilma Effect" (Jalalzai and Dos Santos, 2013). Currently, allegations of corruption led to a vote in the lower house of Congress requesting the Senate to impeach Rousseff, a timely reminder that women leaders are not infallible (Jacobs 2016).

Future challenges

Brazil's constitution promotes equality yet current practice remains challenging and Brazil has the seventh highest rate of violence against women in the world (Andrade 2013). Another study indicates that between 2001 and 2009, more than 54,000 Colombian women were victims of sexual violence (Palau 2016).

Although female representation on boards and executive committees approximates the Latin American average, corporate gender diversity is the lowest in the region. The wage gap—more pronounced than Colombia's average—is similar in the public and private sectors, yet few women hold government positions (only 9% of parliamentary seats). Similar to Colombia, literacy rates of Brazilian women and men are equal at 90%.

The World Economic Forum's Global Gender Gap Report (2013) ranks Brazil 62nd out of 136 countries, yet the survey reveals that women's unemployment is twice that of men.

Reproductive rights are a critical issue in Brazil because of historical resistance by the Catholic Church to contraception and abortion. Until the legalization of contraception, Brazilian law grouped contraception, abortion and immorality together. Brazilian legislation allows women 120 days of paid maternity leave versus only seven days paternity leave for men, illustrating that women are expected to play the major role in childcare. Interestingly, the church in Colombia has been part of advocating for women's reproductive rights within marriage (Roldán 2014). Abortion is illegal in Brazil, but is estimated at more than a million abortions annually.

Colombia

Historical context and dominant ideology

Colombia, also a Catholic state, was highly influenced by religion, which imposed a strict patriarchal social order on society, delineating the roles of women (Gonzalez 2000). Within this religious framework, the role of woman and mother was to protect the moral integrity of the family, and by extension, the nation. Colombia has been beset by conflict for over fifty years (Vietor and White 2015). As a result, the women's movement's aim of greater representation socially, as well as in business and government, has been hindered by conflict associated with violence against women.

According to Gonzalez (2000), the Latin American women's movement lagged behind that of the West, with Colombia being the penultimate Latin American country to gain female suffrage, in 1957. This struggle for the right to vote was part of a broader struggle for civil and political rights (Velandia and Otero 2013). During World War II, Colombian women linked their struggles with democracy and posited feminism as a defense against fascism.

For Hofstede (2001), Colombian culture reflects "high power distance and collectivism and a masculine orientation" (Oilivas-Luján et al. 2008, 229). According to Buchely (2013), most Colombian women are not full participants in the economy, working primarily in unpaid labor tasks associated with caregiving or in the informal sector or receiving a lower salary for skilled work than their male counterparts.

Key milestones

It was only in the 1930s that middle- and upper-class women began to call for change. In 1932, ahead of their Brazilian counterparts, married women were awarded the right to "own and administer their property, appear in court, and engage in economic activities" (Gonzalez 2000, 697). In January 1945, the constitution was amended, to include women aged 21 and over as citizens, and in 1962 women won equal pay for equal work (Velandia and Otero 2013).

In 2011, legislation ensured that 30% of all electoral candidates and senior government positions be held by women (Alsema 2012). There is also a High Presidential Council for Gender Equity which aims to secure and grow gender equity and women's rights. In 2010, statistics showed that 51% of women were economically active, compared to 74% of men (UNDP 2011).

Future challenges

For Buchely (2013), female inequality in the Colombian economy is evident in three areas, namely education levels, division of labor/time, and the workplace. Women achieve more throughout school without this reflecting in their economic performance, with an average wage gap of 23% (Buchely 2013, 318). Furthermore, with regard to division of labor, it is evident from legislation, which provides 12 weeks of maternity leave for women and eight days of paternity leave for men, that the burden of childcare rests clearly with the mother (Buchely 2013). This is similar to the situation in Brazil. The imbalance also serves to make the employment of women more costly, as they require more extended periods of paid absence than men.

McKinsey (2013) highlights Colombia having the highest level of female representation on executive committees and boards in South America, yet "only 12% of seats in national parliament held by women" (Ørstavik and Lizcano 2013). A further challenge is that women in political leadership roles have almost exclusively been from a politico-economic elite, requiring diversity in economic standing to give voice to women across class lines (UNDP 2011).

The Inter-Parliamentary Union (IPU) (2016) ranks Colombia 91 out of 191 countries for female inclusion in political entities. In 2011, Colombia developed the National Policy on Gender Equity for Women, in which it committed to equality as part of the president's overall development objectives (Women's Forum 2014). Issues around crime levels and unsafe geographies within Colombia result in difficulties in policing labor legislation (Alsema 2012). It is thus critical that equality and rights are enforced and not merely features of legislation. Similarly, the 30% legislated "quota" for women in senior positions should be steadily increased to grow the number of women leaders and encourage the development of a strong talent pipeline (UNDP 2011).

Africa and Middle East: featuring South Africa and the United Arab Emirates (UAE)

South Africa

Historical context and dominant ideology

The journey of women in South Africa is strongly intertwined with the diverse and tumultuous political history of the country. A history of patriarchy, as well as the apartheid era and its legacy, have played a role in their continuing journey of emancipation. Women's struggle for equality in South Africa has been against both gender discrimination and racial oppression (Gouws 2012).

Suffrage for white women in South Africa was influenced in 1899 by the establishment of the Women's Christian Temperance Union (WCTU) and on May 19, 1930, white South African women were granted voting rights (South African History Online 2015). The African National Congress (ANC) played a pivotal role in the country's transformation and emancipation since its inception as far back as 1912 (MacKinnon 2014). Charlotte Maxeke founded the first formal black women's organization in 1918 (Ginwala 2002).

In 1948, the Afrikaner National Party obtained power and formalized the policy of apartheid to segregate the various race groups, which resulted in constant political unrest. According to Meintjes (2012, 5), "the nature of the racial divisions under apartheid meant that at an ideological level, both race and masculinity shaped the discourse on both sides of the racial divide". Due to the key role that women played in the struggle, the ANC Women's League (ANCWL) was formed in 1948, with Ida Mtwana as its first president (Suttner 2012). The mobilization of women across the country was a key catalyst in the struggle against apartheid in the years to follow. Segalo (2014) observed that even though there were government restrictions on the various women's movements, they nevertheless challenged the oppressive system through various marches and demonstrations.

In 1954, the Federation of South African Women (FSAW) was established to serve as a platform for the mobilization of women from across the various affiliated organizations. It drew up a Women's Charter to pledge an end to pervasive discriminatory laws (Cunningham 2000). With continued political turmoil and unrest, South Africa faced increasing pressure, both internally and internationally, and various politically active women and organizations were banned. Prominent female activists left the country and went into exile.

Key milestones

In 1991 the Women's Charter was finally completed and incorporated into South Africa's constitution. It championed the importance of gender equality, and was further reinforced through its alignment with the Bill of Rights of the Constitution of the Republic of South Africa (RSA) (Act 108 of 1996) (Gouws 2012). Apartheid was abolished in 1994, when the first multi-racial democratic elections were held. South African women could now focus more extensively on gender issues without their importance being overshadowed by critical political priorities. As a result, many women leaders returned from exile to join key political leadership roles (South African History Online 2015).

South Africa implemented the Employment Equity Act no. 55 in 1988. It gives preference to previously disadvantaged groups based on race, gender and physical disability. In 1996 a new constitution, with provision for women's rights, was instituted. Further historical impact was achieved when Phumzile Mlambo-Ngcuka became the first woman deputy president of South Africa on June 22, 2005.

According to the International Women's Forum held in 2011 (IWFSA 2011), South Africa has shown considerable improvement with regard to the equality of women in the workplace. Even though South Africa has made significant strides and progress, Oliphant (2015) argues that the country is unstable in its gender focus, reflected in the fluctuations against international women's empowerment measures and indices. He also highlights that most organizations in South Africa have focused on numerical targets at the expense of effective upskilling and cultural desensitization. As one of the women we interviewed noted:

> When we presented to certain funders, they automatically listened more attentively and spoke directly to my male counterpart.
> (Stacey Brewer, co-founder of SPARK Schools in South Africa)

Future challenges

Despite the consistent efforts and the progress made, the majority of women in South Africa continue to face discriminatory practices influenced by embedded social norms and gender stereotypes. Despite the dramatic shift from apartheid to democracy, the entrenched gender mindset continues to dominate. Moletsane and Reddy (2010) research on women in poverty highlights that there are continuing disparities in income between the genders.

Of the 293 JSE-listed companies surveyed by Lewis-Enright, Crafford and Crous (2009), only seven had female CEOs. According to Zinn (2016), even though, in comparison to the other BRICS, South Africa is a top performer, there remains insufficient representation across the workforce. Women are only represented at executive level in 8.79% of the JSE-listed corporations and they only have 25% or more women directors. Figure 3.3, based on the Business Women's Association of South Africa (BWASA) 2015 census, highlights the strong differences in gender representation across the workforce. At executive management level and above, men still have 70% to 97% representation in comparison to women. Women are underrepresented, at 29.3% of executive managers, 21.8% of directorships, 9.2% of chairpersons and 2.4% of CEOs. This is concerning as it reflects strong embedded patriarchal power and decision-making structures (BWASA 2015).

Even though the Employment Equity Act supports diversity, organizational culture still has a long way to go before there is widespread acceptance. Women are still stereotyped as the weaker sex, which limits equal participation and decision-making authority. The future seems optimistic despite the many challenges outlined above. However, sustainable progress will be dependent on the mobilization of both women and men in South Africa. It requires a strong cultural shift away from centuries of gender-entrenched mindsets and stereotypes.

United Arab Emirates (UAE)

Historical context and dominant ideology

It is imperative to know something of the background of the UAE, its history and its cultural context, to understand women's movements in this country. The UAE was established in December 1971 as a federation of seven sheikhdoms, each with its own ruler. In 2013, the country's population was 9.2 million. The UAE is not an electoral democracy; political organizations and political parties are illegal and both men and women have limited political rights (Freedom House 2013; Metcalfe 2011). Morgan Stanley Capital International (MSCi) classifies the UAE as an emerging market and it is among the world's wealthiest nations (Tlaiss 2013). Islam is the official religion of the UAE.

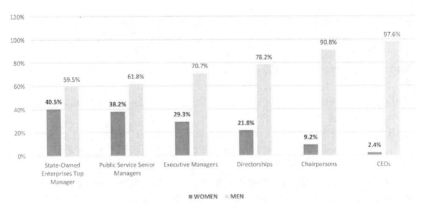

Figure 3.3 Women's workforce representation in South Africa (BWASA statistics)
Source: With permission adapted from www.bwasa.co.za/news/bwa-women-in-leadership-census-media-release.

The Sharia-based personal status law is applicable for Muslims, and non-Muslim expatriates are subject to Sharia rulings on marriage, divorce and child custody (Kirdar 2010). Islamic interpretation is highly variable and confusion exists between what Islam is and what is culturally associated with Islam (Metcalfe 2011). Scholars observe that what maintains inequality among Arab men and women in a patriarchal Arab society has less to do with Islam and more to do with traditional values and beliefs (Sikdar and Mitra 2012).

Traditionally, women have always stayed close to home and focused on biological and social reproduction (Hasso 2014). The Arab society has traditionally placed very little value on women's participation in activities outside the home (Ahmed 2011; Metcalfe 2011; Tlaiss 2013).

Key milestones

Since 1971, three elections have been held in the UAE (2006, 2011 and 2015). Citizens vote for half of the 40-member Federal National Council (FNC) and in 2015, of the 20 members elected, 19 were men and one was a woman. Men and women have limited suffrage in the UAE and women have been able to vote since the first election in 2006. In contemporary UAE, girls and boys are equally represented at primary and secondary school level, while at tertiary level, women outnumber men. More than 70% of Emiratis in federal higher education institutions are women (Kemp 2012; Ridge 2011). Emirati men generally leave the country to study abroad, while women cannot leave the country without the permission of their male guardians.

Government employment of Emirati women increased from 11.6% in 1995 to 66% in June 2007 (UEA Ministry of State and Federal National Council Affairs 2007). While big strides have been made with regard to women in the workplace in the UAE, there is still reluctance on the part of husbands and male relatives for women to participate beyond junior level positions (Kirdar 2010). There has been a slight increase in the number of women in the workforce, as a percentage of the total labor force, from 12.8% in 2011 to 13.1% in 2014 (World Bank 2015). In the UAE, 30% of women hold senior management positions and run their own enterprises (Al Jassmi 2016). Al Jassmi (2016) believes the success of women can be attributed to the UAE government's strong support for women empowerment across the region. In UAE businesses, women leaders display high levels of "agentic" (assertiveness, decisiveness and risk-taking) characteristics typical of the male gender stereotype and low levels of "people orientation" traits associated with the female gender stereotype, resulting in successful women breaking through the glass ceiling and increasing the number of women leaders in the UAE (Sikdar and Mitra 2012).

Future challenges

Although the constitution endorses the principle of equal treatment of all citizens, it does not specifically address gender-based discrimination and contains references that primarily identify women as wives and mothers (Kirdar 2010). Among the government's top priorities is women's advancement and empowerment (Salama 2015), but despite this support there is still a long way to go for women in the workplace (Swan 2016). Programs are needed at schools and universities to assist girls to develop more confidence in their abilities. The private sector also needs to remove barriers and create enabling environments (Swan 2016).

Gender inequality is still a severe problem in Arab society where men and women are considered suited for different roles and only certain careers are deemed suitable for women (Sikdar and Mitra 2012). Tlaiss (2013) asserts that, given the importance of family in the lives of Arab Middle Eastern women, organizations need to adopt women-friendly practices such as flexi-time and daycare facilities on site that would allow women employees to realize their desired career objectives. Metcalfe (2011) argues for the development of individual human rights so that women can take responsibility for creating their own feminist agendas, premised on Arab cultural values. Female entrepreneurship in the UAE is an under-researched area with tremendous economic potential and should be given special attention. Women's roles in society may need to be re-examined by policy-makers to enable them to better contribute to the social and economic development of their country Ahmed (2011).

Women in a number of other Middle Eastern countries share the challenges faced by those in the UAE. As one of our interviewees observed:

> The Middle East is quite different from other mature markets or from Europe, where I had experience. The Middle East is not like that, so there are a lot of other factors that are as important, and it becomes more important.
>
> (Isabel Neiva, UAE)

Other Middle Eastern countries, like Egypt and Turkey, have a different history when it comes to women's movements. Kamal (2015) described the four waves of the Egyptian women's movements and their quest to include women's rights in the new constitution in Egypt, prior to the revolution in 2012. Al-Ali (2002, 4), in turn, compared the women's movements of Turkey and Egypt and discovered similarities and differences due to the fact that Turkey, unlike Egypt, has not been colonized in modern times. She contends that "they are similar in that they share several historical and political factors, such as their links to nationalist movements, their links to processes of modernization and development, and tensions between secular and religious tendencies". She found, however, that the specific ideology of Turkish nationalism employed by the Kemalist regime differs decisively from Nasserist and Arab nationalist ideologies associated with the Egyptian state.

Nonetheless, women's movements in both countries have in recent years challenged prevailing notions of political culture and institutions. The women's movements in the Middle East are "potential agents for demo-cratization, yet they are highly constrained by prevailing social and poli-tical structures, lack of clear institutional targets and ambiguous state policies" (Al-Ali 2002, 4). Al-Ali also points out that a number of tradi-tions in present-day Egypt have their roots in pharaonic times. As a result, they are often not rooted in religion, and while most Middle Easterners are Muslim, there exist differences between Sunni and Shi'a Muslims as well as other Muslim groupings, such as the Alawite minority in Turkey. Moreover, women belonging to minority religious groups, such as the Copts in Egypt, are generally exposed to similar or the same cultural and social codes and traditions as their Muslim counterparts of the same social class. These points highlight the need to be careful of generalizing about women's issues across regions.

A comparison with Western women's movements

In contrast to the women's movements in emerging markets, the first wave of Western women's movements started in the early 1900s, when increasing numbers of women in the West began demanding the legal and political rights—such as the right to vote and to hold property—that democracies had denied them. They were militant, and in 1919 secured the vote for women in the UK and in 1920, the US (Reeves 2010). We mentioned the film, *Suffragette* in Chapter 2, which describes the English suffrage move-ment. The demands for equality for women did not extend to the work-place in those early days. Most women did not work, and those who did were restricted to a narrow range of jobs, such as primary school teaching and nursing.

Well-known icon, Rosie the Riveter, illustrated the abilities of women that enabled them to perform jobs that had previously been done by men, particularly during World War II. However, with the return of millions of soldiers at the end of World War II, men were given priority when it came to hiring in the West. The gender role expectation was that women would go back to being homemakers, especially during pregnancy or while rais-ing children. In the economic stagflation of the 1960s, women eagerly entered the workforce to supplement their family's income and improve their education levels. The second wave of women's movements rejected the notion that women were especially suited for homemaking. The Afri-can American Civil Rights Movement in the 1960s became a blueprint for second-wave feminism. Women's movements advocated for a broader, more inclusive conception of what it means to be female. The first United

Nations World Conference on Women was held in Mexico City in 1975. Attention shifted from the concerns of white women to the empowerment of all women.

In the US the representation of women in management increased from 4% in 1990 to 45% in 2000. Also in the US, from 2006 to 2007, 58% of all degrees were awarded to women and 56% of all master's degrees. The EU calls for a 60% employment rate for women. In EU countries, women earn 15% less than men (Reeves 2010).

Women's movements in the US and Britain have been well documented and there are historical accounts that can serve as a baseline against which trends in emerging markets may be benchmarked. This enabled us to compile the following:

Figure 3.4 depicts the women's movements in the countries under review and shows similar trends across the movements, where suffrage was generally the first wave. The waves also illustrate that development does not necessarily follow a straight line. The Russian women's movement, in particular, demonstrates the fits and starts in which it progressed. The waves also illustrate that women's liberation has been influenced by external factors, in addition to its own efforts. Malaysian independence from British rule is one such external factor. Each wave is embedded in its unique socio-political and economic context, and illustrates the interdependence and systemic nature of the various variables impacting women's liberation.

As the following table illustrates, Western women's movements appear to have contributed to the higher ranking of their gender index scores, leading to higher gender equality. It seems that the ranking on the World Economic Forum's Gender Index is thus related to gender gap scores. For

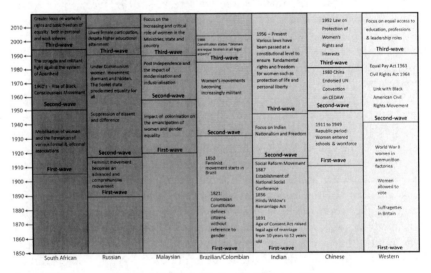

Figure 3.4 Waves of women's movements in selected countries
Source: Authors' own (2016).

example, Poland has a higher ranking, and its equality score is also higher, than India, with its low ranking and, accordingly, *low equality score*.

The voices of the South African women we interviewed did not necessarily echo the high equality scores for South Africa. For example, one anonymous South African interviewee observed: "I think it was definitely a barrier just being in the minority in a very male-oriented culture."

Conclusion: general trends and implications

While investigating women's movements in certain emerging markets, we identified some overarching general themes, with specificities and differences. We will highlight three significant trends. First, women's movements were embedded in particular socio-political and economic contexts that influenced the emergence, development and/or endorsement of these movements. A systemic view is thus essential to comprehend trends across our sample countries. Interestingly, historical events such as world wars opened up opportunities, previously impossible, for women to work in ammunition factories in the West and in Russia.

Second, our choice of regions created some difficulties as there turned out to be huge differences within them. For example, Southeast Asia, India, China and Malaysia each had unique characteristics, and even within those countries there were vast differences. For example, an Egyptian scholar notes that "there is no archetypical Middle Eastern woman"

Table 3.1 Global ranking of gender equality

	WEF Global Gender Index Ranking (2015) Out of 145 countries*	*WEF Gender Gap Score* 1= perfect equality 0= total inequality*
Russian Federation	75	0.694
Poland	51	0.715
India	108	0.664
Malaysia	111	0.655
China	91	0.682
Brazil	85	0.686
Colombia	42	0.725
South Africa	17	0.759
UAE	119	0.646
Egypt	136	0.599
UK	18	0.758
USA	28	0.740

Note: *World Economic Forum (WEF) "Global Gender Gap Index 2015" http://reports. weforum.org/global-gender-gap-report-2015/the-global-gender-gap-index-2015/.

(Al-Ali 2002, 7). Even though the historical trajectories of the women's movements in some of the countries—such as Brazil and Colombia—revealed similarities, they vary in terms of their current ideas and practices. Yet they share certain historical and political factors, such as tension with the Catholic Church. In turn, women's movements such as Sisters of Islam, mentioned in the Malaysian section, share common goals with women's movements in Egypt, the UAE and Turkey.

Third, we observed dissonance between formal legislative reality and practical experience in both our interviews and the literature we consulted. Consequently, while significant progress has been reported in relation to voting rights, inheritance and family planning (contraceptive and abortion) rights today, subtle discrimination still exists. Duality was evident in Brazil, Russia, South Africa, India and Malaysia, for example, where the formal dictates of the law prescribe equality for all, yet in reality women experience inequality.

Meyerson and Fletcher (1999) contend that the 1962, 1977 and 1985 Western feminist movements used radical rhetoric and legal action to drive out overt discrimination. They warn that "the barriers that persist today are insidious and deeply embedded in organisational life" (1999, 127). These researchers were referring to women's movements in the West, as if those were the only ones to consider. Mohanty et al. (1991) accuse research of representing a white middle-class women's ethnocentric perspective, while Nkomo and Ngambi (2009) declare that women leaders in Africa have been largely invisible in scholarly research. To avoid this kind of criticism, we ensured that our sample represented diverse dimensions, such as ethnicity, age, geographical location and industry sector. We hope this book will help to change scholars' mindsets and contribute to a more inclusive perspective.

Our research nevertheless revealed similar issues to those quoted by researchers focusing on the West, such as "women typically bear a disproportionate amount of responsibility for home and family and thus have more demands on their time outside the office" (Meyerson and Fletcher 1999, 127). Lamentations around the paternalistic, masculine societal norms and organizational cultures are echoed in the literature about emerging markets. Their situation is similar to that in the West, when discrimination became more nuanced and less obvious (Reeves 2010). Consequently, overt and covert resistance to legitimizing women's leadership requires the continuation of women's movements. Gender equality is therefore a global point of contention. The International Labour Organization stresses that, worldwide, half of all working women are in vulnerable jobs, which in turn lessens the likelihood of them having a voice at work or even basic human rights (International Labour Organization 2008). Gaciarz (2011) notes that, worldwide, access to a female talent pool will assist companies meet the huge demand for qualified skills in knowledge-intensive industries. The consequences of a lack of skills in emerging markets could mean that women's skills are more important and highly valued than in developed markets, where general education levels are higher.

The voices of women in the emerging markets would be amplified if we developed a joint force of unified women's movements, where experiences and resources could be shared and alliances over particular issues, such as the plight of domestic violence victims, rural women and migrant workers, could be formed. Ban Ki-moon, the UN secretary-general, urged the 80 world leaders at the Global Meeting on Gender Equality and Women's Empowerment on September 27, 2015 to finance and implement gender equality policies, monitoring progress for the next conference in 2030. In the same way, we, the authors, urge emerging market leaders to unite behind game-changing actions to achieve gender equality and to hold one another accountable. An emerging market network of women's movements would have great impact and enable progress to be monitored.

We advocate for, and urge, synergy between women's studies departments at universities and research institutions in emerging markets, and through this book endeavor to open up scholarly conversations between these emerging markets on enablers for and barriers to women's leadership. Ghemawat (2011, 27) states that, unfortunately, the "current levels of interconnectivity are no greater than they were in the past." However, globalization provides increased opportunities to learn and engage with other countries in relation to best practice and successful women's leadership initiatives.

In closing, we applaud the declaration of Phumzile Mlambo-Ngcuka, executive director of UN Women, on September 27, 2015, that by adopting the sustainable development agenda for 2030, UN leaders had taken personal responsibility for the empowerment of women. They had taken the first firm step towards September 25, 2030.

We support this giant step because the emergence of our markets is impossible unless we attend to gender equality as a matter of urgency.

References

Aaltio, I. and H. Peltonen. 2009. "Portraits of Russian Women Entrepreneurs: Identification and Ways of Leadership." *Journal of Enterprising Culture* 17(4): 443–471.

Abdullah, S. N. 2014. "The Causes of Gender Diversity in Malaysian Large Firms." *Journal of Management and Governance* 18(4): 1137–1159.

Adam, K. 2009. "The Role of Department Heads as Change Agents in the Implementation of Educational Reform in the United Arab Emirates." University of South Africa. http://uir.unisa.ac.za/bitstream/handle/10500/1758/02CHAPTER2.pdf?sequence=10.

African National Congress. 2011. Retrieved from www.anc.org.za/show.php?id=206.

Ahmed, S. Z. 2011. "Evidence of the Characteristics of Women Entrepreneurs in the Kingdom of Saudi Arabia: An Empirical Investigation." *International Journal of Gender and Entrepreneurship* 3(2): 123–143.

Al-Ali, N. S. 2002. "The Women's movements in Egypt, with Selected Reference to Turkey." *Civil Society and Social Movements* 5 (April): 1–43.

Al Jassmi, J. 2016. "Enhancing UAE Women's Leadership in Banking, Financial Services." *Khaleeji Times*, January 31. Accessed May 2, 2016. www.khaleejtimes.com/business/banking-finance/enhancing-uae-womens-leadership-in-banking-financial-services.

Al Junied, S. and M. Khairuddin. 2013. "Against Multiple Hegemonies: Radical Malay Women in Colonial Malaya." *Journal of Social History* 47(1): 166.

Alsema, A. 2012. "Gender Policy is Failing Women in Colombia." *Colombia Reports* (July).

Alston, M. and A. Alamgir. 2012. "Women's Rights in Malaysia." *International Policy Digest, Asian Studies* 37(2): 249–266.

Amar, S. 2015. "Feminism Movement in Malaysia Ensnares the Future of the Country's Women and Children." The Khilafah. Central Media Office of Hizb ut Tahrir. www.hizb-ut-tahrir.info/.

Andrade, S. 2013. "Violence and Women in Brazil: What Happens Indoors Stays Indoors." *The Independent*, September 24.

Anuar, K. K. 2015. "Do Women Have Equal Rights in Malaysia?" *KPUM Human Rights Law Journal*. http://hrlj.kpum.org/index.php/2015/10/08/are-women-equal-in-malaysia/.

Anwar, Z. 2007. "Zainah Anwar on Domestic Violence Campaign in Malaysia." *YouTube*, December 8.

Beaman, L., E. Duflo, R. Pande and P. Topalova. 2012. "Female Leadership Raises Aspirations and Educational Attainment for Girls: A Policy Experiment in India." *National Institute of Health* 335(6068): 582–586.

Bryans, P. and S. Mavin. 2003. "Women Learning to Become Managers: Learning to Fit in or to Play a Different Game?" *Management Learning* 34(1): 111–134.

Buchely, L. 2013. "Overcoming Gender Disadvantages. Social Policy Analysis of urban middle-class women in Colombia." *Revista de Economia del Rosario* 16(2): 313–340.

Budrina, I. 2012. "Phenomenon of Women-Leaders in Romania and Russia: Equal Gender Opportunities in Emerging Markets." *Review of International Comparative Management* 13(5): 849–860.

BWASA (Businesswoman of the Year Award). 2015. BWA Women in Leadership Census. www.bwasa.co.za/news/bwa-women-in-leadership-census-media-release.

Chaen, R. 2015. "Ranking in % of Women in Management: China, Malaysia, Hong Kong, Singapore." *Robert Chaen*, March 2. https://robertchaen.com/2015/03/02/9582/.

Chiu, J. 2013. "The Women's Movement in China." *Herizons* 27(2): 16–19.

Country Watch. 2011. "Status of Women: Social Overview." *Russia Review 2011*: 249–251.

Cunningham, A. M. 2000. "Inventory of the Records of the Federation of South African Women 1953–1963." University of the Witwatersrand Department of Historical Papers, Johannesburg.

Dahlerup, D. 1986. *The New Women's Movement: Feminism and Political Power in Europe and the USA*. London: Sage.

De Beauvoir, S. 1949. *The Second Sex*. Translated and edited by H. M. Parsley in 1997. London: Gallimard.

De Paula, M. 2015. "Brazil: Women's Participation in Elections." Gunda Werner Institute for Feminism and Gender Democracy. Accessed May 2, 2016. www. gwi-boell.de/en/2015/05/21/brazil-womens-participation-elections.

Devani, R. K. 2011. *An Analysis: Rights of Women Under the Indian Constitution.* Surat: Veer Narmad South Gujarat University.

Dickson, M. W., D. N. Den Hartog and J. K. Mitchelson. 2003. "Research on Leadership in a Cross-Cultural Context: Making Progress, and Raising New Questions." *The Leadership Quarterly* 14(6): 729–768.

Dongchao, M. 2011. "From Men–Women Equality to Gender Equality: The Zig-Zag Road of Women's Political Participation in China." *Asian Journal of Women Studies* 17(3): 7–24.

Dos Santos, P. 2012. "Gendering Representation: Parties, Institutions, and The Under-Representation of Women in Brazil's State Legislatures." Doctoral thesis. University of Kansas.

Edmonson, L. H. 1977. "Feminism in Russia 1900–1917." Doctoral thesis. University of London.

Elliot, C. and V. Stead. 2008. "Learning from Leading Women's Experience: Towards a Sociological Understanding." *Leadership* 4(2): 159–180.

Esposito, J. L. and N. J. DeLong-Bas. 2001. *Women in Muslim Family Law,* 2nd ed. Syracuse, NY: Syracuse University Press.

Euromonitor International. 2016. "The Outlook for Major Emerging Markets in 2016." *Euromonitor International,* March 24. http://blog.euromonitor.com/2016/03/the-outlook-for-major-emerging-markets-in-2016.html.

European Commission. 2012. "The Current Situation of Equality in Poland: Country Profile." http://ec.europa.eu/justice/gender-equality/files/epo_campaign/country_profile_poland_en.pdf.

Everett, J. M. 1981. *Women and Social Change in India.* New Delhi: Heritage.

Fiedler, A. M. and R. I. Blanco. 2006. "The Challenge of Varying Perceptions of Sexual Harassment: An International Study." *Journal of Behavioral and Applied Management* 7: 274–291.

Forbes. 2014. "The World's 100 Most Powerful Women." *Forbes,* www.forbes.com/sites/carolinehoward/2014/05/28/ranking-the-worlds-100-most-powerful-women-2014/#22b843e1fe7e.

Frank, A. K. 2012. "Factors Motivating Women's Informal Micro-Entrepreneurship: Experiences from Penang, Malaysia." *International Journal of Gender and Entrepreneurship* 4(1): 65–78.

Freedom House. 2013. "Freedom in the World 2013: Democratic Breakthroughs in the Balance." Country Report. www.freedomhouse.org/sites/default/files/FIW%202013%20Booklet.pdf.

Fuszara, M. 2000. "Feminism, the New Millennium and Ourselves: A Polish View." *Signs: Journal of Women in Culture and Society* 25(4): 1069–1075.

Fuszara, M. 2005. "Between Feminism and the Catholic Church: The Women's Movement in Poland." *Czech Sociological Review* 41(6): 1057–1075.

Gaciarz, B. 2011. "Women in the Workplace in Poland: From Egalitarian Economic Necessity to Elite Freedom of Choice and the Pervading Inequality in Status." *International Journal of Sociology* 41(3): 68–94.

Gangoli, G. 2007. *Indian Feminisms: Law Patriarchies and Violence in India.* Farnham: Ashgate Publishing Company.

Gazeta.ru. 2012. "Freed Pussy Riot Member Interviewed on Feminism, Patriarch, Life in Jail." *BBC Worldwide*, October, 17.

Ghemawat, P. 2011. "World 3.0: Global Prosperity and How to Achieve it." Boston, MA: Harvard Business Review Press.

Ginwala, F. 2002. "Charlotte Maxeke, the Mother of Freedom." *ANC Today* 2(31): 2–8. www.sahistory.org.za/sites/default/files/Thozama_April_paper.pdf.

Gonzalez, C. C. 2000. "Agitating for Their Rights: The Colombian Women's Movement, 1930–1957." *Pacific Historical Review* 69(4): 689–706.

Gorst, I. 2015. "Gender and Income Equality in the Russian Workplace." *Financial Times*, March 5. www.ft.com/cms/s/0/91be6ca0b83b11e486bb00144feab7de. html#axzz46SaVA3nX.

Gouws, A. 2012. "Reflections on Being a Feminist Academic/Academic Feminism in South Africa." *Equality, Diversity and Inclusion: An International Journal* 31(5/6): 526–541.

Grant Thornton. 2012. "Global Dynamism Index." www.grantthornton.ee/wp -content/uploads/2012/11/GDI2012-Final-Report.pdf.

Grant Thornton. 2016. "31% of Businesses in Malaysia Have No Women in Senior Management: Highest in ASEAN." www.grantthornton.com.my/en/press/press-re leases-2016/women-in-senior-management/.

Green, J. C. 2013. "Indira Gandhi: India's Destined Leader." History theses, no. 23. History and Social Studies Education, State University of New York College, Buffalo.

Grosse, R. 2015. "AIB Initiatives in Emerging Markets." *AIB Insights* 15(1): 3–4.

Hahner, J. E. 1979. "The Beginnings of the Women's Suffrage Movement in Brazil." *Signs Journal of Women in Culture and Society* 5(1): 200–204. www. jstor.org/stable/3173553.

Hai, A. 2003. "Departures from Karachi Airport: Some Reflections on Feminist Outrage." *Meridians* 4(1): 142–164.

Hall, S. 2000. "The Question of Cultural Identity." In *Readings in Contemporary Political Sociology*, edited by K. Nash. Oxford: Blackwell Publishing.

Hammond, A. 2008. "Saudi Scholar Finds Ancient Women's Rights." *Reuters*. Edited by S. Ledwith. www.reuters.com/article/us-saudi-women-idUSL136115520080501.

Hare, D. 2016. "What Accounts for the Decline in Labor Force Participation Among Married Women in Urban China, 1991–2011?" *China Economic Review* 38: 251–266.

Hasso, F. S. 2014. "Bargaining with the Devil: States and Intimate Life." *Journal of Middle East Women Studies* 10(2): 107–134.

Hofstede, G. 2001. *Cultures' Consequences. Comparing Values, Behaviours, Institutions and Organisations Across Nations*, 2nd ed. Thousand Oaks, CA: Sage.

HSBC. 2016. "What are Emerging Markets?" Accessed March 3, 2016. https:// investorfunds.us.hsbc.com/investing-in-emerging-markets/map-at-night/default.fs.

International Encyclopedia of Marriage and Family. 2003. "Women's Movements." *Encyclopedia.com.* Accessed May 2, 2016. www.encyclopedia.com/doc/1G2-3406900 450.html.

International Labour Organization. 2008. "World of Work Report 2008: Income Inequalities in the Age of Financial Globalization." www.ilo.org/wcmsp5/group s/public/@dgreports/@dcomm/@publ/documents/publication/wcms_100354.pdf.

Inter-Parliamentary Union. 2016. "Women in National Parliaments." www.ipu. org/wmn-e/classif.htm. Accessed April 1, 2016.

IWFSA (International Women's Forum South Africa). 2011. "The Status of Women in South Africa: A Preliminary Report Incorporating the Findings of Consultative Roundtable Discussions on Women Empowerment in South Africa." Prepared by Frontier Advisory. www.iwfsa.co.za/index.php/.../3_d3c47dc5de9c83a beac5ad81458c59c5.

Jacobs, A. 2016. "Brazil's Lower House of Congress Votes for Impeachment of Dilma Rousseff." *New York Times*, April 17.

Jalalzai, F. and P. G. Dos Santos. 2013. "The Dilma Effect: Symbolic, Descriptive, and Substantive Representation of Women Under Dilma Rousseff's Presidency." Annual Meeting Paper, American Political Science Association.

Jalalzai, F. and P. G. Dos Santos. 2015. "The Dilma Effect? Women's Representation Under Dilma Rousseff's Presidency." *Politics and Gender* 11(1): 117–145.

Johnson, K. 1993. "Chinese Orphanages: Saving China's Abandoned Girls." *Australian Journal of Chinese Affairs*, 30(July): 61–88.

Johnson, J. E. and A. Saarinen. 2013. "Twenty-first-century Feminisms Under Repression: Gender Regime Change and the Women's Crisis Center Movement in Russia." *Journal of Women in Culture & Society* 38(3): 543–567.

Kamal, H. 2015. "Inserting Women's Rights in the Egyptian Constitution: Personal Reflections." *Journal of Cultural Research* 19(2): 150–161.

Kanap'ianova, R. M. 2008. "Women in Structures of Authority." *Sociological Research* 47(4): 61–73.

Karpinski, E. C. 1995. "Do Polish Women Need Feminism? Recent Activity of the Parliamentary Women's Group." *Canadian Women Studies* 16(2): 91–95.

Keith, R. C. 1997. "Legislating Women's and Children's 'Rights and Interests' in the People's Republic of China." *China Quarterly* 149(March): 29–55.

Kemp, L. 2012. "Progress in Female Education and Employment in the United Arab Emirates Towards Millennium Development Goal 3: Gender Equality." *Foresight* 15(4): 264–277.

Kholi, P. 2015. "Emerging Markets: The United Arab Emirates, More Than Just an Airline" *Nasdaq*, October 27. www.nasdaq.com/article/emerging-markets-the-united-arab-emirates-more-than-just-an-airline-cm534873#ixzz42y29dhU4I.

Kirdar, S. 2010. "United Arab Emirates." In *Women's Rights in the Middle East and North Africa*, edited by S. Kelly and J. Breslin. New York: Freedom House.

Koo, O. 2010. "Regional Approaches to Trafficking in Women in South East Asia: The Role of National Human Rights Institutions and the New ASEAN Human Rights Body." *Australian Journal of Human Rights* 15(2): 59–82.

Korabik, K. 1993. "Managerial Women in the People's Republic of China: The Long March Continues." *International Studies of Management and Organisation* 23(4): 47–64.

Krishnaraj, M. 2012. "The Women's Movement in India: A Hundred-year History." *Social Change* 42(3): 325–333.

Kumar, R. 1998. *The History of Doing*. New Delhi: Kali for Women.

Kutz, M. 2008. "Towards a Conceptual Model of Contextual Intelligence: A Transferable Leadership Construct." *Leadership Review* 8(Winter): 18–31.

Lawson, S., D. Heacock and A. Stupnytska. 2007. "Beyond the BRICS: A Look at the 'Next 11'." In Goldman Sachs, *BRICS and Beyond*. New York: Goldman Sachs, pp. 161–164. www.goldmansachs.com/our-thinking/archive/archive-pdfs/brics-book/brics-chap-13.pdf.

Lee, M. H. 2011. "The One-Child Policy and Gender Equality in Education in China: Evidence from Household Data." *Journal of Family Economic Issues* 33: 41–52.

Leones, M. J. A. 2014. "Brazil on the Way to Gender Equality." *iKNOW Politics*, August 29. Accessed May 2, 2016. http://iknowpolitics.org/en/knowledge-library/opinion-pieces/brazil-way-gender-equality.

Lewis-Enright, K., A. Crafford and F. Crous. 2009. "Towards a Workplace Conducive to the Career Advancement of Women." *Journal of Industrial Psychology*. 35(1): 1–9.

Lidia, R. and L. G. Feng. 2014. "Cultural Profile of Russian Leadership: A Female Leader in Russian Business." Harbin School of Management Science, Harbin.

Lôbo, Y. L. 2010. *Bertha Lutz*. Recife, PE: Fundação Joaquim Nabuco.

MacKinnon, A. 2014. "The Founders: The Origins of the ANC and the Struggle for Democracy in South Africa." *International Journal of African Historical Studies* 47(3): 507.

Maluf, S. W. 2011. "Brazilian Feminisms: Central and Peripheral Issues." *Feminist Review*: e36–e51. Accessed May 2, 2016. www.palgrave-journals.com/fr/conf-p roceedings/n1s/full/fr201128a.html.

Marion, M. 2010. "Culture, Context and The Qur'an." *East-West Connections: Asian Studies Development Program's Association for Regional Centers* 81–106.

Marody, M. 1993. "Why I am Not a Feminist: Some Remarks on the Problem of Gender Identity in the United States and Poland." *Social Research* 60(4): 853–864.

Masuku, N. 2005. *Perceived Oppression of Women in Zulu Folklore: A Feminist Critique*. Pretoria: University of South Africa.

McKinsey. 2011. "Women at the Top of Corporations: Making it Happen." www. mckinsey.com/business-functions/organization/our-insights/women-at-the-top-of-cor porations-making-it-happen.

McKinsey. 2012. "Women Matter: Making the Breakthroughs." www.calstrs. com/sites/main/files/file-attachments/women_matter_2012_making_the_breakthr ough.pdf.

McKinsey. 2013. "Women Matter: A Latin American Perspective." www.femtech. at/sites/default/files/Women%20Matter%20Latin%20America.pdf.

Meintjes, S. 1996. "The Women's Struggle for Equality During South Africa's Transition to Democracy." *Transformation Critical Perspectives on Southern Africa* 75(1): 107–115. www.researchgate.net/publication/236810776_The_wom en's_struggle_for_equality_during_South_Africa's_transition_to_democracy.

Meintjes, S. 2012. *Rebuilding Peace: The Case of South Africa*. Cape Town: Pambazuka Press.

Merkin, R. 2009. "South American perspectives on Sexual Harassment: The Standpoint in Argentina, Brazil, and Chile." *Journal of Behavioral and Applied Management* 10(6): 357–376.

Metcalf, A. C. 1990. "Women and Means: Women and Family Property in Colonial Brazil." *Journal of Social History* 24(2): 277–298.

Metcalfe, B. D. 2011. "Women, Empowerment and Development in Arab Gulf States: A Critical Appraisal of Governance, Culture and National Human Resource Development Frameworks." *Human Resource Development International* 14(2): 131–148.

Meyerson, D. and J. K. Fletcher. 1999. "A Modest Manifesto for Shattering the Glass Ceiling." *Harvard Business Review* 78(1): 127–136.

Mkhize, M. and P. Msweli. 2011. "The Impact of Female Business Leaders on the Performance of Listed Companies in South Africa." *South African Journal of Economic and Management Sciences* 14(1): 1–7.

Mohanty, C. T. 1988. "Under Western Eyes: Feminist Scholarship and Colonial Discourses." *Feminist Review* 30(Autumn): 65–88.

Mohanty, C. T., A. Russo and L. Torres (eds). 1991. *Third World Women and the Politics of Feminism*. Bloomington: Indiana University Press.

Moletsane, R. and V. Reddy. 2010. "Gender and Poverty Reduction: Voice, Dialogue and Targeting." Human Sciences Research Council, Pretoria. www.hsrc. ac.za/en/research-data/ktree-doc/5932.

Morrison, A. M., R. P. White and E. Van Velsor. 1987. *The Center for Creative Leadership, Breaking the Glass Ceiling*. Reading, MA: Addison-Wesley.

MSCI (Morgan Stanley Capital international). "Morgan Stanley Capital International Emerging Market Index." www.msci.com/market-classification.

Neft, N. and A. D. Levine. 1997. *Where Women Stand: An International Report on the Status of Women in 140 Countries*. New York: Random House, pp. 210–220.

Ng, C. W. and R. Pine. 2003. "Women and Men in Hotel Management in Hong Kong: Perceptions of Gender and Career Development Issues." *Hospitality Management* 22(1): 85–102.

Nkomo, S. M. and H. Ngambi. 2009. "African Women in Leadership: Current Knowledge and a Framework for Future Studies." *International Journal of African Renaissance Studies* 4(1): 49–68.

Oilivas-Luján, M. R., S. I. Monserrat, J. A. Ruiz-Guiterrez, R. A. Greenwood, S. M. Gomez, E. F. Murphy and N. M. Santos. 2008. "Values and attitudes towards women in Argentina, Brazil, Colombia, and Mexico." *Employee Relations* 31(3): 227–244.

Oliphant, P. 2015. "South Africa Falling Short in Gender Equality Standards." *Mail & Guardian*, May 4. http://mg.co.za/article/2015-05-04-south-africa-fa lling-short-in-gender-equality-standards.

Ørstavik, S. L. and A. R. Lizcano. 2013. "Colombia's Gender Problem." *World Policy Blog*, November 25. www.worldpolicy.org/blog/2013/11/25/colombia s-gender-problem.

Osava, M. 2010. "Rights: Women's more Educated, Not More Equal." *Inter Press Service*, March 1. www.ipsnews.net/2010/03/rights-women-more-educated-not-m ore-equal.

Palau, M. 2016. "Colombia's Revolutionary Women: Talking to Heal." *Aljazeera*, Women's Rights. March 24. www.aljazeera.com/indepth/features/2016/03/colom bia-revolutionary-women-talking-heal-160314085744399.html.

Patel, V. 2010. "Women's Struggles & Women's Movement in India." *Europe Solidaire Sans Frontieres*. Originally published in *New Left Review* (September/ October) 1985. www.academia.edu/656077/Womens_Liberation_in_India_by_ vibhuti_Patel_New_Left_Review_I_153_September-October_1985.

Penciliah, Y. 2005. "How Far Have We Come? Integrating Women in Management in the South African Public Service." *Journal of Public Administration* 40(3): 341–351.

Pitanguy, J. 2002. "Bridging the Local and the Global: Feminism in Brazil and the International Human Rights Agenda." *Social Research* 69(3): 805–820.

PwC. 2013. "Women Leaders in Russian Business." www.pwc.ru/en/hr-consulting/women-in-business.jhtml.

Rahi, A. 2015. "Gender Discrimination in India and its Solution." *International Journal of Multidisciplinary Approach and Studies* 2(4): 69–173.

Raman, A. S. 2009. *Women in India: A Social and Cultural History.* Santa Barbara, CA: Praeger.

Rayner, K. 2015. "Examining Prospects in Global Emerging Markets." *Professional Adviser*, March 19: 22–23.

Reddy, E. S. 1993. *The Struggle for Liberation in South Africa and International Solidarity: A Selection of Papers Published by the United Nations Centre Against Apartheid.* New Delhi: Sterling.

Reeves, M. 2010. *Women in Business: Theory, Case Studies and Legal Challenges.* New York: Routledge.

Rhein, W. 1998. "The Feminisation of Poverty: Unemployment in Russia." *Journal of International Affairs* 52(1): 351.

Ridge, N. 2011. "Why Women Graduates Outnumber Men in the UAE." *Gulf News*, April 14. Accessed May 2, 2016. http://gulfnews.com/gn-focus/why-women-graduates-outnumber-men-in-the-uae-1.790849.

Rohana, A. 1999. "Feminism in Malaysia: A Historical and Present Perspective of Women's Struggles in Malaysia." *International Journal of Women Studies* 22(4): 417–423.

Roldán, M. 2014. "Acción Cultural Popular, Responsible Procreation, and the Roots Of Social Activism in Rural Colombia." *Latin American Research Review* 49 (Special Issue): 27–44.

Saha, S. C. 2015. "Breaking Boundaries at Work." *Human Capital Online*, November 22. www.humancapitalonline.com.

Sako, M. 2015. "Technology Strategy and Management: Competing in Emerging Markets." *Viewpoints, Communications of the Association for Computing Machinery* 58(4): 27–29.

Salama, S. 2015. "UAE Leaders Support Women's Advancement and Empowerment, Xerox Chairman and CEO Says." *Gulf News*, August 27.

Saleh, N. 2012. "A Brief Study on the Positive Attentions to Muslim Women's Rights in Malaysia." *International Journal of Business, Humanities and Technology* 2(2): 163.

Samah, A. A. 2010. "The Suhakam Report: The Status of Women's Rights in Malaysia." Human Rights Commission of Malaysia, Kuala Lumpur. www.suhakam.org.my/wp-content/uploads/2013/11/SUHAKAM-Report-on-The-Status-of-Women-s-Rights-in-Malaysia-2010.pdf.

Sebola, M. 2015. "Achieving Gender Equity in Leadership of South African Institutions of Higher Learning: Is Woman Empowerment Mission Impossible in Universities?" *Business and Management Review* 6(5).

Segalo, P. 2014. "Embroidery as Narrative: Black South African Women's Experiences of Suffering and Healing." *Agenda* 28(1): 44–53.

Sen, A. 2001. "The Many Faces of Gender Inequality." *Frontline* 18(22). www.frontline.in/static/html/fl1822/18220040.htm.

Sharma, R. 2012. *Breakout Nations: In Pursuit of the Next Economic Miracles.* London: Penguin.

Sikdar, A. and S. Mitra. 2012. "Gender-Role Stereotypes: Perception and Practice of Leadership in the Middle East." *Education, Business and Society: Contemporary Middle Eastern Issues* 5(3): 146–162.

Singariya, M. R. 2014. "Dr. B. R. Ambedkar and Women Empowerment in India." *Journal of Research in Humanities and Social Science* 2(1): 1–4.

Skiles, C. M. 2012. "Gender-Specific Prison Reform: Addressing Human Rights Violations Against Women In Russia's Prisons." *Pacific Rim Law and Policy Journal* 21(3): 655–689.

Smedley, T. 2015. "Women in Leadership Roles: The West Finds Itself Outshone." *Financial Times*, September 15. www.ft.com/cms/s/0/8a5b7c664cc711e5b5588a 9722977189.html.

Smith, B. C. 2003. *Understanding Third World Politics: Theories of Political Change and Development*, 2nd ed. London: Palgrave Macmillan.

Snider, C. M. 2013. "Get to Know a Brazilian: Bertha Lutz." *Americas South and North*, May 12. Accessed May 2, 2016. https://americasouthandnorth.wordpress.com/2013/05/12/get-to-know-a-brazilian-bertha-lutz-2/.

South African History Online. 2011. "White Women Achieve Suffrage in South Africa." Last modified May 19, 2015. www.sahistory.org.za/dated-event/white-women-achieve-suffrage-south-africa.

South African History Online. 2015. "A World Chronology of the Recognition of Women's Rights to Vote and to Stand for Election." www.ipu.org/wmn-e/suffrage.htm.

Statistics South Africa. 2013. "Gender Statistics in South Africa, 2011." www.statssa.gov.za/publications/Report-03-10-05/Report-03-10-052011.pdf.

Steen, A. 2012. "Emerging Markets: Worlds Away, Money Management." *Financial Times*. http://search.proquest.com/docview/1018684035?accountid=14717.

Suttner, R. 2012. "The African National Congress Centenary: A Long and Difficult Journey." *International Affairs* 88(4): 719–738.

Swan, M. 2016. "There's Still Work to be Done for Equality, Women in Dubai Hear." *The National*, March 8. Accessed May 2, 2016. www.thenational.ae/uae/theres-still-work-to-be-done-for-equality-women-in-dubai-hear.

The Economist. 2011. "China's Population: The Most Surprising Demographic Crisis." *The Economist*, May 5. www.economist.com/node/18651512.

The Economist. 2014. "Wedge Beyond the Edge: Money is Leaving Emerging Markets for Riskier Bets at the Investment Frontier." *The Economist*, April 5. www.economist.com/news/finance-and-economics/21600132-money-leaving-emerging-markets-riskier-bets-investment-frontier-wedge.

Thomas, A. 2000. "Poverty and the End of Development." In *Poverty and Development into the 21st Century*. Oxford: Oxford University Press.

Tlaiss, H. A. 2013. "Women Managers in the United Arab Emirates: Successful Careers or What?" *Equality, Diversity and Inclusion* 32(8): 756–776.

Tokman, V. E. 2010. "Domestic Workers in Latin America: Statistics for New Policies." WIEGO Working Paper 17. http://wiego.org/sites/wiego.org/files/publications/files/Tokman_WIEGO_WP17.pdf.

Torregrosa, L. L. 2011. "Paving a Way for Women in Brazil." *New York Times*, November 15.

Turbine, V. 2012. "Locating Women's Human Rights in Post-Soviet Provincial Russia." *Europe-Asia Studies* 64(10): 1847–1869.

UAE Ministry of State and Federal National Council Affairs. 2007. "Women in the UEA." www.uaeembassy.org/sites/default/files/Women_in_the_UAE_Eng.pdf.

Ufen, A. 2009. "Mobilising Political Islam: Indonesia and Malaysia Compared." *Commonwealth and Comparative Politics* 47(3): 321–322.

UNDP (United Nations Development Programme). 2011. "Human Development Report: Sustainability and Equity." www.za.undp.org/content/dam/south_africa/docs/Reports/Project%20Documents/HDR_2011_EN_Complete.pdf.

UNDP (United Nations Development Programme). 2014. "Colombia: Case Study." Gender Equality and Women's Empowerment in Public Administration, June 3. www.undp.org/content/undp/en/home/librarypage/democratic-governance/public_administration/gepa.html.

United Nations. 2013. "United Arab Emirates." Social Institutions and Gender Index. www.genderindex.org/sites/default/files/datasheets/AE.pdf.

UN Women. 2015. "World Leaders Agree: We Must Close the Gender Gap." *UN Women,* September 27. www.unwomen.org/en/news/stories/2015/9/press-relea se-global-leaders-meeting.

Valerio, A. M. 2010. *Developing Women Leaders: A Guide for Men and Women in Organisations.* New York: Wiley-Blackwell.

Van Klaveren, M. K.Tijdens, M.Hughie-Williams and N. R. Martin. 2009. "Work and Employment in Brazil." Amsterdam Institute for Advanced Labour Studies, University of Amsterdam.

Vasavada, T. 2012. "A Cultural Feminist Perspective on Leadership in Nonprofit Organisations: A Case of Women Leaders in India." *Public Administration Quarterly* 36(4): 462–503.

Velandia, E. and A. Otero. 2013. "Women, the Workforce, and Entrepreneurship in Colombia." *Career Planning & Adult Development Journal* 28(4): 9.

Vietor, R. H. K. and H. White. 2015. "Colombia and the Economic Premium of Peace." Harvard Business School Case Collection. Boston, MA.

Walker, C. 1991. *Women and Resistance in South Africa.* Cape Town: David Philip.

White, A. 2005. "Gender Roles in Contemporary Russia: Attitudes and Expectations Among Women Students." *Europe-Asia Studies* 57(3): 42–455.

White, L. and L. Brown. 2014. "Dynamic Markets: Advancing the Notion of Emerging Markets Through an Empirical Measure of Institutions." Gordon Institute of Business Science, University of Pretoria. http://web.isanet.org/Web/Conferences/FLACSO-ISA%20BuenosAires%202014/Archive/ae038518-94df-4e03-84e0-d6252690444d.pdf.

Women's Forum. 2014. "BRAZIL 2014: The role of Colombian Women." May 21. Accessed February 17, 2017. www.womens-forum.com/stories/brazil-2014-the-r ole-of-colombian-women/150.

World Bank. 2015. "Labor Force, Female (% of Total Labor Force)." Accessed May 3, 2016. http://data.worldbank.org/indicator/SL.TLF.TOTL.FE.ZS.

World Economic Forum. 2015. "World Economic Forum Gender Gap Index 2015." Accessed May 2, 2016. http://reports.weforum.org/global-gender-gap-rep ort-2015/economies/#economy=ARE.

Yiping, C. A. I. 2013. "Re-Ritalize, Re-Strategize and Re-Politicize the Chinese Women's Movement in the New Era." *Asian Journal of Women Studies* 19(1): 113–126.

Zhou, J. 2003. "Keys to Women's Liberation in Communist China: An Historical Overview." *Journal of International Women's Studies* 5(1): 67–77.

Zinn, S. 2016. *Swimming Upstream.* Johannesburg: KR Publishing.

Zuo, J. and Y. Bian, Y. 2001. "Gendered Resources, Division of Housework, and Perceived Fairness: A Case in Urban China." *Journal of Marriage and Family* 63(4): 1122–1133.

4 Women leaders in education

Sunny Stout-Rostron

Introduction

Progress in science and technology is advancing at an ever-increasing rate—yet we still live in a world torn by political strife, social inequalities, injustice, poverty and violence. To bridge the apparently widening gap between technological and social development, what new wisdom and leadership are needed for the twenty-first century?

Contemporary research highlights the nature of global leadership and the roles that women play at senior levels in organizations. As educational institutions struggle more than ever to find effective leaders, there are concerns about the shortage of women leaders in higher education. Internationally, women continue to be under-represented in senior academic or managerial positions in higher education, and experience a range of barriers to higher leadership positions.

This chapter shares the stories of ten remarkable women from six different regions who play powerful leadership roles at senior levels in education. What can we learn from their personal stories that will help us build a new model of leadership for the twenty-first century? The chapter follows a social constructivist approach, in which meanings are constructed by the participants from their own stories.

The first part of the chapter explores contemporary research into leadership development, noting the emergence of a new leadership paradigm strongly influenced by women's global contribution to the workplace. This is followed by the stories of women in senior leadership roles in education around the world. Every story brings its own unique voice and powerful dynamic. The women speak about their personal and professional difficulties and how they have refused to be kept back by glass ceilings, prejudice, trouble in acquiring education or limiting societal assumptions. Their stories dramatically alert us to the possibilities women have to make a difference in every aspect of society.

Narrative enquiry is concerned with analyzing and interpreting the stories we tell, as well as the myths that are embedded in our social interactions (Webster and Mertova 2007, 7). Stories have been used by communities from time immemorial and influence how our identities are formed and transformed. They help us to "remember and organize our past, communicate and negotiate our present, and envision and act into our future" (Drake 2015, 105). These narratives reference a range of "social, cultural and economic contexts" which "test dominant meta-narratives of educational leadership" where the male leader is the norm (Blackmore 2006, 186).

As contemporary literature reveals that women in higher education are less likely than men to participate in upper levels of administration (Kiamba 2008, 11), these narratives help us to understand the experience of senior women. By telling their life stories, these women are able to reconstruct their identities and gain not only self-knowledge but also authenticity (Day et al. 2014, 73). For each story, core themes and behaviors emerge which help us to understand the strategies of women leaders today. The chapter is completed with a summary of these core themes and behaviors and a conclusion which indicates a way forward.

Distributed leadership

Leadership is a process that involves influence and goal attainment and occurs within a group context (Ardichvili and Manderscheid 2008, 620). Historically, empirical studies into leadership have focused on the behaviors and skills of the individual leader. However, there is growing recognition that leadership development is complex and includes interactions between the leader and their social and organizational environments, embracing a more systemic and collective framework (Dalakoura 2010, 433–438).

The traditional "heroic leader" is typically associated with the leader who single-handedly leads their organization to greatness. In education, it would be the head of a school or university who spearheads their way through the educational labyrinth to establish excellent standards, turning out high-performing students. In contrast, the concept of "distributed leadership" suggests that leadership "practice" comprises a series of interactions between educational leaders, followers and their situation, rather than being the culmination of one leader's competence and knowledge. Leadership is thus seen as an activity that is "distributed" across multiple leaders, rather than inherent in the role of one educational leader (Spillane 2005, 145). Distributed leadership emphasizes leadership practice rather than leadership roles but does not necessarily imply an absence of hierarchy (Heikka et al. 2012, 34).

According to Harris (2013), the two main concepts in distributed leadership are task distribution and the view that leadership is about the distribution of influence as social interaction. Heads of schools are only part of the equation, as in any educational institution there are many sources of influence and direction. More importantly, with the strong emergence of women into organizational and educational leadership roles, distributed leadership offers a way through the glass ceiling.

Critical scholars have questioned the concept of "distributed leadership" because teachers and principals are strongly controlled by both market constraints and managerial accountability (Blackmore 2006, 194) and the lack of a strong link between distributed leadership and the two significant goals of educational leadership—school improvement and leadership development (Mayrowetz 2008, 424). Today, a growing number of studies are focusing on the impact of distributed leadership on teaching and learning processes and outcomes (Harris 2013). More research is needed into *how* leadership is distributed and its systemic impact on educational institutions and their ability to improve teaching and academic achievement.

The feminization of leadership

Rather than adding to the existing plethora of leadership definitions, the purpose of this chapter is to understand the need for a global perspective and the inclusion of women leaders' voices in a field that has been historically dominated by men.

The feminization of leadership can mean that women increase their share of management positions, or that management jobs are redesigned to coincide with "women's work", or that leadership requires a more "feminine" style of management (Storvik 2012, 156). In this chapter, feminization of leadership is taken to refer to the spread of traits and qualities generally associated with women in the process of leading organizations and women's entry into a customarily male occupation (Chatwani 2015, 137).

The twentieth century focused on the individual leader, command and control, power and authority, rational and analytical thinking and strong managerial influences. In contrast, the emerging paradigm in the twenty-first century emphasizes human relationships and shared goals. Within contemporary research, a substantial body of opinion holds that leadership in modern organizations needs to be non-coercive, based on teamwork and adept at building deep relationships (Pounder and Coleman 2002, 122).

Companies are under pressure to improve their competitiveness by transforming themselves into continually improving organizations in ways requiring more interactional, relational and participative management styles. This has led some researchers to conclude that "the modern manager is now encouraged to surrender control and share responsibility, help and develop others, and build a connected network of relationships" and that leadership has both "masculine and feminine components" (Johanson 2008, 735). New leadership is "process-oriented, transformative, value-centered, non-coercive and collaborative" (Dugan 2006, 217–218), and "leadership theorists have suggested that leaders should demonstrate new, arguably feminine, leadership behaviors" (Johanson 2008, 784). As Thorp et al. (1998, 56) have argued, "We need to encourage feminine styles of leadership, not to replace, but to balance masculine styles." Consequently, organizations globally are increasingly selecting women to serve in senior leadership positions because their unique skills can make important contributions to organizational management.

Women have been socialized to develop values and characteristics that produce leadership behaviors based on relationships, encouragement and support, which differ from the traditional competitive, controlling, aggressive leadership behaviors of men (Pounder and Coleman 2002, 124–125). Female leadership behaviors have been labelled as "consideration behaviors", which show concerns for people's feelings and include the need for satisfaction, participation and friendship (Johanson 2008, 785). Female leaders emphasize a more democratic leadership style grounded in strong interpersonal skills, using a people-oriented and team approach focusing on interaction, while men rely more on task-related behaviors and are considered to be paternalistic, authoritarian and goal-oriented. Women's skills and behaviors demonstrate "relationship-building, process-orientation, connectedness, and the ethics of care and concern of transformed leaders" who perform more like coaches and teachers—demonstrating transformational behaviors such as "clearly communicated values, motivation, optimism, willingness to consider new perspectives, and attention to individual needs" (Dugan 2006, 218).

In an Australian study of women leaders in higher education, the women's leadership behaviors were identified as "nurturing, communicators and relationship-focused", while "male leaders were admired for their hard skills" that "contrasted negatively with the perceived soft skills of women" (Gallant 2014, 213). In studies in Canada and the UK, female school principals were more likely to employ the "power through and power within" approaches associated with empowerment and participation, rather than a "power over" approach, which is associated with control, dominance and a more masculine image of power (Pounder and Coleman 2002, 125).

However, the general perception remains that the norm for management style is male, with a negative perception of women as leaders in many cultures. Most women around the world tend to be entrenched in environments that are "deeply conflicted about whether, when and how women should exercise their leadership authority" (Chatwani 2015, 142).

Women leaders in education

Due to the extreme challenges facing higher education around the world, leadership development has reached critical importance. Leaders in education "must now have an exceptional set of capabilities and competencies to help their institutions rise to new levels of excellence and innovation"

(Madsen 2012, 4). As a result, higher education institutions are finding it more difficult than ever to find qualified and effective people to fill senior leadership positions such as president or chancellor, vice-president or vice-chancellor, dean, director, and head of department.

One reason for the lack of prepared leaders is that there are fewer women positioned to take on such critical roles (Madsen 2012, 4). There is a growing recognition that women are under-represented in both higher and further education leadership (Gallant 2014, 203). Women represent less than 30% of board members on US college and university boards, and there has been little progress in closing the salary gap between men and women (Madsen 2012, 5).

There are many possible explanations for the under-representation of female senior leaders in all sectors. These include the glass ceiling, work–family interruptions that influence the choice not to pursue leadership positions, and fewer opportunities for women as opposed to men to ascend into more senior roles. Influential factors preventing women from stepping into leadership positions have included educational disadvantages, religious beliefs, familial circumstances, unexpected opportunities, peer group pressure, lack of mentorship and role models, training and development experiences and prior job challenges (Arvey et al. 2007, 694). The challenges women still face in taking leadership positions include "the barriers related to culture and cultural expectations; the choice and/or balance between work and family; and the stress that accompanies positions of leadership as experienced differently by men and women" (Kiamba 2008, 7).

Explanations for gender barriers have focused on the "pipeline problem", which blames women's family responsibilities and the tendency for women to visibly display fewer traits and motivations that are needed to achieve success in high-level positions—particularly their modesty about self-promoting behavior (Eagly and Karau 2002, 573 and 584). The barriers to advancement for women in university settings are five factors known as "leaks in the pipeline": work relationships, university environment, invisible rules, proactivity and personal circumstance (Madsen 2012, 5). Research has shown that these gendered workplace structures are why so few women break through the glass ceiling (Gallant 2014). Despite this, women are increasing in number in senior management positions and are breaking through the glass ceiling (Peterson 2015).

A better metaphor for what confronts women in their professional careers is the labyrinth, which conveys the idea of a complex journey toward a goal that is full of twists and turns, both expected and unexpected (Eagly and Carli 2007, 3). For women who aspire to senior leadership positions, we need to understand the various obstacles that make up this labyrinth and discover how some women have found their way around them. Another metaphor used in higher education management is that of the "glass cliff". This describes the phenomenon where women are more likely to be appointed to precarious leadership roles under circumstances where there is an increased risk of negative consequences, evoking the "dangers of falling from the heights of leadership", with some studies showing that women are being set up to fail (Peterson 2015, 114).

It has been noted that internationally there is a "dearth of information on leadership development programs that focus on the needs of women leaders, and virtually no information on emerging women leaders" (Harris and Leberman 2012, 30). Many universities in New Zealand and Australia have been implementing leadership development programs for women since 1992, with the objective of increasing the number of women in senior academic and general staff positions (Harris and Leberman 2012, 31). Two key benefits of leadership development programs for women are increased self-confidence and the ability to access and develop networks of relationships. Traditionally, women have less access to developmental relationships within organizations, often due to the exclusivity of male networks. Connections are crucial for leaders, both within and outside their institution. According to Gallant (2014, 214), there is thus a proactive trend occurring in higher education with formalized leadership programs being developed for women, but there is a critical need to "deconstruct" gendered notions of leadership and to construct positive leadership identities.

Removing gender obstacles to senior leadership positions

The glass ceiling has historically represented the promotion of men over women into senior leadership positions. Some countries have managed to overcome this barrier; for example, the European Commission found that in 2010, 43 percent of Swedish university vice-chancellors were women, the highest proportion in Europe. This demographic feminization in Swedish university leadership has been attributed to political pressure in the form of goals and policies, quantitative targets for women in academia, top-level commitment to gender equality goals, and a national network to support and encourage women to become managers in higher education (Peterson 2015, 113).

Although women are breaking through the glass ceiling, it does not yet indicate that they are at parity with men. Studies show that the feminization leadership process may occur under conditions of cultural, political and economic change, in which certain occupations become defined as "women's work" and are simultaneously changed into less prestigious work, with limited opportunities for advancement and reduced job security (Peterson 2015, 113–114). Women are still segregated vertically in terms of the career ladder and horizontally into a "velvet ghetto" of particular jobs seen as less valued and considered "gendered", such as in human resources, public relations and marketing (Gatrell and Swan 2008, 11–12). Although glass cliff appointments in higher education may include management positions which embrace a loss of prestige and status, research has shown how some women have been willing to accept promotion to senior positions "out of a sense of duty to their gender", because even glass cliff appointments give them an opportunity to contribute to change (Peterson 2015, 123).

Demographic feminization of leadership in the world of academia is complex and the glass cliff theory helps us to understand situations when women are appointed to management positions under circumstances not only different from those of men, but with increased risk—being appointed in a financial downturn or when an organization is performing poorly (Peterson 2015, 114). However, one explanation for the increase in women's leadership in senior management positions in academia may be due to "external pressure to promote women" (Peterson 2015, 120). One study illustrates that gender stereotypes include beliefs linking women leaders with change and men with stability, with the result that if change is needed for an organization to survive adverse circumstances, female leadership may be favored over male leadership (Peterson 2015, 115).

Researchers argue that women leaders may be as effective as men and also that there is a potential third gender role for leadership—androgyny. The androgynous leader demonstrates "both masculine and feminine characteristics" and captures "behavioral flexibility" which ultimately leads to success as a leader (Johanson 2008, 785). Androgynous leaders combine the best of male and female leadership traits, and this is a style that is "multi-gender, multinational and multi-social" (Pounder and Coleman 2002, 128): Contrary to previous findings that identify "female deficiencies" as a reason why few women have made it to the top, the emergence of androgynous leadership characteristics suggests that feminine traits do not decrease an individual's chances of emerging as a leader as long as the individual also possesses masculine characteristics. If women are more able to behave in "androgynous" ways, they may have a better chance of rising to leadership status (Appelbaum et al. 2003, 45). A key question is how to define "androgyny". Is it simply an integration of male and female behaviors, and how do we overcome the typical rewarding of stereotypical masculine behaviors, such as "being domineering, tough-minded and powerful" (Appelbaum et al. 2003, 47), as opposed to women's relational, team-based, collaborative and intuitive style of leadership?

What is clear is that when women "act as men" they are considered to be less than women—and when there is merit in what would normally be considered a "female" approach, men tend to adopt it as their own; what was considered weak is now thought of as flexible; what was emotional now brings balance (Appelbaum et al. 2003, 49). We need a new debate and dialogue as to what is leader effectiveness and to question seriously how we should train women leaders to step more confidently into their positional power in the corporate, institutional and governmental arena. More research is needed into the emergent "androgynous" style of leadership.

As is shown by the stories of women leaders in this chapter, the patriarchal systems, traditional beliefs and cultural attitudes in African, South American and Asian contexts can make it difficult for women to rise to positions of leadership. Women academics are also seriously hampered by institutional and educational leadership practices. It is therefore important to design leadership development programs which can effectively prepare women to move into higher positions. It is essential to understand that different approaches to women leaders are crucial. An important aspect of future research should be to examine why there is a need to differentiate coaching for men and women, identifying what makes a strong woman leader—and, critically, to develop an original model for women's leadership development. Women professionals need coaching at various stages in their careers. This would include providing advice for younger women starting out in their careers and for women struggling to move beyond middle management, as well as identifying the most important factors needed for women to reach senior leadership and executive positions.

Women's voices: their stories

The stories included in this chapter are of contemporary women leaders in education, with diverse and extraordinary cultural, civic and organizational backgrounds. Their compelling narratives, in which difference is celebrated as potential, help us to understand that we need to include the perspectives and experiences of women leaders. These women are excellent role models—as people, as teachers and as leaders—sharing authentically from their own experience and how they have shifted throughout their personal and professional lives.

Martha Cecilia Bernal Uribe (Colombia)

Martha Cecilia Bernal Uribe is director of executive education at the University of the Andes in Bogotá, Colombia. She holds a PhD in law and an Executive MBA from the Universidad de los Andes.

Born in Bogotá, Colombia, into a "very Catholic" family, Bernal Uribe untypically went to a French school in Bogotá, then moved to a Colombian school at 14 and boarding school in the US at 16. Returning to Colombia, she completed a university degree in law and a postgraduate degree in public economic law. She needed to complete a practical component for her postgraduate degree, so got a job in the Organization and Methods department of a bank. Ever innovative, she developed a system of internal norms or "laws" for the bank, which proved so successful that a vice-president of the bank attempted to persuade her to stay on and replace her boss.

While studying for her final examinations she was recruited by a fellow student's mother, an important artist who had been appointed minister of culture, to be her personal assistant. Inspired by the minister's "revolutionary" approach to culture, Bernal Uribe was not afraid to move from law and business to a completely different field, because as "an entrepreneur, I have always followed my heart". She had her first child, and resigned from the Ministry of Culture to breastfeed her baby, which was not logistically feasible at work. Apart from spending time with her daughter, she worked as president of the alumni at her university, offered free legal advice to the poorest of the poor in Colombia, the Chocó Indians, and also ran the family business. The business was losing money, so she sold it and had her second child. Her driver is her sense of service— doing something that "gives value, adds value to the community, to the society, to the people, to the country".

She had three main mentors. The first advised her to study law; her second mentor was the founder of an association of Colombian industrialists, New Industrial Colombia; and her third mentor was a cousin and owner of one of the most important industrial groups in Colombia. Bernal Uribe found money for New Industrial Colombia, worked on various initiatives including helping academic institutions to work together with government on industrial development projects, and became its vice-president. Her third child was born when she was at New Industrial Colombia, and she was ill for six months carrying the child. "This is something men do not struggle with! I am always pushing. I am an entrepreneur." She resigned from New Industrial Colombia and worked in the Department of National Planning for two and a half years. She then became president of the Bogotá telephone company, but had to leave to avoid a conflict of interest when her husband was appointed to an important regulatory position in the public sector.

Bernal Uribe and her husband were a nationally prominent and highly visible couple. They went through a difficult divorce, which was a great personal crisis for her. She subsequently moved to Miami to be director of the Colombian Trade Bureau. Bernal Uribe eventually returned to Colombia to work on building a "Movement of Citizen Culture", and the University of the Andes asked her to oversee its Executive Education program.

Bernal Uribe said that she came to work at the university because she needed to learn patience and humility. Whereas previously she was a public figure and a very important person, today everything is harder, including her financial situation. But the university needs her to keep working there and keep developing new projects—including building an innovation network all around Latin America. Her biggest learning has been "to learn how to be, to have coherence with what you say and what you think". Further, she believes that the most important role of a leader is to set an example. She feels that to experience difficulty is important, because "It is always a hard life when you grow. You do not grow in comfort."

Stacey Brewer (South Africa)

Stacey Brewer started her career as a social entrepreneur by introducing a model of teaching called "blended learning" to South Africa and now owns a network of privately managed primary schools. Originally from Johannesburg, she went to Rhodes University in Grahamstown, then worked overseas in Europe and the US, returning to start an MBA. Through the MBA process she became intensely interested in education:

> I didn't realize how bad it was in the country. I went to a private school and normal university. Education was never an issue for me. During my MBA at GIBS, the professors kept saying, 'You as the future business leaders of South Africa, what are you doing to sort out the education crisis?' I then started doing further research and finding pretty horrific stats ... the state is really in dire straits. I came across this whole emergence of low-fee private schools, where parents are ... sending their children to private schools [rather than] free government schools, and I found that a very interesting concept. I then did my master's thesis on a sustainable financial model for low-fee private schools.

Brewer set up SPARK schools with a fellow MBA student to provide high-quality education at an affordable cost. She claims their students are performing a year ahead of their peers in other schools. Brewer explained that "South Africa spends one of the greatest proportions of their national budget, and yet we still perform bottom of the world in terms of education according to the global competitiveness report."

What shaped her career as a leader has been working with her male co-founder. "I learned a lot from him not being so emotional, being very pragmatic. I have also taught him a lot, about being more empathetic." However, she discovered that her voice was not being heard. "Depending on the target audience, you will get somebody who prefers working with males. When trying to speak to people about money it was as if I wasn't even in the room. They spoke directly to my business partner." She also found that working with men from strong faith communities sometimes meant not even being able to shake hands with them because of her gender. "And you can't do business if you don't have a relationship."

Brewer advocates diversity, both in race and gender, as important in any organization:

> At the moment we are very female-dominated, especially in primary schools. So I would like to start seeing more men leading. But ethnicity and culture are important for the children's exposure, for staff exposure, to represent what South Africa is and how to deal with diversity. Start-ups are very conscious about creating this culture of acceptance and integration, and diversity as a key driver to success.

Brewer is also conscious of developing a culture of managing big issues such as maternity leave, health and wellness.

Brewer's main challenges are more about being a leader than being challenged as a woman. She explained that there are internal barriers such as lacking confidenc and needing support systems—yet by questioning everything you develop both soft and hard skill sets. She explained that:

> you naturally become harder, because you have to. You have got to manage yourself. I'm conscious that I'm not the same person I was three years ago. If you want to describe it as a masculine leadership trend, I have hardened-up and get on with it.

Brewer explained that in terms of differences between male and female leadership styles, "I would say the males at SPARK get to the point and are not so sensitive. Women I find are a lot more sensitive. Male leaders get to the point very quickly, we females have got to go around a little bit and then you get to the point." She explained that women naturally embody the softer skills, particularly relationship building. "At the end of the day, if you have no social cover, you are not going to get anywhere." But she thinks that women underplay their value. "For men it is accepted to be powerful and to be successful in their career. But for women it is not like they are accepted at all. Don't be apologetic about who you are."

In terms of leadership, she said:

> know exactly what you are good at and what you are bad at, and actually be okay with it. Now we employ 110 staff, and will employ over 300 by the end of the year. I have to lead through others and empower others. When I am the most effective is when I focus and set the vision and the "why", and allow people to figure it out.

Barbara Creecy (South Africa)

Barbara Creecy has been member of the executive council (MEC—that is, provincial government cabinet minister) for finance of Gauteng province in South Africa since May 2014, and was previously MEC for education and for sports, recreation, arts and culture. She was a member of the South African Students' Press Union at university and used her journalism skills in underground structures of the then banned African National Congress (ANC) movement fighting to liberate South Africa from the "apartheid" system of institutionalized racial oppression.

Creecy's identity revolves around:

> the values of human rights and democracy, and that people are equal and have equal chances. All those values were family values, and we were encouraged to think and be critical. I was actively involved in

anti-apartheid politics. My family were politically conscious people and anti-apartheid, which I think was unusual for white people in those days.

Her father was a conscientious objector during World War II and in prison for much of the war; her parents subsequently immigrated to South Africa and her father died when she was eight years old:

> My mother brought me up that there is nothing that needs to be done in the world that women cannot do. My father sent me to Roedean [an exclusive private school for girls in Johannesburg based on the original version in the UK] and there were lots of financial problems after my father died. I started working on Saturdays when I was 13 years old and became a surrogate adult at a very young age.

Interested in politics from the age of 13, Creecy noted:

> I was very clear then what I wanted to do with my life … . My first year at university was 1976. One day, 16 June [now officially commemorated as Youth Day], we heard that there had been a shooting [by police] in Soweto [then a large black "township" or segregated ghetto south-west of Johannesburg]. When we got back to class the lecturer said, "Two children were shot in Soweto this morning. There is some paper and paint, make yourself a placard and go out onto Jan Smuts Avenue and demonstrate." The rest, as they say, is history.

Creecy joined the ANC underground in 1979 and spent the 1980s in overt and covert struggles. She left South Africa in 1987 and "went to the Soviet Union for military training, coming back in early 1989 as the negotiation process [between the apartheid government and anti-apartheid groups towards a political resolution] speeded up."

She gave birth to her children in the early 1990s, after the unbanning of the ANC:

> In 1994 I was elected to the [Gauteng provincial] legislature. I used to go everywhere with a three-year-old, a newborn baby and a baby minder, because I was breastfeeding. … I think being a working mom is tough, for everyone it is tough. I think that women's emancipation hasn't delivered on all fronts.

Creecy made a very conscious decision to be a mother, and would leave work to go home to bathe her children and read them a story. She spent ten years as a member of the Gauteng provincial legislature before being appointed to the provincial executive and has been an MEC for 12 years. Early on she was involved in education struggles, and was founder member of the National Education Union, later renamed the South African Democratic Teachers Union (SADTU):

> Education has always been very politicized. When I was appointed in 2009, one of the big barriers towards achievement of African working-class children was that in a suburban school, children were getting seven hours of teaching and learning a day, but in a township school if they were getting three they were lucky. When I was appointed MEC for education I was instructed by the premier and the ANC leadership to stabilize the education system and implement a culture of learning and teaching. The way that I approached it was from the start to mobilize parents, both on a school basis from governing body formations, but also in communities through ANC structures.

Her most difficult experience was in July 2010, during a strike by public sector workers, including teachers. "We set up classes covertly from behind the picket lines with matrics [final-year high school students]. Once the ANC had taken a decision to put the future of the matrics first, everybody fell into line."

In speaking about her leadership style, Creecy said, "I always try to develop a vision and get everybody to buy in to what the goal is. That requires a team approach and an inclusive approach." Barriers related to being a woman?

> My leadership style is very values-based. I want to be a team person, because if you can get everybody to pull together you get better outcomes. ... The ANC has shaped me. To be an effective leader you have to deal with your own baggage. As a young person I didn't have a lot of self-confidence. I have had to deal with my perfectionism. I have really had to battle, because it makes me controlling and impatient.

Creecy's vision for herself going forward is to leave active politics and write up her experiences. "I would like to give back some of the leadership lessons I have learned, maybe through playing a coaching role."

Barbara Dale-Jones (South Africa)

Barbara Dale-Jones, originally from Zimbabwe, is the CEO of BRIDGE, a non-profit organization (NPO) started in 2009 to improve the South African education system in an impactful and sustained manner. Dale-Jones says that her entire professional life has been in education, for which she has a passion. Starting off in an academic role, she lectured for many years in English at Rhodes University in Grahamstown, then went into publishing consulting for education—she even ran an e-learning company for a while. She says she has developed a "strong conviction around using my knowledge and skills in order to help social development". She was influenced by Anne Lamont, CEO of Convene Venture Philanthropy, with whom she worked to address challenges for orphans and vulnerable children in South Africa.

Another education project became the NPO Bridge, which uses "communities of practice as spaces where we can get people to engage collaboratively", cultivate stakeholder relationships and maximize resources to influence the educational system. Dale-Jones is extremely passionate about this work and believes:

> very strongly in the idea of collaborative engagement in the workplace. I engage my board. I engage consultants around me. I like to think in a fairly democratic way with the staff. Strategic sessions are sessions where we co-create strategy—where it is not just about what I think. But the buck stops with me.

Dale-Jones's leadership style is:

> driving a particular kind of visionary hope for the organization. Partly because of the conviction of wanting to walk our talk, we talk in collaboration, and in a fairly non-hierarchical engagement. ... I think people have a sense of my passion for education and change, and my belief in a values-driven approach. I think I am less of a micro-manager than I used to be—I have learned to allow a certain amount of space to people.

Dale-Jones has been reasonably lucky from a gender point of view:

> I think I have felt the voices of one's history, not being quite certain in the way that perhaps men are certain about their capacity. It took me some time before I realized that I wanted to lead. My father and my grandfather were both headmasters, and I had a lot of personal discomfort growing up with the sense of autocratic masculine leadership. I really had to try and carve a different form of leadership style.

She thinks that the more consultative listening style of leadership—a more integrative style—comes more easily to women than men. "Men tend to be figures who are followed—and women provide more of a connecting role in an organization."

Dale-Jones's role models have been playing a kind of mentorship role for her. One man had headed up many NGOs, and was a change-maker in South African education and social development. She worked closely with him, and "he helped unlock some of my leadership potential". She also worked with Anne Lamont, a visionary who thinks about how to change systems and work in innovative ways with respect to social development.

"She has a style of strategic thinking that was enormously powerful. It changed the way I thought." And Dale-Jones's current chair of the board is a very good leadership role model who provides guidance and a consultative style. "What I hope I role-model is visioning about what is possible and then setting out to achieve that." Dale-Jones believes that it is through collective engagement that individual empowerment will happen.

Being a female principal is a very difficult thing. "I never felt strongly disadvantaged because of being a woman. But I do think that for women in more traditional cultures it is very difficult to be a leader." She also feels that there is "a woundedness in men as much as there is a prejudicing of women, and that leadership is difficult for both". Her final words, "We want bold leadership with a clear vision in education in South Africa."

Cheryl de la Rey (South Africa)

Cheryl de la Rey became vice-chancellor and principal of the University of Pretoria in South Africa in November 2009. She is a qualified psychologist, and was previously deputy vice-chancellor of the University of Cape Town and CEO of the Council of Higher Education.

De la Rey's first important defining moment was to pursue a lifelong career—influenced by her mother, who said, "It is important for a woman to have a career and to be independent." Her second defining moment was to move away from her roots and family network to pursue an academic career. Her third defining decision was to move from an academic department into an administrative executive role. What de la Rey's leadership brings to the university is focus—staying focused on what is important and being able to say yes and no. She brings the experience of having worked in academia and also as an executive director with a budget. She said that "leaders in general have to be comfortable that you will face criticism and that not everyone is going to like you. Young girls get socialized into being nice. You cannot be nice all the time."

De la Rey's first challenge was to learn the organization and get to know the people. "For some men it was a big change to work with a woman." She spent her first year listening to people's concerns, fears and hopes for the future. Her second stage was implementation, and her style changed from listening to creating a greater sense of urgency. "I became a lot more direct and assertive." The vice-chancellor asked for a "perception inventory" and discovered that some in her team were intimidated—so "I have tried to modulate a little more". She described her leadership style as direct, persuasive and engaged, listening to different views.

"To get your voice heard in a predominantly male space is the key issue which we have not dealt with. We still have to overcome that." But she said that she has seen a shift in women becoming more assertive, even though women leaders still seek approval and require regular affirmation:

Sometimes approval and affirmation can be a barrier, because if you are constantly seeking affirmation, you are not going to get the business of the business done. And it means that you are reluctant to take hard decisions or have crucial conversations.

De la Rey has reflected on whether she should be more visible publicly. "I prefer the personal engagement, giving talks. I go and talk to people. I am a very private person." To reach a younger audience through women's magazines, she is willing to be interviewed about her career but not about her favorite perfume, which "simply reinforces stereotypes". She also wants to acknowledge the double standards. "When a male leader is praised for 'having the balls' to do something, he has got strength. When a woman does that, she is aggressive, a bully, intimidating. But women are part of the change process." Moving into a leadership position as a CEO requires taking decisions, and not taking a decision is also a decision. "We do get socialized to be the nurturer, to be nice. I do not want to undermine those qualities." She talked about the importance of creating an environment to encourage other women, and to take individual responsibility and ownership of all the issues that come with the past—but organizations must provide support mechanisms:

> There is a generational shift. The new generation of young women is much better prepared for taking on leadership challenges, and shows much more confidence about their potential to do so. One thing that has not shifted is the tendency for women to get defined mostly by their sexual attractiveness, or sexuality—in a way that male leaders do not have to deal with.

Although women have more freedom than before, a second thing that has not shifted sufficiently "is men taking responsibility for family and domestic life". And she is concerned about abuse: "The issue of power is fundamental in those men who are abusive, and these are serious ongoing challenges that the next generation faces. There is a real absence of a gender equality movement now, and the silence is quite concerning."

Elena Escagedo Suarez de Bustamante (Spain)

Elena Escagedo strives to achieve results and to bring people along through participation. She is an economist by training, having completed her MBA at the IE Business School (formerly the Instituto de Empresa or IE) in Madrid, Spain. She worked for the IE from 1983 to 1987 as marketing professor, running the Executive Education department. From 1987 to 1990 she was hired by the Institute for International Research in the conference sector for executives, then moved to the USA until 1992. In 1993 she returned to IE Business School, and is currently director of open enrolment programs in executive education. Her responsibility is to achieve revenue and margins while managing and motivating 20 staff. She described her identity as one of perseverance. "I am very committed and I always fight until I get what I want. I am a hard worker. I also had to work in other areas like controlling my temper."

Her leadership style is participative, even if she has a clear idea of how to go forward. "I think it better to listen to others' perspectives, because there might be a simpler or different way to get there." She can be more directive if the person is less mature, has less expertise or is new. In dealing with difficulties, she tends to move forward positively. She feels she is an achiever and that people can rely on her. However, she thinks her internal barriers are common to many women: "We tend not to communicate what we do. We never talk about the process, we only present the results." Her executive committee is mostly men—and she thinks the barrier for her is not giving enough importance to the process of achieving results. "That is what men usually do."

She does not feel she has faced any external barriers, but rather internal ones. Through a coaching program she had to unlearn making limiting assumptions and judgments. She had to learn to see different perspectives and to understand other people—developing empathy. Now, "I tend to be more open to understanding what other people think or feel." An effective leadership scenario for her was cutting 100 executive programs down to 60. She finds that her way to accomplish something within a team is to repeat things many times, as people understand things differently—for example, understanding either the economic, the emotional or the reward side.

She finds her tendency to see solutions rather than problems as problematical. In the coaching program she had to learn how to understand other people's situations, seeing not just "with my own glasses but with other people's glasses". She is demanding and wants results. And although it is empowering to encourage people to participate in the solution, it is also stressful. Escagedo observed that her team was demotivated and fought for the women to be able to work at home with flexible hours a few days a week. "The moment they had to do everything from their home it was incredible, the way it worked." Due to her leadership style, she gave them an opportunity—she trusted them and they repaid her with results.

For her, effective leadership is a very clear vision communicated with lots of clarity and the "determination to push through". In Escagedo's job, most high positions are held by men, but comparing herself to others harmed her in her twenties. Her advice to women is: compare yourself only to yourself. "I must be happy with what I do, not with what others do." She doesn't blame men. In Spain, there is a required quota of women for senior positions, but it is still a male-oriented environment. She said women are more transformational and men more transactional. "Women tend to have a more democratic style, and men are more autocratic or directive. Women think differently to men. Sometimes men are not empathetic enough to understand other people." Most important for women is to "walk the talk, and women do more of that than men. Men like to give orders or give directions. Involve yourselves to get results."

Nicola Kleyn (South Africa)

Nicola Kleyn is dean of the Gordon Institute of Business Science (GIBS). In addition to her responsibilities at GIBS, she lectures on various marketing-related academic and company-specific short courses and also consults for a number of organizations seeking to grow customer, brand and reputational equity.

Kleyn thinks that she arrived in her current role through "a balance of personal attributes, a balance of environmental enablers—and an element of seriously hard work, luck and timing". Enablers for her start with a person's own innate characteristics. She said she is intensely curious and always chose interesting work over and above a career—until she realized she could do both. "I was not willing to spend time jumping through someone else's hoops if it was not a contribution to what I saw as my own growth and development and learning."

Home-schooled before eventually attending an all-girls Catholic school, Kleyn grew up in a strong female household but with a very present father:

> Looking back, there were never any of the scripts that I see sometimes playing out with my children. There was never any sense of what might be a female versus a male role in our household. My father worked. My mother worked. In the school I went to, I was encouraged to have a voice.

She explained that there was a definite assumption that "you were going to get married and have children. But there was also a constant narrative that education is a privilege and you must give back to society. You must give back to the world—that was the script for me."

She fell "in love with marketing, because suddenly business was about serving customers, adding value to people's lives". She became a junior lecturer at the University of the Witwatersrand in Johannesburg and claimed to have never been consciously discriminated against as a woman—she was more conscious of being a junior. One potential derailer she finally put to bed was: "Am I really qualified to do this? Do I really know what I am talking about? Should this be me here?"

What definitively shaped her was working in the retail clothing sector. She wanted to go into marketing but was signed up as a trainee store controller. Finishing a six-month job inside of six weeks, Kleyn was told she needed to go find something to keep herself amused. "It was a death knell for me. I lasted nine months in that environment, but it taught me that you have a right to grow yourself." Kleyn returned to academia, got married, and took up a position at Investec, a leading South African financial institution. She was told that her job "was to add value so go and figure out what you are going to do". It was a very male-dominated environment, but after nine months she was asked to head up their business school. "I could really add value."

When her first baby was born she was hit by the most "debilitating postnatal depression. My confidence was absolutely shattered." A sustaining enabler for Kleyn was the "notion that I can absolutely define my identity through work". GIBS rang, and she started out as a program manager. Tragedy struck with the death of her brother and sister-in-law and then the suicide of her mother. "Deaths are hard. I have been shaped far more by the occurrences that have happened in my personal life than in my work life." The loss of her mother was "a very profound learning in what you can control and what you cannot control, but ultimately how we are responsible for our own destinies". She and her husband had one child in 1999, another in 2001, and adopted her niece and nephew in late 2002—making a jump from one to four children in a year. Her husband's business went into financial difficulties and "that was quite a wake-up. What more can I do to make sure that financial security is going to work? And what I realized was, I love this academic environment. I had better get a doctorate and build up a consulting practice."

What was more difficult was finding herself as a woman leader with children and the responses she received from non-working mothers, who disapproved of her working. (In contrast, she received "wonderful supportiveness" from other working mothers.) "I probably would have had my doubts about whether I was doing the right thing," but by "having the script that says I have to become financially independent, it gave me permission to actually reach for anything. I think it hits women more as they are moving up senior leadership positions."

Having completed her doctorate, she became assistant professor and was encouraged to apply for the position of head of academic programs. She had feedback and a profound insight that she was seen as quite critical—which enabled a personal shift. Kleyn describes her leadership style as creating an environment in which people can make their best possible contribution—a path that you jointly believe in and jointly co-create. "It is collaborative; it is inclusive. This notion of authentic leadership is that ability to also admit to your own shortcomings. I do not have to pretend to be someone I am not."

Sheba Maini (India)

Since October 2008 Sheba Maini has been the director of SOL (Spirit of Leadership) management consultants in New Delhi, India. She works in leadership development in the corporate and education sectors through performance and developmental coaching, team facilitation and training. Maini has worked for the last 17 years in the field of leadership development, working with multinationals in India and the Far East. When she completed her last corporate post at Levi Strauss, she took a year off to travel round India teaching in schools, subsequently moving into an NPO in leadership development in education. After eight years she set out on her own, working in the education and corporate sectors through training, coaching and facilitation—particularly working with women in leadership:

> Getting women to find their voice here is an important part of what I do, and I believe forms a strong part of my identity. Part of my identity is very strongly inclined towards bringing up women's leadership in India, because it is a largely patriarchal society. It is still very male-dominated—the positions of power are largely held by men.

Although Maini acknowledged that India had a woman prime minister before other countries, "the conditioning of the society is still very male-dominated. Women are so deeply conditioned that they don't realize they can explore different identities and mark out something for themselves besides being mothers and wives."

Her leadership style, in her own words, is collaborative, building consensus and moving forward through delegation and coaching. "It is tough because it is a very competitive environment, and male characteristics are still very predominant." And she's learned that "if you trust someone and they let you down, it doesn't mean that trust is wrong, it just means you need to find the right people and build on that". She learned this the hard way when she had an opportunity for a promotion and discovered that women don't always support each other. Someone else took the credit for her work and gained the promotion instead. "I learned how to be politically savvy in order to save myself from politics!"

What enabled her to reach her current position is a combination of authenticity and courage plus:

> finding who you are, finding your voice, finding your strengths and staying with that. I have learned over time that people treat you the way you treat yourself. If you treat yourself with dignity and respect, and ask for what you think you deserve and need, the universe and the world responds to you in the same manner.

Her most effective leadership was when the organization within which she was working was shut down and they had to retrench 30 women:

> The way I handled that, giving these women other opportunities, helping them to ride over their feeling of loss. We managed to place 95

percent of them in good organizations. I had a very good leader who demonstrated this behavior, so it was easy to stand on her shoulders.

Her least effective leadership moment was due to inadequate communication:

> I was not very open in my communication, and would not talk about what the team was doing. Some of them had high needs of recognition, which I did not see. I wasn't promoting their work, or standing up and saying things. It was bad handling on my part, and when I lost some really good people, I woke up, and changed my communication style.

Maini described India as an exciting place to be. But "it is still very hard for women, and they have to put on behaviors which are typically male in order to move ahead. It is changing, but not fast enough." She explained that women don't realize that they don't have to be men to succeed, but they need to start building their own networks within the organization and find sponsors. "It's blinders on both sides" because the conditioning is so deep for both genders.

Stella Nkomo (African-American in South Africa)

Stella Nkomo is deputy dean for research and postgraduate studies at the University of Pretoria. Previously she was in the Department of Human Resource Management, and prior to joining the University of Pretoria she was Bateman Professor of Business Leadership at the Graduate School of Business Leadership at the University of South Africa (UNISA). Her internationally recognized work on race and gender and managing diversity appears in numerous journals.

Most of Nkomo's academic career was in the USA before she moved to South Africa in 2000 with her husband. "I built a very successful academic career in the US, and thought I am not coming as the trailing spouse—I am coming on my own—and so I came in 1999 to look for an academic post." Nkomo experienced the lack of women in the business schools and economic and management sciences faculties at universities in South Africa:

> What depressed me was repeating experiences I had previously encountered in the United States. African-Americans in the US are a minority; as an African-American woman I was usually the only black woman in my business school classes. When I did my doctorate I was the only black woman. When I took my first academic post at the University of North Carolina at Charlotte I was the only black woman. I thought, I am coming to a majority black country, and I didn't expect to have the same experience. I got to UNISA as a professor, and I was the only black senior professor.

She was disappointed that her fellow women academics were primarily fulfilling administrative roles despite holding academic posts. What she found most disturbing was that "women didn't speak up for themselves and were literally afraid. Our power lies in our collective knowledge—knowledge that we can use to spur change."

Lecturing on leadership, Nkomo walked into a class of 400 students. The audience began whispering as she began to lecture. Students later came up to tell her what was being said: "Oh no, here is one of those BEE [Black Economic Empowerment, a statutory affirmative action policy] people they have put in here to teach us." How her women peers responded to her was even more surprising. "They were surprised by what they thought was aggressive behavior towards my male colleagues—but it was normal behavior for me." Nkomo supported her women colleagues to find their scholarly voices.

Nkomo was born in Georgia into a family of ten children, who moved to New York City when she was four. Her mother had education up to Grade 8 and her father up to Grade 6. In junior high school, children were allocated by the school authorities to an academic, commercial or vocational track, and because her family was on welfare (social grant) she was advised to take the commercial track to learn shorthand and typing to support them. At 16 she graduated from high school and started working as a personal banker's secretary—but was so bored she asked her boss how she could train to do more. He told her to get a bachelor's degree and an MBA, so she started going to night school. She had a break when she was offered a scholarship. "I realized that education would change my life; through education I could help other people transform their lives. I came from a very poor background. I was not supposed to be sitting where I am sitting now." After completing her MBA she started teaching at the University of Rhode Island. The head of department advised her to get a PhD. She and her husband completed their doctorates, which she says was "the best decision I ever made in my life".

She first recognized the leader in herself as a teenager, when she refused to accept the decision of her (mainly white) church in New York City not to send a bus to enable members to join the March on Washington with Dr Martin Luther King. In response, Nkomo and a few others organized a demonstration at the church—and the church elders did not react well: "I had never seen people so angry. From that day I go to church only for weddings and funerals. I couldn't take the hypocrisy. If you feel strongly you must speak up, because injustice can happen to anyone":

> I help a young student to be the first person in her family to get a degree and perhaps even a postgraduate degree. I tell all my students you can also be a leader. ... I believe my job is helping people find their scholarly voices—the research questions they wish to study, acquire the skills and confidence to research them well, and to obtain

their doctorates. As a young doctoral student, I really wanted to research the experiences of women and black people in corporate America, which at the time was predominantly male and white. I was told "You cannot do that topic." I did a good PhD and published out of it. However, my best work came when I focused on women in leadership, which was my passion.

South Africa is an emerging market with barriers and difficulties for women wanting to step up:

Many women cannot get access to water, safe living conditions, and education. I call these the fundamental human dignity issues. We still have the glass ceiling at universities, in corporations. Those are old issues—men wanting to hold onto power, people not thinking that women are competent. I call it the double bind. Women can also self-destruct or fail to support other women. We as women need to do a better job of recognizing the power of collective action. I would like to see the women in parliament engage in even more advocacy around issues that are peculiar to the condition of women. I have seen this problem in the corporate setting, where senior women worry about being seen as biased towards women if they advocate for gender equality and give special attention to issues encountered by women. There is a need for a different type of leadership in the twenty-first century. A softer, inclusive leadership, leadership that can build relationships. The romance of leadership is the idea that leadership is masculine: the heroic leader who comes in and single-handedly fixes everything. However, the heroic leader prototype is being replaced by a call for a different kind of leadership in today's complex world—a world characterized by uncertainty, diversity and volatility. The belief that women have to play certain roles and men have certain roles is a very deep one. In South Africa there is progressive legislation in terms of the constitution, but there is the romance of culture. Cultural beliefs are sometimes evoked to substantiate gender inequality.

Mónica Sacristán (Mexico)

Mónica Sacristán has been dean of executive development and university extension at Instituto Tecnológico Autónomo de México (ITAM) in Mexico City since 1999. This area reports directly to the university rector and is responsible for all the non-degree programs in the university, meaning executive education (representing 90 percent of the operation) and continuing and distance education. She joined ITAM in 1996 as associate dean for MBA programs and as a faculty member teaching strategy and finance.

Sacristán has had a diverse and rich life. She trained as a research chemist and at 21 fell in love and married a high-ranking politician. She completed her master's in chemistry and got divorced, toting a one-and-a-half-year-old baby. Putting herself through business school as a chef and head of a restaurant, she was hired by McKinsey, an international consulting firm, after completing her MBA. For the past 16 years she has been dean of executive education at ITAM in Mexico City—a small, prestigious private university. The loves of her life are her daughter and second husband.

Her greatest challenge was taking over the executive education program 16 years ago with a department suffering from "broken morale, broken staff and no information". She had to win the respect of 400 faculty members who were "grief-stricken that their beloved boss had been fired". At the age of 33 she succeeded by rolling up her sleeves and increasing revenue 40 percent.

"I have had all these different lives and I think that shaped me, from being a risk-adverse, controlled person to having to be resilient. I realized that you cannot control everything; you have to adapt and learn." Although ITAM is well positioned in government, Sacristán is more comfortable in the business sector and likes to teach if the CEO of an important company is personally involved in a program. "I like challenges and am considered a leader. I am very outspoken, very clear, and consider myself to be tough, but fair." Teaching is her passion and she embraces a teaching leadership style.

Sacristán explained that she has always worked with men, mostly teaches men, and most of the CEOs she works with are men. She feels she can be a bit harsh, almost losing a long-standing CEO client by contradicting him in front of his team. She was frustrated at having to apologize in public—but it worked. She has had to change her leadership style over time as "command and control does not get you anywhere. I have people talk to each other and see how many things you get if you treat people as people."

Sacristán says she is willing to learn and has had a boss for 16 years who trusts her. But the executive education program is a business with revenues and profit margins, and he would not trust her if she did not deliver. She is direct, cuts to the chase, and believes in being clear but not rude. She thinks that "being a woman is a barrier in a macho society where there is still a lot of discrimination. Being too straightforward and direct is a barrier in Mexican culture, which is more about face-saving." Another barrier is not having a US PhD, which she needs to be promoted above her current position. There are also "the family constraints, being a woman. I am very involved with the care of my parents and daughter."

Sacristán has experienced many difficulties: getting divorced at 28, leaving chemistry, managing surgery for cancer—all of which softened her. "You lose a little bit of self-control. That was a big identity change."

Going to Stanford to experience being a participant in an executive program, she discovered top-notch women with whom she became friends. It was life-changing and taught her to be herself. Sacristán is considering eventually consulting in the learning and development arena, and hoping to obtain certification as a coach.

Themes emerging from women's stories

This series of interviews with ten women leaders in emerging markets across the globe from Colombia and Mexico to Spain, South Africa and India has helped us to learn from their varied and wide-ranging experience in the field of education. These are the most important themes emerging from their stories.

Following one's passion

Only some interviewees explicitly mentioned the idea of following their passions, although they have evidently all done this. Bernal Uribe described how the "revolutionary" approaches of people in fields as diverse as industry and culture inspired her to work with them, because "I have always followed my heart". Dale-Jones said that her entire professional life has been spent in education because she is very passionate about it and has a fundamental interest in and commitment to the sector. Kleyn explained that she is intensely curious and has always chosen interesting work over and above a career (particularly in marketing, with which she fell in love), until she realized she could do both. Following one's passion is evident in the stories of all the interviewees and it is clear that none of them would play such demanding leadership roles if they did not feel passionate about their work.

Sense of service

A sense of service was a key driver for most interviewees. Bernal Uribe, whose family was part of her country's social and political elite, defined her sense of service as "doing something that adds value to the community, to the society, to the people, to the country". Her sense of service and commitment to her latest role as director of a large university program, despite the personal sacrifices it entails, is rooted in her spiritual life: "I believe in God and I live for that. And that is why I understand all this."

The sense of service of the South African interviewees is rooted mainly in their commitment to addressing the legacy of apartheid. Creecy was interested in politics since childhood due to her parents' unusually progressive views and said her identity revolves around "the values about human rights and democracy and that people are equal and have equal chances". Brewer, from a relatively privileged background sheltered from the harsh realities of apartheid, was prompted by her university lecturers to address the dismal quality of state-run education for poorer South Africans by developing a network of high-quality, low-fee private schools. Similarly, Dale-Jones was driven by a strong conviction to use her knowledge and skills to help social development in the country, and founded a non-profit organization to improve the South African education system. Kleyn attended a Catholic private school which provided "a constant narrative that education is a privilege and you must give back to society."

Nkomo was born in New York City into a large and poor black family and raised by parents from the southern US state of Georgia with very limited education. As a result, she views her role in life as helping people in minority or otherwise marginalized communities "find their silent voice" through education. A strong part of Maini's identity is getting women to find their voices in the largely patriarchal society of India.

Enterprise, initiative and self-direction

A critical attribute of effective leadership is an enterprising spirit, a willingness to take the initiative, the ability to motivate and direct oneself. Bernal Uribe needed a practical component for her university degree, so at short notice and with no prior experience, beat a hundred other candidates to get a job in a bank—and then developed a successful system of norms and standards for the organization. She has never been afraid of change or of moving into new and unknown fields, because as "an entrepreneur" the subject of her work does not matter to her. She has always followed her own path and left positions when she felt it was time to move on.

In a similar spirit, Kleyn said, "I was not willing to spend time jumping through someone else's hoops." De la Rey demonstrated an enterprising spirit when she moved away from her roots and family network to pursue an academic career, and later moved from an academic department into an administrative executive role. Nkomo graduated from high school at 16 and started secretarial work to support her impoverished family, but attended night school to complete the high school courses required for entry into higher education, secured a college scholarship, completed a bachelor's degree and MBA, became a university lecturer, and ultimately completed a PhD. This progression reveals a remarkable level of drive and self-motivation.

Overcoming adversity

Adversity can take many forms in a person's life—structural or circumstantial, personal or work-related. Nkomo's drive to improve the quality of her life through education helped her overcome the disadvantages of growing up in an impoverished minority community and a public school system which explicitly limited the career horizons of children from poor backgrounds. Creecy's family was financially straitened after the death of her father, so she started part-time work when she was 13. She later demonstrated the same resolve as provincial minister of education, being determined to improve the quality of schooling in the face of militant opposition from the teachers' union and students' organization. Kleyn experienced personal tragedy with the deaths of her brother, sister-in-law and mother. After adopting her orphaned niece and nephew, her husband's business ran into financial difficulties, putting greater pressure on her to become the family's major breadwinner.

Bernal Uribe had to cope with some dysfunctional bosses but nevertheless made a success of her various positions. She suffered through a difficult divorce, but carried on with her career and raising her children. She feels that experiencing difficulty is important, because opportunities occur in challenges. Sacristán has experienced many personal difficulties, such as getting divorced at 28 and undergoing surgery for cancer. She nevertheless managed to put herself through an MBA, and overcome another major challenge when she revitalized a demoralized university department.

Gender barriers

Several of the interviewees have experienced both explicit and less overt gender barriers. Maini explained that, although India had a woman prime minister before other countries, the society is still very male-dominated, with positions of power largely held by men. A critical result of this is that "Women are so deeply conditioned that they don't realize they can explore different identities and mark out something for themselves besides being mothers and wives."

In Mexico, Sacristán thinks that "being a woman is a barrier in a macho society where there is still a lot of discrimination". An added complication is that it can be problematic for a leader to be too straightforward and direct, as face-saving is very important in Mexican culture. Escagedo pointed out that while quotas have been mandated for women in senior positions in Spain, the environment is still very male-oriented. After moving to South Africa, Nkomo was depressed to encounter the same lack of progress of black women that she had seen in the US. She found that she was the only senior black professor in the university she joined, that senior women leaders were simply acting as administrators, and that "women didn't speak up for themselves and were literally afraid".

De la Rey voiced similar issues concerning gender barriers in South Africa: "For some men it was a big change to work with a woman." There has been a generational shift among women, with young women now much better prepared for taking on leadership challenges and showing much more confidence about their leadership potential, but "To get your voice heard in a predominantly male space is the key issue which we have not dealt with. We still have to overcome that." De la Rey noted that the tendency for women to get defined mostly by their sexual attractiveness or sexuality has not changed, and she is also concerned about more overt, aggressive and violent abuse of women.

After founding a non-profit organization in South Africa with a male colleague, Brewer experienced gender discrimination deeply rooted in patriarchal culture, and discovered that her voice was not being heard. In contrast, Kleyn claimed to have never been consciously discriminated against as a woman, being more conscious of her lack of experience while still a junior lecturer. Dale-Jones is keenly aware that being a female school principal is a challenging role for a woman in South Africa: "I never felt strongly disadvantaged because of being a woman. But I do think that for women in more traditional cultures it is very difficult to be a leader."

Internal barriers

Barriers imposed by the outside world on the grounds of race, gender, religion and other attributes are naturally important—but the barriers people impose on themselves, often subconsciously and in reaction to their social conditioning and concomitant external barriers, are often just as important. This is highlighted by the experiences of several of the interviewees, who learned to deal with their own limiting assumptions and self-doubts.

Brewer highlighted a critical internal obstacle to effective leadership— lack of self-confidence and the need for external support systems. These obstacles, rather than opposition on gender grounds, have been her major challenges, which she overcame by "questioning everything" and developing the necessary hard and soft leadership skills. Similarly, as a young person Creecy was very shy and introverted and lacked self-confidence— but was also burdened by perfectionism, which made her controlling and impatient. As she pointed out, "To be an effective leader you have to deal with your own baggage." Kleyn was plagued by self-doubt as a junior university lecturer—"Am I really qualified to do this?" Escagedo has had to unlearn major limiting assumptions and judgments. For example, most senior positions in her field are held by men, but she realized that comparing herself to others was harming her.

Children and work–life balance

It is often difficult for leaders, both men and women, to maintain a satisfactory balance between work and personal life. De la Rey deals with this by consciously reserving one day each week to focus on personal and family life. Women leaders face an additional challenge. As de la Rey pointed out, women have more freedom than before (in some countries and some cultures), but one factor that has not changed sufficiently is the unwillingness of men to take responsibility for family and domestic life.

This means that most women leaders still carry a disproportionately heavy share of childrearing and domestic management—quite apart from the physiological and emotional requirements of motherhood. One result is that many women leaders are compelled to either defer having children until more favorable points in their careers or put their careers on hold while they have babies and nurture them through infancy.

These outcomes are evident in the stories of some of the interviewees. When Bernal Uribe had her first child, she decided to resign from her government job because she wanted to breastfeed her baby and it was not feasible to do this at the office. She spent time with her baby daughter— while working from home in three very different and demanding vocations.

Creecy's involvement in the underground anti-apartheid movement in South Africa during the 1980s led her to delay having children until the unbanning of liberation organizations in 1990. After being elected to the provincial legislature in 1994, "I used to go everywhere with a three-year-old, a newborn baby and a baby minder, because I was breastfeeding." Sacristán says that being a woman brings with it family constraints such as caring for children and parents. Kleyn experienced different challenges, when her first baby was born and her self-confidence was shattered by debilitating postnatal depression. The idea that she could still define her identity through work was a key enabler. More difficult were the demands of being a woman leader with children and the disapproval and lack of support she received from non-working mothers. Brewer is conscious of the need for an organizational culture that supports women staff members on issues such as maternity leave.

Mentors and role models

Several of the interviewees have received strong learning from role models and/or support from mentors. Creecy's mother was a strongly feminist role model—"My mother brought me up [to believe] that there is nothing that needs to be done in the world that women cannot do"—and evidently helped her ignore or overcome gender barriers. De la Rey was similarly encouraged by her mother, who held that it is important for a woman to have a career and be independent. In contrast, Dale-Jones experienced considerable personal discomfort at home due to the autocratic masculine leadership imposed by her father and grandfather. This prompted her to consciously develop a completely different leadership style.

Bernal Uribe had three main mentors and Brewer's career as a leader was shaped by working with the male co-founder of her private school network: "I learned a lot from him not being so emotional, being very pragmatic." Similarly, Dale-Jones has been positively influenced by three people with whom she has worked, the third being the current chairperson of her board who provides guidance and has a consultative leadership style.

Leadership style: "male" and "female"

A core focus of the literature review earlier in this chapter was the contrast between archetypally "male" leadership styles (based on competitive, controlling and aggressive behaviors) and archetypally "female" leadership styles (based on relationships, encouragement and support). It was suggested that the most effective style of leadership could be an androgynous approach that combines supposedly masculine and feminine attributes.

One of the most striking themes to emerge from the stories in this chapter is the way in which these women leaders have done precisely that. Regardless of the style they demonstrated when they first became leaders, hands-on experience taught them that effective leadership requires the application of both masculine and feminine behaviors—and they modified their behavior accordingly. So women who started with a more masculine-oriented leadership style learned to adopt feminine leadership traits as well, while women who started with a more feminine-oriented leadership style learned to include masculine traits.

When Creecy was appointed to supervise a team of 20 political activists, her sense of responsibility and perfectionism drove her to organize their work in detail, demonstrating a stereotypically controlling and directive masculine leadership style. However, her extensive political experience taught her to let go of perfectionism, stop micro-managing team members and develop a more consultative and inclusive (that is, feminine) leadership style. De la Rey understood from the outset that "leaders in general have to be comfortable that you will face criticism and that not everyone is going to like you. Young girls get socialized into being nice. You cannot be nice all the time." Her leadership style now combines directness with persuasion, engagement and consultation.

Feedback from Kleyn's colleagues showed her that she was seen as quite critical, which prompted a shift in her approach. She introduced a more collaborative way of doing things in her institution and described her leadership style as creating an environment in which people can make their best possible contribution, based on what they jointly believe in and co-create. Sacristán feels that her leadership style can be too harsh, and has had to change it, as "command and control does not get you anywhere. You have to adapt and learn."

Escagedo said she is very committed and always fights until she gets what she wants. She acknowledged that she has had to work on other aspects of her leadership style such as controlling her temper. She said her leadership style is participative, even if she has a clear idea of how to go forward. She said women are more transformational and men transactional. "Women tend to have a more democratic style, and men are more autocratic or directive."

Dale-Jones said that she is less of a micro-manager than she used to be, having learned "to be more strategic and allow a certain amount of space to people". She believes "very strongly in the idea of collaborative engagement in the workplace". She thinks that the more consultative listening style of leadership—a more integrative style—comes more easily to women than men. "Men tend to be figures who are followed—and women provide more of a connecting role in an organization."

Nkomo understands that there is a need for "a different type of leadership in the twenty-first century. A softer leadership, leadership that can build relationships that can be inclusive." Brewer is conscious that she has had to move from a feminine leadership style to a more masculine style: "You naturally become harder, because you have to."

Conclusion

To date, leadership theories tend to describe the behavior of leaders in the materialistic, Western world, particularly that of the USA, and the behavior of leaders, who are both male and individualistic—curiously, in a world that is largely populated by collective societies and where women are playing an increasingly strong role. Most leadership theories emerge from their own domestic marketplaces rather than developing as universal theories relevant to all countries. This is clearly illustrated by the experiences of the women leaders in this chapter.

Leadership studies that have not emerged from the US model tend to be domestic rather than global—and yet today global leaders need to focus on cross-cultural interactions. Successful management of today's increasingly diverse workforce is one of the most important global challenges faced by political and corporate leaders. The move from homogeneous societies to heterogeneous cultures is an irreversible trend, and many of today's organizational challenges stem from the inability of leaders to fully comprehend the dynamics of diversity and culture.

In addition, the increased emphasis on the feminization of leadership highlights the importance of employee participation, interpersonal and teambuilding skills and people empowerment. This underlines the importance of listening, coaching, dialogue, conflict management and collaboration. Contemporary research points more and more to leadership requiring a feminized approach and indicates that a change is required in the traditional masculine competitive approach. New strategies are required in every region, which may mean assisting women to build their professional networks, mentoring programs to increase board participation, and legislation to encourage promotion to the C-suite.

The individual stories in this chapter vividly illuminate the strengths, characteristics and behaviors that women continue to contribute to global leadership today. However, the feminization of leadership does not mean that women's leadership styles are necessarily more effective. A new model is emerging which suggests that leaders adopt an androgynous, non-gendered, relational and participative, power-sharing style of management—sensitive to people's needs. We ignore this new model to our detriment.

Questions we need to answer are:

- How would you describe the qualities needed to merge male and female management and relationship styles in order to produce a more effective leadership model?
- What would you regard as the key elements needed to enhance these qualities in senior women leaders in higher education?
- How would you develop a program in order to facilitate these desired outcomes?

References

Appelbaum, S. H., L. Audet and J. C. Miller. 2003. "Gender and Leadership? Leadership and Gender? A Journey Through the Landscape of Theories." *Leadership and Organization Development Journal* 24(1): 43–51.

Ardichvili, A. and S. V. Manderscheid. 2008. "Emerging Practices in Leadership Development." *Advances in Developing Human Resources* 10(5): 619–631.

Arvey, R. D., Z. Zhang, B. J. Avolio and R. F. Krueger. 2007. "Developmental and Genetic Determinants of Leadership Role Occupancy Among Women." *Journal of Applied Psychology* 92(3): 693–706.

Blackmore, J. 2006. "Social Justice and the Study and Practice of Leadership in Education: A Feminist History." *Journal of Educational Administration and History* 38(2): 85–299.

Chatwani, N. 2015. "Looking Ahead: The Feminization of Leadership." In *Unveiling Women's Leadership: Identity and Meaning of Leadership in India*, edited by P. Kumar, 137–152. Basingstoke: Palgrave Macmillan.

Dalakoura, A. 2010. "Differentiating Leader and Leadership Development: A Collective Framework for Leadership Development." *Journal of Management Development* 29(5): 432–441.

Day, D. V., J. W. Fleenor, L. E. Atwater, R. E. Sturm and R. A. McKee. 2014. Advances in Leader and Leadership Development: A Review of 25 Years of Research and Theory." *The Leadership Quarterly* 25(1): 63–82.

Drake, D. B. 2015. *Narrative Coaching: Bringing Our New Stories to Life.* Berkeley, CA: CNC Press.

Dugan, J. P. 2006. "Explorations Using the Social Change Model: Leadership Development Among College Men and Women." *Journal of College Student Development* 47(2): 217–225.

Eagly, A. H. and L. L. Carli. 2007. "Women and the Labyrinth of Leadership." *Harvard Business Review* (September): 62–71.

Eagly, A. H. and S. J. Karau. 2002. "Role Congruity Theory of Prejudice Toward Female Leaders." *Psychological Review* 109(3): 573–598.

Gallant, A. 2014. "Symbolic Interactions and the Development of Women Leaders in Higher Education." *Gender, Work and Organization* 21(3): 203–216.

Gattrell, C. and E. Swan. 2008. *Gender and Diversity in Management: An Introduction.* London: Sage.

Harris, A. 2013. "Distributed Leadership: Friend or Foe?" *Educational Management Administration and Leadership* 41(5): 545–554.

Harris, C. A. and S. I. Leberman. 2012. "Leadership Development for Women in New Zealand Universities: Learning From the New Zealand Women in Leadership Programme." *Advances in Developing Human Resources* 14(1): 28–44.

Heikka, J., M. Waniganayake and E. Hujala. 2012. "Contextualizing Distributed Leadership Within Early Childhood Education: Current Understandings, Research Evidence and Future Challenges." *Educational Management Administration and Leadership* 41(1): 30–44.

Johanson, J. C. 2008. "Perceptions of Femininity in Leadership: Modern Trend or Classic Component?" *Sex Roles* 58(11): 784–789.

Kiamba, J. M. 2008. "Women and Leadership Positions: Social and Cultural Barriers to Success." *Wagadu* 6(Winter): 7–26.

Madsen, S. R. 2012. "Women and Leadership in Higher Education: Learning and Advancement in Leadership Programmes." *Advances in Developing Human Resources* 14(1): 3–10.

Mayrowetz, D. 2008. "Making Sense of Distributed Leadership: Exploring the Multiple Usages of the Concept in the Field." *Educational Administration Quarterly* 44(3): 424–435.

Peterson, H. 2015. "Is Managing Academics 'Women's Work'? Exploring the Glass Cliff in Higher Education Management." *Educational Management Administration and Leadership* 44(1): 112–127.

Pounder, J. S. and M. Coleman. 2002. "Women: Better Leaders Than Men? In General and Educational Management It Still 'All Depends'." *Leadership and Organization Development Journal* 23(3): 122–133.

Spillane, J. P. 2005. "Distributed Leadership." *The Educational Forum* 69(2): 143–150.

Storvik, A. E. 2012. "Introducing the Feminist Management Discourse in Organizations." *Review of European Studies* 4(1): 155–166.

Thorp, L., R. Cummins and C. Townsend. 1998. "Women's Self-Perceived Leadership Skills in a Collegiate Agricultural Education Course." *Journal of Agricultural Education* 39(1): 55–62.

Webster, L. and P. Mertova. 2007. *Using Narrative Enquiry as a Research Method: An Introduction to Using Critical Event Narrative Analysis in Research in Learning and Teaching.* London and New York: Routledge.

5 Institution-level interventions in women's leadership

Desray Clark and Verity Hawarden

Introduction

The importance of continued focus on developing women is acknowledged by several studies. Barsh and Yee (2012) assert that organizations should explicitly focus on talent management processes such as mentorship programs, executive coaching programs and additional education. Morahan et al. (2011) recommend that more attention should be given to retain identified talent at mid- to senior-level management. Sherwin (2014) explains that organizations should do more to combine greater development opportunities with encouragement to all senior managers to expand the pipeline of women who are in supervisory and managerial positions.

In terms of institution-level interventions on women leadership, the debate regarding women-only development programs, as opposed to gender-diverse programs,[1] is one that is heavily disputed by academics and practitioners alike (Ely et al. 2011). One Johannesburg-based consultancy focuses specifically on providing advisory services to organizations in the developing market of South Africa that are particularly wanting to create a more gender-balanced working environment. This is partly in response to the UN Women's seven Principles for Responsible Management Education (UN PRME 7)—principle number four recognizes the need to provide education, training and professional development for women (UN Women 2010)—but also related to the increasing strategic focus on women's development by South African organizations. As a result, the consultancy has provided women's leadership development interventions that have either focused on creating learning opportunities solely to women or been gender diverse and included male participants in the learning process.

Both approaches appear to have advantages and disadvantages. The advantages of women-only programs are purported to include the following: women can talk more freely if no men are present; the vulnerability that women can show is increased and therefore the relationships that are built are much stronger; and the issue of the gender dynamic in the room is not present, allowing for women from different cultures to explore these differences in a deeper, more meaningful way. Development programs that focus specifically on creating awareness around the importance of gender balance and which thus include men in the learning process have been found to be helpful in creating a shared understanding between the genders; the women are better able to understand the male perspective and, likewise, the men are better able to understand the women's perspective.

The disadvantages of women-only programs reveal themselves as a backlash from the men who do not attend the program and feel they are at a disadvantage in terms of their development. The disadvantages of gender-diverse programs is that women do not focus on creating networks between themselves and it appears more difficult to explore the cultural differences between women. In addition, women often change in the presence of men and downplay their power, being subservient to the male energy. Women generally find it more difficult to voice strong opinions in the presence of men.

This chapter provides a comparison of the above two approaches. In order to contextualize the comparison and because the programs were delivered to a global multinational information and communications technology (ICT) organization as well as a leading law firm in the country, an overview of the ICT and professional services industries in a developing market (South Africa) is first provided. A review of the literature on organizational response strategies then sets the scene for the comparison of the programme approaches. Besides the two case studies, additional interviews were conducted with further champions for gender inclusivity who have implemented institutional interventions and are representative of the same two industries (Appendix 1). The objective for these interviews was to establish how other organizations have responded, the efficacy of their interventions and the impact on delegates. The emergent themes from these interviews is presented after the literature review and the case studies are then described, highlighting the process followed when delivering both types of programs, as well as exploring the advantages and disadvantages of each approach for the delegates and the firms. In conclusion, a framework for institutional interventions is presented that incorporates the recommended approach for a women's leadership development intervention as well as an approach for creating a gender-balanced firm.

Overview of ICT (information and communications technology) and professional services in South Africa

Dynamics of the ICT sector in South Africa

The growth of the ICT industry has been influenced in South Africa by the policy and regulatory environment (state regulation, telecommunications policies and acts), and the supply of ICT product and services (IT software, telecommunications, IT services and internet services) (James et al. 2001). While the size of the global IT market was forecast to reach almost US\$4 trillion in 2015 (Mahomed 2015), the South African ICT sector, while still demonstrating dynamic growth (Gillwald et al. 2012), had fallen behind due to several macro-environmental and policy factors (Mahomed 2015). It was understood by government that ICT should have become an increasingly key element in its provincial developmental agenda, with the hoped-for result of increased employment creation and better economic involvement by the broader society (Gauteng Province 2010). Despite industry policy constraints and other challenges, the sector continued to remain dynamic.

Dynamics of the professional services industry in South Africa

In comparison with most developing countries, South Africa has an extensive and well-developed market for professional services in general, but particularly for engineering, legal and accountancy services. Statistics South Africa (StatsSA) provided official data indicating that, combined, these three services contribute around 2% of GDP, whereas unofficial data puts the number much higher (many qualified accountants, engineers and lawyers do not work for the specialist service firms measured by StatsSA). The South African legal system includes a number of court structures, namely, the highest court of appeal on non-constitutional matters, the Appellate Division of the Supreme Court, provincial and local divisions of the Supreme Court, lower courts and special courts which deal exclusively with specific matters such as land claims and small claims. Key issues experienced in the legal services profession center mainly around the new laws associated with socio-political transition, as well as the representation of previously disadvantaged groups in the profession (Mbendi 2016; Condon et al. 2009).

Literature review

While the literature to follow focuses specifically on the question at hand, namely the advantages and disadvantages of women's leadership development programs versus gender-diverse interventions, additional theory is interspersed later in the chapter to further support insights that emerged from both case studies.

Leadership development experiences can be helpful during a person's career and thus general leadership development programs serve a critical function. Women-only programs, however, have been shown to yield many advantages that may not necessarily arise from gender-diverse programs. These are a result of a variety of factors, key amongst which are the topics that are discussed at women-only programs (Colantuono 2016; Ely et al. 2011), such as:

- teaching women how to seek and get the "right" kind of mentoring or how to earn sponsorship;
- addressing gender-specific career derailers (such as assertiveness, self-promotion and asking for opportunities);
- understanding how second-generation gender bias[2] manifests in organizations and can derail a woman's leadership transition;
- dealing with gender dynamics (the mindsets of managers that create barriers for women) and how to address them;

There are a number of advantages for women in attending women-only leadership development programs (Ely et al. 2011; Tessens 2008):

- Women feel more comfortable being in a learning environment with other women as they don't fear any potential post-program consequences based on possible vulnerabilities that may be exposed during the program.
- A more nuanced understanding of the subtle and pervasive effects of gender bias, how it may be playing out in their development as leaders and what they can do to counter it, is presented.
- Learning is fostered by putting women in a majority position, in contrast to the traditionally male-dominated work context. This in itself can elicit powerful insights. In addition, these programs create a holding environment in which to rediscover a sense of agency in their ongoing leadership development experiences, which aids in advancing them into more senior roles.
- Subtle cultural and organizational biases can easily turn women's attention inward as they try to reconcile conflicting messages about how to behave as leaders. Women-only leadership development programs can assist women to find their own style of leadership by anchoring on their larger leadership purpose, thus redirecting their attention outward toward who they need to be in order to advance.
- Women-only programs are an effective and appropriate way of beginning to address the underutilization of female human resources.

The advantages of gender-diverse groups are that the issue can then move from a conversation focused solely on gender to a conversation around a lack of inclusion of key stakeholders, a resultant benefit being that funding for such programs is more easily attainable. Additionally, these programs tend to provide an opportunity for greater visibility of women's contributions and the tacit challenges that may be experienced. Furthermore, through this shared learning process, greater awareness around the additional responsibilities held by women is created. The primary benefit is that mixed programs tend to give rise to a general expanded awareness around the overt and implicit challenges faced by women in the workplace (Gurung et al. 2012). Furthermore, De la Rey et al. (2003,

52) established that women-only interventions "exacerbate the gendered leadership problem and contribute to the stereotypical idea that women are unsuccessful and ineffective leaders". The above authors assert that mixed gender programs aim to deter bias against women and aid in dissipating organizational stereotypes that exist around women in the workplace.

Therefore, while women-only leadership development programs are an effective means of developing women leaders, in order for there to be meaningful long-term change, these programs cannot occur in a bubble. Some research questions whether women-only development programs contribute to cultural change for gender equity (Tessens 2008). Additionally, gender-diverse interventions are important in that they create awareness for both women and men around the value of developing support for the women's environment to permit the women's success (Barakat et al. 2011). On their own, women-only programs cannot address the broader long-term cultural, organizational and societal changes that are required to achieve true gender equality. The message provided by Emma Watson of the HeForShe campaign (UNYANET 2014) asserts that "gender equality is not just a women's issue; it's a human rights issue that benefits everyone". A McKinsey report expands on this by stating that "gender equality at work is not possible without gender equality in society" (Woetzel et al. 2016).

Themes emerging from interviews

Additional interviews were conducted with respondents representative of the ICT and professional services industries who have implemented institutional interventions. The objective for these interviews was to establish how their organizations have responded, the efficacy of their interventions and the impact on delegates. The emergent themes follow hereunder.

Organizational interventions to advance women

When asked about specific organizational development interventions to advance women, respondents provided varied examples. Respondent Dion Shango acknowledged that "the need for more women in business and in leadership is a business imperative" and the firm thus had various initiatives in place to address this, namely, ensuring a 50:50 gender split at recruitment stage, a gender advisory council, mentoring programs and flexi-hours arrangements. Respondent Melanie Botha put forward a "women in leadership program" response, which entailed round tables of women leaders meeting to share their experiences. Interventions highlighted by another respondent, Gert Schoonbee, included an ICT academy to empower youth and specifically young women; an internship program where 50% of the interns were women; a supplier development and localization program, which aimed to develop suppliers with a specific focus on black women and black youth, and a "fair share" policy, which sought to address gender equality by increasing female representation in the highest decision-making positions within the business. Another organization created a gender advisory council, an active body at MANCO (management committee) level, which focused on addressing gender-specific issues.

Delving deeper into organizational interventions to advance women, when questioned about the pros and cons of women's leadership development programs versus interventions that were gender diverse and focused on creating gender balance, one respondent believed the pros around women-only leadership development programs were that they create an environment where women have the opportunity to learn and grow in relative safety—thereby entering the leadership arena on a level playing field—and that "they create an environment that embraces diversity and the unique qualities and leadership traits of women" (Schoonbee). Another respondent seconded these themes by stating that these programs provide a platform for women where they can feel safe to explore and learn about women in leadership challenges. In so doing, women also realize that they are not alone and that there are many similar women with similar challenges around them. The respondent continued by saying that "women find it more challenging to network; such a program does open a levelling playing field for women to learn how to network in a safe environment". Finally, such a program "provides an environment for senior women to be more open about their learnings and share more openly, as women would typically not ask questions around these learnings in a normal situation" (Botha).

Regarding the cons around women-only leadership development programs, Schoonbee believed that these programs could "create a mindset of exclusivity and further exclude women; they could be seen as competitive rather than inclusive" and that they could "set women apart as they do not always allow for integration into the mainstream". Botha provided insights around the response of men to such programs, stating that "certain men do frown upon such a program and top-talent men within the organization would ask why the program is also not available to them, resulting in buy-in being prohibited".

Efficacy of organizational interventions to advance women

A respondent commenting on the women-only leadership development program said the program was successful in creating awareness among the participants of the networking opportunities in their field and the potential for the development of supportive collaborative relationships. This realization created a confidence among the participants that was not previously there. When asked how the intervention could be made more effective the respondent suggested improved follow-through of projects to ensure the recommendations were implemented. When commenting on what contributed towards effective interventions, Schoonbee believed that the most effective interventions were those "that had direct sponsorship from an executive perspective", were implemented at board level, had visible achievements and benefits and, lastly, were "aligned with the core business imperatives" as well as within the South African context (National Development Plan). This last point, namely the link back to a macro-environmental context, is supported by examples from Turkey—one of the best-performing emerging market countries when it comes to the advancement of its women—where focused economic reforms have allowed more women to participate in the labor force (Hlalele 2013). When concluding commentary on effective interventions, Schoonbee stated that "stand-alone initiatives that were not relevant to the company, community or country" rarely succeeded. The successful interventions changed the internal perception of the organization with regard to equal opportunities and increased the organization's ability to retain high-level women employees. A further point provided by another respondent on the efficacy of organizational interventions was around the importance of measurement, which is supported by one of the findings of a study by Barsh and Yee (2012) on the factors which contribute towards women advancing to leading positions. Lastly, one respondent stated that a restricted budget due to macro-economic conditions, as well as the EXCO's (Executive Committee's) strategic focus on diversity (which is particularly relevant in the South African context) rather than gender, impacted on the possibility of gender interventions going ahead. Jahan and Mumtaz (1996) established that once institutionalized gender concerns became legitimate, they would receive access to regular budget provisions.

Case studies: gender-diverse versus women-only leadership development intervention

The previous section presented themes that emerged as a result of institutional interventions specific to the advancement of women. The following section describes two case studies of institutional interventions that were rolled out in organizations in South Africa over the period 2012–2015. One intervention was focused specifically around a gender-diverse approach (both genders were included in the exercise) and the other focused solely on women's leadership development.

Case study 1

Context and process of the intervention

One of the leading law firms in South Africa required an intervention that would enable them to become the role model firm in terms of gender balance. In addition, they required the contracted consulting firm to determine the underlying causes for any current gender disparity that might exist within the firm and identify ways in which these might be resolved. The required intervention needed specifically to explore the extent to which race played a role in gender issues, a subject that is of particular relevance in the South African context.

Using widely known change models such as Kotter's eight-step process (Kotter 1996) and the ADKAR model (Prosci 1994) as a base, the consulting company (hereinafter referred to as the consultants) developed a four-phase approach for firms that are intent on creating a gender-balanced environment. The phases are: Decipher; Determine; Design and Develop; Do and Redo. See Appendix 2 for a detailed description of each phase.

The first phase (Decipher) included 22 one-hour individual face-to-face interviews with key role players in order to deeply understand the current gender and racial disparity issues. These interviews were based on the recommendations listed in the findings of a previous transformation study that had been conducted in the firm, as well as on an informal internal survey regarding gender issues, which was conducted by senior women partners in the firm.

During the second phase of the process (Determine), the findings of the Decipher phase were presented to the partners in the firm in order to validate and confirm the current situation and to determine the ideal future scenario. General themes that had emerged from the initial interviews, as well as the latest findings from academic research on gender inclusiveness in the workplace, were also discussed.

The third phase (Design and Develop) involved the detailed design and development of the intervention—enabling the firm to move from its stated current position towards its envisioned future position regarding gender balance. The initiative was designed around small-group interventions that enabled participants to understand the impact and influence of their behavior. A series of facilitated dialoguing workshops was conducted, which aimed to allow participants to share their lived experience of being a white/black/female/male employee at the law firm.

Results of the intervention

INTERVIEWS WITH KEY FEMALE AND MALE ROLE PLAYERS IN THE ORGANIZATION

Four main themes emerged when interviewees were asked why the firm should be concerned with creating a gender-balanced environment. These are presented below with selected insights from interviewees quoted along with each theme.

- The desire to create the best firm: "Women are the future of law and we want to attract the best. This is based on university statistics and the way that the world is going. Law needs women behaving like women and we need to attract the best women."

- Right thing to do—it's a moral imperative: "It would not be a great place to work if you knew that half your staff felt prejudiced against and unfairly treated."
- Future of the firm, and recognition of the industry trends and changing graduate and client profile: "By making it difficult for women we are probably cutting out the best talent. I don't want to work in an environment with racists and bigots. I want robust conversation, accommodating all views. This is my future ideal state."
- Desire to create a firm that values diversity and where everyone feels valued: "It needs to be comfortable for the women who are here so that they are encouraged to stay on in the long term."

Furthermore, gender stereotypes and organizational culture stood out as being the two areas within the firm where the majority of the 19 respondents who completed a ranking exercise felt gender imbalance was most obvious in the firm (Appendix 3):

There is the perception that just because you are a woman you may not be ambitious. Women want kids and a career. Your value to the firm is the fees that you write. If you do not write the fees that you are required to then there is no way you will have any influence.

The perception right through the organization is that women will do the softer work and won't get their hands dirty. For example, as department heads, senior partners assume more litigation work should go to their male colleagues. This perception is also with the clients so the situation is perpetuated.

It is not a culture that tries to promote the importance of women. There was no lady speaking at the year-end function.

It is difficult to build and maintain a close network of women because they leave and then the hard culture is perpetuated.

FACILITATED DIALOGUING WORKSHOPS WITH FEMALE AND MALE PARTICIPANTS THROUGHOUT THE ORGANIZATION

Many participants expressed how valuable the power of shared experiences was during the facilitated dialoguing workshop phase. Participants came to realize that they were not alone in certain lived experiences at the firm and, as a result, their reactions to these experiences were "normalized." Feedback by one of the participants was: "[It was interesting to learn] that men and women have similar experiences and pressures."

The perceptions of both men and women were challenged, and both male and female respondents were surprised by some of the insights shared by their colleagues. Women were surprised that several men felt both vulnerable and anxious in some circumstances, and experienced difficulties in managing careers and families. Men, on the other hand, were surprised that women had to think about when to have a baby and how that decision would impact on their careers. The men were also horrified at the effect that seemingly harmless sexual innuendo and foul language had on their female colleagues. They felt, however, that they did not know how to address these particular issues without alienating themselves from the male "in-group" at the company. "People brought up certain issues that I did not even know were problems or at least serious problems. Certain problems that were brought up are trivialized in an ordinary business day."

Groups appreciated and were pleasantly surprised by each other's willingness to listen and engage meaningfully with topics that had previously been taboo in open forums, and there was a general recognition that racial, gender and age diversity all impacted each individual's experience within the firm. Individuals expressed that, in the workshops, they felt that there was a general appreciation of each other's perspectives:

> It was liberating and very informative to hear the diverging perspectives from participants. It certainly opened my eyes and awareness levels to hear these first-hand and to experience the emotion in many cases. These perspectives and views must be given 'air time' if we want to be an inclusive working environment.

In the last part of each workshop, small-group discussions were facilitated to consider actions that were identified together by male and female participants and to which each participant would commit on an individual, team and organizational level. The general themes were largely representative of current thinking around the general enablers and disablers of women's progress in organizations and did not appear to be influenced by the organization being set in an emergent market environment. However, there were some actions specific to responding to racial discrimination that were specific to South Africa's history.

Insights and analysis

The insights gained by the consultants on conclusion of the intervention, and supported by the feedback received from many participants was as follows.

MORAL OBLIGATION

The majority of interviewees displayed a long-term mindset and a deep sense of obligation and willingness to do their best for the firm, although in some cases there was a perception that respondents were "towing the party line" and responding in a politically correct manner. The majority of people, however, expressed gratitude to management for embarking on the process of creating gender balance. In addition to the recognition of the moral obligation of creating a firm where everyone felt included, there was a deep desire to create a firm that not only tolerated but also appreciated and celebrated diversity. There was insightful respect for the value that women bring to the workplace—and this was from the majority of the male respondents as well as the female respondents. A strong theme that emerged was the imperative to move away from the existing "discriminatory" way of being into a future state where each person could achieve his or her potential.

AWARENESS OF GENDER INEQUALITY AFTER APPOINTMENT

While it was important to understand where respondents felt gender imbalance was most obvious, it was also valuable to acknowledge what was working well. The perception from the interviewees was that the firm had the ability to recruit, train and on-board very equitably; however, once people were in the firm, respondents saw more gender inequality: "As a firm we seemingly have the best and brightest candidates and the women who we recruit are often top of their class. However, within a year or two of coming into the firm, they seem to lose their confidence."

The respondents noted that the five areas where gender equality was most prominent in the firm were around:

- recruitment practices;
- learning and skills development;
- little evidence of the Queen Bee[3] syndrome;
- induction and on-boarding support, which was generally felt to be fair and equitable;
- promotion opportunities.

GENDER STEREOTYPES AND ORGANIZATIONAL CULTURE

As discussed earlier, gender stereotypes and organizational culture emerged as the two main areas within the firm where gender imbalance was most obvious. As a result, it was imperative that to begin creating a gender-balanced firm, the intervention needed to focus on these aspects.

Recommendations

The above process was a useful step in raising awareness around the obvious and hidden realities of people's lived experiences of gender imbalance within the organization. It resulted in participants acknowledging the need to more consciously drive the gender-balance initiative and allow it to keep its momentum. In order to continue momentum, the consultants proposed the following three initial actions for consideration by the firm.

STRATEGIC PROCESS

This would focus on the effective implementation of various policies— namely, flexible work arrangements, a mentor-mentee program and maternity leave conditions. Furthermore, it was noted that it would be valuable to incorporate education around what constitutes sexual harassment in the workplace and the appropriateness versus risk thereof.

SENIOR WOMEN'S VISIBLE SUPPORT NETWORK

Women directors could meet monthly so as to create a very strong network between them, and in the cases where there was already an existing strong network, it would be important for junior women to obtain a sense of the support that senior women provide for each other. This could and should be consciously modeled by senior women so that juniors could learn from the behavior. It could take either an informal or a formal approach.

CONTINUATION OF WORKSHOPS

It was proposed that a two-hour facilitated session be held every two months. This would be open to anyone who had been on a workshop or to anyone who was not able to attend the previous workshops but who was interested in being part of the process. It was proposed that the consultants would provide external facilitators who would touch base around what had shifted, what had been done, what actions (personal, team, organization) had been taken, so as to keep the conversation going. This formed the final phase—Do and Redo.

Conclusion

The firm subsequently contracted the consultants to provide a brief intervention with junior staff, but they decided not to pursue the workshops. They did not provide the official reasons for this decision; however, it appeared as if the driving reason was the lack of true executive support for the initiative. The minority of partners were prepared to really support this initiative, while the rest were most likely "towing the party line" with no real burning platform to drive a sustainable change in this area. It became apparent that the mostly male EXCO (executive committee) was still not convinced about the significant economic opportunity that a more gender-equal environment represents.

Case study 2

Context and process of the intervention

The consulting company was approached by the South African branch of a global IT firm to assist the company in partnering with them in the area of women's leadership development. After establishing the strategic priorities around gender within the organization, the consultants delivered, first, a two-day seminar for 65 women, followed by two consecutive leadership development programs specifically for women. The design principles for the program were underpinned by the latest trends in women's leadership development—namely, in addition to general leadership content, there was a requirement that women's leadership development programs consist of the following elements: a link to higher purpose, the sensitization to second-degree gender bias and the concept of small group coaching circles to anchor the program. A combination of several learning methodologies was used, specifically:

- interrogation of the latest academic research with experts in their fields;
- experiential learning, which heightened the participants' sense of social responsibility, provided an awareness of mentoring opportunities and presented an important view of women's history in South Africa;
- action learning, whereby delegates, working in teams, solved real business challenges using a rigorous research process and presented their solutions to the company executive on conclusion of the program.

The above blend ensured that there was both a personal and organizational return on investment from the program.

Delegates underwent a structured application process in order to be accepted onto the programs. Demand was higher than there were places so the consultants designed a formal written application and facilitated an observed interactive group session. Both programs were held over six months, with classes taking place for one or two full days per month. The content within each two-day module was designed to enable learning about self, the context of being a woman in South Africa, impact on others, and contribution going forward. Several readings were prescribed for each module in order to support the above overarching themes.

In the first module, the theme of women in leadership in South Africa and abroad was introduced. The leadership model used in the program was the "transactional, transformational and transcendental" model based on theory by Cardona (2000) and Sarros and Santona (2001), explaining how different leadership behaviors are appropriate in different contexts. A session on systems thinking early on in the program was fundamental to reinforcing the application of tools in both personal and organizational contexts. During each module, small-group coaching circles took place in which coaches applied different coaching tools throughout the process to help delegates explore themselves and their roles in the organization. The first session explored each delegate's personal history and the leadership skills and behaviors used to overcome personal and business challenges. The aim of this sharing was to create a collaborative support network amongst the delegates in order for them to assist each other in their career paths.

The consultants discovered during the interview process that the majority of delegates had complex personal/work life balance situations that they were grappling to manage, and hence the consultants built in a session on role management during the second module to assist the delegates with managing their complex situations better. From previous experiences, the consultants established that the basis of women's leadership development is centered on their ability to manage and understand their own financial situation, thus a session on financial planning was included. This was complemented by a visioning/dream-boarding exercise that allowed delegates to use the left side of their brains, with the intention of more freely accessing aspects that are not easily retrieved with the right side of the brain. The second coaching circle focused on positive and shadow aspects of each delegate in order to deepen self-awareness and understand why they behave in a certain manner.

Module three opened with a full-day experiential, including the third coaching circle. The experiential learning day had two main aims: first, an immersion into different/unknown contexts, and second, leadership in action. In order to achieve these aims, the immersion took the form of an Amazing Race. The groups worked in their coaching groups and were given a series of tasks that led the delegates from their comfortable northern-suburbs offices into the inner city and somewhat grittier areas of Johannesburg. The element of competition raised the stakes and the teams ended their journey by delivering a business plan to a non-profit organization. Participants were debriefed in the coaching circle, where leadership behaviors were analyzed and discussed.

A session on strategic thinking in module four focused on a practical method of converting strategic thinking into action. The process took the delegates through a set of questions and, by using their own examples, they were able to produce action plans for their strategies. The purpose of this session was to act as a subtle reminder that the program delegates were responsible for leading not only themselves but also the business, and needed to remain aware of their environmental context and the dynamics within an emerging market. The fourth coaching circle allowed some flexibility around content as the consultants wanted to allow the coaches and delegates the opportunity to engage with each other in areas that were specific to the needs of each particular circle. The platform from which the sessions grew was focused on the ability to share honest feedback with each other in order to grow and acknowledge each other's strengths (with individuals sometimes not able to see their own strengths). The next step was to commit to particular actions going forward and allow the group to hold each other accountable for implementation.

Module five included a session on resilience in which the term "resilience" was defined and then the content evolved towards illustrating how resilience could be enhanced, how challenges could be turned into opportunities, how one could leverage change and bounce back from adversity. A session on body brilliance enabled a better understanding of the connection between one's physical and emotional states.

The final module incorporated a session on personal branding and leadership, which touched on the importance of communicating a powerful brand, how to define one's brand through powerful storytelling, the importance of being consistent in expressing one's personal brand, the value of networking and personal and professional interaction.

Throughout all the modules, the delegates underwent an action learning process. The "business challenge" was an opportunity for the delegates to increase and demonstrate their leadership skills via a stretch assignment. Small-group projects, focusing on a genuine organizational challenge, centered around a development process which ensured an application of learning and developed new skills among delegates. Each topic was underpinned by one of the organization's current strategic imperatives and each team had a project sponsor from the executive who supported the team throughout their action-learning journey. During each module of the program, the groups were required to do a five-minute presentation to the class on their progress. This was followed by a peer-feedback session where the other teams provided suggestions for the group to consider going forward. Small-group business challenge coaching sessions were held between each module to allow teams and business challenge coaches to check in on project progress and discuss team dynamics. The final module concluded with the teams presenting their projects to an executive panel which assessed each team against an evaluation rubric, provided feedback and discussed next steps for piloting or implementation of the projects within the organization.

The program was completed with a concluding celebratory dinner and an award process which recognized people who, in the opinion of their peers: 1) contributed most to the learning of the group—that is, the person who challenged the status quo and conventional wisdom by her questions as well as her actions—and 2) demonstrated the most growth in terms of leadership behavior during the course.

In order to cement the potential learning shifts gained from the program, the delegates were asked to evaluate the sessions at the end of each module. They were specifically asked to provide feedback around what they found most useful about the sessions, aspects of the session that could be improved, things that they may be thinking differently about and what they learned about themselves.

Results of the intervention

The general feedback centered around the value of learning about oneself, the value of giving support to and using support from work colleagues, the opportunity to explore possibilities within the organization using different approaches and tools, and also having the courage to do so.

A selection of quotes is noted below.

WHAT DID I FIND MOST USEFUL ABOUT THE SESSION?

"The great wealth of insight in looking at what's composing our systems and the span of control we have in making some positive changes."

"How systems thinking can be applied in solving business/personal problems. How to tackle dilemmas so that you can move away from being stuck."

"Challenged my current thoughts and encouraged me to explore possibilities for the future. Taught me a new paradigm—a new way of thinking about problems. Less narrow view of issues and resolution."

"Strong visual impact with real touching examples."

"How amazing to be exposed to this info and connect with the group in a way I haven't before."

GENERAL COMMENTS

"Opening up, learning that the people you work with all have their own challenges and we are women who need to support each other. I have a new love and appreciation for my coaching circle. It also taught me to be vulnerable and share."

"I am finding a difference already in how my team is responding to the subtle yet important changes I am making."

"The program was a thought-provoking experience and incredible journey for me. It proved to be a valuable outlet to exchange ideas with other women."

"The program has been an experience that I will not easily forget—for many reasons. Today, I truly feel enabled to strengthen my position as a leader in business. I, now, have a great desire to leave a legacy in both my professional and personal life."

"I managed to form new meaningful relationships with women in the business that would otherwise not have been possible without the program."

"Great to meet others in the business who actually helped us with our own roles."

The experiential off-site component of the program provided the opportunity for delegates to hold conversations with women entrepreneurs from the inner city of Johannesburg, learning about their challenges as women trying to succeed in the informal sector and how they, in turn, were supporting and uplifting girls and women in their immediate communities. This experience enabled the delegates to acknowledge that an internal understanding better equipped them to understand and make sense of their external environment, with particular relevance to the specific context of an emerging market.

Upon completion of the program, the delegates appeared to have increased their leadership efficacy, improved their business acumen and had a much deeper understanding of themselves and the environments in which they functioned.

Insights and analysis

The insights gained by the consultants on conclusion of the programs and supported by the feedback received from many participants were as follows.

EXECUTIVE/SENIOR LEADERSHIP SUPPORT

One of the reasons for the powerful and positive impact of the women's leadership development programs at the particular IT firm was that they were a key item on the executive's strategic agenda; the executive team was visible and expressed interest throughout the duration of each program. The research of Mattis (2001) confirmed that retaining and advancing women in corporate management requires a sustained and coordinated commitment from the top of organizations.

Frequent feedback was received from the delegates around their acknowledging the importance of feeling supported by the organization and fellow women colleagues. Mattis (2001) recounts an example from Bank of Montreal that in order to retain and advance women, ongoing support from the bank's chief executive and other senior leaders was practiced. Barsh and Yee (2012) second this by stating that top management must be visibly committed to achieving gender-diversity goals, and senior leaders should be held accountable for developing opportunities for women in their talent pool.

INFLUENCE AND INVOLVEMENT OF SENIOR-LEVEL WOMEN

The women's leadership portfolio at the IT firm was actively driven by a female executive member. Again Mattis (2001) provides an example from Procter & Gamble around their Advancement of Women initiative. A key success factor in the implementation of the initiative was the strategies that Procter & Gamble used to build senior-level commitment and ownership for action. Of particular interest was the fact that a woman general manager led the task force managing the initiative, and a sector president and senior vice-president were active sponsors. Research by Van Heerden (2015) found that female board and executive-level representation is critical to bringing awareness to boardrooms in order for companies to implement structures in support of female advancement in the workplace.

NETWORKING AND MENTORING

The value gained from creating new networks and building supportive relationships was visibly apparent on conclusion of the program. A new system was introduced by the consultants for the second program; namely, that the graduates from the first program each had to mentor a delegate during her attendance for the full duration of the second program. The feedback received from both mentor and mentee confirmed the benefits that were gained from this relationship.

Gordon and Whelan (1998) explain many ways in which organizations can more effectively understand and respond to the challenges facing successful women in the midlife of their careers. Their one particular point focused on the importance of encouraging women to act as mentors to younger women and building a culture that supports networking and leadership roles for women.

Morahan et al. (2011) propose that certain interventions, including equipping women and increasing visibility, were needed to assist women in the management of their career transitions and to advance and sustain the success of women in executive positions. Hewlett and Rashid (2010) state that networking and relationship-building, essential to strengthening engagement and commitment, helped women develop the ties, visibility, and organizational know-how essential to professional success.

Sherwin (2014) discusses the benefit of formal mentoring programs, stating that organizations should work toward getting more senior leaders to give more mentoring and assistance to talented women inside the firm. The organization needs to support the creation of women's groups that can provide opportunities for women to be with those who face the same dilemmas and exchange solutions for coping with these demands.

BARRIERS TO WOMEN'S ADVANCEMENT

While delegates appreciated discovering more about the root causes that have prevented women from being great leaders, these may have been relatively overt and more invisible barriers may not have surfaced (for example, gender bias, corporate culture and stereotypes). The result is that women are not necessarily equipped to recognize and respond to all the barriers to their advancement. This is further aggravated by the fact that the social context, education and economic environments of South Africa were found to be underlying contributors to the failure of women's advancement (Van Heerden 2015).

Conclusion

While it is interesting to note that some of these themes also emerged from the interviews, the above observations are further supported by a McKinsey (2012) study, which found that gender diversity is best supported within an ecosystem consisting of three parts. The first part is management commitment, which includes CEO commitment, senior management commitment, target-setting and actions to increase men's awareness of gender-diversity issues. The second part involves women's development programs and refers to actions such as networking events, external coaches and mentoring programs. Finally, the third part is a set of enablers, including salary differences, attrition rates and overall gender representation.

Recommendations

On conclusion of the project with the client, the consultants noted the following, which would be useful considerations to ensure even greater success in future women's leadership development interventions:

- The "head, heart and hands"(H^3) approach to leadership development contributes to the powerful impact of such a program. Inclusion of academic content encouraged application and reflection at a cognitive level and this was positively countered by the coaching and experiential components, which entailed a deeper emotional response. The action-learning element completed the H^3 triangle with a more action-focused approach.
- Executive commitment and buy-in.
- Pre-program communication to all stakeholders, setting context.
- What about the men who are not participating in the program—how to garner support?
- Should the program include more content and discussion around the invisible barriers and provide mechanisms on how to overcome these (gender bias, corporate culture and stereotypes)?
- It is critical that the experiential exercise in an emerging market in particular is not simply a window-dressing exercise but that it is conducted with positive intent and will result in sustainable impact for the hosting party within the informal sector.

Application: framework for institutional interventions

When considering the merits of the different types of institutional interventions, namely women-only leadership development programs versus gender-diverse women's leadership development interventions, and based on the resultant information from the interviews as well as outcomes from the two case studies, the authors of this chapter strongly recommend a blended approach. This blended approach would include two central components—namely, women's leadership development programs as the foundation, supplemented by gender-diverse dialoguing workshops. This proposed approach is based on women's leadership development global best practice and centers around the themes of leading self, leading others, leading in business and society. The approach follows an appreciative inquiry philosophy—thereby enabling organizations to leverage what is working well in their environments instead of focusing only on what is wrong or what is not working. Firms that harness the collective intelligence of their workforce show better results (Catalyst 2013) and the approach is underpinned with that type of collaborative mindset at its core. The process would typically result in a rigorous learning and development program with measurable outcomes for both the individual and the organization.

Each of the components is expanded on below.

Women's leadership development programs

When considering providing in-depth women's leadership development programs tailored to the different levels of participants (that is, executive, senior leadership group, extended leadership team and lower levels if requested) within the context of an emerging market, the following approach is recommended. The proposed overarching program architecture would, of course, be tailored to the organization; however, it would include content about networking, sponsorship, mentoring, financial acumen, strategic thinking, female and male leadership archetypes, and, where possible, an experiential component so as to provide a deeper understanding of leadership within the context of an emerging economy and the various dynamics emerging therefrom. The experiential learning component would have two main aims: first, an immersion into different/ unknown contexts, particularly relevant in an emerging market, and, second, an opportunity to demonstrate and practice leadership in action. Furthermore, and as expanded on in the second case study, the design principles employed would be underpinned by the latest trends in women's leadership development and the program design would combine several learning methodologies.

What has proved to have resounding impact in such programs is the small-group coaching circles, which create an environment where relationships with trusted peers can emerge—a vital link in enabling women to identify themselves as leaders. In this space, delegates are provided with the opportunity to reflect on their impact, become more aware of their strengths, development areas and blind spots, and learn how their invisible intentions translate into visible behaviors. The benefits of the coaching circles are that delegates appear to become much more reflective and aware of their impact on others.

The action-learning component provides an opportunity for real business problems to be solved by the delegates, enabling them to work on their identified development areas and reflect on their general process of learning. This provides the delegates with an opportunity to increase and demonstrate their leadership skills and it contributes a visible return on financial investment for the organization.

In order to blend the previously two opposing approaches it is recommended that one of the modules within the above program is a gender-diverse dialoguing workshop.

Gender-diverse dialoguing workshops

Within the women's leadership development program, a series of workshops is recommended in order to gain stakeholder buy-in and provide an environment where dialogue can take place, which will enable a deeper understanding of others' lived experiences. Workshops would be facilitated by a pair of facilitators, each pair being gender and racially diverse (this being particularly relevant within a South African context). The aim of the workshops would be for participants to share their lived experience of being a white/black/female/male employee at the organization. Based on previous successes, the suggested tools and methodology to design and support the process would be as follows:

- a combination of academic theory and tools provided by the Organization and Relationship Systems Coaching (ORSC) method;
- theory focusing on Arnold Mindell's work around rank, power and privilege;
- integration of the McKinsey (2012) findings on corporate culture being the most important barrier when trying to create a gender-balanced workplace.

Finally, it is important to note that the initial program should be followed up at least every four to six weeks by a session that embeds the initial concepts and assists individuals, teams and organizations to overcome the current reality of a lack of female representation at all levels of the business.

Conclusion

To conclude, this chapter has focused on a comparison of institution-level interventions in women's leadership by reviewing some of the literature, presenting themes that emerged from interviews with key figures in particular industries in South Africa and providing case studies of how two organizations responded to the opportunity to advance their women into leadership positions in order to create a more gender-balanced workplace. The two contrasting approaches were analyzed and the resultant deduction presented in this chapter is that the two approaches do not necessarily oppose each other and are more powerful in combination. The chapter is closed by offering practical ideas to readers about how they may wish to design and implement such institution-level interventions within their own context.

Appendices

Appendix 1: The consulting company's bespoke four-phase approach for firms that are intent on creating a gender-balanced environment

1   Decipher: This phase includes face-to-face interviews with key role players in order to deeply understand the current gender and racial disparity issues. These interviews are based on any recommendations emerging from any internal transformation studies, as well as an informal internally conducted survey regarding gender issues.

2   Determine: During the second phase of the process, the findings of the Decipher phase are presented to a wider audience (as decided by the steering committee) in order to validate and confirm the current situation and to determine the ideal future scenario. Frequently, at this point, the consulting company is asked to identify the steps likely to occur in phase 2. Because these are heavily influenced by the outcomes of phase 1, it is difficult to predict these with certainty, but this step typically involves a series of workshops in order to gain stakeholder buy-in—the critical mass in order to gain buy-in is typically 75% of staff. The optimal number of staff per workshop is usually between 12 and 16. The required number of workshops would be determined by a steering committee and the decision would be based on the level of the firm that the intervention needs to address. The most important outcome of phase 2 is the development of a powerful coalition of true change agents—those formal and informal leaders within the firm who will drive the gender-balance initiative and allow it to keep its momentum.

3   Design and Develop: This step involves the detailed design and development of the intervention—enabling the firm to move from its stated current position to its envisioned future position regarding gender balance. The initiatives would typically be based on the latest research regarding creating gender-balanced firms and would include interventions such as sensitization to second-generation gender bias as well as small group interventions that enable participants to understand the impact and influence of their behavior. The outcomes of this phase are a clear future vision for what a gender-balanced firm would look like, the culture and the environment of the firm.

4   Do and Redo: During this step, the plans that were designed and agreed upon in the previous step are implemented and constantly evaluated in terms of efficacy and suitability, and the necessary changes made as circumstances dictate.

Appendix 2: Ranked dimensions of gender imbalance of Abbellard (2016)

Rank	Dimension
1	Gender stereotypes
2	Organizational culture
3	Mentoring and sponsorship
4	Family responsibility (flexible time)
5	Networking
6	Excessive modesty (lack of ability to promote oneself)
7	Committed leadership
8	Accountability and representation
9	Work allocation
10	Performance appraisal and management
11	Equal pay
12	Promotion opportunities
13	Induction and on-boarding support
14	Queen Bee syndrome
15	Learning and skills development
16	Recruitment practices

With permission from: Clark, D., and Hawarden, V. 2016. Unpublished consulting documents from Abbellard, "Ranked dimensions of gender imbalance." Abbellard Consulting, Johannesburg.

Notes

1 Gender-diverse program/intervention: in the context of this chapter, this refers to a program or intervention that includes both female and male participants and which is designed specifically around the topic of creating gender balance and/or women's leadership development within organizations.

2 Second-generation gender bias: Ibarra, Ely and Kolb (2013) established this as the primary cause of women's persistent under-representation in leadership roles. They stated that this bias erects powerful but subtle and often invisible barriers for women that arise from cultural assumptions and organizational structures, practices, and patterns of interaction that inadvertently benefit men while putting women at a disadvantage. Among them are a paucity of role models for women, gendered career paths and gendered work, women's lack of access to networks and sponsors, and "double binds" (the mismatch between conventionally feminine qualities and the qualities thought necessary for leadership puts female leaders in a double bind).

3 Queen Bee syndrome: Baumgartner and Schneider (2010) discovered that women who experience difficulty breaking through the glass ceiling turn to the successful women in management for support, only to find that it does not exist. Queen Bee syndrome is described as the phenomenon whereby women who have made it to the top find reasons not to help other women aspiring to break through the glass ceiling. Orser, Riding and Stanley (2012) found that gender issues arose from other women as well as from men, and that once women have broken the glass ceiling, they quickly seal it shut to other women.

References

Barakat, S., Rigozzi, M., Boddington, M. and McLellan, R. 2011. "Enterprise-WISE: Making WISE women more enterprising?" Working paper presented at the Institute of Small Business and Entrepreneurship conference, Cambridge, November 2012.

Barsh, J. and Yee, L. 2012. In Van Wyk, R. 2012. "Women in Executive Positions: Managing Career Transitions." MBA thesis, Gordon Institute of Business and University of Pretoria, South Africa.

Baumgartner, M. S. and Schneider, D. E. 2010. "Perceptions of Women in Management: A Thematic Analysis of Razing the Glass Ceiling." *Journal of Career Development* 37(2): 559–576.

Cardona, P. 2000. "Transcendental Leadership." *Leadership and Organization Development Journal* 21(4): 201–206.

Catalyst. 2013. "Why diversity matters." Accessed September 30, 2013. www.catalyst.org/knowledge/why-diversity-matters.

Clark, D. and Hawarden, V. 2016. Unpublished consulting documents from Abbellard on "Ranked dimensions of gender imbalance." Abbellard Consulting, Johannesburg.

Colantuono, S. 2016. "News and Insights about Closing the Leadership Gender Gap." Accessed February 10, 2016. www.leadingwomen.biz/blog/bid/73237/Recipes-for-Mentoring-Success-CAKE-and-PIE.

Condon, N., Stern, M. and Truen, S. 2009. "Professional Services in South Africa: Accounting, Engineering and Law." *Development Network Africa.* Accessed May 2, 2016. www.dnaeconomics.com/assets/Usegareth/SA_Professional_Services.pdf.

De la Rey, C., Jankelowitz, G. and Suffla, S. 2003. "Women's Leadership Programs in South Africa: A Strategy for Community Intervention." *Journal of Prevention & Intervention in the Community* 25(1): 49–64. Accessed May 8, 2016. http://repository.up.ac.za/bitstream/handle/2263/14298/DeLaRey_Womens(2003).pdf?sequence=1.

Ely, R. J., Ibarra, H. and Kolb, D. M. 2011. "Taking Gender into account: theory and design for women's leadership development programs." *Academy of Management Learning and Education* 10(3): 474–493.

Gauteng Province. 2010. "Gauteng ICT Development Strategy Draft." Accessed January 19, 2016. www.ecodev.gpg.gov.za/policies/Documents/Gauteng%20ICT%20Strategy.pdf.

Gillwald, A., Moyo, M. and Stork, C. 2012. "Understanding What Is Happening in ICT in South Africa." Evidence for ICT Policy Action Policy Paper 7, Research ICT Africa. Accessed January 19, 2016. www.researchictafrica.net/publications/Evidence_for_ICT_Policy_Action/Policy_Paper_7_-_Understanding_what_is_happening_in_ICT_in_South_Africa.pdf.

Gordon, J.R. and Whelan, K.S. 1998. "Successful Professional Women in Midlife: How Organizations Can More Effectively Understand and Respond to the Challenges." *Academy of Management Executive* 12(1): 8–27.

Gurung, J., Hytönen, L. and Pathak, B. 2012. "Scoping Dialogue on the Exclusion and Inclusion of Women in the Forest Sector". Summary Report. September, 22–24, Kathmandu. Accessed May 9, 2016. http://theforestsdialogue.org/sites/default/files/tfd_eiw_nepal_co-chairssummary_en.pdf.

Hewlett, S.A. and Rashid, R. 2010. "The Battle for Female Talent in Emerging Markets." *Harvard Business Review* 88(5):101–106.

Hlalele, A. 2013. "The MBA as a key contributor towards women's career advancement: an emerging versus developed market perspective." MBA thesis. Gordon Institute of Business and University of Pretoria, South Africa.

Ibarra, H., Ely, R. and Kolb, D. 2013. "Women Rising: The Unseen Barriers." *Harvard Business Review* 91(9): 60–66.

Jahan, R. and Mumtaz, S. 1996. "The Elusive Agenda: Mainstreaming Women in Development." *Pakistan Development Review* 35(4): 825–834.

James, T., Esselaar, P. and Miller, J. 2001. "Towards a Better Understanding of the ICT Sector in South Africa: Problems and Opportunities for Strengthening the Existing Knowledge Base." Trade and Industry Policy Strategies. Accessed January 19, 2016. www.tips.org.za/files/towards_a_better_understanding_of_the_ICT_sector_in_south_africa.pdf.

Kotter, J. 1996. "The 8-step Process for Leading Change." *Kotter International.* Accessed January 19, 2016. www.kotterinternational.com/the-8-step-process-for-leading-change/.

Mahomed, F. 2015. "S. Africa's ICT sector lacks critical skills." *CNBC Africa.* Accessed January 19, 2016.www.cnbcafrica.com/news/southern-africa/2014/11/18/south-africa-ict-skills-shortage/.

Mattis, M. C. 2001. "Advancing Women in Business Organizations: Key Leadership Roles and Behaviors of Senior Leaders and Middle Managers." *Journal of Management Development* 20(4): 371–388.

MBendi. 2016. "Professional Services in South Africa: Legal Services." Accessed May 3, 2016. www.mbendi.com/indy/psrv/lawf/af/sa/p0005.htm.

McKinsey. (2012). "Women Matter 2012: Making the Breakthrough." Accessed January 31, 2016. www.mckinsey.com/client_service/organisation/latest_thinking/women_matter.

Morahan, P. S., Rosen, S. E., Richman, R. C. and Gleason, K. A. Cited in Van Wyk, R. 2012. "Women in Executive Positions: Managing Career Transitions." MBA thesis, Gordon Institute of Business and University of Pretoria, South Africa.

Orser, B., Riding, A. and Stanley, J. 2012. "Perceived Career Challenges and Response Strategies of Women in the Advanced Technology Sector." *Entrepreneurship and Regional Development* 24(1/2): 73–93.

Prosci. 1994. "ADKAR Change Management Model Overview." Accessed January 19, 2016. www.prosci.com/adkar/adkar-model.

Sarros, J. C. and Santora, J. C. 2001. "The Transformational—Transactional Leadership Model in Practice." *Leadership and Organization Development Journal* 22(8): 383–394.

Sherwin, B. 2014. "How Companies Can Get More Women In Leadership Roles." *Business Insider.* Accessed January 31, 2016. www.businessinsider.com/how-companies-can-advance-women-in-leadership-2014-1.

Tessens, L. (2008) "A Review of Current Practices in Women-only Staff Development Programs at Australian Universities." University of Western Australia, Perth.

Thomas, S. 2015. "FM Fox: An incredible journey. Profile: Dion Shango." *Financial Mail.* Accessed January 21, 2016. www.financialmail.co.za/fmfox/2015/11/26/profile-dion-shango.

UN Women. 2010. "UN Global Compact: UN Women—Women's Empowerment Principles." Accessed October 13, 2015. www.weprinciples.org/Site/PrincipleO verview/.

UNYANET (United Nations Youth Associations Network). 2014. "Why Gender Quality is Everyone's Issue." Accessed February 15, 2016. http://blog.unyanet. org/why-gender-equality-is-everyones-issue/.

Van Heerden, A. 2015." An Investigation into the Organizational and Behavioural Factors that Influence the Advancement of Women to Senior Positions in the Workplace." MBA thesis. Gordon Institute of Business and University of Pretoria, South Africa.

Woetzel, J., Madgavkar, A., Ellingrud, K., Labaye, E., Devillard, S., Kutcher, E., Manyika, J., Dobbs, R. and Krishnan, M. 2016. "How Advancing Women's Equality Can Add $12 Trillion to Global Growth." McKinsey Global Institute. Accessed February 15, 2016. www.mckinsey.com/global-themes/employment-a nd-growth/how-advancing-womens-equality-can-add-12-trillion-to-global-growth.

6 Workplace barriers faced by women leaders in emerging markets

Jasmien Khattab and Ashleigh Shelby Rosette

Introduction

Given a plethora of gender and leadership research over the past few decades, we now understand a great deal about the various obstacles that can prohibit women from advancing in their careers to top leadership positions. Women who aim for high positions in their respective organizations must navigate a labyrinth of leadership barriers filled with complexities and challenges (Eagly and Carli 2007), contend with the proverbial glass ceiling (Catalyst 2016; Cook and Glass 2014; Glass and Cook 2016), and struggle with appointments to precarious leadership positions (i.e. the glass cliff; Ryan and Haslam 2007; Ryan et al. 2011; Ryan et al. forthcoming). However, much of the existing research is overwhelmingly based on Western populations from developed countries and the predominant norms and values of Western culture (Cuddy et al. 2015). Whether women in emerging markets who have successfully worked their way to the top of their organizations experience comparable or distinct barriers compared to women in developed countries warrants investigation.

On the one hand, women in emerging markets may be presented with more opportunities than their female peers in developed markets. For example, several developing countries, such as Brazil, Chile, and South Korea, each have a female head of state, suggesting the possibility of substantial career advancement opportunities for women. Additionally, a *Financial Times* report (Khalaf 2014) shows that in emerging markets, a greater number of boards of directors of large public companies are chaired by a woman, compared to industrialized markets. Similarly, higher percentages of women occupy senior executive positions in Africa (27%) and in Asian countries, such as Indonesia (36%) and China (30%), than in North America (23%) or the European Union (24%) (Grant Thornton, 2016).

On the other hand, in developing markets, women's rights and opportunities can be severely limited. Discriminatory national policies in emerging markets—compared to industrialized markets—more often form barriers to education, financial access, and equal pay for women. Societal and cultural norms and family- and female-nonfriendly business environments can also constrain women's societal and organizational status (*The Economist* 2012). For instance, in China, family pressures and expectations for women to prioritize their children and the elderly in the family can cause women to leave their jobs (Khalad 2014). Moreover, women in developing countries are still lagging behind men in terms of educational opportunities (Khalad 2014).

While these cited media reports provide some insights into the rate of women's promotion to top positions in emerging markets, the contradictory reporting can be confusing and does not capture women's personal experiences on the job. Therefore, we focus on specific cases of women who have successfully worked their way to the top of their respective organizations. Our research findings suggest that women from emerging markets in our sample face comparable barriers to those experienced by women leaders in developed countries. This chapter provides an overview of the obstacles encountered by the interviewed women in their ascent through the organizational ranks in order to gain a better understanding of the collective experiences of women leaders in emerging markets. The result of our extensive analysis is a qualitative account of the barriers that the women featured in this book have faced and continue to encounter in the workplace.

Gender bias in the workplace

Social science research provides plenty of evidence suggesting women's experiences of significant barriers that prevent them from achieving workplace equity. Not only do women receive less pay for the same work (Christofides et al. 2013; World Economic Forum 2015), they are also underrepresented in senior and top leadership positions. This skewed representation is frequently caused by biased processes in the workplace. For example, stereotypes can influence much of the social interaction at work and the development of organizational policies (DeRue et al. 2015; Lanaj and Hollenbeck, 2015; Rosette et al., forthcoming) and can result in discrimination (Dipboye and Colella 2013; Hoobler et al. 2014; Koch et al. 2015; Umphress et al. 2008). Moreover, because competence and masculinity perceptions are associated with leadership, men tend to emerge more quickly as leaders (DeRue et al. 2015; Lanaj and Hollenbeck 2015). This situation occurs despite research findings that stereotypical content about what *effective* leadership entails has shifted from a more masculine prototype to a prototype that now prominently includes feminine characteristics (Paustian-Underdahl et al. 2014). Gender biases can lead to discrimination, such as hiring more men than women for organizational positions when both are comparably qualified (Koch et al. 2015; Umphress et al. 2008) or managers' withholding of developmental opportunities for women due to managers' lower assessment of women's career motivation compared to men (Hoobler et al. 2015), all of which in turn limit women's professional advancement.

From these research accounts, women evidently face struggles that are distinctly tied to their gender in their ascent to top leadership positions. To better understand the experiences of the women from emerging markets featured in this book and to situate their experiences in the context of existing gender and leadership research, we first scoured the transcribed interviews and extracted examples of leadership barriers that could be linked together to form larger and more inclusive concepts. Next, we extensively reviewed the gender research literature on career barriers. Most of these studies have been conducted in developed countries. A Web of Science search using different keyword combinations, such as *gender* and *women*, with terms including *barriers, constraints, management, leader, career, glass cliff, glass ceiling, labyrinth of leadership*, and *role congruity*, yielded over 1,000 empirical and theoretical articles and books from disciplines such as psychology, organizational behavior, and sociology. To capture the most widely acknowledged barriers, we selected the most influential articles (by citation count and each journal's impact factor) from each search combination, generating 49 scholarly articles, management trade articles, and books, on which we based our literature review.

We then compared the broad concepts identified from the transcripts with the most prevalent barriers reported in the existing literature. From this extensive literature review and subsequent comparison, five categories of gender-related barriers emerged, as follows: gender-based stereotypes, work–life conflict, self-imposed constraints, social network limitations, and biased organizational policies. In addition, three categories that are not as prominently considered in existing gender and leadership research also emerged from our analysis of the transcribed interviews: non-gender-based discrimination, inadequate qualifications, and minimal female representation. Next, the barriers described by the top women leaders in emerging markets were classified under one of these eight categories. The next section describes each of the eight categories in more detail.

Types of career barriers

Each interviewed leader was asked about the barriers she had experienced throughout her career. The question was purposely phrased to convey a broad view of barriers, avoid leading the respondent, and solicit answers that were not influenced by the question (Ritchie et al. 2013). The women leaders' responses provide the basis of this chapter. Additionally, each interview was reviewed in its entirety. If any barrier was mentioned in response to an alternate question, the answer was included in our analysis.

One hundred and forty-eight quotes that referenced experienced barriers were extracted from 22 transcribed interviews. Each quote was indexed under one of the eight barrier categories, as follows: (1) gender-based stereotypes (n = 54), (2) work–life conflict (n = 21), (3) self-imposed constraints (n = 19), (4) social network limitations (n = 15), (5) biased organizational policies (n = 11), (6) non-gender-based discrimination (n = 18), (7) inadequate qualifications (n = 5), and (8) minimal existing representation of women (n = 5).

Gender-based stereotypes

Gender-based stereotypes can be sources of a great deal of bias against women in the workplace, resulting in significant barriers to their leadership. Gender stereotypes tend to describe women as relationship oriented, warm, kind, nurturing, and helpful, and men as independent, confident, assertive, and decisive (Abele 2003; Eagly and Karau 2002, Fiske and Stevens 1993). Gender bias can derive from both descriptive (i.e. what women and men *are generally like*) and prescriptive stereotypes (i.e. what women and men *should be like*) (Prentice and Carranza 2002). Descriptive gender stereotypes, such as "women are warm" and "men are strong" (Bem 1981), form the basis of what society deems desirable for women and men (Auster and Ohm, 2000). Prescriptive stereotypes represent behavioral norms that individuals should uphold to avoid negative perceptions (Gill 2004). These descriptive and prescriptive stereotypes can sometimes determine how women and men are evaluated in the workplace (e.g. Eagly and Karau 2002; Fiske et al. 2002; Ridgeway and Smith-Lovin 1999).

Women are generally perceived as lacking the characteristics that are stereotypically associated with effective leadership, while the stereotype associated with men encompasses leadership attributes (Schein 1973, 1975). As a result of this lack of fit between the female gender stereotype and the leadership stereotype (Heilman 2001), men are expected to be better leaders and are consequently more often favored for top positions than women (Heilman 2012). In fact, bias deriving from gender stereotypes is the most often cited barrier (*n* = 54) by the interviewed women leaders. We have further categorized the selected interview excerpts under four sub-themes: (1) subjected to low expectations (i.e. women leaders are not expected to perform as well as men), (2) experiencing double standards of competence (i.e. stricter performance requirements are applied to women compared to men), (3) navigating a male standard of leadership (i.e. managing the notion that women are not expected to be leaders), and (4) withstanding gender backlash (i.e. negative evaluations of women leaders who behave counter-stereotypically). Each subtheme is discussed below.

Subjected to low expectations

Women leaders are scrutinized, often as a result of low expectations about their leadership abilities. These low expectations not only shape interpretations about female leaders' behaviors but also influence evaluations of female leaders—irrespective of their behaviors. Women are frequently expected to be less effective than men (cf. Heilman 2012) even when they have not been given the chance to prove themselves. An interviewee shares this story about how others expected a female manager to fail before she even started the job:

> So [name of female associate] is the vice or actually the president of the region for [a division in our company]. A really amazing skill and title to have. [W]e knew that there was going to be a new leader, and she was going to be a woman. And there were a lot of questions as to, wow, is she going to cut it, and it is a male environment. We have never had a female leader in this position before. What will happen to the company? And the general expectation was that it would go south. That she would not be able to maintain, let alone grow it. [...] And she felt that there was mistrust or initially a default position of failure.
>
> (Aneshree Naidoo)

Another interviewee explains that women in leadership positions are expected to fail because they are considered less smart:

> Being a woman in a very macho society [is a barrier], and there is still a lot of discrimination. For example, I was working with my [...] most important client, and [...] I was calling, you know, that we have this program, and we have been very few women, and he said, well, yes, that is because there are not very many women who are smart, and stuff like that. So, your being a woman is a barrier.
>
> (Monica Sacristan)

This quote echoes the findings from Thomas-Hunt and Phillips' (2004) series of experiments on perceptions about expertise and actual expertise of women and men. The results show that possessing more expertise is positively related to the amount of influence held by men in a group setting, while expertise is negatively related to influence in the case of women. Moreover, women are sometimes perceived as possessing less expertise, the more expertise they actually have.

Experiencing double standards of competence

People's information search and processing tend to be biased. They often look for information that confirms their stereotypical beliefs, and they interpret it in a way that fits in their frame of reference, which is also partly shaped by stereotypical beliefs (i.e. confirmation bias; Koriat et al. 1980; Kruglanski, 1980). The same information about men versus women can lead to very different interpretations or evaluations (cf. Kunda and

Sherman-Williams 1993; Thomas-Hunt and Phillips 2004). According to Foschi's (2000) double standards of competence model, the competence of women and men can be inferred by using different standards. Such standards are usually much stricter for women, resulting in their being evaluated as less capable than men even when both perform equally well. Because women start off with such a stereotypical disadvantage, being "good enough" is often insufficient. Specifically, women's expertise needs to be unequivocal for others to recognize it (Wood and Karten 1986). In Lyness and Heilman's (2006) study, women who have been promoted have received higher performance ratings than men, suggesting that women need higher scores than men to be considered for advancement in the hierarchy. The following quote reflects that no matter how much women prove themselves, others may not recognize and trust their leadership abilities:

[W]e groom people, but the moment that they take on those roles, there would be a lot of sentiment around. They still do not have executive maturity; they are still not ready. So […], you know, women have to bake and bake and bake until they are eventually black, and they are still not ready to take on the roles.

(Melanie Botha)

Another interviewee recognizes how being a man enhances status more than mere capabilities do:

So, even though you have got equally strong or sometimes even better capable attorneys who are women, […] and you are interacting with [clients], that differential comes through. [There is almost an ingrained] client perception of wanting to deal with a white male […], even though he doesn't have to be senior, versus wanting to interact with you, […] that perception [is almost tangible].

(Deepa Vallabh)

Apparently, being a man signals more expertise and capability compared to a woman, regardless of the actual expertise and capability of both men and women. These stereotypical perceptions are deeply ingrained in society and held by both genders.

Navigating a male standard of leadership

Many of the interviewed women are pioneers, being among the first female leaders in a male-dominated work environment. As such, the standard and culture of leadership are mainly masculine, regarding both representation (i.e. the number of men in leadership roles; e.g. Zweigenhaft 2014) and the norm (i.e. what is expected; e.g. Eagly and Karau 2002; Garcia-Retamero and López-Zafra 2006). Established norms can be quite difficult to change

(Hofstede 2001), and attempts to reform an organizational culture usually encounter much resistance (Alvesson and Sveningsson, 2015). One interviewee shares her perceptions of how working in a male-dominated environment can be challenging for women:

> The industry is very male dominated. It very much is. The legacy of the gas, oil industry, and men's world and engineering worlds, also mainly. And so it has not really lent itself to embracing women and [especially] women in leadership positions. [This is] by legacy [despite] all the hype that is going [on] around developing women.
>
> (Lerato Mosiah)

The leadership style that women have introduced in male-oriented cultures has often differed from traditional leadership approaches, which could cause resistance to female leaders (Peterson 2014). An interviewee mentions how deeply ingrained the traditionally masculine culture is in her field:

> I think it is interesting because it will come to even the language, where you will see a lot in the languages described in the masculine form. And it appears to just be assumed that we are all men, you know.
>
> (Phuti Mahanyele)

Gender backlash

Gender backlash comprises negative implications for women who do not behave according to the stereotypical gender expectations (Rudman 1998). It represents negative social and economic experiences from behaving in a manner that is more akin to the male rather than the female gender role. When there is a discrepancy between an expectation and an action (i.e. when women demonstrate masculinity or are not feminine enough), women suffer adverse career outcomes (Heilman et al. 2004; and Burnette 2013; Rudman 1998; Rudman and Glick 2001) and are frequently perceived as less likable (Amanatullah and Tinsley 2013; Eagly and Karau 2002; Heilman et al. 2004), which also causes professional setbacks. Several interviewees describe negative experiences of women when they display masculinity:

> [I]n fact, society often regards [women's ambitions] quite negatively. There could be a misjudgment that the ambition is kind of being selfish, thinking too selfish, being too self-centered. And sometimes women, ambitious women, get judged as aggressive.
>
> (Cheryl de la Rey)

> Well, I mean, there is the typical thing about [...] the man being tough and the woman [as] the bitch.
>
> (Susan McNerney)

Next to being judged for being "too masculine", women also suffer back-lash if they violate the gender role by not being feminine enough. When women do not play the female role as prescribed by societal expectations (e.g. take care of the children), people tend to find this surprising:

> [P]eople, generally speaking, expect women to be [the same in their] work life as they are [in] their personal life, like the care takers. They seem to be sometimes a bit surprised when they are exposed to a woman [who] has a more aggressive style about, like, more like a man, to use those words. And so, on that hand, I think there is this stereo-type that people expect women to be, continue to be a caretaker even on the work side.
>
> (Aneshree Naidoo)

In fact, when an interviewee stands up to one of her clients whom she has known for over twenty years, he is not amused:

> He actually called me Joan [of Arc]. He says my new name is Joan because he is going to tie me to the stake and burn me in the fire. [...] I do not like to say that, but I had to use the feminine part and sort of play it down, and now he loves me.
>
> (Monica Sacristan)

Only by manifesting her feminine side does she manage to ease the tense situation with this client, which only reinforces women's subjection to strict behavioral norms that they should not violate.

Summary of gender-based stereotypes

Gender-based stereotypes suggest that women are perceived differently and should behave differently from men (e.g. Eagly and Karau 2002). Moreover, these stereotypes are frequently touted as the principal reasons why women leaders do not advance in their respective organizational hierarchies (e.g. Heilman 2001). The research findings presented here sug-gest that these prevailing beliefs plague the experiences of the top women leaders featured in this volume. Whether the barriers are derived from descriptive or prescriptive stereotypes, gender stereotypes clearly serve as the basis for the disparate treatment of these women leaders in their professional careers.

Work–life conflict

When family responsibilities contend with work responsibilities, situations of work–life conflict occur (Greenhaus and Beutell 1985). Experiencing conflicts between work and family demands can lead to lower levels of job and life satisfaction (Kossek and Ozeki 1998). Moreover, women tend to feel guilty about spending time away from their families (Judge et al. 2006; Livingston and Judge 2008). A meta-analysis of the importance of work–family support policies shows that work–family conflict produces more negative work attitudes, in turn causing lower levels of job satisfaction, affective commitment, and intentions to stay, but work–family support policies reduce work–family conflict (Butts et al. 2013).

Many of the top women leaders interviewed for this book mention their experiences of work–family conflict, which entail a lot of careful planning and sacrifice to continue their professional development:

> I have been very selfish. I did not want to sacrifice any [particular] role. So I wanted to be [an activist, I wanted to be a] professional. I wanted to be a wife. I wanted to be a mother. [Doing] all this, and keep[ing up] these roles [is] difficult [but I don't regret the choices I made].
>
> (Geraldine Fraser-Moleketi)

In fact, the lack of careful balance between family and work can have detrimental effects in the workplace, as well as for the family. As described by an interviewee, having a child was a burden for her job performance:

> I gave birth to my son in October 2010. In 2011, I found myself [...] with almost two different worlds to handle. So, it was time to find a balance, a work–life balance. And that, for me, started [affecting] my effectiveness [as a mother] on the scale.
>
> (Lerato Mosiah)

Another interviewee admits how her family suffered from her long work hours:

> My daughter would [stay] beyond aftercare [hours, when] the aftercare teacher [had] to leave, and I [was] not there yet. So, yes, it was difficult.
>
> (Dolly Mokgathle)

Work–life conflict arises when the time devoted to meeting the requirements of one role (e.g. the work role) impedes the fulfillment of the other role's (i.e. the family role) demands. While men are not exempted from experiencing work–life conflict, women mention this issue far more often than men (Hochschild 1997; Wada et al. 2010), making this a barrier that is mostly imposed on women. For instance, studies on work–family conflict describe how career women feel as though a "second shift" waits for them at home—they have to tend to housework and family demands—while men are less likely to experience such pressures at home (Hochschild

1997; Hochschild and Machung 2012). The pressure of taking care of the family that comes from gender-role demands seems to be an issue for women worldwide:

I think there is a critical period of time when the demands for a woman, if the woman has a child or children, [are] very, very tough. And it probably varies by country, but in [named country], I would say that the woman still carries a lot of the [burden] of raising a child. You know, there are husbands [who] help and all that, but here it is seen as a woman's role.

(Silvana Machado)

The complications that can arise from balancing work and family can lead women to pull out from the workplace altogether and focus on their families, as illustrated in the following comments:

[M]y father and my mother were sick already, and I decided [that] the most important thing would be to dedicate to them most of my time and to my kids and to everything.

(Martha Cecilia Bernal Uribe)

Probably, we will never have an equal number of men and women at the top in the future. Because that is also a choice that some women have: [they can] prefer to stay with [their] children [and give up their careers].

(Silvana Machado)

Summary of work–life conflict

Finding a balance between work and family life is difficult, especially for women. Societal role expectations dictate that women should take care of their families, while such strict demands do not apply to men. As the interviewees describe, women have to make tough decisions on how to allocate their time to work and family, which may affect the quality of their work or family life and may make them decide to refrain from pursuing their career ambitions.

Self-imposed constraints

While women can be just as ambitious as men in pursuing their careers (Emrich et al. 2015; Fels 2004; Lang 2012), stereotypical perceptions can lead to self-imposed constraints that can form barriers to women's career advancement. Biases that arise from gender and leadership stereotypes influence not only other people's views about women but also women's self-perceptions. When women internalize biased, stereotypical gender and leadership prescriptions and proscriptions, it may cause them to engage in self-debilitation strategies (Clance and Imes 1978; Spencer et al. 2016), which can hinder their career advancement (Ibarra and Petriglieri 2016). The top women leaders interviewed for this book mention four self-imposed constraints. They cite experiences of their lack of confidence, minimal focus on their career, feelings of guilt, and refusal to ask for help.

Lack of confidence

Stereotype-threatened individuals (i.e. individuals concerned about confirming negative stereotypes (Davies et al. 2005; Spencer et al. 2016)) are at risk of feeling less confident (i.e. have lower self-efficacy) about their threatened domain-specific skills (Chung et al. 2010; Deemer et al. 2014). This is consistent with the imposter syndrome whereby an individual feels inadequate while simultaneously experiencing substantial success and high achievements (Clance and Imes 1978). A leadership setting may elicit feelings consistent with stereotype threat and the imposter syndrome, which may cause women to lack confidence in their leader abilities. For instance, the following quote describes an interviewee's feelings of self-doubt, even after attaining a position in the C-suite:

> When I was facing all the barriers at an early stage of being the CFO, I asked myself often, do I even deserve to be here? Maybe I am not going to be successful. You become your own worst enemy when you do this.
>
> (Aneshree Naidoo)

Other interviewees have observed women around them display such feelings of self-doubt, for example:

> I have met quite a few women of different races, and you can see it in the way they sometimes are too what you call submissive and do not have enough confidence in themselves. Under-sell themselves, you know.
>
> (Melanie Botha)

The idea that they may not be "good enough" for top leadership positions can become a real obstacle for women. One woman describes how it inhibited her functioning in her respective leadership positions:

> I was always thinking that, you know, people [would] come to me and propose promotions, you know. But in the corporate world, apparently, sometimes you have to cry for it, you know, and you have to ask for it. And that's where I think I failed a little bit, on being demanding, you know. On certain positions I always thought, oh no, I mean, I [was] not well qualified for it.
>
> (Barçin Yinanç)

Minimal focus on career

Barçin Yinanç's quote not only describes how a lack of self-confidence can inhibit women's career advancement, it also touches on another theme that has emerged from the interviews—that women can sometimes be less focused on professional growth than men and concentrate more on doing their jobs well. Their lack of confidence in their ability to lead shifts their attention to performing well rather than advancing to leadership roles. The following quote captures this experience perfectly:

> Let me not speak for others, but I think I have felt it for myself sometimes, the voices of one's history, not being quite certain in the way that perhaps men are certain about their capacity to reach. So one of the things that I had to overcome was [the belief] that I wasn't a leader. It took me some time before I realized [it], but I wanted to lead.
>
> (Barbara Dale-Jones)

Another interviewee describes how for a long time she was not even thinking of career progress:

> As women, we probably do not get so caught up in a functional kind of role that we may be [in] and [have not] seen a career progress in that way, but that you actually remove the blinders, and you start to see opportunities outside of the role that you may be currently fulfilling.
>
> (Cheryl de la Rey)

Sometimes women pass up a promotion for fear that it might interfere with their family responsibilities:

> I think [that] she [i.e. a typical woman] is less encouraged to ask for certain positions. She just says, "Okay, I have too much [on my plate]; I am not going to ask for a higher position because a higher position means higher responsibility, less time for [my] family."
>
> (Barçin Yinanç)

Feelings of guilt

The previous quote addresses the issue of women who deliberately forgo a career move because of their families. However, those women who decide to take on the challenge still struggle with internal barriers. Women who need to balance work and family roles often feel guilty when they cannot spend as much time as they would like with their families, a sentiment expressed in the following comments:

> The working mother guilt trip. That was difficult.
>
> (Susan McNerney)

And obviously because we are women, we are nurturers. We are the ones who carry babies, you know. We are the ones [who] feel guilty when we can't [take care of] those babies. I mean, my eldest daughter would be waiting for me in school until about six o'clock, sitting alone in the quad [...]. And you have to make [a] certain decision in your mind about a situation like that and say, what's my contribution to making this part of her life. She has absolutely no responsibility in having a career-driven mother like me. She is supposed to be some-where safe. She is supposed to have been picked up by a mum or a father at a particular time.

(Dolly Mokgathle)

Because balancing work and family means that, at times, a woman has to sacrifice in both areas, feelings of guilt also arise on the work front:

I was feeling guilty as a mother. And feeling guilty as a leader of a team. And just that guilty feeling of not knowing whether I [was] actually in control of [my responsibilities]. Things really fell apart. I could see that I was beginning to become very alienated from my team. And the minute that happens, everything else falls apart. Because they cannot talk to you. They cannot come in and be honest with you. You cannot even deliver on the numbers: I would look at the numbers and I would think, oh, but this is fine, [they are on target]. And I would find every excuse why the profits were not [exceeding targets as I would sometimes have it].

(Lerato Mosiah)

Refusal to ask for help

Awareness of the negative leadership stereotype that is attached to the female gender role can result in another barrier that may interfere with women's career progression. Some women try to avoid asking for help out of fear of confirming the negative stereotype that women are less compe-tent leaders. The following quote describes this internal struggle that women face, while rationalizing this fear:

You have to get over yourself. Because asking for help or having the ability to ask for help, people often see it as, now I am going to show a sign of weakness, and I am not going to make myself vulnerable and allow others to judge me or to judge me on the basis that I should know it all, and I don't actually. I think that fear of judgment, I think that fear of being not only judged but of revealing that I don't know everything, holds people back from [asking for help]. And I think that's sad because that's very limiting. It's a limiting belief, firstly. It's also an unrealistic expectation of yourself.

(Deepa Vallabh)

Summary of self-imposed constraints

The accounts of the top women leaders featured in this book show how stereotypes can be internalized by women themselves and result in self-fulfilling prophecies. These women describe how they often lack confidence or observe other women around them having self-doubts in pursuing a career in leadership. In fact, they may not even realize that focusing on their career growth, in addition to their work, is an available option. The other ways in which internalized stereotypes may inhibit women's professional ambitions are feeling guilty for not spending enough time with their families and refusing to ask for help out of fear of reinforcing the negative stereotype of lower competence. These findings suggest that some of the greatest obstacles to women's career advancement can be self-inflicted rather than externally imposed.

Social network limitations

Social network limitations arise from being constrained in creating useful networks and utilizing existing ones. Research on gender and social networks has identified some restrictions in building a valuable social network, emerging from being a woman in a male-dominated occupation (Ibarra 1993). Given that the quality of a person's social network is positively related to career advancement outcomes (Seibert et al. 2001), being unable to develop a high-quality network forms a barrier to women's professional progress.

Barriers to having or creating beneficial social networks, as well as experiences of lower instrumental value of existing networks, are mentioned by the interviewees. Being a woman has proven to be more difficult in establishing relationships with others, especially with men:

> [Being a woman is] a disadvantage because [establishing] relationships is not as easy or not the same as your colleagues, men, would establish.
>
> (Isabel Neiva)

> The other barrier, of course, is you generally would feel that you are not part of the boys' club. That when you now run home to go and cook, to go and look after the babies and whatever, men have the time to puff the proverbial cigar and have the proverbial glass of brandy. And therefore, there was always within me that feeling, that I wish could be part of that.
>
> (Dolly Mokgathle)

The lack of a useful network can have detrimental results for a person's career (Seibert et al. 2001). Having mentors who provide guidance and show the ropes of the trajectory can be quite valuable for one's career:

> To be [...] successful in [a field where you need to attract clients], you need the support to open up the networks, the support you need to be able to convince important clients that this is the person that you should be able to trust with your work [...]. I realized in my journey, in my current career, that unless I was actively supported and liked by the leadership, I wasn't going to progress beyond where I was.
>
> (Deepa Vallabh)

Without such guidance, the leadership trajectory becomes much more difficult and the probability that one exits the path becomes much higher:

> I didn't have any connections in the business world. I don't come from a family that has any connections [with] the business world [...]. I [had] no network. And that is the biggest reason why a lot of women and [a] lot of black people, black and women, fail or why they don't [...] continue on this trajectory [of furthering their careers beyond a certain point].
>
> (Deepa Vallabh)

Moreover, several interviewees mention that their networks did not support them in the same ways that men were helped by their networks:

> You get allocated to different partners. Everyone was allocated to the young stars or the young partners or the guys [who] have really busy practices and doing really interesting things, and for some reason, I was allocated to a partner who was about three or four years away from retirement. He didn't really care about me, honestly. He didn't care. I was just an irritation in his life. His weeks constituted his golf sessions and then his lunches with his clients, and training a little enthusiastic candidate attorney was not high on his priority list.
>
> (Deepa Vallabh)

Summary of social network limitations

Many of the women featured in the interviews acknowledge the importance of the social network. They also recognize how the lack of a useful and supportive social network forms a barrier to their careers and that this obstacle is often the result of being women. Men often have better access to and receive more support from their networks than women do, which negatively affects women's career advancement.

Biased organizational policies

An additional impediment that has emerged from our literature review is the presence of biased organizational policies—macro-level policies that favor men and/or disadvantage women. Such policies can include those tackling obvious and straightforward differences, including the absence of women's bathrooms, the possibility of parental leave, and setting up flexible work arrangements, as well as policies that at first glance do not seem to exacerbate gender differences but in fact do, such as potentially biased performance reviews (Snyder 2014), (informal) allocation of tasks (de Pater et al. 2009), and the long hours norm (Eagly and Carli 2007; Guillaume and Pochic 2009). For instance, the women interviewed in Guillaume and Pochic's (2009) qualitative study mention that the long-hours norm means making sacrifices in their family life to maintain their career progress. Similar experiences are shared by the interviewees in our study, for example:

> I found that it takes something to make a bet on women for those types of roles [i.e. leadership roles]. Because it is a day-and-night function, you know. You literally work nonstop.
>
> (Melanie Botha)

Not only the long work hours, but also the travel required, are cited as barriers:

> Unfortunately, in the job we were in, we used to travel a lot. And so, we would get told: "You need to go to London tomorrow." And so I remember I would always have to get on the phone and start to figure out the story for my husband.
>
> (Phuti Mahanyele)

When organizations lack the structures that appeal to social groups with different needs than those of the majority, it can obstruct the disadvantaged social groups from achieving similar outcomes as the majority group does, such as job and life satisfaction (Kossek and Ozeki 1998), performance (Biernat et al. 2012), retention (Kalev 2014), and career advancement opportunities (Cabrera 2007). However, organizations often do not recognize the need for work–life policies to level the playing field for both genders. The solution to some issues, such as parenthood, are not considered the responsibility of the organization but of women themselves:

> There are deep scripts that women have, and I think particularly [of] those women who might well have the skills but have stepped out of the workplace for a while. So, [we should be] creating the on-ramps

and off-ramps, creating more accessible positions, encouraging women who are not working but could be working to be working, encouraging those who are working to be stepping up to the plate more fully.

(Nicola Kleyn)

Other issues arise from the workplace being historically a male-dominated space. The first women entering the male-dominated workplace have encountered relatively obvious gender-biased structures, such as the lack of facilities for women or uniforms that are not tailored to female needs:

My first client in the Middle East was in Saudi Arabia, and the entire organization consisted of men only. I was the only woman there. And so […]. No women's toilets. Exactly.

(Isabel Neiva)

So I said, "What is it like working down here [in the mines]?" She said, "It is hell." So I said, "Tell me why?" She said, "I work an eight-hour shift. I don't drink anything. For hours, I am in these hot conditions with no private toilet facilities. The women's overalls are the same as men's and are a one piece. So, for women, you have to take the uniform partially off to go to the loo and you can't actually get the thing off in the cubicle as the cubicle is for a stand-up. So you can't actually go to the loo underground."

(Wendy Lucas-Bull]

Summary of biased organizational policies

Due to the ingrained masculine culture in organizations, which formed naturally over the course of many years when only men were in charge of organizational life, corporate policies often accommodate men's needs and provide opportunities for them. The first women who have encroached into the masculine culture have experienced organizational barriers caused by masculine norms, including the long work hours and the lack of policies catering to the needs of and opportunities for women, such as family-friendly policies and female-oriented facilities. The presence of masculine norms and the absence of female-inclusive policies are mentioned as distinct obstacles to women's ascent to top leadership positions.

Non-gender-based discrimination

It is important to acknowledge that women do not comprise a monolithic category. There may be just as much variation within gender categories as across them. That is, women hold concurrent membership in numerous social categories and these other demographically based categories may also represent barriers along their career paths. For example, culture

(Brown 2002), age (Snape and Redman 2003), and race (Pager and Shepard 2008) may raise hindrances in the ascent to top leadership positions. These were the three non-gender-based sources of discrimination that were identified by the women in our sample.

Cultural discrimination

From the interviews, seven quotes are related to cultural discrimination. Cultural minorities report experiencing more barriers in their careers and less professional advancement opportunities compared to cultural majorities (Fouad and Byers-Winston 2005). Cultural differences among individuals can lead to misunderstandings and conflicts (Stahl et al. 2010), so to successfully navigate the intercultural domain it is important to be sensitive to and aware of cultural differences (Mor et al. 2013). As an interviewee admits, it is not easy to recognize the differences between one's own culture and the cultural norms and values of the environment:

> The most difficult part is, you are not a local. And that means that [...] whether you like it or not, this circumstance pretty much is attached to your Western [background] and to your very rational processes. And here, that is a different perspective. So here, you have a much more, how can I put it, constant social responsibility act. So sometimes it is the changing of mindsets that is more difficult and not necessarily being a woman.
>
> (Isabel Neiva)

On the other hand, awareness of potential cultural differences and applying this knowledge in intercultural settings bring advantages, such as the ability to build trust with culturally different others (Chua et al. 2012). For instance, leaders who are culturally sensitive in intercultural collaborative settings are perceived as more trustworthy by intercultural collaborators, resulting in higher creative performance (Chua et al. 2012). However, until these cultural barriers are overcome, it is difficult to fit in when the dominant culture is different from one's own, as an interviewee states:

> I guess, which I still see now is [that] it was a lot, obviously the cultural barriers. I mean, [...] it is known that the mining environment is a strong Afrikaans environment. So, you know, to fit in has been very difficult. But what has been important is making them understand [the value of the contribution of] what I am bringing. So the cultural barriers in terms of fitting in will [be there for anyone who is different. You have to always consciously revert to what the key objectives are and focus on them and constantly push until there is a shift].
>
> (Sindisiwe Koyana)

Age discrimination

Six quotes extracted from the interviews are categorized as accounts of age discrimination. Being regarded as "too young" or "too old" can result in perceptions of less access to promotions (Snape and Redman 2003). Research on youthful appearances (i.e. baby faces) finds that while a more youthful face is often seen as trustworthy, warm, and innocent (Zebrowitz 1997), it can be a barrier to achieving high-power positions due to stereo-typical perceptions of incompetence and weakness (Rule and Ambady 2008; Zebrowitz and Montepare 2005). Given that women's facial features tend to more often resemble those of a baby face (e.g. big eyes, small nose) than those of men (Keating 1985; Senior et al. 1999), and being youthful is considered an important aspect of women's physical attractiveness, in assessing workplace competence (Marlowe et al. 1996), women are more prone to suffer from stereotypically negative evaluations regarding per-ceptions of their age. An interviewee talks about her interaction with a client who views her youthfulness as a sign of incompetence:

> One thing that I think, especially before at some point, age was a factor. So, when I [became] a manager […], I had responsibility and all that, and sometimes the client would look at me and think, oh, who is this "baby", you know.
>
> (Silvana Machado)

Another interviewee shares how being younger lessens her influence on which topics are discussed during meetings:

> So sitting at the table, actually voicing an opinion, I do feel that because of age sometimes, and when you are the lowest contributing person, the next one may be 10 to 15 [years] older than you, the type of conversation is steered in a different way, based maybe on more mature topics, if you will.
>
> (Aneshree Naidoo)

Racial discrimination

Five interview excerpts refer to racial discrimination, all of which come from nonwhite women. In Western cultures, racial discrimination arises from ste-reotypical perceptions about leaders being White, as demonstrated in a series of experiments (Rosette et al., 2008). This bias results in perceptions of greater leadership effectiveness and potential for Whites versus nonwhites (Rosette et al., 2008). In fact, Greenhaus, Parasuraman, and Wormley (1990) have found that Black managers have lower promotability ratings and are more likely to have reached career plateaus than White managers, indicating that this racial bias forms a real barrier in nonwhites' careers. An interviewee has even experienced racial bias as the most significant obstacle in her career:

I think the first [barrier] would be definitely race, gender, and then most recently, age.

(Aneshree Naidoo)

In the workplace, higher status is accorded to being White, accompanied by more positive views of anticipated performance, and is therefore preferred in workplace interactions (cf. status characteristics theory, see Berger et al. 1972). This racial bias persists in emerging markets although nonwhites do not necessarily constitute a numerical minority in these countries. For instance, 20.8% of US citizens (United States Department of Labor 2016) and approximately 20% of EU citizens are nonwhites, while Brazil counts 47.7% Whites (Censo Demográfico 2010). In South Africa, the country with the largest proportion of Whites in Africa, they only comprise 8.7% of the national population (Statistics South Africa 2013). An interviewee shares her experience with racial discrimination:

I did feel that, to be very honest, in the Middle East, more preference is given to the white skin and not [to] people from colored backgrounds. If you are from India, if you are from the Philippines, you are only a second-class citizen.

(Renuka Methil)

Summary of other types of discrimination

The interviewed women hold simultaneous memberships in multiple social groups, which represent additional obstacles to their professional careers. The top women leaders report experiencing cultural, age, and racial discrimination. These findings suggest that further insights into the experiences of women top leaders can be gleaned by also focusing on the differences that occur within the social category of gender.

Inadequate qualifications

Barriers relating to inadequate qualifications do not necessarily arise from gender bias; however, some research indicates that the lack of qualifications can be the result of gender bias. For instance, women are less likely than men to have line experience, one of the requirements for advancing to the senior management level in certain industries (Oakley 2000). Lacking the right qualifications mostly stems from a lack of knowledge, not having access to information, or from inexperience. For instance, if someone does not know which opportunities are available, one cannot take advantage of them. The following quote comes from an interviewee who decided to pursue an MBA degree later in life:

> I did not know that if I wanted to go into business, I had to do my MBA earlier than I did. That for me [was] a barrier in terms of knowledge and understanding [...] and being informed.
>
> (Lerato Mosiah)

Another interviewee describes how careers reach plateaus when a degree is not obtained in the desired country:

> And the other barrier I have is not having a PhD. So, because I [studied] chemistry, and then I went [on] to a masters in chemistry, and then I [earned an] MBA. And where I work, they will not consider a Mexican PhD. You will need a US PhD. So if I ever want to go to a position above, I will need a US PhD.
>
> (Monica Sacristan)

These women do not recognize their lack of qualifications as a gender-biased barrier per se. However, given that the interviewees work in emerging markets and that women have less access to educational opportunities in those countries compared to men (Khalaf 2014), the lack of qualifications might well be a barrier that is more often faced by women than by men.

Minimal female representation

Underrepresentation of women is not only a result of obstacles that they encounter throughout their careers; some women also recognize it as a barrier in and of itself. The lack of women at the top, or at least the lack of individuals who call attention to gender issues, can prevent the change needed to facilitate women's career advancement. If almost no one voices a different view on gender-related issues, the circumstances will probably remain the same. For instance, Dobbin, Kim, and Kalev (2011) find that the number of women in upper management is positively related to the likelihood that an organization adopts a diversity program, indicating that change may not come naturally. Advocates should be in place, with the power and authority to actually make equality a priority. If most top managers are male, gender inequity will less likely be brought to the forefront, and the conditions will more likely remain the same, as pointed out by an interviewee:

> I think that the biggest thing is the inertia of human systems to stay the same and stay with what is comfortable. And that is the problem, because we are not at that tipping point in numbers yet. So the more comfortable way is to stay the same, which means, the current incumbents (men) surround themselves with and promote more 2men, as that is a known environment, and it is much more comfortable. So, that's I think, the biggest thing. We have not yet got the critical mass of women in senior positions.
>
> (Wendy Lucas-Bull)

However, representation of women in top leader positions does not necessitate support for diversity, as women who have reached upper managerial positions may not have positive views of women who are not there yet. In fact, research shows that women can express stronger negative bias against other women than men do (Ellemers et al. 2004). This has also been the experience of some of the interviewees:

> But there is also some truth to the fact that sometimes, there is more jealousy also among women, you know.
>
> (Barçin Yinanç)

> You never see another woman recommend one. So even at the boardroom table it is not happening, and it is not happening in middle management. I think there is maybe more collaboration and support on the woman-to-woman basis on the shop floor. Once they leave that and move into lower management, middle management, it is lost. And I can only think that it is a competition thing.
>
> (Susan McNerney)

No barriers

Interestingly, when asked the barrier question, 10 women leaders (n = 14 quotes) responded that they did not experience any gender-specific obstacles to their careers. However, based on the review of the entire transcript, most of these women report (earlier or later in their interviews) having experienced various social, political, or organizational boundaries at some point—usually early on—in their professional lives that could potentially be construed as gender-related. Some women emphatically state not having encountered impediments due to their gender:

> If you look at my organization itself, you know, there are as many women as men. I have never, never seen a disparity between men and women in this organization [...]. Even in the top leadership. I have never seen that disparity. They are very, very amenable to female employees. I have never had a concern where I felt, oh, there is gender disparity in some ways.
>
> (Name withheld)

Even when probed to think more critically about gender-specific barriers, they do not change their minds, as illustrated in these excerpts from one interview:

> I have not really faced many external barriers really, no. I do not feel I have had any external barriers. No. I think I have achieved professionally wise whatever I wanted at every moment of my life.
>
> (Name withheld)

[Research indicates that race, ethnicity, and culture might also be barriers to women's progress as they ascend the organizational hierarchies. Has that been your experience? Would you have any examples in that respect?] No, I cannot. I really cannot answer that because [...] I sit on the board for three times a year. So, I do not have enough experience. In my day-to-day work, I do not see any differences because we are all the same.

(Name withheld)

Some women do mention barriers, but they do not consider these gender-specific challenges. They emphasize how they took matters into their own hands and assumed responsibility for their situation, for example:

Yes, we are [in] a male-dominated environment. Yes, we have changed already, a little bit. But I have never seen that as a barrier because it is what you make of it, you know. Yes, there were times [when] you would sit on [the same] level for years, but I deliberately drove it. So, maybe some people could see that as a barrier because they are not moving as fast, as the manager does not see their potential. But I drove it. If I did not drive my career myself, probably it would not have been where it is now. But I did not see that as a barrier.

(Name withheld)

An interviewee recognizes that her racial, ethnic, and cultural background have probably presented obstacles to her career. However, she does not feel that these hindrances have been significant enough to prevent career advancement altogether:

I think, like all barriers, they [race, ethnicity, culture] are all there. There [are] many different barriers. Those are a couple of them. They have been my experience to a large extent. But I don't think that they are so offensive that they will stop careers from progressing.

(Name withheld)

This phenomenon—that is, women downplaying or not recognizing the gender-specific challenges they face in their careers—is consistent with previous research showing that women sometimes work hard to take gender out of the equation as a performance explanation (Crosby 1984). Instead, they make an extra effort to focus on being acknowledged for their skills and talents (Ibarra et al. 2013). However, our study's qualitative results indicate that the women who do not perceive the barriers they have experienced as gender-specific have in fact faced similar obstacles as the women who believe they have encountered gender-specific challenges in their careers.

Conclusion

Research on barriers that women face throughout their careers has mostly involved women from developed countries in the Western hemisphere. In our current study, we find that top women leaders in emerging markets face obstacles similar to those encountered by their female peers in more developed markets. From our review of the transcribed interviews, five types of barriers emerged that were consistent with those identified in our extensive literature review on the barriers that women face in their careers. The five types of barriers were gender-based stereotypes, work–life conflict, self-imposed constraints, social network limitations, and biased organizational policies. Moreover, non-gender-based discrimination, minimal qualifications and lack of female representation are three additional barriers (although not as prominent as the other five in existing gender research) that emerged from the interviews with the women leaders.

While the hindrances mentioned are often recognized as gender-specific challenges that they have faced as women and that men encounter to a (much) lesser extent, several women deny having experienced barriers that are significant enough to influence their careers, or they refute having encountered obstacles at all when directly asked about such barriers. However, these women mention experiences of gender-specific impediments in other parts of their interviews. These results indicate that despite our increasing understanding of gender bias and its consequent barriers, not all women recognize the barriers as such (Ibarra et al. 2013).

In our literature review, we cited empirical research that substantiated broader and well-researched theoretical frameworks. However, our research is not without limitations and it should be noted that the somewhat older empirical references need to be replicated to assess whether the outcomes are still applicable to the state of affairs today. It should also be noted that we did not evaluate or specifically indicate whether the barriers that emerged from the literature review were objective or perceived, nor did we focus on whether the barriers women face in the workplace are also recognized as such by men. Future research should be conducted to address these considerations.

In this qualitative study we have attempted to provide a wide-ranging understanding of the various barriers faced by the women leaders in emerging markets who are featured in this book. Our results illustrate that complex obstacles remain as major aspects of organizational life and continue to influence women in their careers (Ibarra et al. 2013). We hope that our work can inspire aspiring women leaders who encounter comparable hurdles to persevere in their career pursuits and remain steadfast in striving to attain their professional goals.

References

Abele, A. E. 2003. "The Dynamics of Masculine-Agentic and Feminine-Communal Traits: Findings from a Prospective Study." *Journal of Personality and Social Psychology* 85(4): 768.

Alvesson, M. and S. Sveningsson. 2015. *Changing Organizational Culture: Cultural Change Work in Progress*. Abingdon: Routledge.

Amanatullah, E. T. and C. H. Tinsley. 2013. "Punishing Female Negotiators for Asserting Too Much ... or Not Enough: Exploring Why Advocacy Moderates Backlash Against Assertive Female Negotiators." *Organizational Behavior and Human Decision Processes* 120(1): 110–122.

Auster, C. J. and S. C. Ohm. 2000. "Masculinity and Femininity in Contemporary American Society: A Reevaluation Using the Bem Sex-Role Inventory." *Sex Roles* 43(7): 499–528.

Bem, S. L. 1981. *Bem Sex-Role Inventory*. Palo Alto, CA: Consulting Psychologists Press.

Berger, J., B. P. Cohen and M. Zelditch Jr. 1972. "Status Characteristics and Social Interaction." *American Sociological Review* 37(June): 241–255.

Biernat, M., M. J. Tocci and J. C. Williams. 2012. "The Language of Performance Evaluations Gender-Based Shifts in Content and Consistency of Judgment." *Social Psychological and Personality Science* 3(2): 186–192.

Brown, D. 2002. "The Role of Work and Cultural Values in Occupational Choice, Satisfaction, and Success: A Theoretical Statement." *Journal of Counseling & Development* 80(1): 48–56.

Butts, M. M., W. J. Casper and T. S. Yang. 2013. "How Important are Work–Family Support Policies? A Meta-Analytic Investigation of Their Effects on Employee Outcomes." *Journal of Applied Psychology* 98(1): 1.

Cabrera, E. F. 2007. "Opting Out and Opting In: Understanding the Complexities of Women's Career Transitions." *Career Development International* 12(3): 218–237.

Catalyst. 2016. "Pyramid: Women in S&P 500 Companies." Accessed March 23, 2016. www.catalyst.org/knowledge/women-sp-500-companies.

Censo Demográfico. 2010. "População residente, por cor ou raça, segundo o sexo e os grupos de idade." Accessed May 6, 2016. ftp://ftp.ibge.gov.br/Censos/Censo_Demografico_2010/Resultados_do_Universo/tabelas_pdf/tab3.pdf.

Christofides, L. N., A. Polycarpou and K. Vrachimis. 2013. "Gender Wage Gaps, 'Sticky Floors' and 'Glass Ceilings' in Europe." *Labour Economics* 21: 86–102.

Chua, R. Y., M. W. Morris and S. Mor. 2012. "Collaborating Across Cultures: Cultural Metacognition and Affect-Based Trust in Creative Collaboration." *Organizational Behavior and Human Decision Processes* 118(2): 116–131.

Chung, B. G., M. G. Ehrhart, K. H. Ehrhart, K. Hattrup and J. Solamon. 2010. "Stereotype Threat, State Anxiety, and Specific Self-Efficacy as Predictors of Promotion Exam Performance." *Group & Organization Management* 35(1): 77–107.

Clance, P. R. and S. A. Imes. 1978. "The Imposter Phenomenon in High Achieving Women: Dynamics and Therapeutic Intervention." *Psychotherapy: Theory, Research & Practice* 15(3): 241.

Cook, A. and C. Glass. 2014. "Above the Glass Ceiling: When are Women and Racial/Ethnic Minorities Promoted to CEO?" *Strategic Management Journal* 35(7): 1080–1089.

Crosby, F. 1984. "The Denial of Personal Discrimination." *American Behavioral Scientist* 27(3): 371–386.

Cuddy, A. J., E. B. Wolf, P. Glick, S. Crotty, J. Chong and M. I. Norton. 2015. "Men as Cultural Ideals: Cultural Values Moderate Gender Stereotype Content." *Journal of Personality and Social Psychology* 109(4): 622.

Davies, P. G., S. J. Spencer and C. M. Steele, 2005. "Clearing the Air: Identity Safety Moderates the Effects of Stereotype Threat on Women's Leadership Aspirations." *Journal of Personality and Social Psychology* 88(2), 276–287.

Deemer, E. D., D. B. Thoman, J. P. Chase and J. L. Smith. 2014. "Feeling the Threat: Stereotype Threat as a Contextual Barrier to Women's Science Career Choice Intentions." *Journal of Career Development* 41(2): 141–158.

de Pater, I. E., A. E. Van Vianen, M. N. Bechtoldt and U. C. Klehe. 2009. "Employees' Challenging Job Experiences and Supervisors' Evaluations of Promotability." *Personnel Psychology* 62(2): 297–325.

DeRue, D. S., J. D. Nahrgang and S. J. Ashford. 2015. "Interpersonal Perceptions and the Emergence of Leadership Structures in Groups: A Network Perspective." *Organization Science* 26(4): 1192–1209.

Dipboye, R. L. and A. Colella, eds. 2013. *Discrimination at Work: The Psychological and Organizational Bases.* Hove: Psychology Press.

Dobbin, F., S. Kim and A. Kalev. 2011. "You Can't Always Get What You Need: Organizational Determinants of Diversity Programs." *American Sociological Review* 76(3): 386–411.

Eagly, A. H. and L. L. Carli. 2007. "Women and the Labyrinth of Leadership." *Harvard Business Review* 85(9): 62.

Eagly, A. H. and S. J. Karau. 2002. "Role Congruity Theory of Prejudice Toward Female Leaders." *Psychological Review* 109(3): 573.

Economist Intelligence Unit. 2012. "Women's Economic Opportunity: A Global Index and Ranking." Accessed April 25, 2016. www.eiu.com/Handlers/WhitepaperHandler.ashx?fi=WEO_full_report_final.pdf&mode=wp&campaignid=weoindex2012.

Ellemers, N., H. Heuvel, D. Gilder, A. Maass and A. Bonvini. 2004. "The Underrepresentation of Women in Science: Differential Commitment or the Queen Bee Syndrome?" *British Journal of Social Psychology* 43(3): 315–338.

Emrich, C., N. M. Carter and A. Beninger. 2015. "The Promise of Future Leadership: A Research Program on Highly Talented Employees in the Pipeline." *Catalyst*. Accessed May 19, 2016. www.catalyst.org/knowledge/promise-future-leadership-research-program-highly-talented-employees-pipeline.

Fels, A. 2004. "Do Women Lack Ambition?" *Harvard Business Review* 82(4): 50–60.

Fiske, S. T., A. J. Cuddy, P. Glick and J. Xu. 2002. "A Model of (Often Mixed) Stereotype Content: Competence and Warmth Respectively Follow from Perceived Status and Competition." *Journal of Personality and Social Psychology* 82(6): 878.

Fiske, S. T. and L. E. Stevens. 1993. *What's So Special About Sex? Gender Stereotyping and Discrimination.* Thousand Oaks, CA: Sage Publications.

Foschi, M. 2000. "Double Standards for Competence: Theory and Research." *Annual Review of Sociology* 26: 21–42.

Fouad, N. A. and A. M. Byars-Winston. 2005. "Cultural Context of Career Choice: Meta-Analysis of Race/Ethnicity Differences." *Career Development Quarterly* 53(3): 223–233.

Garcia-Retamero, R. and E. López-Zafra. 2006. "Prejudice Against Women in Male-Congenial Environments: Perceptions of Gender Role Congruity in Leadership." *Sex Roles* 55(1/2): 51–61.

Gill, M. J. 2004. "When Information Does Not Deter Stereotyping: Prescriptive Stereotyping Can Foster Bias Under Conditions That Deter Descriptive Stereotyping." *Journal of Experimental Social Psychology* 40(5): 619–632.

Glass, C. and A. Cook. 2016. "Leading at the Top: Understanding Women's Challenges Above the Glass Ceiling." *The Leadership Quarterly* 27(1): 51–63.

Grant Thornton. 2016. "Women in Business: Turning Promise Into Practice." Accessed April 25, 2016. www.grantthornton.global/globalassets/wib_turning_p romise_into_practice.pdf.

Greenhaus, J. H. and N. J. Beutell. 1985. "Sources of Conflict Between Work and Family Roles." *Academy of Management Review* 10(1): 76–88.

Greenhaus, J. H., S. Parasuraman and W. M. Wormley. 1990. "Effects of Race on Organizational Experiences, Job Performance Evaluations, and Career Outcomes." *Academy of Management Journal* 33(1): 64–86.

Guillaume, C. and S. Pochic. 2009. "What Would You Sacrifice? Access to Top Management and the Work–Life Balance." *Gender, Work & Organization* 16(1): 14–36.

Heilman, M. E. 2001. "Description and Prescription: How Gender Stereotypes Prevent Women's Ascent Up the Organizational Ladder." *Journal of Social Issues* 57(4): 657–674.

Heilman, M. E. 2012. "Gender Stereotypes and Workplace Bias." *Research in Organizational Behavior* 32: 113–135.

Heilman, M. E., A. S. Wallen, D. Fuchs and M. M. Tamkins. 2004. "Penalties for Success: Reactions to Women Who Succeed at Male Gender-Typed Tasks." *Journal of Applied Psychology* 89(3): 416.

Hochschild, A. 1997. "The Time Bind." *WorkingUSA* 1(2): 21–29.

Hochschild, A. and A. Machung. 2012. *The Second Shift: Working Families and the Revolution at Home*. London: Penguin.

Hofstede, G. 2001. *Culture's Consequences: Comparing Values, Behaviors, Institutions and Organizations Across Nations*. Thousand Oaks, CA: Sage Publications.

Hoobler, J. M., G. Lemmon and S. J. Wayne. 2014. "Women's Managerial Aspirations: An Organizational Development Perspective." *Journal of Management* 40(3): 703–730.

Hoyt, C. L. and J. L. Burnette. 2013. "Gender Bias in Leader Evaluations Merging Implicit Theories and Role Congruity Perspectives." *Personality and Social Psychology Bulletin* 39(10): 1306–1319.

Ibarra, H. 1993. "Personal Networks of Women and Minorities in Management: A Conceptual Framework." *Academy of Management Review* 18(1): 56–87.

Ibarra, H., R. Ely and D. Kolb. 2013. "Women Rising: The Unseen Barriers." *Harvard Business Review* 91(9): 60–66.

Ibarra, H. and J. Petriglieri. 2016. "Impossible Selves: Image Strategies and Identity Threat in Professional Women's Career Transitions." INSEAD Working Paper No. 2016/12/OBH. Accessed January 27, 2017. http://papers.ssrn.com/sol3/papers.cfm?abstract_id=2742061.

Judge, T. A., B. A. Scott and R. Ilies. 2006. "Hostility, Job Attitudes, and Workplace Deviance: Test of a Multilevel Model." *Journal of Applied Psychology* 91(1): 126.

Kalev, A. 2014. "How You Downsize is Who You Downsize: Biased Formalization, Accountability, and Managerial Diversity." *American Sociological Review* 79(1): 109–135.

Keating, C. F. 1985. "Gender and the Physiognomy of Dominance and Attractiveness." *Social Psychology Quarterly* 46: 61–70.

Khalaf, R. 2014. "Women in Business: Emerging Markets." *Financial Times*, March 7. Accessed April 25, 2016. http://im.ft-static.com/content/images/0724cd16-d149-11e3-bdbb-00144feabdc0.pdf.

Koch, A. J., S. D. D'Mello and P. R. Sackett. 2015. "A Meta-Analysis of Gender Stereotypes and Bias in Experimental Simulations of Employment Decision Making." *Journal of Applied Psychology* 100(1): 128.

Koriat, A., S. Lichtenstein and B. Fischhoff. 1980. "Reasons for Confidence." *Journal of Experimental Psychology: Human Learning and Memory* 6(2): 107–118.

Kossek, E. E. and C. Ozeki. 1998. "Work–Family Conflict, Policies, and the Job–Life Satisfaction Relationship: A Review and Directions for Organizational Behavior–Human Resources Research." *Journal of Applied Psychology* 83(2): 139.

Kruglanski, A. W. 1980. "Lay Epistemology Process and Contents." *Psychological Review* 87: 70–87.

Kunda, Z. and B. Sherman-Williams. 1993. "Stereotypes and the Construal of Individuating Information." *Personality and Social Psychology Bulletin* 19(1): 90–99.

Lanaj, K. and J. R. Hollenbeck. 2015. "Leadership Over-Emergence in Self-Managing Teams: The Role of Gender and Countervailing Biases." *Academy of Management Journal* 58(5): 1476–1494.

Lang, I. H. 2012. "The Ambition Gap Myth." *Catalyst*. Accessed May 19, 2016. www.catalyst.org/zing/ambition-gap-myth.

Livingston, B. A. and T. A. Judge. 2008. "Emotional Responses to Work–Family Conflict: An Examination of Gender Role Orientation Among Working Men and Women." *Journal of Applied Psychology* 93(1): 207–216.

Lyness, K. S. and M. E. Heilman. 2006. "When Fit is Fundamental: Performance Evaluations and Promotions of Upper-Level Female and Male Managers." *Journal of Applied Psychology* 91(4): 777.

Marlowe, C. M., S. L. Schneider and C. E. Nelson. 1996. "Gender and Attractiveness Biases in Hiring Decisions: Are More Experienced Managers Less Biased?" *Journal of Applied Psychology* 81(1): 11.

Mor, S., M. W. Morris and J. Joh. 2013. "Identifying and Training Adaptive Cross-Cultural Management Skills: The Crucial Role of Cultural Metacognition." *Academy of Management Learning & Education* 12(3): 453–475.

Oakley, J. G. 2000. "Gender-Based Barriers to Senior Management Positions: Understanding the Scarcity of Female CEOs." *Journal of Business Ethics* 27(4): 321–334.

Pager, D. and H. Shepherd. 2008. "The Sociology of Discrimination: Racial Discrimination in Employment, Housing, Credit, and Consumer Markets." *Annual Review of Sociology* 34: 181.

Paustian-Underdahl, S. C., L. S. Walker and D. J. Woehr. 2014. "Gender and Perceptions of Leadership Effectiveness: A Meta-Analysis of Contextual Moderators." *Journal of Applied Psychology* 99(6): 1129.

Peterson, H. 2014. "Someone Needs to Be First: Women Pioneers as Change Agents in Higher Education Management." *Gender Transformation in the Academy* 19: 395–413.

Prentice, D. A., E. Carranza. 2002. "What Women and Men Should Be, Shouldn't Be, Are Allowed to Be, and Don't Have to Be: The contents of Prescriptive Gender Stereotypes." *Psychology of Women Quarterly* 26(4): 269–281.

Ridgeway, C. L. and L. Smith-Lovin. 1999. "The Gender System and Interaction." *Annual Review of Sociology* 25: 191–216.

Ritchie, J., J. Lewis, C. M. Nicholls and R. Ormston, eds. 2013. *Qualitative Research Practice: A Guide for Social Science Students and Researchers.* Thousand Oaks, CA: Sage Publications.

Rosette, A. S., C. Z. Koval, A. Ma and R. Livingston. Forthcoming. "Race Matters for Women Leaders: Intersectional Effects on Agentic Deficiencies and Penalties." *The Leadership Quarterly.*

Rosette, A. S., G. J. Leonardelli and K. W. Phillips. 2008. "The White Standard: Racial Bias in Leader Categorization." *Journal of Applied Psychology* 93(4): 758.

Rudman, L. A. 1998. "Self-promotion as a Risk Factor for Women: The Costs and Benefits of Counterstereotypical Impression Management." *Journal of Personality and Social Psychology* 74(3): 629.

Rudman, L. A. and P. Glick. 2001. "Prescriptive Gender Stereotypes and Backlash Toward Agentic Women." *Journal of Social Issues* 57(4): 743–762.

Rule, N. O. and N. Ambady. 2008. "The Face of Success Inferences from Chief Executive Officers' Appearance Predict Company Profits." *Psychological Science* 19(2): 109–111.

Ryan, M. K. and S. A. Haslam. 2007. "The Glass Cliff: Exploring the Dynamics Surrounding the Appointment of Women to Precarious Leadership Positions." *Academy of Management Review* 32(2): 549–572.

Ryan, M. K., S. A. Haslam, M. D. Hersby and R. Bongiorno. 2011. "Think Crisis–Think Female: The Glass Cliff and Contextual Variation in the Think Manager–Think Male Stereotype." *Journal of Applied Psychology* 96(3): 470.

Ryan, M. K., S. A. Haslam, T. Morgenroth, F. Rink, J. Stoker and K. Peters. Forthcoming. "Getting on Top of the Glass Cliff: Reviewing a Decade of Evidence, Explanations, and Impact." *The Leadership Quarterly.*

Schein, V. E. 1973. "The Relationship Between Sex Role Stereotypes and Requisite Management Characteristics." *Journal of Applied Psychology* 57(2): 95–100.

Schein, V. E. 1975. "The Relationship Between Sex Role Stereotypes and Requisite Management Characteristics Among Female Managers." *Journal of Applied Psychology* 60: 340–344.

Seibert, S. E., M. L. Kraimer and R. C. Liden. 2001. "A Social Capital Theory of Career Success." *Academy of Management Journal* 44(2): 219–237.

Senior, C., M. L. Phillips, J. Barnes and A. S. David. 1999. "An Investigation into the Perception of Dominance from Schematic Faces: A Study Using the World-Wide Web." *Behavior Research Methods, Instruments, & Computers* 31(2): 341–346.

Snape, E. and T. Redman. 2003. "Too Old or Too Young? The Impact of Perceived Age Discrimination." *Human Resource Management Journal* 13(1): 78–89.

Snyder, K. 2014. "The Abrasiveness Trap: High-Achieving Men and Women are Described Differently in Reviews." *Fortune,* August 26. Accessed May 19, 2016. http://fortune.com/2014/08/26/performance-review-gender-bias/.

Spencer, S. J., C. Logel and P. G. Davies. 2016. "Stereotype Threat." *Annual Review of Psychology* 67: 415–437.

Stahl, G. K., M. L. Maznevski, A. Voigt and K. Jonsen. 2010. "Unraveling the Effects of Cultural Diversity in Teams: A Meta-Analysis of Research on Multi-cultural Work Groups." *Journal of International Business Studies* 41(4): 690–709.

Statistics South Africa. 2013. "*Mid-Year Population Estimates.*" Accessed May 6, 2016. www.statssa.gov.za/publications/P0302/P03022013.pdf.

The Economist. 2012. "Women's Economic Opportunity: A Global Index and Ranking from the Economist Intelligence Unit." Accessed April 25, 2016. www.eiu.com/Handlers/WhitepaperHandler.ashx?fi= WEO_full_report_final.pdf&mode=wp&campaignid=weoindex2012.

Thomas-Hunt, M. C. and K. W. Phillips. 2004. "When What You Know is Not Enough: Expertise and Gender Dynamics in Task Groups." *Personality and Social Psychology Bulletin* 30(12): 1585–1598.

Umphress, E. E., A. L. Simmons, W. R. Boswell and M. C. Triana. 2008. "Managing Discrimination in Selection: The Influence of Directives from an Authority and Social Dominance Orientation." *Journal of Applied Psychology* 93: 982–993.

United States Department of Labor. 2016. "Employed Persons by Occupation, Race, Hispanic or Latino Ethnicity, and Sex." United States Census. Accessed May 6, 2016. www.bls.gov/cps/cpsaat10.pdf.

Wada, M., C. L. Backman and S. J. Forwell. 2010. "Theoretical Perspectives of Balance and the Influence of Gender Ideologies." *Journal of Occupational Science* 17(2): 92–103.

Wood, W. and S. J. Karten. 1986. "Sex Differences in Interaction Style as a Product of Perceived Sex Differences in Competence." *Journal of Personality and Social Psychology* 50(2): 341.

World Economic Forum. 2015. "The Global Gender Gap Index." Accessed April 25, 2016. www3.weforum.org/docs/GGGR2015/The%20Global%20Gender%20Gap%20Index%202015.pdf.

Zebrowitz, L. A. 1997. *Reading Faces: Window to the Soul?* Boulder, CO: Westview Press.

Zebrowitz, L. A. and J. M. Montepare. 2005. "Appearance DOES matter." *Science* 308(5728): 1565–1566.

Zweigenhaft, R. L. 2014. "Diversity Among CEOs and Corporate Directors: Has the Heyday Come and Gone?" *Who Rules America?* Accessed December 23, 2014. www2.ucsc.edu/whorulesamerica/power/diversity_among_ceos.html.

7 Women's leadership in entrepreneurial contexts

Yogavelli Nambiar and Renuka Methil

Introduction

> I think I was fortunate enough to be brought up by a mother, and in fact by women; surrounded by women [who] never let societal rules dictate what they did with their lives, with their careers.
>
> Polo Leteka

Risk and business: the two key words characterizing every entrepreneur's journey. Loosely defined, an entrepreneur identifies a gap in the market, takes risks in challenging environments, works hard to implement a particular idea or innovation, creates jobs, contributes to the social fabric of society and, along the way to business triumph, makes mistakes and often faces failure. Entrepreneurs are the engines powering the economy. Countries hold entrepreneurship summits; governments, private sector and civil society relentlessly woo entrepreneurs; business schools vie with each other offering sought-after courses on how to become entrepreneurs, while these new entrants to the market continue to create a new lexicon of business, with words like sharing economy, crowdfunding and angel investing increasingly gaining currency in management parlance.

Originating from the French word "entreprendre", meaning "to undertake", entrepreneurship—and the myriad of subsequent definitions that have been ascribed to this concept—links to the initial thinking of doing something to meet a need amidst much risk to reap a reward. Entrepreneur, venture capitalist and academic, Daniel Isenberg calls entrepreneurs "contrarian value creators" who see opportunity where others see only a dead end (*The Economist* 2013).

According to the World Bank, "formal SMEs contribute up to 45% of total employment and up to 33% of national income (GDP) in emerging economies which increases significantly when informal SMEs are included" (Bell and Teima 2015). In India, small- and medium-sized businesses are estimated to contribute anywhere between 17% and 37% to the country's GDP and about 40% to jobs (*Economic Times* 2013). In Chile, SMEs are said to contribute close to 86% of jobs; and in Panama, they add 60%

to the country's GDP (Ayyagari, Beck and Demirguc-Kunt 2007). It is clear that small business is really big business.

Yet, with rising levels of unemployment and inequality, South Africa and many other developing countries contend with insufficient opportunities or platforms for the integration of women into the mainstream economy, leaving a significant segment of the population jobless and disenfranchised. The differential in terms of labor participation versus economic benefit derived was reinforced by former US president, Bill Clinton, who once stated that women perform 66% of the world's work and produce 50% of the food, yet only earn 10% of its income and own a mere 1% of the land (OECD 2012).

The fact is that women comprise more than half of the world's population, and while men have had a historical head start over women in business, the number of female entrepreneurs across the world is rising. However, total global gender equality, as per new research, is still a century away. The World Economic Forum (WEF) in its Global Gender Gap Report 2015 says it will take another 118 years for the world to be fully gender equal (WEF 2015). At an International Women's Day event in New York City in 2015, American politician Hillary Clinton called equal rights for women and girls "the great unfinished business of the 21st century" (*Newsweek* 2015). Former president of India, A. P. J. Abdul Kalam, added that "empowering women is a prerequisite for creating a good nation, when women are empowered, society with stability is assured" (Masood 2011).

This chapter seeks to question why there is still this glaring disparity, especially in emerging economies and patriarchal societies, where female potential has not been fully tapped to take the nation forward through entrepreneurship. Entrepreneurship is a journey of risk and responsibility. An entrepreneur carries the burden of every key decision in the business being dependent on her while she also juggles other priorities. This challenge is further compounded by having to support the livelihoods of staff and, in many cases, needing to contribute to the financial welfare of the entrepreneur's own family in the absence of a fixed and stable income—all while attempting to achieve her own dreams.

The women profiled in this chapter are a testament to the complexity of being an entrepreneur and, specifically, the determination required for women to succeed in environments not always conducive to or encouraging of entrepreneurship.

Evolution of women's entrepreneurship

While women entrepreneurship in practice is centuries old, the emergence of women's entrepreneurship as a topic of research is just over three decades old (Jennings and Brush 2013). The bulk of this research has been in more developed contexts.

Sadly, the history of entrepreneurial women over the ages has also not been explored and recorded so these women could be lauded and taught in the present day, encouraging young women and girls to follow their pioneering examples. This is especially true in developing countries, where the history books often fail these "heroines" of the business world, in contrast to the exhibition held in 2003 and 2004 by Harvard Business School, Enterprising Women: 250 Years of American Business, which recognized the indelible mark women made through their innovation and courage. The Smithsonian and the National Women's History Museum also honored American women in business over the centuries as a means of understanding the unique challenges they faced and overcame.

The literature in developing countries also largely ignores the historical socio-economic landmarks that have driven women entrepreneurship forward, such as World War II, when European women created alternate sources of income to address shortages in financing that were exacerbated by the primary breadwinner being away from the home (Berend 2013).

The authors for this chapter are based in South Africa, a country that also understands great strife, having experienced apartheid up until 1994. For black women, it was not just a fight against racism but also a gender fight for their rightful place in society. These struggles were inextricably linked. In the present day, women in emerging economies form a part of the global workforce; not just confined to office desks, but piloting planes, working the pickaxe in mines, driving tractors and running countries and conglomerates. However, there is still a glaring imbalance in the numbers of women in comparison to men in senior or executive positions.

Significance and impact of women's entrepreneurship

The world's youth population (aged 15–24) is currently around 1.8 billion, with 87% living in developing countries (Langley and Liddle 2014). According to the African Development Bank, Africa has more than 200 million people in the same age group, and about 65% of the continent is made up of millennials, making it the youngest continent in the world. Demographic forecasts show that this figure will double by 2045 and become an invaluable engine of the global economy in decades to come. However, the African Development Bank also reports that only a quarter of young African men and just 10% of young African women manage to get jobs in the formal economy before they reach the age of 30, and "the vast majority of young Africans will continue to have precarious employment" (*The Economist* 2014). This is the foundation for the concern that the highly popularized concept of a "youth dividend"—to maximize the assets of a youthful African population—would be compromised due to the lack of employment opportunities.

Startling statistics around unemployment in many emerging countries, such as South Africa's 26% in 2016 (closer to 35% if those who have given up looking for work are counted) (Statistics South Africa 2015), demonstrate the critical need for a strong entrepreneurial culture, especially for women who have even further restricted access to the mainstream economy than men (Statistics South Africa 2016). Research shows that prevalence rates of female entrepreneurship tend to be relatively higher in developing than in developed countries as a result of women facing higher barriers to entry in the formal labor market and hence having to turn to entrepreneurship as a way out of unemployment and poverty (Minniti and Naude 2010).

Besides being seen to be a solution to these challenges, entrepreneurship is also key to an economy's productivity and competitiveness. A simple analogy lays bare the gaps in the propagation of a workplace or market that excludes women. If a country is likened to a company that has 100 productive workers but chooses to effectively utilize only 48 of them, can it be expected to operate at maximum efficiency or create optimal value?

Entrepreneurship has widely been recognized as having an impact on a country's wealth and job creation, through economic activity and an increased tax base, as well as its accumulation of innovation capital. Further, female entrepreneurship is now increasingly being acknowledged as making a significant contribution to economic growth and employment generation (Rabbani and Chowdhury 2013; Brush and Cooper 2012; Maphalla, Nieuwenhuizen and Roberts 2009; Nmadu 2011). According to the United Nations Industrial Development Organization (UNIDO 2014):

> When men and women become more equal, economies grow faster, fewer people remain in poverty, and overall well-being increases. Studies have reported that raising female employment to male levels can have a direct impact on GDP growth rates, increasing it by as much as 34% in some countries, and that countries' productivity can increase by as much as 25% if discriminatory barriers against women are removed.

According to the Global Entrepreneurship Monitor (GEM) 2012 Women's Report, 126 million women were starting or running new businesses in 67 economies around the world (Kelley et al. 2013). Women entrepreneurs represent approximately one-third of all new business activity and one-fourth of established business activity in countries around the globe (Terjesen and Elam 2012). This proliferation of women-owned businesses has ensured its growing popularity as a focal point for international research.

The literature has identified a distinct gender bias in entrepreneurship in relation to the numbers, types and business growth levels of entrepreneurs, with men having founded or owned a great number and diversity of businesses and having higher representation in the ownership numbers of more sophisticated and larger businesses (Herrington, Kew and Kew 2014). The majority of enterprises headed by women tend to be found in the retail and personal service sectors and are under-represented in the manufacturing, extraction and business services sectors (Jennings and Brush 2013).

There also exists a gendered discrepancy in the types of challenges faced and in the availability of and accessibility to support mechanisms provided. The life of a female entrepreneur is still riddled with the rhetoric of clichéd stereotypes, cultural demands and archaic entry barriers and challenges.

It is thus no wonder that across the 59 economies participating in the GEM report, only Ghana had more women entrepreneurs than men and only a few had almost equal numbers of women and men entrepreneurs, while most had more men than women (Kelley et al. 2013). In a study on women entrepreneurs in developing countries within Asia, it was found that the majority of women entrepreneurs create businesses due to the push factors of poverty, unemployment, the need to have a greater revenue to support the family's expenditure and as a precaution against potential risks to their primary income (Tambunan 2009).

Such compelling arguments make any effort to develop and sustain female enterprise pertinent—especially in emerging economies where women, when included, can improve businesses, a fact widely endorsed by research and those companies that believe in diversity. The benefits of greater inclusion of women are widely acknowledged by billionaire philanthropists and the planet's most powerful advocates for women. Melinda Gates calls women's issues the "hard issues" (Howard 2016).

Globally, despite the disappointing, gender-skewed figures on business ownership, a World Bank–Goldman Sachs study entitled "Women hold up half the sky" (2012) found that women entrepreneurship leads to better-educated children, healthier families and more empowered communities. As heads or managers of households, women tend to spend more on household health, nutrition and education than men and also employ proportionately more females compared to male-headed firms (Nichter and Goldmark 2009).

It is thus viewed as an integral component in the overall development of communities and nations. Women tend to "pay it forward": in an impact study on a women entrepreneurship program entitled the Goldman Sachs "10,000 Women" initiative, nine out of 10 women trained paid forward the education and support they received by supporting other women and girls in their communities. It is popularly believed that in viewing wealth differently, women when employed use 90% of their income for their family or community, compared to the 30% men use (OECD 2009). Thus, women go further in their efforts to empower others, and help to create stronger communities and nations. Putting wealth in their hands could thus have a significant multiplier effect. South African Entrepreneur Polo Leteka, the owner of IDF Capital in Johannesburg, said:

> In emerging economies, primarily you are trying to solve social problems. But on the other hand, you are also trying to grow your

economy and somehow you want to infuse the two. You want to say that through economic growth, I will then invariably solve social problems. So your policy framework has to be very different to that, because it is not just about saying, let's open our doors to the world for us to trade with. You need to understand how then does that affect the ability of us creating, say, small businesses who are going to be creating jobs for these unemployed people. So, I think the conversation is very different.

In large part, the dominant paradigm of patriarchy is common in many emerging markets. Yet, in the face of complex and non-conducive environments, many women are finding innovative products or services to contribute to the market and braving many challenges to improve the circumstances of their families and communities.

Take, for instance, Essma Ben Hamida, who is the founder of Enda Inter-Arabe, the first and leading microfinance institution in Tunisia. According to the women entrepreneurship group, Lionesses of Africa, Enda has a staff of 1,300 people working out of 79 branches and, as of January 2016, had served 270,000 micro-entrepreneurs (70% of these are women and 40% live in rural areas) with a US$150 million loan portfolio and a repayment rate above 99%. In response to the needs of the community, Enda developed non-traditional lines of credit and specialized products, which included education, housing and agriculture loans, as well as start-up loans for unemployed youth to launch their own businesses. Through its work, Enda has had an impact on over half a million Tunisians formerly excluded from access to the economy.

It is clear that innovative and resourceful women who either have no access to the mainstream job market or see an opportunity to meet a market need have stepped up to create an impact in a myriad of ways. Their significance is felt through direct contributions to the economy and the livelihoods of others and makes a palpable difference to the living conditions of their own families.

Characteristics and motivations of women's entrepreneurship

Who are these female entrepreneurs? What is the perception of them? The Global Entrepreneurship and Development Institute (GEDI) created the Female Entrepreneurship Index to understand this further and indicated that the subject is approached quite broadly, including everyone "from informal petty traders and shopkeepers to founders of high-tech start-ups" (Terjesen and Lloyd 2015).

Entrepreneurial activity ranges from survivalist businesses motivated by necessity, mainly in the informal sector, through to opportunity-based businesses created through the identification of a niche in the market (Herrington, Kew and Kew 2014). In relation to the size of the business, lifestyle-based businesses are run at a size and level that is comfortable for the entrepreneur without any aim to grow. High-growth businesses are those that are based on a higher level of innovation and where scalability is a key priority of the entrepreneur (Herrington, Kew and Kew 2014).

According to the 2013 GEM report, it is established businesses that create jobs, and it is thus vital to ensure that women-owned businesses are supported to grow sustainably. Yet, as the level of business sophistication and size increases, women's ownership decreases (Herrington, Kew and Kew 2014).

The sub-Saharan Africa and MENA/Mid-Asia regions show high levels of necessity motives among women entrepreneurs: on average, 37% and 36%, respectively, started their businesses out of necessity (Kelley et al. 2013). The majority of women entrepreneurs in developing economies are "locked in" to the informal sector; this has been found to be the case in South Africa as well (Chaney 2014; Nmadu 2011). It appears that businesses owned by women either fail or remain very small, especially within low-income communities. The South African Department of Trade and Industry released a special report in 2005 entitled "Women Entrepreneurs: A burgeoning force in our economy", which acknowledged that while women made up half of the business force, their contribution was not adequately nurtured.

Today, the numbers around women entrepreneurship in these emerging contexts remain unimpressive and reaffirm that insufficient impact has been achieved in this regard. The demographic of women entrepreneurs at different business sizes has remained the same (Herrington, Kew and Kew 2014; Chaney 2014). As a business goes through the growth phase of its lifecycle, the demands on the entrepreneur spike and they are faced with conflicting priorities; women especially are forced to make hard choices (Sharma 2014). Women are generally the primary caregivers in their household and the support systems to enable them to manage the personal or family demands while also building the business are frequently limited. This often means an early exit or discontinuance of the business (Sharma 2014; Schindehutte, Morris and Brennan 2003).

In terms of business sector, women entrepreneurs tend to stay within services-based industries, mainly hospitality, due to the lower barriers to entry in terms of skills, capital, infrastructure and resources required to get started. While numbers have increased in certain traditionally male-dominated sectors, this is still not significant enough to make substantial change.

The collective evidence found internationally is that females are much less likely than males to be involved in various forms of entrepreneurship. Some of the reasons for this relate to education, culture or exposure.

A study on women entrepreneurship in India indicated that some women started their own businesses to take on new challenges or maximize opportunities for self-fulfillment, as a response to success stories of friends and relatives, or out of need for employment, additional income or independence (Sharma 2014).

Many women focus on work that is customized around their household priorities—and so growth of the business becomes difficult. Ambition is also often perceived to be a negative trait, thus discouraging women from being aggressive with business growth. Culturally, women tend to be encouraged to remain quiet, passive and non-ambitious. Growth and success are sometimes perceived to be unfeminine. Typically, they may be encouraged, especially in more traditional environments, to enter "safe" professions such as teaching or nursing. Reports suggest as much as four-fifths of women entrepreneurs in sub-Saharan Africa operate in the consumer sector, whereas men often show much more diversity in industry sector participation (Kelley et al. 2013).

Whether in traditional "woman-friendly" sectors or those that are generally male-dominated, there are examples of women who have pushed the boundaries and been able to create successful businesses. Through the research and the interviews conducted with women leaders for this book, specific themes emerged, including mindfulness and resilience. This chapter explores these two attributes in more detail, looking at how they helped these women stay the course and enabled them to face and overcome adverse circumstances with dignity and grace.

The ecosystem for women entrepreneurs

The 2015 Global Entrepreneurship Monitor (GEM) survey (Herrington, Kew and Kew 2016), which assessed the quality of entrepreneurship ecosystems across different geographic regions, found that the entrepreneurship ecosystem is most developed in North American economies and least developed in African economies.

In the same year, the top 10 countries for female entrepreneurs were the United States, Australia, the United Kingdom, Denmark, the Netherlands, France, Iceland, Sweden, Finland and Norway (Terjesen and Lloyd 2015). The 2015 Female Entrepreneurship Index (Global Entrepreneurship and Development Institute 2015), which identified factors enabling high-potential female entrepreneurs, noted that sub-Saharan Africa needs to improve women's access to bank accounts and financial training programs. There is a growing body of research that echoes this reality.

While women's entrepreneurship has grown in popularity as an area for support by leading companies and public sector institutions in emerging countries, the general consensus is that the support is insufficient. Two of the larger programs of support are the Goldman Sachs "10,000 Women" initiative, which saw 10,000 women entrepreneurs from 42 countries provided with scholarship-based business education and support; and the Coca-Cola 5by20 program, which aims to economically empower five million women entrepreneurs around the world by 2020. The International

Labour Organization (ILO), an agency of the United Nations, ran the Women Entrepreneurship Development (WEDGE) program, which provided women entrepreneurs with training and mentorship services. The tools developed were extended to 25,000 women entrepreneurs in 15 countries.

Governments have also become more proactive around the creation of customized initiatives to support women entrepreneurs. In South Africa, the National Home Builders' Registration Council (NHBRC) created a skills and support program for women who own businesses in construction or related sectors. Part of the drive is to ensure that there is a structure to support women in this male-dominated sector. As part of its transition into democracy, South Africa developed specific legislation called the Broad-based Black Economic Empowerment Codes (B-BBEE), which consists of five elements of support, one of which is Enterprise and Supplier Development (ESD). This was specifically included to ensure corporate and institutional support for small businesses. Specific support for black South African women entrepreneurs is a vital part of the South African government's goal to address historical disempowerment of black South African entrepreneurs, and as a parallel effort to enable women to progress in business (Bradford 2007). This effort received a boost by women-owned businesses being weighted and scored higher within the B-BBEE Codes' ESD element.

Despite this legislative and institutional drive, women entrepreneurs continue to face negative prevailing socio-cultural attitudes and gender discrimination. There has not been significant change in reconstituting the societal framework or mindsets to create a supportive environment for women entrepreneurs. This brings into focus the media's role in celebrating entrepreneurs through the creation and promotion of female role models. This was highlighted in the eight-township study on the psychosocial support ecosystem for women entrepreneurs in South Africa, undertaken by one of the authors in 2015. It was found that one of the key barriers of entrepreneurship amongst women was the lack of female role models, creating the perception that entrepreneurship had a "male" image and that in order for a business to be successful, it needed to be owned and run by a man (Nambiar 2015). In Bangladesh, where women form only 10% of the country's total entrepreneurs, the image of successful entrepreneurship has been found to be male (Rabbani and Chowdhury 2013).

Arising from these and other studies on the institutional framework needed to support women entrepreneurs are several key recommendations for public and private sector interventions. These are often categorized under education, opportunity recognition, registration of businesses, equal legal rights, financing, business skill development, access to markets and networks, family support systems and socio-cultural factors.

The Kauffman Foundation (Robb, Coleman and Stangler 2014), which has a strong research focus on entrepreneurship internationally, offered the following approaches to the promotion of women entrepreneurship:

- family-friendly policies that allow women to have their children cared for in order to pursue entrepreneurship policies;
- profiling success stories of women entrepreneurs;
- providing opportunities within various sectors for women entrepreneurs to participate;
- more opportunities to learn about how to start and grow a business.

Khumbar (2013, 192–200) summarized the inhibitors to women entrepreneurship in India as follows:

women face (an) absence of balance between family and career obligations, no awareness about capacities, low ability to bear risk, problems of work with male workers, lack of self-confidence, mobility constraints and lack of interaction with successful entrepreneurs are major problems of women entrepreneurship development in India.

Further, institutional and legal barriers such as the lack of direct ownership of property or financial freedom, negligence by financial establishments in the provision of financing and a gap in professional education were also cited as inhibiting factors. This leads to a paradox of entrepreneurial skill and finance in economically rich and poor women (Khumbar 2013).

Many women in other developing countries would also identify with this experience and often express similar frustrations in interviews conducted for both mainstream media and academic studies.

The experience of the female entrepreneur

The women interviewed for this chapter are entrepreneurs drawn from various different sectors and separate business contexts and geographies. They have all risen despite adverse circumstances, driven by a strong sense of purpose, profit and philanthropy. There is limited empirical evidence and discourse on female entrepreneurs in emerging economies, which makes it important to focus on the enablers and barriers in their journeys to becoming significant players in the mainstream economy.

According to American entrepreneur, Erica Nicola, who left the corporate world to start *YFS Magazine*, "The glass ceiling that once limited a woman's career path has paved a new road towards business ownership, where women can utilize their sharp business acumen while building strong family ties" (Forbes 2012). But is that the case for millions of women in emerging contexts who still encounter different and perhaps more inhibiting environments? In many areas, young women and girls find it difficult to consider entrepreneurship as a career option. This is linked to several factors: a lack of support for the entrepreneurship within the country and community, resulting in a negative perception of self-employment; few appropriate role models; the lack of education faced by many females in developing countries, which is linked to a deficit in business skills; and the lack of exposure to opportunities, markets and financing.

The motivation for women entering the entrepreneurial path is extremely diverse. Often, the inspiration for success can be adversities experienced in childhood that drive a woman to reverse her fortune. The traits that get these women through are resilience and mindfulness in the face of punishing circumstances. Turkish businesswoman Neri Karra (as profiled in *Forbes Woman Africa* (Methil 2014/15)) sells an eponymous range of luxury handbags in plush boutiques around the world. Her family were refugees who landed on the Turkish border from Bulgaria, and she still recalls the day she arrived there at the age of 11, penniless and homeless. It was then that the little girl grew up and got her first impression of "living out of a suitcase". Today, Neri shuttles between offices in Istanbul and London, overseeing her multi-million-dollar business. She has a PhD in management, has published two academic books and often teaches at universities in London. During the personal interview, she recalled her childhood in Turkey when the family had limited means. She attended a "ghetto school"; her father was a welder, her mother a factory-cleaner. There were days when the family went to bed hungry. She studied very hard to rise above her circumstances and became the first person in her family to go to university—that, too, in the United States—after which she embarked on her first entrepreneurial venture at 22, setting up her first showroom in Bulgaria.

Poverty is a huge driver in the lives of some of the women we interviewed. It was the prime determinant of success later in life. Another example is South African entrepreneur and corporate leader, Sindisiwe Koyana, who was raised on the border of Durban in Umlazi, a township in South Africa's KwaZulu-Natal province. What made her determined to change the course of her life and that of her family? She used the word "mindful":

It was the poverty. It was what I saw around me. Yes, it was a difficult journey. But basically, having to go to school with my mother's nursing shoes which I had to dye black ... . And Sundays after church was time to mend socks and other old clothes that needed to be restored for use to go to school. This taught me a good sense of routine, discipline and order ... . When the first shopping center was opened in Umlazi, I was in that queue when they were looking for students who were going to do stock-taking over the weekends. Doing accounting at school at the time came in handy. This too, instilled a strong culture of independence and get things done yourself instead of waiting for handouts. So I was very mindful of what I am seeing around me. And I made a pact with myself that I will get out of here. Not on my own, but I will take my family out of this situation. So that drove me ... throughout my life, the adversity raised me up.

And when she forayed into a career as a chartered accountant, she discovered it was a condescending environment for a young, black woman:

> I must say again, in that environment, I didn't really feel the hostility [...] I guess the patronizing was probably the big issue if I look back. I was young. I was a woman. I was black. So people would look at me like this little girl. So I would then do things in such a manner [to show] that "I am not a little girl."

The "little girl" image is often used to dismiss women in male-dominated environments—yet another demonstration of the stereotyped male perception of female newcomers in business. As the owner of the business, women entrepreneurs often speak of feeling that they're "not being taken seriously." Despite being armed with multiple degrees and an iron will, Namibian oil and gas entrepreneur Selma Shimutwikeni—interviewed for *Forbes Woman Africa* (Methil 2015b)—also faced this prejudice. The daughter of liberation fighters, Selma was born in Russia, raised in Angola as a refugee and witnessed the independence of her country, Namibia. In her case, it was her parents, both of whom were lawyers, who instilled in her the confidence to rise above inequalities. One of only two mineral lawyers in Namibia, she is CEO of Rich Africa Consultancy. In the course of her journey she was often confronted by skepticism from the men in the male-dominated sector who thought that because Namibia is a frontier territory in the oil and gas arena, such an undertaking was too big for "a petite young woman".

Women are invariably kept out of the smoky alcoves or golf courses of the big boys' clubs, where networks are formed and gainfully used. Because of the historical lag women have had in entering business, men boast better business relationships, and they are also adept at using them to advance their careers—and keep winning. As there are fewer women at the top, women also have the added hurdle of lacking role models they can look up to in business. In some cases they have turned to familial support systems, as parents can be role models too, and—as in Selma's case—strong in-family mentors have helped guide them on their path to success,.

In a personal interview for *Forbes Woman Africa* (Methil 2015a), Ethiopian entrepreneur Mahlet Afework revealed that she had no role models whatsoever, in either family or society, and had to find her own way. Her shop, Mafi, is in a busy commercial complex in Addis Ababa. She was only eight, the youngest of five children, when her mother left them to go to Israel for medical treatment. A year later, their father died. Her mother did not return until she turned 18. But by then, Mahlet was already a designer, working as a rapper with radio stations in Ethiopia playing her music to make ends meet. Today, she showcases her designer wear on the ramps of New York and has been quite the game-changer in Ethiopia's fashion industry.

Often, men can take on the mantle as friend, philosopher and guide to women in business. Take the men along in your journey, is the mantra for the UN Women's HeForShe solidarity campaign for gender equality.

South African entrepreneur Stacey Brewer is a success story by herself. But she too admitted to learning a lot from her male business partner. While studying for her MBA she was challenged by her professors at the Gordon Institute of Business Science (GIBS) in Johannesburg to effect change in the education system in South Africa. In January 2013, Brewer and her business partner Ryan Harrison did just that, opening the doors of their school, SPARK, and bringing the blended learning model to the continent. As she put it:

> I wouldn't say necessarily as a female leader but just as a leader it is huge. I have learnt so much from Ryan, co-founder of SPARK. I learned so much from him in terms of the business [...] I learned a lot from him about not being so emotional and to be more pragmatic about things. So I would say he has been a key influence in shaping my leadership skills, especially for the business world.

Examples abound where women can also be strong role models for women. Gil Oved, co-founder of The Creative Counsel, a South African advertising and activations company that employs 80% women, admitted to having many female mentors, one of whom had her own production company and offered Gil his first break in television. Gil said:

> I am often in awe at how strong women really are. There is no question in my mind that in the next hundred years or however long, women will incomparably rule the world. And the logic is very simple. The only reason that it is a man's world now is because brawn mattered more than brain mattered [...] Things like emotional maturity, collaboration, empathy, and you know, deep communication, all these things that women are way more involved in, is what becomes more powerful, more necessary in today's society [...] I think it is probably the best time in the history of man to be a woman.

And when a country itself rallies behind its women, the results are path-breaking too. Rwanda is exemplary in that respect. Take the story of Rosette Chantal Rugamba, whose parents fled from Rwanda to Uganda in 1959 during the liberation struggle. She grew up as a refugee with her seven siblings. Her father was a brewer and her mother a teacher. She worked very hard at university and destiny took her from Africa to the United Kingdom. In 2002, after stints at Harrods and British Airways in London, she was asked by the Rwandan president Paul Kagame to return to Rwanda and turn the country's tourism infrastructure around as its tourism head. "I asked myself, 'What value can I add?' I am eternally grateful to the president that he unleashed the potential I never knew I had," said Rosette, who was six months pregnant when she was offered the role in a country she had never lived in. "It was really, really challenging," said Rosette, who is today an entrepreneur in the luxury travel, tourism and conference industry in Rwanda. She arrived from a developed market to a post-conflict economy, facing the concomitant challenges head-on, saying, "there is nothing that is impossible". She was very aware of the impression she made: "I was a manager and immediately I had to change my wardrobe. I wanted to wear a three-piece suit, I wanted to carry a specific briefcase. I talked differently."

For most women occupying senior roles, part of the "hard work" is also looking the part, often adopting the masculine model of leadership, in attire and attitude. Polo Leteka found that:

> as a woman, when I become assertive, I am accused of being aggressive. But when a man behaves in the exact same way that I do, they say he is firm, he is assertive. So with men, it is seen as positive. With women, it is seen as a negative.

Interestingly, many of the women entrepreneurs interviewed for this chapter did not see themselves as "traditional" women or view their leadership style as particularly "female"—raising the question of whether being a feminine leader is perceived to be inhibiting to success.

Female millennials have turned around masculine models of leadership and convention—better than the demographic cohorts that have gone before. Millennials are people born between 1980 and 2000, also commonly referred to as Generation Y. This generation does not conform to nine-to-five schedules for too long, and they have a proclivity to take risks and be their own bosses—a culture and attitude that might be more suited to entrepreneurship. Gil Oved concurred:

> Fifty years ago, if you had asked a typical 16-year-old if they know the name of one CEO of one company, they wouldn't be able to tell you. Not even the company that their dad works for. Now, 50 years later, it is the coolest job to have. Not soccer star. Not *Idols* singer, but CEO.

Many of these young people may seek to attain this position by creating their own businesses rather than following the traditional route of seeking employment.

Take the case of Archel Bernard, a twenty-something millennial CEO with a little boutique in downtown Monrovia. She was raised in Atlanta in the US, as her family lived there in exile during both the first and second Liberian civil war. Archel moved to her family's hometown in Liberia in 2011 in search of opportunities. This was where she chose to remain. She is today a socialite and fashion designer with a label called "It's Archel". For a young educated woman with bright ideas, the country offers few incentives, but Archel is bent on changing the image of Liberia. The climate for businesswomen is especially challenging for entrepreneurs: most times there is no electricity or running water, she said, but she has chosen to look beyond these issues. She now works with female Ebola survivors who help sew her clothes and sell them to the world.

One of the barriers stalling women from ascending heights could be other women—or a woman's own mental makeup when she sets high expectations and internal standards for herself. Owning a successful business and being ambitious about its growth may not be perceived as "suitable" for a woman. "I think women's biggest enemy is women," said Gil:

> One is, they themselves create their own barriers in their minds. I have mentored a lot of women in my business who don't believe that they are worthy. And my biggest challenge is convincing them that I am not bullshitting them when I say that I believe in them and that they can do it [...] So the first problem is that I think they were brought up in this culture where women are not allowed to succeed. The second problem is other women in a workplace would sooner see a man succeed and a man promoted than their own peers [...] There is a terrible vindictiveness and huge jealousy if another woman succeeds.

Further cultural barriers to women running their own businesses are age and race. For instance, Polo Leteka said age, gender and race were the three "negatives" she carried with her, although she always wanted to be an entrepreneur and her own boss:

> I think I made a decision very early on that actually that is not my problem. It is really the problem of everybody else who might be thinking of those things. And I learned very quickly that I needed to occupy a space. So when I walk into a room, I need not feel like I don't belong, or I should not be apologizing for being there. And it is something you learn with time [...] I have also learned that because of those prejudices and the role that they can play in you becoming successful or not in whatever it is you are trying to do, unfortunately you have to work harder than everybody else.

The challenges experienced by women entrepreneurs

Parallel to the case for greater mainstreaming of female entrepreneurs in the economy is the issue of financial inclusion and access to finance. An

Iranian study on differences in reasons for business failure between male- and female-owned businesses showed that the main cause for the former was management deficiency while for women it was related to financing, business management training and support (Arasti 2011).

A vast majority of women in Africa still remain unbanked and have limited financial literacy. There are echoes of this across the developing world. Gender imbalance in business financing is correlated to a lack of high-growth women's entrepreneurship (Robb, Coleman and Stangler 2014).

The World Bank's Global Findex provides gendered data on access to basic financial resources. Its 2014 database shows that while there has been progress, many people around the world, particularly women, still do not have bank accounts. "The gender gap in account ownership is not narrowing … in developing economies, the gender gap remains a steady 9 percentage points", states the report (World Bank 2014).

In the initial stages of rampant nation building it was most often women who led in the financial empowerment of less privileged women. South Africa's best example is WIPHOLD, an all-woman investment company formed in the days after apartheid ended (with a new African National Congress government keen on transformative policies). WIP-HOLD encouraged women in small towns and villages to invest their savings in the country's biggest companies. It gave them a sense of ownership they had not experienced before (Methil 2014).

The Cherie Blair Foundation for Women, which also works in Africa to empower women to gain financial independence, focuses on developing women's micro, small and medium-sized enterprises to help them grow into sustainable businesses. On its website the foundation refers to the vital development of this "missing middle" of the economy. This mass of untapped potential is clearly a missing link. A 2015 McKinsey Global Institute report indicated that "in a full potential scenario in which women play an identical role in labor markets to that of men, as much as $28 trillion, or 26 percent, could be added to global annual GDP by 2025" (Woetzel et al. 2015).

Stacey Brewer, the entrepreneur who founded SPARK Schools, spoke of the "invisibility" she experienced in her initial funding meetings with male startup investors. They would specifically address her male co-founder, which led her to realize that a relationship with these potential investors would not work if they could not value her role.

According to Terjesen and Elam (2012), "even in the most advanced economies where large numbers of women start and build formal businesses, women are often silent partners in business ventures, especially as minority owners of family businesses, and are less likely to register their business than men".

The emphasis now has to be on conceptualizing practical solutions to address the inhibitors to growth of women-owned businesses. The motivation for the creation of a business is viewed as similar across genders, but women face particular challenges that have been evidenced by extensive research in this area. Dependent on the socio-economic level, geographic location, environmental and societal context, and institutional support available, women face varying degrees of support (or lack thereof).

Solutions that address these challenges have been proposed by numerous academics, practitioners and policymakers with little increase in actual numbers. This may be indicative of a further layer of intricacy that is being missed by the many enterprise development support providers.

Despite a scarcity of appropriate entrepreneurial role models, women entrepreneurs tend to have a more positive outlook on failure within business. The theme of resilience that emerged in the interviews and in the literature review pays tribute to women having to "pick themselves up and get on with it".

Women have been found to face a number of obstacles and challenges during their entrepreneurial journey, from lack of experience and lack of both financial and social capital, to gender discrimination rooted in stereotypical views on traditional roles of women, and domestic issues (Ascher 2012). Research into the issues and challenges faced by women entrepreneurs in India found several problems or constraints mentioned as inhibitors to business growth—among them were male-dominated societal norms, women's poor education levels, lack of self-confidence and not "being taken seriously" (Sharma 2014). This was further expounded in a discussion of the time and emotional burdens arising from the dual responsibilities of entrepreneur and traditional homemaker. These expectations were found to impede the "ambition, self-confidence, innovativeness, achievement motivation and risk-taking ability" of the women entrepreneur (Sharma 2014). In an article entitled "Women entrepreneurs: 'we cannot have change unless we have men in the room'", the argument is made that it is essential to integrate the gender dimension into discussions on entrepreneurship (Kamberidou 2013).

In addition to the business challenges customarily mentioned by small business owners, women entrepreneurs face the additional societal pressure of gender discrimination. The Indian study suggested that patriarchal bias inhibited entrepreneurial traits such as ambition, self-confidence, innovativeness, achievement motivation and risk-taking ability (Sharma 2014). However, the personality traits generally aligned to those who choose an entrepreneurial career are; assertiveness, self-governance and being positive and proactive (Mordi et al. 2010). The question then arises how these positive characteristics might be maintained in the midst of the emotional challenges mentioned above. Despite the growth in the number of women-owned small businesses, "gender asymmetry" persists—a study on entrepreneurs and motherhood showed that women are not usually relieved of household responsibilities and remain the "primary parent, emotional nurturer, and housekeeper" (Schindehutte, Morris and Brennan 2003). The study argued that there are several factors that cause conflict for the woman entrepreneur, including gender, work-role overload, parental demands, family involvement, and informational and emotional support (Schindehutte Morris and Brennan 2003).

Research conducted by one of the authors in eight townships in South Africa indicated that insufficient attention was being paid to the psycho-social challenges faced by women entrepreneurs, which was often a contributing factor to the failure of their businesses. The top five challenges that emerged were: jealousy of and lack of support from the community, sometimes resulting in physical and emotional intimidation; gender-related discrimination by employees, suppliers or clients; unsupportive family or friends due to them being discouraging of entrepreneurship; a critical or discouraging husband; and a lack of confidence in one's own ability to run and grow a business (Nambiar 2015).

The study demonstrated that there were layers of complexity and challenge faced by this group connected to gender, the difficulties related to being entrepreneurs and the infrastructural barriers of townships. Gender-related difficulties were felt unilaterally by all participants, ranging from "not knowing her place" to "the community is more passive-aggressive. They know what I do but won't give me business. They would rather say I'm not going to assist; if she succeeds, she succeeds on her own." Women rely on family, friends, peer- and faith-based groups for support; however, each group acts as both enabler and barrier for these women. Such challenges are largely ignored by public and private institutional support role-players when designing initiatives for support, as they opt for standard interventions due to convenience or affordability (Nambiar 2015).

Lessons for aspiring entrepreneurs

The women interviewed and featured in this chapter have seen and overcome adversities and have a wealth of pertinent learning to share. In the words of the dynamic South African entrepreneur, Johanna Mukoki, who started the award-winning business, Travel with Flair and was profiled in *Forbes Woman Africa* (Methil 2015): "If you have an idea that keeps you awake at night and you think about it all the time—that means you are passionate enough to make it work. You need an opportunity, passion and a great funder!" (Ravanona 2015). And Sindisiwe Koyana said:

> Unpack the noise and be able to focus on what needs to be done. Walk with it. But then, know when you realize that there are no more lessons to be learned. Be authentic and true to yourself. Don't be driven by emotions, don't be so angry that you can't unpack the real issues.

South African wine entrepreneur Wendy Appelbaum had advice for women in the boardroom: "If you are with men, be gruff, you have got to be prepared to play their game, you have got to be prepared to swear, as often, those techniques are used to intimidate women. So give it back" (Methil 2015).

Conclusion

Women entrepreneurs have an integral role to play in the health of families, in building a stable society and in driving national growth. There are economic, psychological, human rights-based and economic arguments for the inclusion of women in the economy and ensuring they are at the forefront of creating businesses in their respective countries. Support for women's development and entrepreneurship support is no longer seen as "nice to have"; it is now a necessity if emerging markets intend to grow significantly.

If the full potential of women as growth-oriented entrepreneurs is realized, it will prompt greater economic and employment growth, which will support the drive to alleviate poverty. Governments, corporates, academics, business development service providers and other bodies cannot afford to ignore the importance of women's potential contribution.

To the women entrepreneurs, the overriding message that appears to emerge can be encapsulated in Johanna Mukoki's assertion: "Do not let your gender hold you back from being your best version of yourself" (Ravanona 2015).

References

Arasti, Z. 2011. "An Empirical Study on the Causes of Business Failure in Iranian Context." *African Journal of Business Management* 5(17): 7488–7498.

Ascher, J. 2012. "Female Entrepreneurship—an Appropriate Response to Gender Discrimination." *Journal of Entrepreneurship, Management and Innovation* 8(4): 97–114.

Ayyagari, M., T. Beck and A. Demirguc-Kunt. 2007. "Small and Medium Enterprises Across the Globe." *Small Business Economics* 29(4): 415–434.

Berend, I. T. 2013. *Case Studies on Modern European Economy: Entrepreneurs, Inventions, Institutions.* London: Routledge.

Bradford, W. D. 2007. "Distinguishing Economically from Legally Formal Firms: Targeting Business Support to Entrepreneurs in South Africa's Townships." *Journal of Small Business Management* 45(1): 94–115.

Brush, C. G. and S. Y. Cooper. 2012. "Female Entrepreneurship and Economic Development: An International Perspective." *Entrepreneurship & Regional Development* 24(1–2): 1–6.

Chaney, A. 2014. "Black Female Entrepreneurs in Post-Apartheid South Africa: Achieving Female Economic Empowerment in the Formal and Informal Sectors." PhD diss. ProQuest Dissertations and Theses Database (UMI 3641734).

Forbes. 2012. "Entrepreneurship Is The New Women's Movement." June. www.forbes.com/sites/work-in-progress/2012/06/08/entrepreneurship-is-the-new-womens-movement/#6c4b363c6922.

Global Entrepreneurship and Development Institute. 2015. "2015 Female Entrepreneurship Index." https://thegedi.org/2015-female-entrepreneurship-index/.

Goyal, M. 2013. "SMEs Employ Close to 40% of India's Workforce, but Contribute Only 17% to GDP." *The Economic Times*, June 9. http://articles.economictimes.indiatimes.com/2013-06-09/news/39834857_1_smes-workforce-small-and-medium-enterprises.

Herrington, M., J. Kew and P. Kew. 2014. "Global Entrepreneurship Monitor: South African Report 2013." Graduate School of Business, University of Cape Town.

Herrington, M., J. Kew and P. Kew. 2016. "Global Entrepreneurship Monitor: South African Report 2015." Graduate School of Business, University of Cape Town.

Howard, C. 2016. "The First Woman of Women." *Forbes India*, January 14: 96.

Jennings, J. and C. G. Brush. 2013. "Research on Women Entrepreneurs: Challenges to (and from) the Broader Entrepreneurship Literature?" *Academy of Management Annals* 7(1): 663–715.

Kamberidou, I. 2013. "Women Entrepreneurs: 'We Cannot Have Change Unless We Have Men in the Room'." *Journal of Innovation and Entrepreneurship* 2(1): 1–18.

Kelley, D. J., C. G. Brush, P. Greene and Y. Litovsky. 2013. "Global Entrepreneurship Monitor: 2012 Women's Report." Babson College, Boston. www.babson.edu/Academics/centers/blank-center/global-research/gem/Documents/GEM%202012%20Womens%20Report.pdf.

Kumbhar, V. M. 2013. "Some Critical Issues of Women Entrepreneurship in Rural India." *European Academic Research*, 1(2).

Langley, K. and J. Liddle. 2014. "The Importance of Entrepreneurship by Jeremy Liddle, President of the G20 Young Entrepreneur's Alliance." *The Asian Entrepreneur*, 7 July. www.asianentrepreneur.org/the-importance-of-entrepreneurship-by-jeremy-liddle-president-of-the-g20-young-entrepreneurs-alliance/.

MacNeil, N. 2012. "Entrepreneurship is the New Women's Movement." *Forbes*, June 8. www.forbes.com/sites/work-in progress/2012/06/08/entrepreneurship-is-the-new-womens-movement/#15d824116922.

Maphalla, S. T., C. Nieuwenhuizen and R. Roberts. 2009. "Perceived Barriers Experienced by Township Small-, Micro-, and Medium-Enterprise Entrepreneurs in Mamelodi." PhD diss., University of Johannesburg.

Masood, R. Z. 2011. "Emergence of Women-Owned Businesses in India: An Insight." *Researchers World* 2(1): 233.

Methil, R. 2014. "To the Power of Three." *Forbes Woman Africa*, April/May: 16–22.

Methil, R. 2014/15. "The Girl on the Border." *Forbes Woman Africa*, December/January: 48–49.

Methil, R. 2015a. "Singer. Seamstress. Survivor." *Forbes Woman Africa*, April/May: 44–45.

Methil, R. 2015b. "Young, Overqualified and a Woman." *Forbes Woman Africa*, November: 70.

Minniti, M. and W. Naude. 2010. "What do we Know About the Patterns and Determinants of Female Entrepreneurship Across Countries?" *European Journal of Development Research* 22(3): 277–293.

Mordi, C., R. Simpson, S. Singh and C. Okafor. 2010. "The Role of Cultural Values in Understanding the Challenges Faced by Female Entrepreneurs in Nigeria." *Gender in Management: An International Journal* 25(1): 5–21.

Nambiar, Y. 2015. "The Psychosocial Support Ecosystem for Women Entrepreneurs in South African Townships: Barriers and Enablers." Masters diss., University of Pretoria.

Newsweek. 2015. "Hillary Clinton Talks Gender Equality, Not Politics, at Clinton Foundation Event." *Newsweek,* World, September. http://europe.newsweek.com/hillary-clinton-champions-gender-equality-clinton-foundation-event-312433?rm=eu.

Nichter, S. and L. Goldmark. 2009. "Small Firm Growth in Developing Countries." *World Development* 37(9): 1453–1464.

Nmadu, T. M. 2011. "Enhancing Women's Participation in Formal and Informal Sectors of Nigeria's Economy Through Entrepreneurship Literacy." *Journal of Business Diversity* 11(1): 87–98.

OECD (Organisation for Economic Co-operation and Development). 2009. "Gender Equality: Empowering Women so that Development is Effective." www.oecd.org/dac/gender-development/42310124.pdf.

OECD (Organisation for Economic Co-operation and Development). 2012. "Women's Economic Empowerment." www.oecd.org/dac/povertyreduction/50157530.pdf.

Rabbani, G. and M. S. Chowdhury. 2013. "Policies and Institutional Support for Women Entrepreneurship Development in Bangladesh: Achievements and Challenges." *International Journal of Research in Business and Social Science* 2(1): 31–39.

Ravanona, A. 2015. "An Interview with Johanna Mukoki, Group CEO, Travel with Flair." *Global Invest Her.* http://blog.globalinvesther.com/women-leaders-in-the-spotlight/an-interview-with-johanna-mukoki-group-ceo-travel-with-flair/.

Robb, A., S. Coleman and D. Stangler. 2014. "Sources of Economic Hope: Women's Entrepreneurship." Ewing Marion Kauffman Foundation. www.kauffman.org/~/media/kauffman_org/research%20reports%20and%20covers/2014/11/sources_of_economic_hope_womens_entrepreneurship.pdf.

Schindehutte, M., M. Morris and C. Brennan. 2003. "Entrepreneurs and Motherhood: Impacts on their Children in South Africa and the United States." *Journal of Small Business Management* 41(1): 94–107.

Sharma, K. L. 2014. "Women Entrepreneurship in India: Issues and Challenges." *International Journal of Entrepreneurship & Business Environment Perspectives* 3(4): 1406–1411.

South African Department of Trade and Industry. 2005. "South African Women Entrepreneurs: A Burgeoning Force in Our Economy." http://pmg-assets.s3-website-eu-west-1.amazonaws.com/docs/2006/061114entrepeneur.pdf.

Statistics South Africa. 2015. "Work & Labour Force: 2014." www.statssa.gov.za/?page_id=737&id=1.

Tambunan, T. 2009. "Women Entrepreneurship in Asian Developing Countries: Their Development and Main Constraints." *Journal of Development and Agricultural Economics* 1(2): 27–40.

Terjesen, S. and A. Elam. 2012. "Women Entrepreneurship: A Force for Growth." *International Trade Forum* 2(16).

Terjesen, S. A. and A. Lloyd. 2015. "The 2015 Female Entrepreneurship Index." Global Entrepreneurship and Development Institute, Washington, DC.

The Economist. 2013. "Crazy Diamonds." *The Economist*, July. www.economist.com/news/business/21581965-true-entrepreneurs-find-worth-worthless-and-possibility-impossible-crazy-diamonds.

The Economist. 2014. "African Demography: The Dividend is Delayed." *The Economist*, March 8. www.economist.com/news/middle-east-and-africa/21598646-hopes-africas-dramatic-population-bulge-may-create-prosperity-seem-have.

UNIDO (United Nations Industrial Development Organization). 2014. "Empowering Women: Fostering Entrepreneurship." www.unido.org/fileadmin/user_media_upgrade/What_we_do/Topics/Women_and_Youth/Brochure_low_resolution.pdf.

Westcott, L. 2015. "Hillary Clinton Talks Gender Equality, Not Politics, at Clinton Foundation Event." *Newseek*, March 9. http://europe.newsweek.com/hillary-clinton-champions-gender-equality-clinton-foundation-event-312433?rm=eu.

Woetzel, J., A. Madgavkar, K. Ellingrud, E. Labaye, S. Devillard, E. Kutcher, J. Manyika, R. Dobbs and M. Krishnan. 2015. "How Advancing Women's Equality can Add $12 Trillion to Global Growth." McKinsey Global Institute, San Francisco. www.mckinsey.com/global-themes/employment-and-growth/how-advancing-womens-equality-can-add-12-trillion-to-global-growth.

World Bank. 2014. "Global Findex 2014: Measuring Financial Inclusion Around the World." www.worldbank.org/en/programs/globalfindex.

World Bank. 2015. "Small and Medium Enterprises Finance." www.worldbank.org/en/topic/financialsector/brief/smes-finance.

World Bank–Goldman Sachs. 2008. "Women Hold Up Half the Sky." Global Economics No. 164. www.goldmansachs.com/citizenship/10000women/about-the-program/index.html.

WEF (World Economic Forum). 2015. "The Global Gender Gap Report 2015." http://reports.weforum.org/global-gender-gap-report-2015/.

8 Women in professional services

Cecily Carmona

Introduction

This chapter aims to examine how women leaders in a range of professional services (accounting, consulting, law, engineering and medical professionals) have managed to navigate their careers and be promoted to the highest levels in their organizations or professional working environments. It examines the dynamics of professional services organizations in relation to women, the barriers women face in rising to the top and the common themes to which women who have been successful, attribute their success. Finally, we look at what professional services organizations are doing to promote women, what we envisage for the future, and what actions can be taken towards the achievement of these goals.

As input to the chapter we interviewed a number of women in the professions noted above from across different emerging markets, including Brazil, Bulgaria, India, Middle East, Russia, South Africa and Uganda.

The context of professional services

Professional services exist due to the demand for problem-solving competence on behalf of the client (Kaiser and Ringlstetter 2011). Some professional service providers, such as architects, auditors, engineers, doctors and lawyers, require professional licenses. For the purposes of this chapter, we have restricted the definition of professional services to accountants, consultants, lawyers, engineers and medical professionals.

Professional services practitioners, as the name indicates, offer their services to companies or individuals and are remunerated on a fee basis. They may do this as part of a wider firm or as individuals, providing a service to another organization or entity. This construct of offering brings with it many interesting dynamics, with professional services providers needing to convince their clients to buy the services and then deliver those services to the acceptable standard, within time and budget. There are two major steps required in this process: the *sale* and the *servicing* that happens after the sale.

The *sale* requires the lead partner (be it lawyer, consultant, engineer or accountant) to convince their prospective client that their approach, skill, experience and expertise is the best and that there is a good fit between the professional services firm (or team on the job) and the corporate. When the relationship between the two parties is a new one, the decision on the part of the corporate requires a certain level of *trust, connection and belief* that the service provider will do the job and will be worth the (usually significant) money spent on the job.

The *servicing* requires that the client team and the professional services team and leadership work harmoniously together to deliver the results. There may be some persuasion required to convince the client that the recommendations are the right ones, and the two leadership teams need to be in sync in terms of process and outcome of the work.

Building this kind of trust in the sales and service process requires a number of things: areas of common ground, shared experience and a track record, recognition of similarities in background and an ability to communicate in a manner that both parties understand.

According to Paliszkiewicz (2011), the concept of trust has become popular in public debate and academic analysis. Trust has been identified as a major factor influencing things such as investment, marketing, cross-learning and cooperation. Trust management is also becoming very important inside the organization and in the services the organization uses.

When these two touch points (client and services provider) are both men there may be a number of areas upon which to build the trust: similar schools, both being husbands or dads, sports teams, favorite hang-outs and similar thought patterns and language. For women professionals working for a male corporate client, it is definitely *possible* to find these areas of commonality, but it is much more difficult and takes skill and perseverance.

The women who have been successful in professional services have learned ways of navigating their paths and careers to build trust with their clients; to outperform on delivery and hence (particularly in engineering) overcome the bias of having a woman lead the team.

The professional services working environment typically includes tight deadlines, long working hours and high pressure to maintain performance. These pressures, and the significant travel required for the job, push women out of professional services firms after a time, especially as their roles and responsibilities outside the workplace increase.

While these are a few of the dynamics common to many professional services organizations, there are some that are specific to particular services.

Accountants

The accounting profession is one of the best recognized of the professional services and is often seen as having a clear progression path to CFO or

CEO positions. Accountants can branch off after their rigorous training into lucrative areas such as private equity, finance functions in corporates and even entrepreneurship. By providing diverse career options and being so well recognized, accounting has a healthy pipeline of young women entering the profession.

In developed markets, women and men qualify in accounting more or less equally (in 2013 there were 61% female chartered accountants in the USA, and in Canada, 49%). In emerging markets, however, fewer women than men graduate in the profession (34% in 2015 in South Africa, from 27% in 2009).

The nature of the accounting profession requires a high level of attention to detail and accountants' recommendations or findings usually mean high stakes for the companies involved. Leaders within firms are usually male and the female accountant has to find a balance between being technically excellent and being able to communicate difficult or uncomfortable messages to an audience that is largely different from her (that is, male).

The drop in numbers of women in finance and accounting occurs at the typical time of starting to have a family, usually about five to ten years into a woman's career. Whether still part of an audit firm or having moved into commerce, maintaining the demands and rigor of a corporate structured job often doesn't suit the lifestyle choices that women want to make—they still want to contribute, but they also wish for the flexibility, autonomy and freedom to play multiple roles. Female accountants thus often choose to move out of the big corporates, typically starting their own companies or working in small businesses or ventures, to allow for more lifestyle choice. This leads to fewer women officially in top finance or accounting leadership roles in big corporates or accounting firms.

Despite these difficulties, women in accounting do have some support. Accounting in most countries is governed by a regulatory body (for example, the South African Institute for Chartered Accountants—SAICA—and the Institute of Chartered Accountants of India—ICAI), which usually has a strong women's organization that is supported at executive level. This helps to ensure that removing the barriers to women's progress is kept on the agenda.

This may be part of the reason why improvements have been made in both number of senior women accountants in organizations and parity of pay scale:

> The good news is that, today, female CAs enjoy greater parity with their male counterparts—particularly in the areas of pay and promotion—than in most other professions. The 2013 Stott and May/ICAEW Chartered Accountants Salary Survey of UK-based CAs found that the pay gap between younger male and female accountants has narrowed, with the average basic salary earned by female accountants

now 97% of their male counterparts, up from 92% in 2012. Female chartered accountants now also fill more senior management roles. The 2013 Grant Thornton International Business Report (IBR) revealed that while only 28% of South Africa's senior management roles are currently filled by women, this year the number of female chief financial officers (CFOs) rose 128%, from 14% in 2012 to 32%.

(Brent Personnel n.d.)

Consultants

Consultants come from a range of different specialisms, including engineering, medicine and finance, and most move into consulting via business school. Consulting firms recruit individuals with a specific skillset: the ability to conduct rigorous analysis, solve complex problems, utilize fact-based logic and demonstrate extremely strong interpersonal skills. They are client facing and need a high level of gravitas, along with well-developed intellects and problem-solving mindsets, in order to advise clients on their most critical business issues. This requires them to have confidence in their ideas, as well as finely tuned communication skills to enable them to listen to and interpret clients' needs and respond in a convincing and compelling manner. Trust is a key component of successful consultant-client relationships, and building that trust requires time spent networking in order to understand the clients' needs and build a common view of the problem and solution.

Delivery of consulting services can be anywhere, any time, to suit the client's agenda. It often involves significant travel pressures and time away from family and home. In addition, there is continual pressure to demonstrate excellence in output, since consultants sell advice and not tangible things. These factors contribute to the high-pressure environment in which consultants operate.

While across the world the intake of new business analysts into consulting is often made up of a nearly equal number of women and men, there is a critical point, generally four to five years later (and increasing after that), when significant numbers of women leave consulting, leading to low numbers of women in senior positions—that is, partners or directors and principals. This turnover results in a lack of diversity in the firms' leadership, and consulting firms have found that it can cause discontinuity of client relationships and significant costs to replace this top talent (Hewlett and Luce 2005).

Consulting companies, and thus consultants, usually provide their services to large corporates where, more times than not, the clients are male. A number of dynamics are at play in this relationship:

1 *Forming relationships*: it is easier and more natural for men to "bond" with other men in a social situation as topics of conversation that appeal to men are frequently different from those that appeal to

women. Forming a trusting relationship based on mutual understanding and shared experience is therefore often easier for two men.

2   *Being remembered*: with women in such a minority, both as colleagues and as clients, they are often remembered simply due to their scarcity. This can actually play in women's favor as they stand out from the crowd.

3   *Teamwork*: traditional models of consulting require a high degree of teamwork, working long hours on site with the client to deliver to tight deadlines. There is a sense of being sure that each team member "pulls their weight", shares equally the responsibility to deliver and can be relied on. This demanding environment means that women who are trying to find different and more flexible models of working may struggle to manage the demands of the client, the team and the pull to do things outside of work.

A stark look at these multiple requirements and demands makes it easy to understand why some women decide not to continue along this path, particularly as their roles outside of work expand, and opt to develop their careers elsewhere.

Engineers

"Engineers apply the principles of science and mathematics to develop economical solutions to technical problems. Their work is the link between scientific discoveries and the commercial applications that meet societal and consumer needs" (SDSU College of Engineering n.d.). This intersection between science and commercial application could be extremely suitable for young girls with strong mathematical and scientific thinking skills, yet it does not typically attract young women out of school as a career choice. The reasons for this are many. Engineering is not a profession that is easily accessible to the outsider—lacking consumers as the end users, it is neither visible nor well known unless a familial link to an engineer exists. With so few women engineers, girls lack female engineering role models, and the work environment (on site, in mines or plants) is unsuitable for job-shadowing opportunities. As a result, and in contrast to accountants, lawyers and consultants, there are significantly fewer women than men at graduation—below 30% in developed markets and even lower in emerging markets (SDSU College of Engineering n.d.).

The industries in which engineers operate are usually demanding physical environments and working conditions may be harsh. Extractive and process industries and construction and building industries, where engineers are predominantly found, are extremely male dominated and female engineers need a specific skillset to manage in these conditions.

In 2009, the University of Wisconsin-Milwaukee conducted a nationwide longitudinal study to investigate women engineers' experiences in technical workplaces (Fouad et al. 2012). By 2012, when the paper was published, over 5,500 women who had graduated with an engineering degree had engaged with the study. While the study was in a developed market, the insights apply equally to the emerging markets we examined.

The study indicated that women typically leave engineering because of various issues relating to workplace climate, including harsh working conditions, the organizational culture or the nature of the boss: "Nearly half of women left engineering because of working conditions: too much travel, lack of advancement, or low salary" (Fouad et al. 2012).

The study further found that women who stayed in engineering were most satisfied when they were in an environment that recognized their contribution and which invested in their professional development. However, they were more likely to exit the organization if they felt pulled too sstrongly in different directions by the demands of work and home. "The greater the conflict between work and non-work roles, the greater the intention to leave the organization as well as the profession" (Fouad et al. 2012). Thus, particularly when having a family, women felt immense pressure. These women are forced to choose between work and family—and often they choose family.

Given the harsh, male-dominated working conditions, women engineers have to fight to find their place, but according to the study, "many women choose to leave without fighting the uphill battle … . It is a self-sustaining cycle" (Fouad et al. 2012).

As schools and educational institutions are increasingly encouraging girls to be excited about science, some of the social stereotypes concerning women and science are being challenged. But the change is not yet great enough and still very few women choose to study engineering. In consequence, women who do study and work in engineering need a high degree of resilience to bias and an ability to survive in a culture where they may not feel entirely at home. Women who survive have found a way of working where they either mimic the male styles or carve out a space in which they can be more themselves. But diversity in design team is critical to excellence in delivery: "Every time an engineering problem is approached with a pale, male design team, it may be difficult to find the best solution, understand the design options, or know how to evaluate the constraints" (Wulf 1998). Further work therefore needs to be done by firms and the engineering profession as a whole to enable the integration of women and other minorities.

Lawyers

Like accountants, lawyers undergo a four-year degree course plus rigorous on-the-job training and board exams to finally become full-fledged practitioners. They need to be individuals who are detail-oriented, able to absorb large amounts of written content and have strong deductive reasoning abilities.

Those who opt to work for a large law firm will experience a similar working environment to that of consultants, with a high proportion of male lawyers and predominantly male clients.

There is, however, a slight difference between consultants and lawyers. Although both work under billable time and use this as a strong measure of performance, lawyers work under a billable *hour* structure. In this model, a law firm charges the client per working hour of each lawyer working on the matter, often with no cap on fees charged, depending on the practice. Law firms, by definition, will make more money the more hours per day each lawyer bills to a client (Barrett 2014). Billable hours are therefore a strong measure of performance in this profession. The more time a lawyer spends at work and bills to a client, the more profitable is the lawyer to firm and partners. In a highly competitive environment, these professionals will try to log as many billable hours a day as possible. In order to justify each minute billed to the client, the lawyer has to log every activity as it occurs. A simple phone call to follow up on a matter to the court is not just a phone call. It is logged and detailed for content and duration. A drive to the client is logged for duration and cost by the professional. The lawyer model is a cause of anxiety, depression and high turnover rates (LexisNexis 2012).

As in consulting, women flee this profession at a faster rate than men. They start out as candidate attorneys equal in numbers to their male counterparts but, as family responsibilities become increasingly important, few make it to partner level. As in emerging markets, the ratio of male to female lawyers in developed markets at partner level is below 26%, with the number of managing partners even lower at below 4%.

With few women either in their own organizations or as their clients, female partners in law firms find themselves in a tough working environment. They are also required to sell to clients (who are largely male) and mentor younger lawyers, both male and female.

Like their male counterparts, female partners are driven by the time constraints of their profession and want to get through the work as quickly, efficiently and accurately as possible. Females, however, are more likely to pause and be cognizant of the context of their mentees. They are more likely to recognize that the driver for higher performance from younger colleagues is not necessarily promotion but may be lifestyle related. These leaders will encourage younger colleagues to take time off or take breaks during stressful working periods. They are more supportive of their mentees' contexts and needs. According to John Gerzema and Michael D'Antonio in *The Athena Doctrine* (2013), these kinds of leadership traits, which are traditionally associated with women but which may also be displayed by men, create more effective leaders and organizational strategies in today's society.

Medical professionals

Historically, medicine was dominated by men, but women and men now graduate from medical school in equal numbers. Since 2000, in South African medical schools, women have outnumbered men in intake, with figures ranging between 52% and 63% at seven of the eight medical schools in 2005 (Brieir et al. 2008). However, specialization shows a different picture, with certain areas attracting more men and others more women. The University of Cape Town postgraduate enrolments shows that females had increased to 42% of MMed enrolments in 2005. However, female postgraduate students were concentrated in disciplines such as pediatrics and psychiatry and comprised no more than 11% of enrolments in the surgical disciplines between 1999 and 2005 (Brieir et al. 2008).

To obtain a place at medical school a student must have top grades, have undertaken community service, and show an aptitude for people and sciences. Once in medical school and thereafter, the medical professional requires serious commitment over a long period of time, with several years of training, plus extensive hours of on-call duty, community service and emergency-room practice. For those doctors choosing to specialize, a further two to six years of additional training is required. Besides academic excellence and knowledge of the biomedical sciences, doctors are often judged by their interpersonal skills or "bedside manner". As noted in an article titled "Gender Biases and Discrimination: A Review of Health Care Interpersonal Interactions" (Govender 2007), "A good interpersonal relationship between a patient and provider—as characterised by mutual respect, openness and a balance in their respective roles in decision-making—is an important marker of quality of care."

The working environment of medicine is fast-paced, demanding and pressurized. Having to make life-threatening decisions about people on an everyday basis adds an element of stress beyond that experienced by other professional services. It requires decisiveness and, particularly in some disciplines, such as surgery, the ability to make decisions under extreme pressure. Working hours are particularly demanding for young doctors, with their grueling call rosters, but for most specializations this continues well into the senior years.

This type of working environment is possible, albeit trying, during the early years of medicine. However, once the doctor starts a family, these schedules become more difficult to maintain. The many practicing women doctors with families sometimes choose specializations like hematology or radiology, where the hours are more predictable and accommodative of family life. In contrast, very few women chose to study surgery. In line with international trends, Brieir et al. (2008) found that:

> Enrolments in the surgical disciplines ... declined from 101 in 1999 to 80 in 2005, falling as low as 73 in 2003 (at the University of Cape

Town). Women formed no more than 11% of enrolments in any of the seven years reviewed, and some surgical disciplines had no women students.

A recent meta-analytic review of 29 publications investigating the effects of physician gender in medical communication during consultations in the USA found notable differences (Roter, Hall and Aoki 2002 in Govender and Penn-Kekana 2007). Although the review found no gender differences in the biomedical information provided during the consultation, female physicians did engage in significantly more active partnership behaviors, positive talk, psychosocial counselling, psychosocial question-asking and emotionally focused talk, and spent on average two minutes (10%) longer with clients compared to male physicians (Govender 2007). According to Govender (2007):

> While the gender of the patient is important in defining access, we would argue that the *gap* between the provider and patient with respect to gender, class, caste, ethnicity and other social stratifications (i.e. the social distance) might be even more important in shaping the interaction.

Looking at the dynamics within the professional services described above, it is clear that these are fast-paced, highly competitive and male-dominated professions. However, the women who have "made it" into senior positions in professional services firms show that this is not only possible but that many women are maintaining successful careers in these roles. An important question is whether women can be leaders in their professional lives without compromising their personal lives and the many other roles they play outside of work. This was succinctly articulated by one of our interviewees, Edith Kikonyogo, an engineer in Uganda, who said:

> It is easy to become a successful career women, well not easy, but very possible with the right attitude, aptitude and hard work. What is not that easy is to achieve all that while still balancing your other roles, like being a mother and still being present in your children's lives.

Catalysts for creating leading professional services women

Women leaders from around the world have different stories of how they chose their careers (for the purposes of this chapter, in the particularly male-dominated area of professional services), what drove them to achieve and how they came to rise to the top as leaders in their organizations.

The women in professional services whom we interviewed were extremely diverse in terms of geographical origin and all were in leadership positions within their firms or industries. They had clearly "made it to the top".

Our interviews revealed three common and important ingredients in their successful leadership journeys: a catalyst in childhood, positive role models, and an inner drive. We will look at each of these in some detail.

A catalyst in childhood

One fascinating finding was that the vast majority of our sample of women in professional services in emerging markets came from somewhat disadvantaged environments: a small town in Russia, a mining town in South Africa, a village in Portugal, communist Bulgaria, a township in Kwa-Zulu Natal (South Africa), a poverty-stricken city in Uganda, a large sprawling city in Brazil, to name but a few. Most of these interviewees grew up in an environment with constraints—socio-economic, political, sometimes emotional. All of our interviewees aspired to something better.

One of our interviewees, Daniela Chikova, said:

> I was born and grew up in Bulgaria. Bulgaria is, you know, one of the ex-communist countries, which changed after 1999. And at that time I was 12 years old and so probably at the right age in order to embrace all the opportunities that the fall of the communist regime in Bulgaria. The biggest opportunity was that of being able to travel freely abroad. After 1999, opportunities in terms of travel, education and working abroad opened up, which was absolutely fantastic for a lot of young people in my generation.

The catalyst for Daniela was the initial complete restriction of travel as she grew up, followed by the opening of borders. This gave her the drive to be educated elsewhere and travel widely across the world as part of her career.

This scenario was reflected in many other interviews: the women observed the environment around them and had an inner resolve to make it better—in many cases not only for themselves but also for others living in the same circumstances. Sindi Koyana grew up in the townships of Kwa-Zulu Natal. For her, the extremely poor socio-economic circumstances she grew up in were the catalyst for wanting to succeed: "It was the poverty. It was what I saw around me. Yes, it was just a difficult journey." She wanted better for herself and she wanted better for her family, present and future:

> So I was very mindful of what I was seeing around me. And I made a pact with myself that I will get out of here. I will, not on my own, but I will take my family out of this situation. So that drove me.

In some instances, the impoverishment was not so much socio-economic as emotional: young girls saw their mothers constrained by their household roles and duties, bound by the fact of *not* being the breadwinner. This gave a feeling of being trapped, unempowered and unable to fulfil their potential. We viewed this as a kind of childhood catalyst for women who did not want to repeat the cycle in their own lives.

Challenging adverse circumstances like these experienced by women, particularly in emerging markets, can drive finding an inner desire and a resolve to beat the system, to achieve in the face of adversity. As one of our interviewees stated: "From adversity comes strength."

We are well aware that schooling and background, networks, social credentials and family status have long been the foundation on which people have grown their careers. Businesses globally, including in emerging markets, are filled with people at the top, mainly men, who have outstanding connections and affluent and privileged backgrounds. So why is there this theme of successful businesswomen in emerging markets coming from challenging backgrounds? Perhaps it is the nature of the environment of emerging markets, in which challenging circumstances are more common. Perhaps it is that women who grow up in affluent circumstances have the financial means not to *have to* work and can fully take on the role of mother or homemaker. Perhaps adverse circumstances do exist for women in developed markets, but they may be less visible and more subtle experiences or emotions that are not spoken or heard about.

Positive role models

Without exception, and without specific prompting in this regard, our interviewees noted that they had had significant support, input and/or guidance that contributed to their belief in themselves and/or their resolve to achieve. While this support usually came from their mothers or fathers, in some instances it was from another caregiver or adult in their community. The role models had extremely important functions.

Instilling strong values

These role models came in different guises. One interviewee indicated that her mother's unwavering moral compass and values were the foundation on which she grew her desire to succeed. Despite what could be considered strict and restrictive rules in the home, Sindi Koyana's mother said, for example, "Your only friend is your book." Sindi also had a school principal who reinforced the strong values instilled at home. His belief in her planted seeds of belief in herself, which she would later use in her journey. Prominent South African businesswoman Shirley Zinn, in her book *Swimming Upstream* (2015), speaks of how her grandmother inculcated a rigorous sense of discipline in the children: "There was a time to play, a time for chores, a time for homework and a time to go to bed." While this may have been resented at the time, ultimately it was felt that they were central to a work ethic and resolve that were essential later on for tackling the tough barriers to establishing a career. Eketerina Sheremet from Russia noted that her parents always taught her to reach for the top and, regardless of what you do, to be really good at it. Phatho Zondi, a medical doctor, learned the importance of hard work from a young age: "My mother showed me that one should never stop learning and stretching oneself, so I continue to seek ways to grow and refine underdeveloped skills."

Daniela Chikova grew up in Bulgaria and told the story of how her father used to travel to East Germany. He would come home and tell her about things he had seen and places he had visited. He would speak to her in other languages, bringing the world into their home, in a country that was otherwise limited and isolated. She was sent to a German school, which opened her eyes and ears to different ways of being and created a desire in her to do what she needed to do to see the world. Daniela's father introduced the attractions of discovery and exploration and this was a spark that began her journey. She resolved to ensure that she always performed well so that she would have the luxury of choice regarding where to live and what to do.

Working parents

For those of our respondents whose mothers worked, working mothers were the norm. In Eastern Europe there were no gender-stereotypical jobs for women and jobs for men, and both mothers and fathers worked. This led to less conflict and less of a question for young girls as to whether or not they would work—the only question was what they would do. In Brazil, the stereotypical roles of women and men, mothers and fathers, still exists: "I would say that the woman still carries a lot of the responsibilities of raising a child and running the home," said Silvana Machado from Brazil.

In many African countries and in situations of poverty, finding and keeping work was not a question of developing a career; it was a necessity of economic survival. Grandparents in these circumstances had an important role raising children, while parents went far away to find work in different cities. In other instances, children witnessed their mothers not working, but instead playing the important role of running the household and childrearing.

Our interviewees experienced all of these variations of working parents, with different effects on different respondents. On the one hand, women whose mothers did work knew and understood that women *can* work and drew inspiration from that. On the other hand, women whose mothers did not work felt that this was not a situation they would like for themselves and made every effort to have a career, to ensure financial freedom. Whichever combination, the women leaders we interviewed vividly remembered comments from their childhoods which settled in their minds and molded their thinking: "I was pushed to perfection," said one interviewee, who felt she was living out her father's dream in an effort to please. "I'm going to raise you not to be dependent on any man," said another's father, even though her mother didn't work and was entirely dependent on her husband. These statements helped to cement ideas of what these girls, later women, wanted to achieve in life.

Words of affirmation

Besides the crucial role parents play in developing leaders, many of our interviewees also mentioned other role models who made a significant impact in their lives. For example, one of our male leaders said that he was born to a loving and devoted but very young, uneducated mother. He grew up a shy child and, due to his impoverished family life and some early issues that were identified by his school, he was overseen by a social worker. The social worker visited them at home over a number of years to check on them both and ensure that his health and socio-economic status were properly monitored. After many years of intervention the social worker was ready to "discharge" him. On her last visit, she patted him on the head and said, "*Jy is a slim seun*," meaning, you are a clever boy. These words stuck in his mind as it was the first time that someone expressed belief in him. It was a turning point in his life; he acquired a resolve to succeed and started the journey of developing his own self-belief and drive to achieve.

Most of the women leaders interviewed referred to similar instances at some point in their lives, involving either a parent wanting the best for them or community members, aunts, uncles or grandparents. Rania Anderson, in her book *Undeterred*, found that self-confidence can be traced back to how success and failure are viewed by the family (especially fathers). For the women interviewed, the positive influence mostly came from words expressing confidence in their abilities and potential as young girls, affirming that success was indeed possible for them.

Inner drive

Millions of people from around the world grow up in adverse circumstances and many people have strong role models to look up to, but only a few, and particularly few women, actually rise to the top, drive through the bias, take care of their other roles and develop successful careers. The third component of what we found to be key for success was a steel-strong resolve to succeed. While the resolve to succeed may have been ignited by the women's background and the right role models, we believe it that it is also an innate quality, backed up by the capability to succeed.

Daniela Chikova told of how she was a perfectionist from as far back as she can remember. When she was seven years old she was told in class that she did not write the number two properly. That night Daniela went home and wrote and rewrote the number. She filled page after page until it was perfect. This demonstrated her will to achieve perfection and her ability to do the hard work required to get it right.

Other respondents spoke of going above and beyond in an effort to get the best marks, to do more than was expected, to deliver against all odds. This commitment to excellence, success and achievement was there in all our respondents. It was something they demonstrated from when they were very young, right through to where they are today.

The impact of bias

The women we interviewed had a sense that although always being in the minority might have some advantages, on the whole it presents a significant challenge. Each of the professional services disciplines described above has its own dynamics, which affect the ease of women operating in those environments, but it is fair to say that it takes particular perseverance and energy to do what it takes to become a leader in the especially male-dominated professional services.

In addition to often being the only woman in the room, many of the interviewed women were also part of a minority in other ways—cultural or ethnic. Being the only Asian woman round a boardroom table of white men, or the one black woman on a mining site with all Afrikaans-speaking white males, or the only Western woman amongst Arab men in the Middle East, is challenging and requires sustained energy to manage.

Many of the structural barriers of "being the only woman" have been slowly dismantled over time. Issues such as having no female toilet on the executive floor, no steel-cap boots in women's sizes on site, offices with pictures of naked women on the back wall of the working room—all situations that the women we interviewed experienced over their careers—have, on the whole, been tackled. Apartheid is destroyed, the Berlin Wall has fallen and there is an awareness and inclination to embrace diversity.

But at many levels in emerging markets the prejudice remains. Thus, while many of the external structural barriers have been broken down, unconscious bias persists in the form of language and culture. This is experienced by our female interview respondents in the kind of responses their ideas get in board meetings, the kind of reactions male clients make to having a female lead engineer allocated to build their refinery plant, and the often condescending language used to address them. An example was given by one of our interviewees, who said that even now that she is a senior professional, clients who don't know her still sometimes ask her to make them tea!

As described above, networking, a key component in professional services, happens most naturally when there is a "good fit" between individuals, an affinity based on common interests. This means that in male-dominated environments, despite the need for and acknowledgement of diversity, male networks are easier to form and tend to be stronger than male–female engagements. Successful women professionals have pushed through these biases. They understand that these biased behaviors come from deeply entrenched cultural beliefs and societal norms that will likely take centuries, not decades, to undo. Thus, they push for technical excellence beyond what is required and find ways to build networks through the male constructs to develop connectivity and become recognized.

One of the women we interviewed, Phatho Zondi from South Africa, had chosen her specialization in a typically male medical field, that of sports medicine. Her sporty nature, combined with a family love for sport, sparked her interest in the field. Not only did Phatho specialize in sports medicine, but early in her career she became the doctor for the provincial rugby team, the Blue Bulls. This required complete dedication, a great deal of travel and ongoing weekend work. Phatho also had to overcome the prejudice querying how a young, black female could be at the helm of a high-performing provincial rugby team. People often assumed she was the nurse, and Phatho had to constantly prove her credibility and worthiness to play this important role. As she put it: "The only way to overcome prejudice is by excellence." She worked out that bias often comes from historical preconceptions and that finding a connection and being outstanding at what you do gradually starts to dismantle the layers of bias.

However, being a woman in an all-male environment can have its advantages. Many of the women interviewed said that being the only woman in the room means that are you are likely to be remembered, while you may remember only a few male clients. One of the consultants noted: "Clients enjoy talking to me because I am the only woman." There can be what some described as a "fascination factor" in being a woman who has made it in a male-oriented environment. Ramyani Basu from United Kingdom said, "Actually I would not say I have faced barriers. I felt the fact that I am from a different ethnicity, different accent, different viewpoint, a different personality than a British woman, has acted as a positive for me. Not a negative."

Isabel Neiva, a consultant working in the Middle East, had a balanced view, finding that in some instances:

> being a woman is an advantage and in others being a woman is not. You bring a different perspective to the table [...] Whether they like it or not. Women have a different way of thinking and a different perception [...] So that for me is an advantage.

She said that networking and forming relationships with clients is an essential part of professional services work, but that it is difficult to do, particularly as a woman in the Middle East.

Some interviewees felt that race and gender played less of a role in their career progression than age. A female partner in Brazil, Silvana Machado, said, "When I started my career, I was already a manager. Sometimes the client would look at me and think, 'Who is this baby'? A client that I had, called me 'daughter'. It was not badly intended." In Silvana's experience, the consulting environment was very open to different genders and races. However, she also noted that people's perceptions of race and economic standing—along with gender—are inextricably linked in emerging markets like Brazil, making for a prejudice that has considerable power even if it is not explicit. Simply put by Ekaterina Sheremet of Russia and felt by most of the women we interviewed: "You are always the minority and that's kind of a challenge." Being a woman in the male-dominated professions is difficult.

Women leadership trends in professional services

Women's styles in professional services have evolved over time. While women used to feel a need to mimic masculine leadership qualities and behaviors, we know from research this is often not successful: women displaying male-like behaviors are not perceived in the same light (that is, not as positively) as their male counterparts. As Shirley Zinn says in *Swimming Upstream* (2015), "when women step up and want to have their voices heard, they're often seen to be too aggressive, too outspoken, and too pushy".

Our women professionals noted a move in favour of leadership qualities that come more naturally to women, including being more collaborative and more engaging in interactions with staff and clients. These "feminine" traits, which may also be displayed by men, are important not only in leadership but also in career management and self-improvement, as well as in the management of change (Gerzema and D'Antonio 2013). Indeed, the interviewees argued that many of the qualities of an ideal modern leader might be considered feminine.

The women interviewed acknowledged the importance of exploring different ideas with the aim of bringing more creativity and innovation to their solutions. While this may be harder and take longer to do, the benefits are thought to be worthwhile. As mentioned by Silvana Machado from Brazil, leadership is about finding the best approach to different types of people and working out how best to engage them.

As stated in the paper "The Female Economy in B2B: A Lens on South Africa" (A. T. Kearney 2014), with more women rising to the top of organizations, they are more often at the end of business-to-business buying decisions. The paper sets out to understand how this may or may not affect the buying process. This is directly relevant for women in professional services, who, as they rise to the top, are required to take on business development and client relationship roles.

Understanding that individuals—men and women—have an array of different business styles, the paper illustrates three main ways in which men and women differ in their approach to decision-making.

Intuition, facts and other dynamics

Women tend to be more intuitive than men in decision-making. Men are persuaded by facts and figures, while women are more interested in understanding the broader picture, including cultural fit, strength of the relationship and the values and beliefs of the service provider. Our interviews also revealed that working in the emerging markets requires more than just factual, logic-based arguments for both men and women. Different perspectives and consideration of other factors—such as politics—are necessary.

Relationships, cultural fit, and value systems

As stated in the A. T. Kearney paper (2014), when making decisions, women consider relationships, cultural fit and the alignment of value systems more than most men, bringing a balance of emotions and intelligence to create win-win situations. "Women place much greater emphasis on the holistic fit," explained Sindi Koyana, executive chairperson for Advanced Capital.

Inclusion, collaboration and consultation

Female executives often use the terms "inclusive" and "collaborative" to describe their decision-making behavior. This management style is sometimes misinterpreted as indecisive and is often seen as women's biggest weakness. However, it can actually be a major strength: even when a woman is confident she has an answer to a question, she will often seek broader views—and ideally consensus—from the rest of her team. This can help develop a hands-on, collaborative environment. Having a collaborative, enquiry-based approach is a common theme and one that seems to lead to success, particularly in emerging markets where it is often necessary to fill more than one role in an organization. Edgar Schein described this as "Humble Enquiry", which is "the fine art of drawing someone out, of asking questions to which you do not know the answer, of building a relationship based on curiosity and interest in the other person" (Schein 2013). Similarly, the women we interviewed thought that being a coach to your team, rather than being purely directive, helped bring out more from team members, although an adaptive approach is often required and a more directive style may be necessary to achieve a result. Women who are successful are able to seamlessly navigate these two styles.

Women in professional services have had to learn to "sell" in a way that demonstrates more of the masculine characteristics of decision-making, making their propositions fact and value based, with graphs, charts and financial benefits, oriented around outputs. As their clients' profiles change (with the rise of women in senior positions), their sales approach too will start to change. Women will be able to call on their natural intuition, relationship-building skills and cultural fit and values, as well as their preference for inclusion and consultation, and will find levels of understanding they have not, on the whole, experienced much of to date. This could result in collaboration between service provider and client, with the result co-created for best outcome.

Key to success

While there is clearly no single recipe for success for women in professional services, we have explored the elements that make up fertile ground for leaders. In addition to these, the women we interviewed spoke of five factors as key to their success in professional services: authenticity; confidence; work ethic, drive and ambition; perseverance and resilience; and a supportive organization (see Figure 8.1). Two of the areas we defined as "pull characteristics", as these are what make the leader "attractive" to others: their confidence and authenticity draw followers and people to them, people who believe in them. Two other factors—work ethic, drive and ambition; and resilience and perseverance—are what we call the "push characteristics", that is, attributes that people need to have to get their skills and abilities into the market and survive the harsh conditions typical of professional services. Clearly these are underpinned by the fifth factor, a supportive organization, as no leader can thrive unless she lands on fertile ground.

Authenticity

Being true to oneself, or authentic, was something that many of the women we spoke to believed was central to their success, especially as they became more senior. Being clear about their values and using them for guidance assisted them in their choices and decision-making as leaders. As Silvana Machado from Brazil said, "Being authentic and speaking your mind will ultimately help you." Ekaterina Sheremet from Russia echoed this: "Act normal and be yourself—that makes you feel relaxed and able to be the best you."

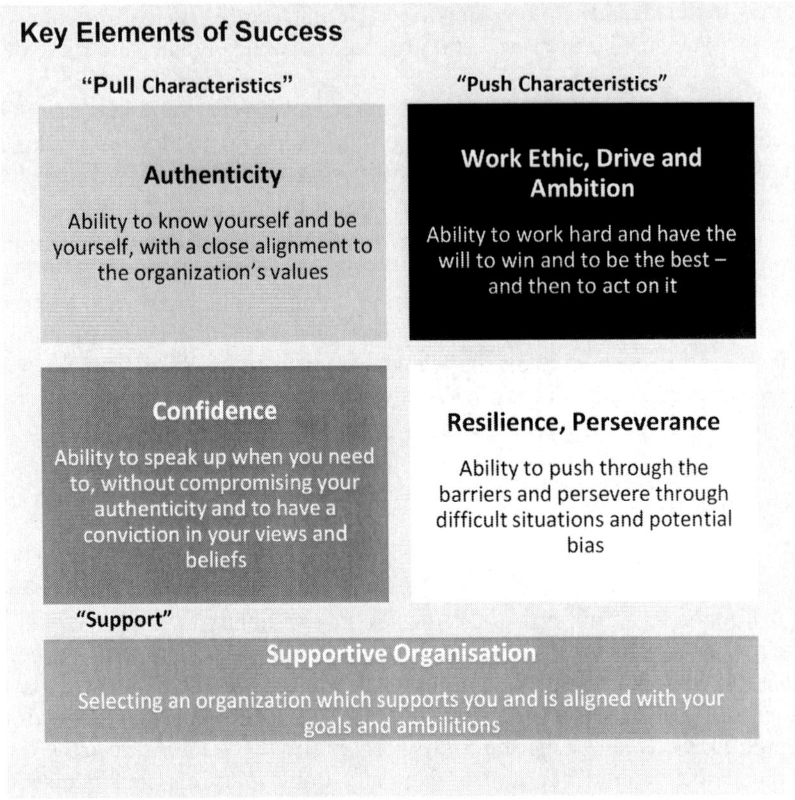

Key Elements of Success

"Pull Characteristics"   "Push Characteristics"

Authenticity

Ability to know yourself and be
yourself, with a close alignment to
the organization's values

Work Ethic, Drive and Ambition

Ability to work hard and have the
will to win and to be the best –
and then to act on it

Confidence

Ability to speak up when you need
to, without compromising your
authenticity and to have a
conviction in your views and
beliefs

Resilience, Perseverance

Ability to push through the
barriers and persevere through
difficult situations and potential
bias

"Support"

Supportive Organisation

Selecting an organization which supports you and is aligned with your
goals and ambilitions

Figure 8.1 Key elements of success

Confidence

While taking your authentic self to work each day was critical for the
women interviewed, developing a confidence in who you are was an
essential part of that. Our interviewees recognized that, at times, the
internal barrier of lack of confidence can hinder a woman's progress.
Especially after taking a career break to have children or for another
reason, women may suffer a severe loss of confidence coming back to
work—particularly when they know they will need to operate within a
male cultural environment that may no longer be congenial. Our interviewees recommended that women put shyness aside and speak up; not be
afraid of what people think and tackle any issues confidently one by one
without losing authenticity. Women need to push past the internal barrier
of lack of confidence and cultivate a belief in their own abilities. Self-belief
will give them the confidence to take risks and thus continue to move their
career forward.

Work ethic, drive and ambition

Hard work is essential for success for professionals. Male and female leaders alike put in sustained hard work to achieve their success. However, enjoyment in and passion for the role is also important. As stated by one of our interviewees, "You have to put in the hard work and have the passion for it. If you don't, it will be hard to put in the hours and work needed." Another said, "The work ethic at the beginning gives you grounding and understanding and lets you develop as a leader." One of the leaders put it in quite a straightforward manner: "There are no shortcuts—nothing requires talent. If you want something, you just need to work for it."

Alongside this strong work ethic, which was demonstrated by our women leaders from a young age, there was clarity around what was important to them and what they wanted to achieve. Finally, dedication and loyalty were also deemed to be important components.

Ambition was also key. As discussed, many of the professional services women came from disadvantaged backgrounds. For them, this sparked a flame of dedication, commitment and drive and was a spur for developing ambition. In other cases, seeing their mothers' need to be more independent created that ambition. Whatever the origin, it was absolutely clear that senior women in professional services know what they want to achieve and are driven to achieve it.

Perseverance and resilience

Given the many barriers and challenges discussed, it is easy to understand that high levels of perseverance are required to push through and achieve success. One interviewee noted, "I got to where I am today because I don't give up easily." Another respondent said, "Don't let things bother you for too long; learn from them and move on." One of the other women interviewed pointed out how she turned potential prejudices into advantages.

It is also necessary to push past the prejudices regarding traditional roles. One interviewee—an engineer—described a time when she felt despondent about the reaction she got when she started a new job and was introduced to clients as the lead engineer. The clients' faces would drop and they would initially treat her with disdain, lacking confidence in her abilities. One evening she spoke to her husband about how that wears her down. Her husband responded by saying:

> Imagine you want to take your little two-year-old son to crèche. You search for the best crèche in town and find a highly expensive but highly acclaimed one in your neighborhood and decide to go for it. On the first day you take your two-year-old there to meet his teacher, and out walks a Rastafarian man to welcome your little son. He

might be the best carer in the world, but your initial bias will hinder the development of your trust. Only as he proves himself over time, and with demonstrated success in caring for your son, will your trust in him grow.

Her experience was the same and since then she has taken the bias that she experiences less personally. She uses it as a way to surprise the client positively with the excellence of her technical skill. She realized that people needed to see her output before they could trust and appreciate her.

This story demonstrates how the ability to exceed expectations is an important part of perseverance and resilience. Many women described how being met with skepticism in their typically male roles makes them feel that they have to deliver over and above the normal requirement to prove their capabilities. Some of the individuals we interviewed indicated that they specifically endeavor to deliver results early in order to overcome the expectations of their clients. As Edith Kikonyogo from Uganda said, "Prejudice falls away in the face of excellence."

Supportive organization

Some of our interviewees suggested that the role the organization plays in supporting and backing up their female leaders was central to their success. As seen in the study of engineering, "Stemming the Tide" (Fouard et al. n.d.), many women left the industry because they felt the environment was not supportive of their advancement. In contrast, the successful women we interviewed clearly indicated that the support of their organizations and the openness with which they were welcomed into leadership roles contributed to their success. Of course, it is not only the organization as a whole but also the individual support of male leaders within the organization that may be crucial. As stated by Johan Aurik, Global Managing partner of A. T. Kearney, "Men need to actively sponsor high potential women to help propel their success," and, "Men's comments/ support can help or hinder you up the ladder."

Dion Shango from South Africa had the same view:

If men are perceived to be the ones in the driving seat currently, I think they have a bigger role to play in making sure that the cause of women is advanced. So, I am under no illusions as to the responsibility I have in that regard and it is one of my key objectives if I look at my own firm. It is a criticism that I take head-on, that our people tell me all the time, you know, why aren't there more women partners in the firm? And I say to them, look, I don't have an answer yet, it is a massive problem, it is a fair, fair criticism, it is factual. And not only a problem for us here in South Africa, but it is a global problem for our firm.

Shirley Zinn notes in *Swimming Upstream* (2015):

> Women make a huge difference when they're empowered to do what they need to do within the organization. Smart organizations have worked this out. When you interpret this in a systemic and thoughtful way, you can realize results you never imagined possible.

The resulting positive impact is that with more women in leadership roles, there will be more role models and more opportunity to further reach into the organization in terms of understanding people and their needs. Dion Shango also noted: "I have no doubt that by getting a better gender diversity within the leadership structures, communication and connectivity will improve."

What professional services firms are doing

According to Johan Aurik, Global Managing partner of A. T. Kearney, clients are increasingly looking for innovative, distinctive and inspiring solutions to their business issues. The only way to deliver these is to have diverse teams doing the thinking and generating the solutions. Women are a key element of diversity and it is absolutely key that programs exist to encourage their participation in business work.

With the number of women in the boardroom increasing particularly slowly, companies are taking action to understand the needs and actively support the careers of women while promoting healthy work/life integration.

Components of women's programs

Large professional services firms are, almost without exception, investing in women's programs and initiatives to help to increase their diversity, including (and in some cases especially) at top levels. Six main elements recur in these programs (although only the most progressive organizations include as many as five; most include between one and three):

1   *Flexi-time and discretionary-time programs*: these include reduced working hours, flexible working arrangements (for example, work from home) and sometimes reduction on travel for a period—particularly when adjusting to a growing family. An example of this is A. T. Kearney's "Success with Flex" program, which allows consultants to work part-time according to their needs. This program is available to men and women, and increasingly, men are taking it up as they begin to have more of a role in the home.

2   *Sponsorship and mentoring programs*: these are official initiatives to link high potential women with senior leaders in the firm who are usually male, in order that the sponsor might raise the profile of the

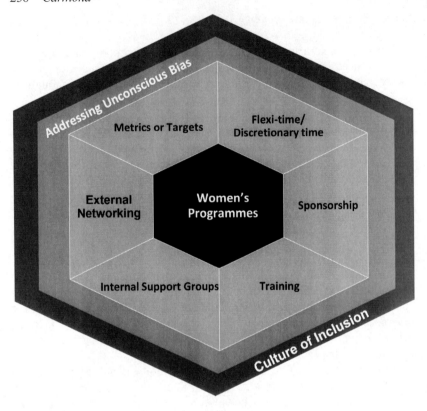

Figure 8.2 Components of women's programs

women within the organization and formalize what is often an informal networking mechanism.

3 *Formal women's training programs*: these include women-specific courses that explore topics such as credibility, ambition, negotiation and communication, executive presence and managing difficult situations. More recently some of the firms have started to develop specific programs for mothers returning to work: for example, Webber Wentzel's "Maternity Support Program" (2016) has a combination of training and support for managing the re-integration into the workplace.

4 *Internal support groups*: typically internal networking forums for women, these are a good place for identifying the issues women face and crafting the solutions. They are often at the center of these programs, but in some cases have a specific purpose; for example, supporting mothers re-entering the workplace after maternity leave.

5 *External networking*: this usually pertains to the professional services women who run networking events with their female clients or

prospective clients. These act as a useful forum for building trusting client relationships. Some firms, particularly engineering firms, are looking at these types of program to help attract and retain female talent and utilize their strong networking capabilities.

6   *Metrics and performance targets*: while firms are increasingly adopting targets for women entering their profession, only a few have targets for increasing the number of senior women in their leadership teams and the number of women being promoted—that is, committing to change at the top level. The results for those few firms show a positive impact.

Two areas that are an essential part of successful programs but often not included are:

1   *Addressing unconscious bias*: one of the most difficult things to do, and only undertaken by some professional services firms, is addressing people's unconscious bias. Such bias affects not only women but indeed most minorities. There is often a lack of awareness that the bias exists and the process of unveiling it is the first step in properly tackling the barriers to women in organizations.
2   *Creating a culture of inclusion*: this means addressing the language and practices pertaining to women of the firm or organization and ensures that the organization is a place that allows all people to thrive—and is not set up to consciously or unconsciously create barriers for women or other minorities. Again, while many firms indicate they are doing this, very few have programs to specifically address the cultural area.

As stated by Robert Waring in his article, "Will the Workplace of the Future 'Lean In' to Women and Parents?" (Waring 2013), the requirements for innovative ways of working go beyond the needs of women and will be particularly important as the millennial generation becomes more senior: "With the aging of the millennial generation, generous leave policies and flexible work hours could become more important than large salary packages." However, he believes that we are still far from finding these innovative models and that indeed it might get worse before it gets better: "Many commentators have indicated that workplace flexibility will not become popular until more men start to use them. But flexing men often face even worse career stigma."

Other programs include options like Dial Up or Dial Down that enable professionals to make choices about the pace of their careers depending on their life stage. While these programs are definitely steps in the right direction, in many cases they do not address the underlying unconscious bias and structural and cultural barriers that are part of the systemic problem relating to the promotion of women in businesses. In addition, many of the organizations have programs that are piecemeal and sporadic. Isolated programs such as these do not address the fundamentals and are not likely to have the impact that is truly required.

The vision for the future

It is hard to imagine what a completely diverse and gender-balanced (and in some cases racially/ethically balanced) organization might look like, but we have described what we would like to see within organizations to bring about more balance than we have at present.

Our vision for the future of women in professional services in particular is that organizations are keen to create an environment where *all people* can thrive equally. That means that culture, values, structure and practices are as welcoming to women (and other minorities) as they currently are to men.

Our vision for the future is that society sees and understands the importance of the multiple roles—homemaker, carer ... *and* breadwinner—that are required to hold up our society and that society develops a balanced and forward-thinking view of how these roles could be filled by men and women.

Our vision is that women make choices about the jobs they do because of their aptitude, passion and capabilities, not because the environments in which they find themselves are hostile to women professionals.

Our vision is that women work with men, but particularly other women, in a way that nurtures them and gets the best from them, and also that people address their unconscious biases, which reinforce the culture and structures that hinder the progress of many female leaders in emerging markets.

Finally, our vision is that young girls and boys in emerging markets equally hope and believe that they can build a better world for themselves and their families with mutual understanding and joint accountability across the different roles they play in society.

Practical steps to build a better future

The workplace is a completely different environment from what it was twenty years ago. This shows the immense progress that has already been made, not least by professional services firms. While there is no single action that can be taken to "put it all right", attending to some of the following areas will help ensure that professional services firms nurture more women leaders for the future:

1   *Education and raising awareness* is required to explain why diversity in general and gender diversity in particular are important to deliver on the goals of the future; and that the current state does not provide

an environment where all people can thrive equally, by its setup and nature.

2 *Tackling the bias (conscious and unconscious)*: men and women need to look at themselves to understand what barriers their own biases could be placing on their own progress or the progress of their female colleagues. As part of Deloitte's program to address women, they began with dialogue as the platform for change, requiring everyone to attend intensive workshops to reveal and examine gender-based assumptions in their own and their clients' organizations (McCracken, 2000).

3 *Systemic integration of women's initiatives/programs*: we need to move away from isolated programs to more integrated holistic strategies aligned to business imperatives, which address all the elements of progress for women, including acknowledging that culture is at the core of creating an environment where women can thrive.

4 *Commitment from the top*: top leadership needs to show absolute commitment, understanding and humility to make the necessary scale of changes and unleash the organization's potential. In the HBR article "How Ernst & Young Keeps Women on the Path to Partnership" (Hewlett and Luce 2005), it was noted that E&Y's chairman from 1994 to 2001 made it his priority to retain and promote women. He created a task team on diversity and an "Office of Retention." Subsequent chairmen have strengthened this focus (Hewlett and Luce 2005).

5 *Support each other:* women and men need to work harder at supporting the progress of women in their organizations, even if it means going out of their way to do so and tackling their own fears and biases in the process.

Conclusion

So much has changed in the world of women in professional services since our mothers (or fathers) were in these roles twenty to forty years ago. There are more women at the top, fewer women acting like men and bias of all sorts has become untangled. But barriers do still exist and the professional women leaders we interviewed indicated that their ability to persevere despite the barriers—alongside their technical excellence, authenticity, confidence and hard work—was key to their success. Professional services organizations in emerging markets that are alive to the kinds of environment where all people, including women, can thrive will play a significant part in producing outstanding leading women for the future.

References

Anderson, R. H. 2015. *Undeterred: The Six Success Habits of Women in Emerging Economies.* Kansas, MO: The Way Women Work Press.

A. T. Kearney. 2014. "The Female Economy in B2B: A Lens on South Africa." Accessed August 11, 2016. www.atkearney.com/documents/10192/4371002/The +Female+Economy+in+B2B+-+A+Lens+on+South+Africa.pdf/6044cabd-ba07-4 2f5-aa61-7451e5012e34.

Barrett, P. M. 2014. "How Billable Hours Changed the Legal Profession." *Bloomberg.com.* Accessed August 11, 2016. www.bloomberg.com/news/articles/ 2014-12-04/how-billable-hours-changed-the-legal-profession.

Bosch, A. 2013. *The SABPP Women's Report 2013.*

Breir, M. and A. Wildschut. 2008. "Changing Gender Profile of Medical Schools in South Africa." *South African Medical Journal* 98: 557–560.

LexisNexis. 2012. "An Investigation of the Billable Hour." *LexisNexis Legal Newsroom*, April 10. Accessed August 11, 2016. www.lexisnexis.com/legalnews room/lexis-hub/b/careerguidance/archive/2012/10/04/an-investigation-of-the-billa ble-hour.aspx?Redirected=true.

Catalyst. 2016. "United Kingdom: Women in Accounting." *Catalyst*, March.

Catalyst. 2016. "United States: Women in Accounting." *Catalyst*, March.

Financial Reporting Council (FRC). 2015. "Key Facts and Trends in the Accountancy Profession." FRC, June. Accessed February 6, 2017. www.frc.org.uk/ Our-Work/Publications/Professional-Oversight/Key-Facts-and-Trends-in-the-Ac countancy-Profes-(1).pdf.

Fouad, N. A., R. Singh, M. E. Patrick and J. P. Liu. 2012. "Stemming the Tide: Why Women Leave Engineering." *Journal of Vocational Behavior.* 83: 346–355.

Gerzema, J. and M. D'Antonio. 2013. *The Athena Doctrine: How Women (and the Men Who Think Like Them) Will Rule the Future.* Hoboken, NJ: Wiley.

Govender, V. and L. Penn-Kekana. 2007. "Gender Biases and Discrimination: A Review of Health Care Interpersonal Interactions." World Health Organization. Accessed February 6, 2017. www.who.int/social_determinants/resources/gender_ biases_and_discrimination_wgkn_2007.pdf.

Grant Thornton. 2013. "Women in Senior Management: Setting the Stage for Growth." Grant Thornton International Business Report 2013. Accessed February 6, 2017. www.grantthornton.ae/content/files/women-in-senior-managem ent-ibr-2013.

Hewlett, S.A. and C. B. Luce (2005) "Off-Ramps and On-Ramps: Keeping Talented Women on the Road to Success." *Harvard business Review* 88(3): 43–54.

ICAEW (Institute of Chartered Accountants in England and Wales). 2014. "ICAEW Salary Survey 2013" *ICAEWJobs.* Accessed August 11, 2016. www. icaewjobs.com/article/icaew-salary-survey-2013-/.

Kaiser, S. and M. J. Ringlstetter. 2011. *Strategic Management of Professional Service Firms: Theory and Practice.* Heidelberg, New York: Springer.

Manoharan, T. N. n.d. Personal interview by D. Murali. [T. N Manoharan is the former president of the Institute of Chartered Accountants of India.]

McCracken, D. 2000. "Winning the Talent War for Women: Sometimes It Takes a Revolution." *Harvard Business Review* 78(6): 159–167.

Paliszkiewicz, J. O. 2011. "Trust Management: Literature Review." *Management* 6(4): 315–331.

Brent Personnel. n.d. "Female Chartered Accountants and the Glass Ceiling." *Brent Personnel.* Accessed August 11, 2016. www.brent.co.za/Pages/news-view.asp x?iID=76e0ad8a-1b77-4cd7-9029-6cfdf775b853&title=Female+Chartered+Account ants+and+the+Glass+Ceiling&v=t&ID=f2f10d4b-bded-4625-b311-4c5baac54ad3.

PwC. n.d. "What are Professional Services?" *PwC.* Accessed August 11, 2016. www.pwc.co.uk/industries/government-public-sector/education/higher-apprentice ships/higher-apprenticeships-what-are-professional-services.html.

SAICA (South African Institute of Chartered Accountants). 2009. "Celebrating Women Chartered Accountants [CAs(SA)]—SA's Women CAs(SA) Are Creating a New Glass Ceiling Mould." *SAICA,* August 5. Accessed February 6, 2017. www.saica.co.za/News/NewsArticlesandPressmediareleases/tabid/695/item id/1760/pageid/20/language/en-ZA/language/en-ZA/Default.aspx.

Schein, E. H. 2013. *Humble Inquiry: The Gentle Art of Asking Instead of Telling.* Oakland, CA: Berrett-Koehler.

SDSU (San Diego State University) College of Engineering. n.d. "Careers & Job Placement" page. Accessed August 11, 2016. https://newscenter.sdsu.edu/engi neering/careers_job_placement.aspx.

Waring, R. (2013). "Will the Workplace of the Future 'Lean In' to Women and Parents?" *Great Place to Work,* June 20. Accessed February 6, 2017. www.grea tplacetowork.com/blog/487-will-the-workplace-of-the-future-lean-in-to-women-a nd-parents.

Webber Wentzel. 2016. "Webber Wentzel Launches a Maternity Support Programme: Another First for the South African Legal Industry." *Webber Wentzel,* February 29. Accessed February 6, 2017. www.webberwentzel.com/wwb/con tent/en/ww-most-popular?oid=55219&sn=Detail-2011&pid=35793.

Wikipedia. 2016. "Professional Services." *Wikipedia.* Accessed August 11, 2016. https://en.wikipedia.org/wiki/Professional_services.

Wulf, W. 1998. "Diversity in Engineering." *The Bridge: Competitive Materials and Solutions* 28 (4).

Zinn, S. 2015. *Swimming Upstream.* Johannesburg: K. R. Publishing.

9   Women's leadership in corporate enterprises

Maxine Jaffit and Kelly Alexander

Introduction

In emerging markets, women in corporate enterprises face a unique set of challenges and opportunities. These women assume responsibilities and face pressures that are atypical in terms of cultural norms and values around the role of women in society. Challenges around access to talent in emerging markets may result in a greater number of women being engaged in corporate enterprises, yet not all women make it to positions of leadership within these organizations. Furthermore, these emerging markets are often characterized by heterogeneity in national cultures, which requires sensitivity and cultural agility when dealing with different stakeholders (Hofstede 1980).

The ten women interviewed for this chapter were all distinctive in terms of their strong sense of personal and professional identity and their unwavering sense of mission and purpose. This corresponds with the notion that "People become leaders by internalizing a leadership identity and developing a sense of purpose" (Ibarra, Ely and Kolb 2013). Authenticity is also the hallmark of successful women in corporate enterprises. Women leaders are self-aware and unapologetic in terms of tackling issues head on, particularly when their beliefs and values about social justice issues are challenged. All of the women interviewed were clear about tackling undercurrents, and their career trajectories were characterized by hard work, commitment and a strong focus on building relationships.

Literature review

Social cognitive theory views the development of individuals as a result of the assimilation of cues in the form of positive or negative reinforcement regarding behavior. The theory examines "the psychological mechanisms that enable people to interact effectively with the environment, to assign personal meanings to their actions and to plan and execute courses of actions in accordance to their own personal goals and standards" (Caprara et al. 2013, 145). In this way, the transmission of gendered identities occurs, leading to the construction of and adherence to gender roles, norms and values in society. This is aligned with Butler's notion of gender performativity, with its question: "Does being female constitute a 'natural fact' or a cultural performance ...?" (Butler 1990, viii).

As noted in Chapter 2, gender is a social construct that is reproduced and maintained in daily activities (Gherardi and Poggio, 2001). For Bussey and Bandura (1999, 676), gender roles take "on added importance because many of the attributes and roles selectively promoted in males and females tend to be differentially valued—with those ascribed to males generally being regarded as more desirable, effectual, and of higher status". Thus, there is less value ascribed to attributes that are typically described as being "female", which legitimates the exclusion of the majority of women from senior roles in corporate enterprises. Social dominance theory was developed in order to begin to understand how "group-based hierarchies are formed and maintained and its premise includes the idea that discrimination occurs across various levels and is coordinated to favor the dominant group by legitimizing society's shared social ideologies" (Pratto et al. 2006 in Kiser 2015, 601). Furthermore, as "perceptions are guided by preconceptions" there exists a tension between traditionally male-centric corporate enterprises, and the abundance of broader societal gender roles reinforcing "traditional gender conduct" that serve to regulate behavior (Bussey and Bandura 1999, 687). This is particularly true for women in emerging markets who need to contend with patriarchal societal norms.

Social cognitive theory is a useful framework for understanding how the creation of gendered selves in the workplace impacts the way in which women structure their reality and create their identity. The decisions people make around work, structure their realities and ultimately impact on their satisfaction and the quality of their work life (Bussey and Bandura (1999, 692). Social cognitions influence the nature of goals and standards that are set by individuals, based on their self-perceptions (Mccormick and Martinko, 2004). Thus, the way in which girls and women are socialized impacts their perceived ability to achieve certain goals and may in fact limit the degree to which they believe senior leadership positions are within their reach. Bussey and Bandura (1999) suggest that the choice of occupation is highly influenced by gender and preconceptions regarding individuals' ability to perform the required tasks. Notably, women are more likely to judge that they are best suited to "typically" female occupations. It is thus important to consider the individual characteristics of women in leadership positions and identify the factors contributing to their achievement and career paths.

When considering decision-making relative to occupation, Bandura (1991, 278) states that "self-regulation of conduct is not entirely an intrapsychic affair, nor do people operate as autonomous moral agents impervious to the social realities in which they are enmeshed". Social norms have a profound impact on women's career decisions by limiting the choices women feel are open to them.

With the above theoretical context in mind, what follows is an investigation of the ways in which current female leaders were able to develop—personally and professionally—and attain their current positions, despite the broader gender stereotypes that exist. The key themes and insights that emerged from the interviews focused on specific early-childhood factors and how these factors have informed the identity and leadership approach of these women. We analyze the respondents' unique personality characteristics in terms of how they have defined their leadership "signature". Additionally, specific ideas relating to the role to be played as a leader, networking and advice for other women—specifically, women transitioning into senior positions in corporate enterprises—is referenced.

Background to women interviewed

The women interviewed for this chapter include CEOs of corporate enterprises, philanthropists and executive women in a variety of sectors, including those who are excelling in traditional male-dominated sectors such as mining and financial services. While the interviewees work in a multitude of business sectors, none of them experienced any pressure to perform gendered work or pursue a gendered career path. Examples of typically "female" sectors would include healthcare and education. All ten respondents have a global view of business gained from working internationally or representing their organizations and professional associations internationally. A number of the women interviewed are recognized globally as distinctive in their field of endeavor.

Common themes emerging from the interviews

Early childhood

It is interesting to note that respondents had varied childhood experiences. Some of the women came from impoverished backgrounds while others came from more privileged families and environments. However, they were all taught from a young age that hard work was imperative for success. Many of the women experienced challenges that molded them and seem to have defined them, often very painfully. These challenges included growing up in poverty-stricken families and communities—sometimes with absent or deceased parents. Many respondents were required to do part-time work in order to pay for their studies from a young age. Further examples include growing up within communist regimes where they were unable to express their opinions.

Ekaterina Sheremet, from Eastern Europe, described her parents' influence, saying, "They actually made me very responsible and accountable."

This reflects many of the women's earliest parental or authority figures' expectations of their behavior. Daniela Chikova from Bulgaria described her parents as providing the best basis for her no matter what she studied: "Just to speak foreign languages and understand that my life does not need to be limited to the place where I was born or grew up." Isabel Neiva grew up in Portugal and now works in Dubai. She described her parents as open and encouraging, clear about choices and consequences. Sindisiwe Koyana referred to her mother as her role model of hard work and tenacity.

In their formative years, all the women interviewed had significant role models who impacted on and shaped their personalities and their drive to succeed. These role models were not gender specific; it was later on that male role models were significant in terms of advancing their careers within communities and organizations. In some instances it was people who recognized their potential that influenced the interviewees' lives; these included school principals and teachers. These important role models created the belief that the women were capable of achieving. According to Caprara et al. (2013, 145), one of the key factors in influencing behavior is "self-efficacy beliefs, namely judgements people hold about their capacity to cope effectively with specific challenges and to face demanding situations". A number of the women interviewed went to all-girls' schools and learned about being competitive through their various sporting activities. Phuti Mahanyele describes "a hunger—to know more and to grow", and Melanie Botha stated that, growing up, "I did not know anything but work. I had dreams and visions of becoming a leader."

As stated in Chapter 2, a central tenet running through the entire research project is awareness of social justice—with female leaders across regions highlighting awareness of the broader context of inequality. Many of the women interviewed confronted, or were aware of, social injustice in their early years, and all were aware of the social and political environments in which they were raised. Within an emerging market context, issues of racial discrimination and class inequality were key factors that shaped them as people and later on as leaders. For example, some of the women reported that growing up in apartheid South Africa enabled them to deal with levels of complexity. This complexity characterizes emerging market contexts and remains prevalent within corporate enterprises. None of the women saw themselves as particularly disadvantaged due to their gender and were taught by their parents, teachers, mentors or peers to simply "get on with it". Sindisiwe Koyana describes her experience as one in which "adversity raised me". This highlights a common theme of resilience, which is a key characteristic in all of the respondents.

The result of their childhood experiences—such as dealing with the injustice of apartheid in South Africa or the transition from communist rule in Eastern Europe—translated into a leadership style that was cognizant of their responsibility as citizens and their role in their respective societies and organizations. Many of these early discussions on injustice took place in the privacy of the home, and Daniela Chikova, growing up under a communist regime, learned at a young age that politically charged conversations could not be held in public.

The respondents are highly aware of the impact they have, both as role models for other women and in terms of the value and impact of their organizations on broader society. Thus, the women leaders, through exposure to the levels of complexity growing up, are able to translate this into a unique leadership style in corporate enterprises and beyond the boardroom. This style of leadership is referred to by Pearce and Conger (2003 in Fletcher 2004, 648) as a "more relational concept of leadership, one that focuses on dynamic, interactive processes of influence and learning intended to transform organizational structures, norms and work practices".

Individual characteristics

A study completed in the USA, UK and Germany revealed the factors that drive women to strive for positions of leadership. They include the ability to flourish, excel and gain mastery, plus the desire to have meaningful, purposeful work, to be empowered and empower others, and finally, to earn well (Hewlett and Marshall, 2014).

Emerging market economies are often characterized by informal relations and a way of doing business based on patronage and affiliation. However, the women interviewed unanimously stated that in every situation they try to make the biggest difference or positive impact. Botha spoke of supporting her team and stated, "I will walk the extra mile in fighting for them if there is injustice against them or if there are wrong perceptions." Again, the importance of authenticity and a strong values base characterize the women interviewed. Respondents all have a well-developed sense of identity and internal locus of control that is evident in their self-confidence and willingness to be outspoken on issues. In a related study on enterprise leaders, women in leadership positions displayed a persistent desire to control their destiny (Weidenfeller 2012).

This internal locus of control and desire to manage their own futures is evident in Barçin Yinanç (from Turkey), who described her work discipline and ethics as central. She believes in having a "stance" (point of view), being very meticulous and "not running after quick successes". Furthermore, all these women have learned to deal with conflict and to confront directly those issues that may be uncomfortable for others to raise. For example, for Wendy Appelbaum, "There are few elephants in the room when I'm in the room … . I take them out, but I have learned that to do this, one needs to be prepared to deal with the consequences."

This ability to tackle issues, and fearlessly, emerged as a key leadership trait shared by respondents. As Wendy Ackerman stated, "I suppose I am a feisty person. I have learned to speak my truth with no hidden agendas." This comment is also an example of the honest, straightforward style of communication required by leaders. At the same time, these women have a high level of personal insight, an acute awareness of themselves and of their impact on others—and thus, knowing when to act. This is evident in Sindisiwe Koyana's statement: "I am not going to accept nonsense; I am going to nip this in the bud. I have also learned that there are times to actually sit back and just observe before acting."

Respondents also share an intense curiosity and a strong desire to have a big-picture perspective. The women leaders interviewed see themselves as enablers and have a huge passion for what they do. They also see themselves as exceptionally hard workers. Isabel Neiva, for example, indicated that her work "requires a lot of commitment. It requires a lot of effort ... and you really need to enjoy it." These women define themselves as mentors to women, catalysts for organization effectiveness or activists for social change. As noted, they are willing to take a stand on issues related to what they consider improper business practice, despite pressures not to act this way. This tendency may relate to the respondents' awareness of social justice issues noted previously. For example, due to the societal contexts in which they grew up being characterized by duality in terms of wealth and poverty, access and denial, information and secrecy, they may be more aware of the broader consequences of unethical behavior.

A common characteristic of these women is their deep sense of purpose and their commitment to corporate issues beyond their own career development. As noted previously, the complexities of growing up in an emerging market context highlight both the opportunity and the need to adopt a broad worldview. All leaders interviewed derive a great deal of meaning from the work they do and are passionate about it.

Apart from passion and commitment, a number of other key traits emerged in the interviews. For some of these women, the desire to emerge from poverty and adversity has translated into a form of personal resilience that enables them to move forward in spite of challenges and obstacles. For example, Wendy Lucas-Bull stated, "I am fearless with no second-guessing", highlighting her inner locus of control and self-belief. Another defining characteristic is the ability to make sense of issues and deal with multiple levels of complexity—that is, to "connect the dots". These women have a strong focus on information and obtaining all the facts in their need for objectivity and clarity, and are thus unafraid to ask for help to ensure that all the facts are known. They see themselves as having developed an ability to read the situation and make sense of restraining factors. Appelbaum stated that she has an ability "to see the big picture and the detail at the same time".

Relationship to power

The women leaders were very conscious of the power dynamics within corporate enterprises. This is critical in an emerging market context where power dynamics and relations of power are key to understanding the operational and business context. The respondents acknowledged the power they wield in their roles in corporate enterprises and consequently the potential they have to influence others. Although they are all cognizant of their personal power and the power implicit in their role, they each use power differently. For example, Appelbaum stated, "I am very aware of power and I think women collaborate more than men. For me, power is connectivity, and the ability to network and connect with people, although I acknowledge that there is overt abuse of power in emerging markets." This statement on the abuse of power in emerging markets links to the way in which there is often a different world view and culture in these markets. Wanasika et al. (2010) discuss how the factors around poverty and familial and social networks, coupled with instability and often violence, can result in reduced expectations of political and business leaders. As stated in the Journal of World Business on 'Managerial culture and leadership in Sub-Saharan Africa' the low expectations of leaders result in citizens accepting this abuse of power, which can ultimately result in poor leadership becoming entrenched at all levels of society (Wanasika et al. 2010).

This reinforces the notion, discussed previously, of complexity in emerging markets, whereby competing forces impact on the operations of corporate enterprises and influence the actions and behaviors of leaders. Similarly, in an Eastern European emerging market context, Sheremet highlights that "there are not so many ... there are very few female leaders and politicians," which impacts on the ability of those few women to exercise power in that environment: "You are always the minority and that's kind of a challenge."

Some women reported that, as executives, there is perceived power in their role as champions of women's issues in the workplace and in society in general. An additional dimension to the perceived power of successful women is being labelled as celebrities. This was felt to be onerous because of the way it trivializes competence, hard work and identity. Some women reported that they experienced a sense of dissonance between their self-image and identity and some of the descriptors used by others, particularly men. This may be another product of the unusualness of women in leadership positions. The fact that simply being a female leader confers "celebrity status" may contribute to her being seen as exceptional and so create a divide between female leader and "ordinary" female in an industry. Again, this highlights the performativity of gender and the entrenched nature of gender roles in society.

Many women reported that they used their leadership roles to advocate for change at a macro level. Nicky Newton-King is such an example. She works towards building investor confidence through building partnerships across civil society, labor and government in her drive to achieve meaningful and inclusive growth in South Africa.

Leadership style

The factors that have shaped the women leaders in childhood, their sense of self, authenticity and adherence to their values, as well as the power conferred on them—all influence their unique leadership styles.

All the women interviewed had high expectations of themselves and held others to the same standard. They all defined their leadership style as highly collaborative, although some have been accused of being too inclusive in their decision-making processes. Many women described how they have to "learn as they go" because of the many gaps or institutional voids that exist within an emerging market. Consequently, they had to lead and operate at the same time, which made the involvement and inclusion of others in sense-making and decision-making particularly crucial. As noted previously, the respondents all displayed a strong sense of purpose and a passion for their work. This was clearly evident in their leadership style and their ability to motivate their teams and organizations with a clear vision and articulate their metrics of success. Neiva said that her leadership style was "quite inspirational and collaborative. But if I look at how I have evolved throughout the years … I am sometimes much more … assertive and much more directive than I was a few years back."

Context is continually a feature of the analysis of emerging markets. Leadership style is likely to be influenced by the environment a leader is in. Barçin Yinanç in Turkey described her evolving insights about teamwork and collaboration, stating, "Everyone is different, everyone is precious, everyone has a talent, you know. And you have to see through whoever has the skill and make use of these skills accordingly." This was reiterated by Daniela Chikova in Bulgaria who, when describing her decision-making style, stated, "I am always trying to consult and involve the persons around me, in order to make sure that I am seeing the entire picture."

A further aspect of respondents' leadership style was their focus on understanding the environment and being present at the "coalface". They engage with stakeholders and use a variety of strategies to understand their people and the clients they serve. For example, Sindisiwe Koyana stated, "I have learned that you can't sit in some fancy office and get reports done or sent to you. You have to see it for yourself. It's important to be at the coalface in your miner's boots and hat." This was echoed by Botha: "I really get involved. I am in the trenches with the team. I do not sit on the side."

The desire leaders have to see both the big picture (strategy) and the smaller details (operations) translates into their sense-making ability. They also define their leadership style as one where there is a predominant focus on their relationship ability. As well as linking to the effective use of power, this focus on relationships and understanding people's characters and specific skills enables the leaders to select the right kind of people and correctly identify the skills they choose to support. This was seen as particularly important when choosing people for the leadership teams. Phuti

Mahanyele talked of building strong relationships as fundamental to success: "Early on, I understood the importance of forming relationships and not being afraid to talk to influential people in the organization."

A key feature of the leadership style of these respondents was their ability to combine traits such as individualism, control, assertiveness and advocacy—which are socially ascribed to men and generally understood to be masculine (Acker 1990, Calas and Smircich 1993, Collinson and Hearn 1996, in Fletcher 2004)—with traits such as empathy, community, vulnerability and collaboration, generally associated with females, in a new, post-heroic model of leadership, as described by Fletcher (2004).

Role in developing other people

In the discussion above, the respondents identify as enablers, catalysts for organizational and social change. They believe they have the ability to see the big picture and tackle issues greater than their own career development. As a result, developing others is key. Most of these women see their role in regard to developing others as "looking for opportunities for others to push themselves" (Lucas-Bull). This enabling role is echoed by Applebaum, who stated that, "As a mentor, all I do is build up confidence to believe that they deserve those positions, and they can do it. Then I let them do it for themselves." Phuti Mahanyele suggested that what is needed is for young people to be able to access their gifts so these can be grown further. She believes that opportunities are ever-present in spite of the challenges. Mahanyele added that it is important to make sure that all people feel valued in the organization, so that they give their best work. For Sheremet, transitioning from an authoritarian to an inclusive leadership style "required some investment in people—the more you invest, the more you get".

According to Hensvik, in a European-based study, "women obtain more (or better) mentoring by female managers, either because they find it easier to establish mentoring relationships with women or because they receive better mentoring from more similar supervisors" (2014, 397). It is likely that the same is true in an emerging market context, where it has already been noted that relationships are key to success.

The respondents all confirmed that what is vital for any leader—particularly in emerging markets today—is to be contributing to communities outside the business environment. They believe that this aspect of their leadership role offers them an important lens on, and role in, society in that it involves contributing to broader society, while also enabling a fuller understanding of their business context.

Organizational dynamics

According to Chin (2016, 21), "organizational structure refers to the rules and practices which control and shape members' daily interactions in pursuit of organizational goals". Women in corporate enterprises reported that they have worked hard to create inclusive environments where women can be "authentic". In a multicultural emerging market, working with a diverse team, Neiva believes that "authenticity is the key success factor". In corporate enterprises headed by women, such as the Johannesburg Stock Exchange, there has been a deliberate focus on creating a culture within which women can thrive. In such an environment, the "waste of talent in the workforce" noted by Leimon, Moscovici and Goodies (2011) is likely to be less significant. This includes enabling a woman to embrace all aspects of herself by validating the various roles women play, such as professional and mother. For Hensvik, this kind of organizational culture could lead to a greater volume of female talent within the organization, as "it could also be ... that female talented workers may choose to enter women-led firms because they anticipate better career opportunities" (2014, 418). This is in stark contrast to many organizations, where women subjugate some of their roles and identities in order to align with the lived and experienced (as opposed to the espoused) organizational culture.

This includes having to manage a subtle form of prejudice that is difficult for women to raise and resolve. The difficulty is due to the fact that certain prejudicial behaviors, values and attitudes are so entrenched and normalized that they often occur unnoticed. Some respondents discussed the impact of this unconscious bias, which they believe is rooted in a model of patriarchal traditional leadership characteristic of emerging market contexts such as sub-Saharan Africa, Latin America, India, Russia and Turkey. Elliott and Stead (2008) use the concept of multiply constituted gender identities, in which various competing factors influence an individual's identity formation. In an emerging market context—be it Turkey with its modernism/religious tension, Bulgaria's emergence from the Soviet Union or the influence of religion over large parts of Latin America—these unconscious biases interact in various ways with the broader environment, influencing women's ability to attain leadership positions. In spite of these factors, all the women interviewed seem to have accomplished success in their chosen domains through hard work, courage and commitment. Furthermore, by championing women in their workplaces and creating enabling environments for women to succeed in corporate enterprises, the leaders interviewed are actively working toward altering these norms.

The majority of respondents are of the view that men have "opened the doors" to senior leadership positions, while others disagree and believe it was their hard work and competence that enabled them to progress. This may be attributed to different self-perceptions, as well as to different operational environments and organizational cultures.

There was a significant difference of opinion and experience regarding the means of attaining success in the corporate enterprises. Some interviewees believed that women "show their colors and then rise" (Nicky

Newton King), while others believed that competent women are invited by men to join the senior ranks. For a number of women it was important to have had executive male sponsors in the organization who could vouch for them and open doors to opportunity. Botha noted that male mentors had assisted her development throughout her career, stating, "All those mentors really helped me with self-awareness and being more aware of how I operate and what I do."

This was a key research finding for a highly successful South Africa-based financial services company. Women who had joined the senior ranks were of the view that without influential male sponsorship they would not have progressed to the upper echelons of the organization, even with their superior academic and professional credentials. It is interesting to note that the women leaders have now taken on this role for junior women in their organizations. Referring to what corporate enterprises could do to alleviate barriers to women in corporate enterprise, Neiva mentioned sponsorship: "The sponsorship initiative … I think that was one of the things that we needed."

Women's transitions in corporate enterprises

The women interviewed have been promoted to senior positions and discussed their personal insights regarding three key factors that enabled their transition. First, they had spoken to many people, including clients, to develop their understanding of their industries and appreciate different perspectives. Second, respondents had spent some time in reflection and carefully considered the kinds of people with whom they wished to surround themselves. Caprara et al. (2013, 146) indicate that the capacity for self-reflection is critical as it reflects "self-regulatory processes and mechanisms that allow people to reflect upon themselves, to learn from experience, and to accord their behavior to their own pursuits and standards". Finally, the transitions were carefully planned and were indicative of high levels of emotional awareness. Some leaders used the early part of the transitional phases to refocus on understanding their clients' needs and connect with people on the front line. Once more, this highlights the commitment such leaders have to a big-picture understanding of their environments.

Transitioning into a leadership position is experienced as a subtle process and described as moving away from operational detail and observing and embracing the entire political and corporate system dynamic. Transitioning is also referred to as a process of personal and professional transformation that entails developing insight, awareness and skill for tackling tough issues. It involves being mindful of when and how to raise issues and deciding whether to deal with these issues outside the formal meeting process. If issues are serious, the ability to tackle them directly and not remain silent or ineffectually non-confrontational must be acquired. As noted previously, learning to deal with challenging issues is a key characteristic of the leaders interviewed.

Transition in and out of the corporate enterprise

As important for the women leaders as the shift into positions of leadership within corporate enterprises were the transitions within or out of these organizations. Lucas-Bull advised:

> Don't give up too soon. Try to fix it so that you fix it for people who come after you. But there is a point in time where you can say, "I have tried everything; it is not getting better," and then leave.

Similarly, other interviewees suggested that when their ability to impact positively became compromised or limited, it was time to move on. It is important for leaders to know the correct time to exit an organization so as not to become ineffectual in their role.

On the issue of the "second shift"—that is, when women remain primary caregivers – "much has been written on the negative spillover that women's job pressures have on family life but little on how job satisfaction may enhance family life" (Bussey and Bandura 1999, 703). An executive male opined that women who claim to leave corporate enterprises due to "family commitments" are giving a "cop-out reason". He suggested that women leave for a variety of reasons, including the comments of males, the incorrect assumption made by organizations that Women's Day events are a retention strategy for female staff members, and the pressure to perform while managing multiple other commitments—such as family. This corresponds with Fletcher (2004), noted in Chapter 2, and Butler (1990), who expose the performative and continual way in which gender roles are created and reinforced. For Bussey and Bandura (1999, 677) this is important because changing commitments bring about altered expectations and "gender role development and functioning are not confined to childhood but are negotiated throughout the life course". As Botha highlights, this is problematic, particularly when coupled with entrenched cultural norms, as "you cannot (easily) change the culture". These factors highlight the lack of priority given to supporting women in corporate enterprises, particularly with regard to identity shifts, and the importance of organizational dynamics in creating an enabling environment for women leaders to succeed.

Networking

Networking, as mentioned previously, is a critical tool for female leaders, both in their power relations and due to the more relational leadership style described by certain respondents. The women interviewed were clear that networking was important for accessing people and resources for the good of their institution and/or to benefit society as a whole. Thus, networking was not only important for power relations but also contributed to female leaders fulfilling their broader aim of working to decrease inequality in society. A limited number of interviewees used networking to assist them through difficult times and to obtain the support of other women. Networking is commonly referred to as relationship-building and part of leveraging power networks, especially in pursuit of a predefined goal or objective. In the case of women leaders in emerging market contexts, a broad network both facilitates personal career growth and provides fulfilment and purpose through broader societal contributions.

Advice to women in corporate enterprises

Although women leaders are working to alter the organizational dynamics in their companies to ensure a significant pipeline of female leaders, the corporate enterprise environment still facilitates the continuance of unconscious bias in the workplace. As a result, Newton-King urges women, "If life has treated you well, send the elevator down." This is the suggestion that women in corporate enterprises assist other women in their career progression, acting in a similar way to how men may have in the past—acting as sponsors and vouching for individuals. For Hensvik (2014, 418), "Theoretical literature has also argued that female managers may break the glass ceiling for female employees by, for example, serving as mentors and role models for lower-level employees or by eliminating discriminatory behavior." It was also suggested in the interviews that more women need to "put their hands up for small things" and in doing so, counter the disparity between perception and ability—as per social cognitive theory (Bussey and Bandura 1999). Respondents agreed that women need to be more proactive in stepping forward and enabling others to see their abilities. As Sheremet put it, "One thing that [women need to do] is speak up. Because what I have observed is that many women … tend to be shy and they are not aggressive enough."

Wendy Appelbaum recommended that women "stand up and feel comfortable to speak". She added, "When women have the courage to use their voice, their honesty is their most powerful tool … the courage to stand up against what is wrong." This is closely linked to the notions of authenticity discussed previously and the importance of acting in accordance with one's values. Sheremet similarly said, "It is very important that … you continue to act normally, not a male style, but try to be yourself." Furthermore, according to Applebaum:

> We need to change the psyche of women: ambition and confidence are not dirty words. Women naturally consider the consequence of their actions. Women are essentially more cautious and tend to over-intellectualize; they scheme, don't take knee-jerk decisions, but often don't scheme right.

A key theme that emerged in the research—evident in the conceptual framework presented in Chapter 2—was voiced by Wendy Ackerman, who said that women need to have a passion for the job. Ackerman further recommended that emotions be kept out of decisions, adding, "There are no shortcuts and hard work is essential." This corresponds with Wendy Lucas-Bull, who is of the view that everyone needs to equip him- or her-self to be the best that they can be and that this involves not only technical knowledge but also knowledge of ongoing current affairs: "Without contextual understanding of the business environment, women in leadership cannot be effective." Further advice from Wendy Lucas-Bull included having an ability to cut through "the noise", which is linked to issues of gathering facts and sense-making, noted above; to see the real issue, as well as an ability to stay grounded.

Factors specific to emerging markets

There are many levels of complexity specific to women leading in emerging markets. The practice of "learning as you go" is one that stands out in particular, a response to the deficits in skill, infrastructure and systems that characterize an emerging-market context. Leading corporations in contexts where there are socio-political dynamics requires sensitivity—that is, sensitivity to how the history of the country finds expression in the nuances of organizational behavior of employees in those countries. Neiva highlights how in the Middle East, religious and cultural norms create barriers that deter local women from reaching senior positions within organizations, yet expatriate women are often represented at senior levels in the same organizations. One of these norms is evident in Turkey, where, as Barçin Yinanç explained, family ties are very important: "Women have an extra burden of running the family and running the children." She considers this to be a key factor preventing women from taking a more active role in corporations.

For women, the existence of patriarchal leadership models in emerging markets is a serious hurdle for them to overcome, particularly when women are seen as "less than" or inferior to men. Although men believe it is easier to hire women in senior positions in emerging markets than elsewhere, those women require drive, authenticity and unwavering commitment to succeed in order to navigate the complex contextual dynamics coupled with corporate cultures that often obstruct their progress. The women who occupy senior leadership positions in these market contexts are characterized by hard work, strong interpersonal relationship abilities and their belief in a purpose beyond the corporation. They have needed to be entrepreneurial and look for opportunities. This includes looking for finance, as well as proactively seeking partnerships.

It is therefore apparent that strong female leaders are both born and bred. The particular environments in which the respondents grew up presented them with numerous obstacles—in addition to those thrown up by traditional patriarchal and gender norms. Thus, both the corporate enterprise and the broader socio-political environment provide opportunities for women leaders to respond to difficulties and overcome them. In this way, inherent strengths are tested and refined. Our respondents showed that they were able to develop and hone the leadership skills that serve them today.

The ability to network, engage with power and assist others to develop, gain insight and navigate institutional voids through inclusive leadership, coupled with attempts to alter organizational cultures were key themes that emerged from these interviews. Respondents also demonstrated that following their own passions and working in a manner that aligned with their moral values was critical to navigating their careers with integrity and their eventual success.

References

Bandura, A. 1991. "Social Cognitive Theory of Self-Regulation." *Organisational Behaviour and Human Decision Processes* 50(2): 248–287.

Butler, J. 1990. *Gender Trouble: Feminism and the Subversion of Identity.* New York: Routledge.

Bussey, K. and A. Bandura. 1999. "Social Cognitive Theory of Gender Development and Differentiation." *Psychological Review* 106(4): 676–713.

Caprara, G., M. Vecchione, C. Barbaranelli and G. Alessandri. 2013. "Emotional Stability and Affective Self-Regulatory Efficacy Beliefs: Proofs of Integration Between Trait Theory and Social Cognitive Theory." *European Journal of Personality* 27: 145–154.

Chin, L. G. 2016. "Unequal Egalitarianism: Does Organizational Structure Create Different Perceptions of Male versus Female Leadership Abilities?", *Gender in Management: An International Journal,* 31(1):19–42.

Elliott, C. and V. Stead. 2008. "Learning from Leading Women's Experience: Towards a Sociological Understanding." *Leadership* 4(2): 159–180.

Fletcher, J. K. 2004. "The Paradox of Postheroic Leadership: An Essay on Gender, Power, and Transformational Change." *The Leadership Quarterly* 15(5): 647–661.

Gherardi, S. and B. Poggio. 2001. "Creating and Recreating Gender Order in Organisations." *Journal of World Business* 36(3): 245–259.

Hensvik, L. E. 2014. "Manager Impartiality: Worker–Firm Matching and the Gender Wage Gap." *Industrial and Labour Relations Review* 67(2).

Hewlett, S. A. and M. Marshall. 2014. "Women Want Five Things." Centre for Talent Innovation, New York. www.citywomen.co.uk/wp-content/uploads/2015/03/WomenWant-FiveThings_ExecSumm-CTI.pdf.

Hofstede, G. 1980. *Culture's Consequences: International Differences in Work-Related Values.* Beverly Hills, CA: Sage.

Ibarra, H., R. J. Ely and D. M. Kolb. 2013. "Women Rising: The Unseen Barriers." *Harvard Business Review* 91(9): 60–66.

Kiser, A. I. T. 2015. "Workplace and Leadership Perceptions Between Men and Women." *Gender in Management: An International Journal* 30(8): 598–612.

Leimon, A., F. Moscovici and H. Goodies. 2011. *Coaching Women to Lead.* London: Routledge.

Mccormick, M. J. and M. J. Martinko. 2004. "Identifying Leader Social Cognitions: Integrating the Causal Reasoning Perspective into Social Cognitive Theory." *Journal of Leadership and Organisational Studies* 10(4): 2–11.

Wanasika, I., J. P. Howell, R. Littrell and P. Dorfman. 2011. "Managerial Leadership and Culture in Sub-Saharan Africa." *Journal of World Business* 46(2): 234–241.

Weidenfeller, N. K. 2012. "Breaking Through the Glass Wall: The Experience of Being a Woman Enterprise Leader." *Human Resource Development International* 15(3): 365–374.

10 Women on boards

Shirley Zinn, Mpho Nkeli, Cecily Carmona and Hema Parbhoo

Introduction

According to Adams and Ferreira (2009), the board of directors plays an immensely critical role in the oversight, strategic direction and regulation of organizations to ensure both corporate governance and social adherence. Board members are the custodians who continuously manage the delicate interplay between the corporate and shareholder mandate in relation to broader societal responsibility and impact. As a result, board members need an extremely diverse set of skills and tools to be able to effectively navigate inevitable uncertainty.

Given their mammoth responsibilities, Deeb (2014) further asserts that board members collectively need the ability to interrogate, question and challenge multiple stakeholders across multiple platforms and contexts to ensure optimal decision-making outcomes and organizational performance. This requires an immense wealth of business and executive experience. They also require diverse skills that encompass all disciplines, from financial acumen, stakeholder management, strategic leadership capability and insight to dealing with high levels of complexity (Rhode and Packel 2014). In addition, defending shareholder interests, ensuring the executives act in the best interests of the shareholders and providing a level of separation of duty between ownership and control of capital are key elements of boards' responsibilities (Wagana and Nzulwa 2016).

However, McDonald and Westphal (2013) strongly highlight and remind us that historically women have been disadvantaged and given limited opportunities in terms of both education and overall workplace experiences. This directly results in limited opportunity to align with board member criteria and success, leading to minimal gender representation at the corporate leadership level. They further emphasize that as societies continue to evolve and become more diverse in their representation, this has necessitated considerable study of women on boards and the impact of their inclusion on overall organizational and board outcomes.

This chapter aims to explore the context of women on boards by exploring global trends around the issue of gender diversity at board level.

The importance of prevalent challenges and barriers to entry will also be highlighted in the context of broader societal and organizational influences. It also becomes critical to look at current corporate strategies to increase board gender diversity and its direct impact on organizational performance. Furthermore, as several female board members were interviewed, the key themes from their interviews will be integrated and aligned to global best practice research within the emerging markets context. Finally, the chapter will make recommendations regarding key areas of improvement and suggest levers that could be developed and adopted to increase the effectiveness of recruiting more women to boards.

The reality of corporate boards and its impact on gender diversity

The cultural and organizational context

Due to the complexities that board members face and the level of experience this necessitates, the leadership skills required are different from those required of executive leadership. However, executive experience and individual leadership journeys create a great foundation for skilled board members. As a result, board members are often selected from a relatively small pool of retired or former executives (Deeb 2014).

In most emerging markets, this makes for a limited pool of potential candidates to draw from and in the current business environment only a fraction of these are women. Thus, boards remain largely untransformed and women significantly unrepresented around the world, particularly in emerging markets where the prevailing societal norms are also strongly embedded within the organizational culture (Rhode and Packel 2014).

Carrasco et al. (2015) conducted research on women on boards across 32 countries. Their results suggest that two key factors influence the representation of women on boards: (1) cultures where the role of men is valued more than the role of women (generally patriarchal in nature), and (2) cultures in which there is a greater tolerance for inequality in relation to the distribution of power. The countries that exhibited the above cultural characteristics tended to have lower female board representation. The study went on to further assert that it therefore becomes critical to examine both the political and cultural context when considering levels of board diversity.

"In order to survive in competitive environments and acquire legitimacy, organizations must design their organizational structure in line with the set of rules and belief systems that prevail in the country in which they operate" (Carassco et al. 2015, 431). As far back as Hofstede (2001), the concept of institutional theory was explored whereby culture was seen as strongly conditioning the social roles that were assigned to the different genders. Culture also attributed to the promotion of gender stereotypes within an organizational context.

However, as the global workforce changes fast, more women have access to education and are increasingly entering the workplace. Thus, many organizations are beginning to realize the importance of workplace diversity. Governments across the world have updated legislation and governing codes to promote greater gender equality across all management levels and organizations are also placing more emphasis on adherence to corporate governance and business ethics. Despite this need for diversity, particularly gender diversity, women remain dramatically underrepresented across the world on boards and the goal of diversity remains an aspiration (Terjesen and Sealy 2016).

Within the South African context, the King III report can be seen as a good example of how legislation and corporate governance may be used as a supporting tool to promote greater gender diversity on boards. It was introduced by the Institute of Directors in Southern Africa (IoDSA) and its key objective was to serve as a regulating document in terms of best practice corporate governance standards. The King III report recommends that a needs assessment be determined to ascertain the skills that currently exist and those that are missing in order to fill any vacancies that arise on boards. The report further asserts that diversity aspects should be considered along with the key criteria of experience and skills (IoDSA 2011). They even suggest the use of a nominations committee to measure, monitor and report on the progress of diversity within boards. The report further emphasizes that shareholders are the custodians and are ultimately accountable for the composition of the board, and it is in the organization's interest to ensure that the board is constituted taking into consideration skills and representivity (Chapter 2, principle 2.19).

Given the context of the King III report, one can strongly argue that it is the board's responsibility and accountability to demonstrate commitment to fostering a diverse environment that strives for greater gender equality. In order to foster this environment of diversity in all aspects, integrating women into boards becomes an essential component of an effective and sustainable board. This becomes even more critical within the emerging markets contexts due to low levels of existing diversity and ongoing gender equality concerns.

Gender diversity on boards in emerging markets

According to the report of the Organisation for Economic Co-operation and Development (OECD) on women's access to leadership (OECD 2016), women are vastly under-represented around the world at board level. In two prominent "first world" countries, the United States and the UK, women are only represented at board level at 19% and 26%, respectively. In comparison, a country like Japan, which has a more traditional cultural context, has only 3% female board representation.

The low representation appears to resonate around the world. According to Catalyst (2014), women only occupied 16.9% of Fortune 500 company board seats within the United States.

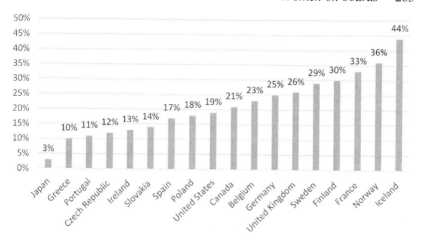

Figure 10.1 Share of female board members, 2015 or latest
Source: With permission from OECD (2016) Conference on improving women's access to leadership, Background Report, 8 march 2016, http://www.oecd.org/corp orate/oecd-conference-women-leadership.htm.

Looking particularly at emerging markets we can observe that at 8.6%, developing Asia has the highest proportion of companies with women on their boards, while developing Europe has the lowest, with 1.1% (Doff et al. 2014). Russia has about 3% of companies with female board members. Brazil presents some interesting contradictions. The country elected its first female president in 2011, and its stock exchange has been particularly focused on promoting transparency in corporate governance standards, which often helps to build diversity within companies. However, despite these positive changes, the percentage of women on corporate boards within Brazil is surprisingly low at just over 5% (Doff et al. 2014). Looking at India, Kishore (2016) points to the New Companies Act of 2013 which makes it mandatory to appoint at least one women director on the board of directors of certain categories of listed companies. As a result, the numbers in India are around 10%, similar to those in Hong Kong.

China is nevertheless first among the emerging economies: more than 550 of its publicly traded companies (about 21% of the total) have women on their boards, and it is home to two of the four listed companies in the world with all-female boards (Doff et al. 2014). According to Jia and Zhang (2011), following its institutional reform China has undergone socio-economic changes that have resulted in changes within the labor market and a greater focus on equal opportunity legislation. All these social, political and economic changes over the years have resulted in increased opportunities for women within the workplace. The one-child family policy and increased workplace child care support systems can also be seen as giving women greater leverage to climb the corporate ladder. As a result, despite its patriarchal cultural context, China has a higher pro-portion of female board members than Fortune 1000 companies in the USA (Jia and Zhang 2011).

Even though South Africa is ahead of the curve in many instances, the figures show that the country still does not have adequate representation of women in JSE-listed corporations. The Businesswomen's Association of South Africa (BWASA) conducts an annual "South African Women in Leadership" census. According to the 2015 results, only 8.79% of JSE-listed companies have 25% or more women directors. Only 5.3% of chair-man's positions and 15.8% of directorships are occupied by women (BWASA 2015). Despite South Africa's pro-female policy framework, which defines an enabling set of legislation enshrined in the South African constitution, there has been slow progress with regard to the appointment of women on boards.

The first country to formally mandate gender equity quotas at board level was Norway in February 2002. They mandated 40% director representation from a gender perspective. There was then a snowball effect, with 14 other countries introducing quotas and 17 more countries instituting voluntary codes for gender representation on boards (Terjesen and Sealy 2016).

Figure 10.2 shows the results of a study conducted by the advocacy group 2020 Women on Boards, which runs a national campaign in the US that aims to increase the percentage of women on boards. Research revealed that when women were responsible for the selection of boards, they were more successful at filling board positions with more women. It showed that when women held key leadership positions, companies employed women in more than 27% of director seats, compared with less than 18% when men were in charge (MSCI 2015).

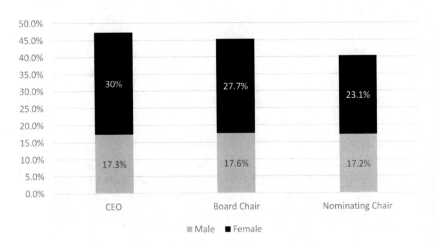

Figure 10.2 When women lead: 2020 women on boards 2016
Source: https://www.2020wob.com/companies/2020-gender-diversity-index.

The above graph demonstrates that when female board members are in positions of power, there is an increase in the number of females hired at senior levels. Thus, higher gender diversity at board levels results in an increased gender pipeline from a sustainability perspective.

Why gender diversity on boards is important

The case for diversity, particularly at board level, has been widely discussed in the literature over the past decade. In recent times there has been a growing emphasis in the corporate community that diversity should be viewed as a key strategic imperative. According to Rhode and Packel (2014) there are two key perspectives for viewing diversity within organizations: first, the financial case, and second, the moral imperative.

Abdullah, Ismail and Nachum (2016) highlight that most government policies are underpinned by the premise that having women at board level has a positive impact on boards' functioning and subsequently on an organization's overall performance. Diversity and inclusion are both viewed as critical to business and wider economic success.

Gender diversity can be viewed as being linked to various business benefits that include improved corporate governance and increased profit margins. Triana, Miller and Trzebiatowski (2014) reinforce that women in emerging markets are generally associated with their strong skills sets when it comes to monitoring activities such as management accountability for performance in comparison to men. As a result, the quality of organizational corporate governance tends to be much higher. Abdullah and Ku Ismail (2013) further highlight that various studies across emerging markets indicate that female boards of directors negatively correlate with earnings management and accounting manipulation and positively correlate with the value and informativeness of the reported financial numbers. They are also seen as contributing to the boards' overall quality of functioning due to access to diverse resources (Abdullah 2014).

Rhode and Packel (2014) highlight several studies where a positive correlation was found between the number of women on boards and boards' financial performance. The best known of these is the study by Carter and Wagner (2011), which ranked Fortune 500 companies according to the percentage of women on their boards and found that, "companies in the highest quartile outperformed companies in the lowest quartile by 53% in return on equity (ROE), 42% in return on sales (ROS), and 66% in return on invested capital (ROIC)". Erhardt, Werbel and Shrader's (2003) research also found a positive correlation between gender representation on boards and return on assets (ROA) and return on investment (ROI). Adams and Ferreira's (2009) study also found a significant positive relationship between the proportion of female directors and financial performance.

However, Wagana and Nzulwa (2016) and Abdullah (2014) provide us with contrary research perspectives and mention that evidence that links firm performance with board gender diversity is inconclusive. While many studies, including but not limited to those listed above, show that there is a positive correlation, others show a negative link. Haslam et al.'s investigations (2010) established a negative relationship between women's presence on boards and specific measures of financial performance.

Besides the clear business case for diversity, Abdullah, Ismail and Nachum's (2016) research looked at various arguments against diverse boards. One concerns the risk within emerging markets of hiring women at board level, asserting that the societal context can often override measured performance. Women in top positions of power can be viewed negatively in some countries, leading to negative market reactions and investment. Another hypothesis looks at how the appointment of female board members will have a negative impact on overall performance in countries with family or government-owned firms. They highlight that in emerging markets shareholders tend to nominate people within their circle and strongly favor personal relationships over business relationships (Bianco, Ciavarella and Signoretti 2015). However, in developed markets like Norway, government pressure results in poor quality female nominations, diminishing overall business impact.

Alongside the conflicting research results, it can be noted that even in studies that do show a positive correlation between women on boards and financial performance, the relationship cannot be said to be a causal one and in many cases it is considered inconclusive (Kakabadse et al. 2015). It may be inferred that high-performing organizations understand the need for diversity of boards and are thus more open and active in appointing women as directors. There is need for further research to examine the complex context of contributing factors at play in the relationship between women board leadership and financial performance of firms (Luckerath-Rovers 2013). Even though the multiple research perspectives provide conflicting views, organizations and governments also take the moral imperative into consideration when promoting the appointment of women on boards.

Choudhury (2014) and Rowley, Lee and Lan (2015) argue that the underlying principles of appointing women as directors should be based not only on economic value but also on equality. Bringing fairness to the fore means acknowledging the cultural history that has led to a lack of women on boards. She further states that female representation needs to be viewed independently, instead of a mere business reform.

According to the Global Gender Gap Report (WEF 2014), people and their talents are two of the core drivers of sustainable, long-term economic growth. If women represent roughly 50% of the population, having so few women at senior level in organizations means that much of the world's talent is underdeveloped or underused and this will never result in the best organizational, social and economic outcomes.

Rhode and Packel (2014) also argue that one of the biggest reasons for including more women on boards is to ensure that women and men (and other minority groups) have equal access to opportunities, that they are personally able to fulfil their own potential and that organizations are able to make active use of the skill, education and abilities of a wider part of the labor market.

Even though the concept of the positive impact of women on boards has been theoretically understood, there is a distinct and concerning lack of practical implementation within the workplace. The question that remains is whether we have moved from a conceptual level of understanding to fully grasping how the successes noted in the prevailing research came about and why it is critical that we nurture and grow the cadre of women on boards in a visible and deliberate way. To add further insight to the inherent value, it therefore becomes critical to understand how the different genders practically experience women on boards in the workplace (Mathisen, Ogaard and Marnburg 2013).

How women and men experience women on boards

Mathisen, Ogaard and Marnburg (2013) conducted a study on how female directors perceive boardroom dynamics. From a social identity perspective they looked at how male directors socially should tend to support those individuals that are similar to them and retract from those they would perceive as being different. Thus, female directors would form part of the out-group and would therefore experience higher levels of task and relationship conflict.

Despite organizations recognizing the importance of gender diversity, many women on boards have and continue to experience gender-based discrimination. All the interviewees were conscious of the gender imbalance in the economy and corporate environment. Many agreed that women have to work much harder for their achievements to be recognized than men and some were surprised by the extent of gender bias they experienced in the work environment despite their constant fight against these stereotypes.

Chizema, Kamuriwo and Shinozawa's (2015) research attempted to better understand the reason behind some of the existing corporate triggers and barriers. They used social theory as a foundation for understanding the justification for board directorship being viewed as an agentic role that, societally, might be considered primarily suitable for men. However, their research also emphasizes the important role of social and national institutions in shifting these stereotypes.

Despite the challenges faced by women on boards, Gert Schoonbee (South Africa) continued to emphasize the importance of having diverse boardrooms. He mentioned in his interview the value of "unlocking the magic of diversity" in his business and that gender diversity is a key component of everything they do within their business. He also said that gender diversity is not only about "goodness", it is also about "relevant and sustainable initiatives for business growth". He strongly emphasized that men and women should be driving gender diversity together and collaboratively. Artigas, Callegaro and Novales-Flamarique (2013) stated that about 60% of their respondents believed that board diversity and diverse leadership teams resulted in higher financial returns.

Dang's (2011) research explores the issue of diversity from an agency and resource dependency perspective. Agency theory concerns the role of board directors when it comes to corporate governance of managers—that is, how one monitors and controls people and activities. As a result, the agency-theoretic perspective looks at how female board directors introduce a different viewpoint through their particular skills and leadership styles. They are known to be more analytical and thorough in problem-solving. As highlighted previously, they are also known to improve the overall quality of corporate governance. Resource dependency theory "views a firm as an open system which is dependent upon external organizations and environment contingencies" (Dang 2011, 96). Therefore the board members' role is to enhance the access to key resources. Based on the above theory, women bring skills, competencies, perspectives and resources that are different to those of their male counterparts.

The interviewees also emphasized the difference in business language and leadership styles in the boardrooms. This included the culture, the decision-making styles and the business structures. They highlighted how more feminine leadership styles utilized more intuition and generally leaned towards collaboration and building communities—a sharing rather than ego-driven approach. As a result they were more integrative and thorough in their overall analysis of situations. The interviewees also believed that female leaders were more authentic and more sympathetic to work-balance issues relating to family responsibilities. Wendy Ackerman, non-executive director of Pick and Pay Holding Limited (South Africa), described when interviewed how she actively changed her organization's work environment to be more accommodating of women with family responsibilities. This was positively received by female employees within the organization.

Gabaldon et al.'s (2016) research analyzed some of the barriers and gender differences that impact board succession. They discovered that women might identify with cultural gender roles and perceive top management roles as being conflictual. Many females might experience work–family conflict and have their time spoken for by family commitments. They experience different types of gender discrimination within the work environment. "This concept is closely related to mistake-based discrimination, the systematic underestimation of women's skills. Along the same lines, taste based discrimination or a preference for male leaders is often ingrained in cultural and social conventions that associate corporate leadership with masculinity" (Gabaldon et al. 2016, 373).

Gabaldon et al. (2016) also looked at how people's biased perceptions of what they believe women can offer undermines their actual level of expertise and capabilities. Lastly, institutional biases and rigidities within the environment produce structural biases that work against gender equality. Despite numerous research studies on the value of diversity and global efforts to increase women's board representation, the overall numbers still remain low. It therefore becomes critical to better understand the board member development path, barriers and triggers and key insights that have impacted on women in their journeys to becoming board members.

The woman's board member journey: key insights

While the need for diversity has been recognized for a range of reasons, not only in emerging markets, but globally, organizations still find it difficult to build and maintain a good base of women on their boards. This may be due to a variety of social, environmental, cultural, institutional, legal and political factors (Grosvold and Brammer 2011).

Organizational mentoring access

McDonald and Westphal's (2013) research focused on why minorities and women continue to be under-represented at higher levels within organizations. They recognize that there are certain norms that dictate success for board members. One of the issues they explored was that new board members are more likely to succeed and find acceptance if other members within the organization provide guidance around board member expectations. They refer to this as 'participation process mentoring', which is informal mentoring from someone with more experience who can guide you to navigate the new terrain and better understand existing organizational behavioral norms. So, within an organizational hierarchy there appear to be other hierarchies linked to experience, power, control and culture.

Mentoring and role models were recurrent themes in the interviews. All the women interviewed had acquired a high level of self-awareness. This took time, and involved self-reflection, humbling events and/or advice from a mentor or sponsor. Most of the women had been influenced by role models during their formative years, and mentors, both formal and informal, existed as far back as people's childhood years. For example, Thandi Lujabe-Rankoe, South Africa's high commissioner for Mozambique, referred to the importance as a young girl of "her parents' example and their encouragement to do homework and the discipline that went with that", adding that women can "learn until [the] grave".

In addition to having role models in their formative years, mentors and sponsors were important to the women in their work environment. They contributed substantially to careers by providing advice or pointing out blind spots. Although the role models from their formative years were not gender specific, it appeared that most mentors and sponsors were males. This may be attributed to the fact that there were limited women in leadership positions in the early 1990s—and this dynamic is now shifting (Branson 2012).

Although the interviewees were all successful businesswomen, they had experienced moments during their journey when significant events forced them to pause, self-reflect and realize that they didn't have all the answers. They learnt to accept that they didn't know it all and to confidently seek help from others. This led them to appreciate the diversity of thought around them without feeling inadequate. As leaders, they now use the strengths of those around them for the overall benefit of the team and the organizations they manage.

Adaptive resilience mechanisms

Torchia, Calabro and Huse (2011) explored how women as a critical mass within the company board structure can positively contribute to corporate value creation and organizational innovation. Their study showed that impact and value is dependent on the number of women present on the board. A self-aware board member can play to her strengths and encourage other board members to tap into theirs too. This gives further insight around boardroom processes, dynamics and interactions. Their study also found that heterogeneous groups had a positive impact in terms of innovation in contrast to male-dominated homogeneous groups.

One can infer from the above research that if a woman is the only female on the board she may face greater challenges and resistance. She may have to be particularly emotionally strong and resilient to get her ideas and inputs supported by the male-dominated board.

Wendy Lucas-Bull, further reinforces the value and importance of being resilient and how she acquired this discipline from a young age to equip her for challenges later on in life. She draws the analogy of the sports field as a metaphor for the corporate work environment:

> ... from the early days I gained that discipline throughout [...] the school situation. I was involved in competitive sport at both a school and provincial level. I think that teaches you resilience. Because you have to be able to lose, be wiped off court and then go on again and play the next match. While you might have been wiped out in singles (tennis match), but then you still have a doubles match and a mixed doubles match, so you can't fall in a heap. You have actually got to steady yourself and move on. It required rigorous training and discipline to succeed. You only actually achieved results with training. So the name of the game was around discipline, put your head down, and put in the hours of training.

Authentic leadership practices

At the EY Women in Leadership Summit, Schreiber (2016) looked at how an authentic leader is defined and developed. Being authentic is best described as aligning one's thoughts, words and actions and not trying to be anyone but oneself. The emphasis was on posing the right questions to able to understand one's current position and future direction.

In various interviews women spoke of the importance of moving from emulating the predominantly masculine behavior in the boardroom to being more true to themselves—that is, giving rein to more of their feminine personality characteristics. This ability to transition and be more authentic was seen as a crucial part of their leadership journey. As these women leaders accepted themselves, they found their voice and developed the confidence to openly share their views. With authenticity came a willingness to learn from others. Monica Sacristan, dean of executive development at ITAM (Mexico), highlighted "the importance of finding your own style, while you may learn from different people".

Phuthi Mahanyele, former CEO of the Shanduka Group (South Africa), also emphasized the importance of authenticity: "It was wonderful learning how to be authentic in your working environment and not trying to be somebody else and that really grew and taught me a lot as an individual." Ekaterina Sheremet (Russia) spoke of the importance of being an authentic leader in order to make an impact and be valued and heard:

> It is very important that if you continue to act normally, not a male style, but try to be yourself. And that is very important, because after that, because then you feel relaxed, they are more likely to accept you as a member of their team.

Enhancing gender parity on boards

Finding strong female candidates

According to Byron and Post (2016) there is a greater focus on the importance of corporate social performance across the globe due to its impact on financial performance. As a result, organizations are actively looking to recruit more females onto boards to leverage their value and their diversity of experience to increase overall corporate social performance. A diverse mix of board members translates into well-rounded, holistically capable boards able to address a wide range of topics and issues. This gives the board and the organization as a whole a competitive edge.

Particularly in emerging markets, well-qualified, competent candidates are in such short supply that companies cannot afford to exclude women candidates in their decision-making and selection processes. Many organizations, instead of making the effort to find the right mix for diversity on their boards, simply find ways of achieving any quota for the sake of compliance. While this may have the impact of (slowly) increasing the number of women on boards, in most instances it results in unsustainable and ineffective appointments of women, which misses the point of the diversity objective (Ahern and Dittmar 2012).

The requirements for appointment to a board often include executive responsibility. In the current business landscape this means that the pipelines for women are limited. Successful women candidates exist, but they are not as easy to find as the many men who currently hold executive positions. Men are greater in number and are therefore easier to identify. The women who do have the right credentials in terms of executive experience often already hold a number of board positions and have reached the limit of how many boards they can serve on (Rhode and Packel 2014).

Selection process

Elstad and Ladegard's (2012) research looked at various different aspects of women on boards. While they acknowledge that quotas have served to increase the number of women appointments, they also mention that business leaders caution against hiring women with limited management experience as this could result in reduced performance and legitimacy.

There has already been reference to Mathisen, Ogaard and Marnburg (2013), who, from a social identity perspective, highlight that the different genders would have a tendency to select those that are similar to them (in-group) and avoid those that are inherently different to them (out-group). This was reinforced by Phuthi Mahanyele, former Shanduka CEO (South Africa):

> I think when you look at many nomination committees on a number of boards, you will tend to find that you will have people who prefer to have other people like them, or people that they feel comfortable with. And unfortunately often it will be people of the same gender, the same race, the same culture, age group, everything.

Structural challenges and cultural biases

To recruit and retain talent—of both genders—we need to tackle deep-rooted issues in our corporate culture. And while structural factors and policy issues certainly represent significant obstacles, cultural biases in the workplace are perhaps even more challenging.

As previously mentioned, Chizema, Kamuriwo and Shinozawa's (2015) research on women on boards indicates that social role theory goes some way to explain the deep-seated prejudices in the workplace with regard to gender stereotypes. Perception of leadership behaviors displayed by women is different to perception of those same behaviors displayed by men. The result is that when women step up and try to have their voices heard, they are often seen as too aggressive, too outspoken and too pushy.

These same behaviors by men are interpreted as assertive and decisive. This type of bias is a threat to the effectiveness of gender-diverse boards where women may not be taken seriously. Board training only includes the technicalities of how boards work, the legalities and fiduciary duties, but there is an urgent need to include the behavioral and attitudinal requirements so that unconscious biases may be properly understood and board members take personal responsibility to end discrimination.

Ekaterina Sheremet (Russia) spoke of how certain stereotypes often make women behave in a particular way to fit into the culture. Her advice was to resist this: "One thing that is clear is to speak up. Very often women under-represent themselves. It is important to speak up and don't be afraid. Don't be afraid to seem aggressive."

Wendy Ackerman (South Africa) mentioned in her interview that her goal was to promote talented women in her enterprise during a time when negative gender stereotypes were very strong. Her approach was to engage with women and encourage meaningful discourse. This resulted in the first gender-focused leadership development program. "Many of these women grew to very senior levels within the enterprise, something I am very proud of, more so because this took place in the early 1990s when South Africa did not have female managers."

In order to continue to enhance and then maintain gender parity on boards one also needs to reflect on the impact and effect of quotas. There are multiple perspectives and the use of quotas can also be rather contentious, depending on context and outcome.

Quotas and policies

While the numbers do not represent a significant shift of gender equality in organizations' boards, much has been done to attempt to rectify this situation. In order to reduce the glaring gender gap, governments and organisations have taken various actions. For example, governments have put in place equal opportunity strategies, legislative changes, reporting requirements and particularly quotas, resulting in the increased representation of women on boards (Sojo et al. 2016).

EY (2014) produced a report looking at the structural mechanisms that have been put in place in countries around the world and what they have achieved. The report looked at the European Council's European Pact for Gender Equality 2011–2020, which acknowledged that gender equality policies were vital to economic growth, prosperity and competitiveness and appealed for action to promote equal involvement of men and women in decision-making at all levels and in all fields. The Council also introduced a directive on improving gender balance among directors listed on stock exchanges.

The report also noted that the Australian government committed to lead by example, announcing a target of 40% of women on boards by

2015. It met this target in 2013. It also established a Gender Equality Agency that continues to work with business. In Norway, the quota imposed by government is 40% and the consequence of non-compliance for listed companies can be dissolution by court order. Germany's quota is 30% by 2016, while the UK took the route of voluntary targets as opposed to quotas, which resulted in women on FTSE 100 boards increasing from 10.5% in 2010 to 20.7% in 2014.

While these examples are for developed nations, the EY report (2014) notes that in India, public companies with five or more directors have to have a minimum of one female board member, although only 4.7% of India's corporate directors were women in 2013. The report also states that the United Arab Emirates, with only 1.2% female corporate directors, similar to India, is also mandating all companies to have at least one woman on the board, though there is no definite timeline.

In South Africa the policy landscape has been shaped by the constitution, the Employment Equity Act and the Black Economic Empowerment codes. These all call for demographic representivity at all occupational levels, but especially at board level. More recently, the Johannesburg Stock Exchange (JSE) has required that all listed companies have a policy on the promotion of gender diversity at board level that must be reported in the annual report of listed companies (Lawrence 2016).

All these efforts should see the increasing representation of women on boards. However, "Quotas are by no means perfect. There's always a risk that companies will appoint a female to the board just to comply with quota regulations, rather than recruiting the best person for the job" (Sullivan 2015). In addition, if government removes the legislation, there is the question of how sustainable board diversity will be in the current corporate culture. Legislation may assist the process, but achieving diversity on company boards needs to make business sense and also become a societal imperative. Genuine, sustainable improvements that grow the pipeline need to be in place. For women to progress on to boards, the pool of senior executive positions needs to be expanded and board succession planning needs to be considered. It is therefore vital to explore some of these sustainable initiatives (Terjesen and Sealy 2016).

The sustainable path ahead

Building organizations on the foundations of equality is a vision that many leaders aspire to create. However, as previously discussed, it is not always practical in reality. The figure below was developed by one of our co-authors, Cecily Carmona, from the research and female board member interviews. It indicates three high-level sustainable components of increasing the number of women on boards.

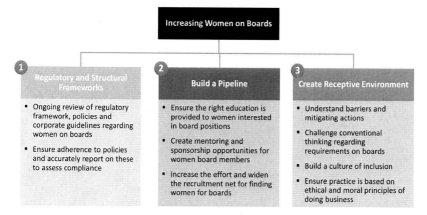

Figure 10.3 Key components of increasing the number of women on boards
Source: Authors' own.

Regulatory and structural frameworks

Branson (2012) formed part of a study group operating across various countries whose key focus was the issue of diversity on corporate boards. They took into account a number of potential benefits, which included (i) positive role modeling for other women within the organization; (ii) the avoidance of groupthink; (iii) considering women's economic market and buying power through market reciprocity; (iv) having the board reflect the diversity of changing times; and (v) increasing international laws and conventions that promote gender equality. However, they also recognized that despite the apparent benefits, the implementation and progress of gender equality has primarily been achieved in countries where there is support through ongoing legislation, policies and regulatory frameworks.

Labelle, Francoeur and Lakhal's (2015, 802) work compared countries that had strong regulatory structures to promote gender diversity on boards with those that did not. Their research identified six characteristics of countries where women are promoted to boards. These included (1) quota laws; (2) certificate and pledge programs; (3) soft law "comply or explain" requirements of stock exchanges; (4) mentoring/sponsorship programs; (5) renewed pressure by institutional investors; and (6) hard law—that is, governmental agency requirements for plenary disclosure. One can infer from the above that countries and organizations that have more stringent regulatory environments have a greater impact on the appointment of women on boards.

According to most of the interviewees, for regulatory frameworks to be effective the policies need to be adhered to and there needs to be accountability processes for non-compliance. This includes compliance with corporate governance guidelines, integrated reporting as set out in directives, and codes of good practice with regard to gender diversity. Organisations need to make themselves accountable for meeting these various business commitments, reporting annually on progress.

Building a pipeline

Mentoring/sponsorship opportunities

McDonald and Westphal's (2013) research alludes to the fact that women receive fewer offers of mentoring and sponsorship than their male counterparts when initially appointed to board level. This is often the result of inter-group biases and has an impact on both career progression and performance. The research strongly supports the positive value of mentoring and considers it an urgent need for newly appointed female board members.

Silvana Machado (Brazil) talked about the importance of people and relationships within the workplace:

> Then you grow and, you know, you move, you realize that things happen because of people, how they interact, how you share your ideas, how you involve others. I see that today, most of my work goes around people, not just people at [company], but also my clients.

Beyond the mentoring, and mentioned by many of the women interviewed, it is critical that women have role models to inspire them to take up a board position. This results in enhanced levels of workplace meaning and purpose. Visible role models who share their stories also encourage women to step more boldly into board roles.

Wendy Lucas-Bull (South Africa) further highlights the value and importance of mentoring within one's career. She states:

> It is quite a lonely journey, and that is the reason why I do so much mentoring now, because I know actually how much easier it would have been if I had had somebody I could bounce ideas off ... I didn't really have a mentor or role models that I could draw from. I just worked flat out.

Barçin Yinanç (Turkey) said further:

> I had support, that's for sure. Some of my superiors, they absolutely have supported me. But supporting is one thing. Creating opportunities, I am sending you to this scholarship, I am sending to this place, etc., is one thing. But you know, sort of assisting, and this is the way we need do things, this is the way you should approach this issue, is another thing.

Continuous learning platforms

As Adams and Ferreira (2009) say, the board of directors play a critical role as custodians of the organisation and as a result must possess a range of skills and competencies. They should be highly educated and/or continuously develop their skills through formal and informal learning platforms. Thus, organizations have to ensure that women are being brought up through the ranks and are constantly growing their skills—building the right "basket" of capabilities and competencies in order to meet high board requirements.

All those interviewed had an unquenchable thirst for learning. Francie Shonhiwa, corporate social transformation manager at PPC Group Services (Pty) Ltd (South Africa) talked about her stand on girl-child education, stating strongly that "the first and best husband for any girl-child is good education". She talked of how learning took different forms for her. These included formal training, reading books, learning from others, seeking advice from others and modeling the behavior of role models. Elena Escagedo (Spain) mentioned the value of ongoing learning for development as a person and a leader: "I did a coaching program at my school and there I learnt how to see in different perspectives, and to understand other people. I gained empathy."

Recruitment practices

Gabaldon et al. (2016) explored gender diversity on boards from a supply and demand (scarcity) perspective and found that it varies across different cultures. They asked the question of whether the inclusion in databases of female candidates would increase their chances of board nomination. They looked at various other research studies and found no conclusive evidence for distinguishing between the attitudes and behaviors of female and male directors. The implication of this is that there should be no difference in terms of performance or skills between the two genders. They also suggested a need for further empirical studies to determine if the actual root cause of low women board member percentages is rooted in the searching and hiring processes within organizations.

This was alluded to by the interviewees, with many of the women saying there should be more effort to develop a broader slate of women who could be eligible to take positions on boards. They all felt strongly that plenty of credible senior women exist; however, there needs to be greater gender collaboration and effort needs to identify, harness and nurture female board potential. They believed that search firms could also play an important role in assisting boards identify and place board members. Recruitment entities should also be committed to redefining their approach and ensuring that they present diverse candidates to the board. Choudhury (2014) suggested creating a central government-run database in order to manage the issues of succession planning at a more national level.

Creating receptive environments

As mentioned several times in the chapter in connection to various research studies, women have endured decades of inequality that have resulted in educational and social disadvantages. In order to promote gender-equal environments, men and women need to collaborate in order to remove the barriers to progressing women on boards. They need to build a transformational culture and an institutional climate that are more enabling for gender equality. Shareholder, investor and broader stakeholder activism could also assist in accelerating the progress towards gender equity (Choudhury 2014).

Based on the interviews, both genders broadly emphasize the importance of purposefully building a culture of inclusion. They believe that inequality inhibits and silences voices that may have significant impact on the direction of business strategy. Organizations also need to be mindful of ethical and moral principles that enable social justice, equity and economic growth. This includes how cultures approach gender equity on boards and how they create an enabling environment to fast-track women into key roles (Kogut, Colomer and Belinky 2014).

Based on the various research perspectives, the authors believe that multi-dimensional human capital strategies need to be implemented within organizations. These include (i) the acquisition of diverse board members; (ii) induction and on-boarding of new members; (iii) promotion strategies; (iv) job rotation opportunities; (v) succession planning; (vi) building bench-strength and the talent pipeline; and (vii) providing opportunities to advance the gender equality agenda.

The authors also believe that the chairman plays a key role in transforming the demographics and capability of the board. Organizations require a clear and systematic set of planned and structured interventions to address gender stereotypes and equity. Unfortunately there is a tendency to conceptualize gender equity as a women's issue to be resolved by women. Organizations need to develop more unified and collaborative gender equity platforms that are spearheaded by both genders. Organization-wide attitudes and practices that restrict and inhibit the attainment of gender diversity objectives also need to be re-examined.

Conclusion

This chapter examined the context of boards, the requirements for diversity and the importance of gender equity. While there is substantial research on the positive financial case for having women on boards, it has also been argued that findings are inconclusive. Thus, further research needs to be conducted to understand the complex issues at play in this correlating relationship. Beyond the business case, a strong rationale also exists for removing the barriers to having more women on boards.

Carrasco et al. (2015) reinforce that although much has been done in terms of policy and structural requirements for having women on boards across emerging markets, the numbers are nevertheless still extremely low. Where women are already in executive and leadership roles, they continue to experience gender-based discrimination in the various environments. Greater emphasis needs to also be placed on growing the pipeline of suitable board candidates and addressing the unspoken biases that continue to exist. The structural incentives that need to be put in place to support greater gender and cultural changes have also to be taken into consideration.

As we look to the future, the positive efforts by individuals, governments and organizations need to continue in order to ensure sustainable outcomes. We need to aspire to and inspire the desired transformation of the hearts and minds of both genders. Regression and maintaining the status quo based on inequality should be strongly prevented. The authors have a collective vision of gender diversity being viewed as a strategic advantage. This vision should be authentically and collectively embraced by all so that we may create a gender-equal and empowering society.

References

Artigas, M., H. Callegaro and M. Novales-Flamarique. 2013. "Survey: Why Top Management Eludes Women in Latin America". www.mckinsey.com/business-functions/organization/our-insights/why-top-management-eludes-women-in-latin-america-mckinsey-global-survey-results. McKinsey & Company. Accessed August 15, 2016.

Abdullah, S. N. 2014. "The Causes of Gender Diversity in Malaysian Large Firms". *Journal of Management and Governance* 18(4): 1137–1159.

Abdullah, S., K. Ismail and L. Nachum. 2016. "Does Having Women on Boards Create Value? The Impact of Societal Perceptions and Corporate Governance in Emerging Markets". *Strategic Management Journal* 37(3): 466–476.

Adams, R. B. and D. Ferreira. 2009. "Women in the boardroom and their impact on governance and performance". *Journal of Financial Economics* 94(2): 291–309.

Ahern, K. R. and A. K. Dittmar. 2012. "The Changing of the Boards: The Impact on Firm Valuation of Mandated Female Board Representation". *Quarterly Journal of Economics* 127(1): 137–197.

Bianco, M., A. Ciavarella and R. Signoretti. 2015. "Women on Corporate Boards in Italy: The Role of Family Connections". *Journal of Corporate Governance* 23(2): 129–144.

Branson, D. M. 2012. "Initiatives to Place Women on Corporate Boards of Directors: A Global Snapshot". *Journal of Corporation Law* 37(4): 793–814.

BWASA (Businesswoman of the Year Award). 2015. "BWA Women in Leadership Census". Business Women's Association of South Africa. www.bwasa.co.za/news/bwa-women-in-leadership-census-media-release. Accessed August 19, 2016.

Byron, K. and C. Post. 2016. "Women on Boards of Directors and Corporate Social Performance: A Meta-Analysis". *Corporate Governance: A Corporate Review* 24(4): 428–442.

Carrasco, A., C. Francoeur, R. Labelle, J. Laffarga and E. Ruiz-Barbadillo. 2015. "Appointing Women to Boards: Is There a Cultural Bias?" *Journal of Business Ethics* 129(2): 429–444.

Carter, N. M. and H. M. Wagner. 2011. "The Bottom Line: Corporate Performance and Women's Representation on Boards (2004–2008)". Catalyst, New York. www.catalyst.org/system/files/the_bottom_line_corporate_performance_and_wo men's_representation_on_boards_(2004-2008).pdf. Accessed August 13, 2016.

Catalyst. 2011–2012. "Increasing Gender Diversity on Boards: Current Index of Formal Approaches". *Catalyst*, New York.

Catalyst. 2014. "Women on Boards: Quick Take". *Catalyst*, New York.

Chizema, A., D. S. Kamuriwo and Y. Shinozawa. 2015. "Women on Corporate Boards around the World: Triggers and Barriers". *The Leadership Quarterly* 26(6): 1051–1065.

Choudhury, B. 2014. "New Rationales for Women on Boards". *Oxford Journal of Legal Studies* 34(3): 511–542.

Dang, R. and D. K. Nguyen. 2011. "Does Board Gender Diversity Make a Difference? New Evidence from Quantile Regression Analysis". IPAG Business School, Working paper 2014-297. www.ipag.fr/wp-content/uploads/recherche/ WP/IPAG_WP_2014_297.pdf. Accessed February 23, 2017.

Deeb, G.. 2014. "How to Structure Your Board of Directors or Advisory Board". *Forbes Magazine*, October 11. www.forbes.com/sites/georgedeeb/2014/10/11/ how-to. Retrieved February 13, 2016.

Doff, N., Z. Hankir and A. Narayan. 2014. "Women No Longer Disabled in BRICs Boards as Ranks Swell. Bloomberg". *Bloomberg*, December 17. www. bloomberg.com/news/articles/2014-12-17/from-one-woman-board-member-in-em erging-markets-to-1-500. Retrieved August 19, 2016.

Elstad, B. and G. Ladegard. 2012. "Women on Corporate Boards: Key Influencers or Tokens?" *Journal of Management and Governance* 16(4): 595–615.

Erhardt, N. L., J. D. Werbel and C. B. Shrader. 2003. "Board of Director Diversity and Firm Financial Performance". *Corporate Governance: An International Review* 11(2): 102–111.

EY. 2014. "Point of View—Women on Boards: Global Approaches to Advancing Diversity". *EY*, July. www.ey.com/Publication/vwLUAssets/ey-women-on-boards-p ov-july2014/$FILE/ey-women-on-boards-pov-july2014.pdf. Accessed August 16, 2016.

Gabaldon, P., C. Anca, R. de Cabo and R. Gimeno. 2016. "Searching for Women on Boards: An Analysis from the Supply and Demand Perspective". *Corporate Governance: An International Review* 24(3): 371–385.

Grosvold, J. and S. Brammer. 2011. "National Institutional Systems as Antecedents of Female Board Representation: An Empirical Study". *Corporate Governance: An International Review* 19(2): 116–135.

Haslam, S. A., M. K. Ryan, C. Kulich, G. Trojanowski and C. Atkins. 2010. "Investing with Prejudice: The Relationship Between Women's Presence on Company Boards and Objective and Subjective Measures of Company Performance". *British Journal of Management* 21(2): 484–497.

Hofstede, G. 2001. *Culture's Consequences: Comparing Values, Behaviors, Institutions and Organizations Across Nations.* Thousand Oaks CA: Sage Publications.

IoDSA (Institute of Directors Southern Africa). 2011. "Institute of Directors Southern Africa (IoDSA) Integrated Report 2011". www.iodsa.co.za/resource/ collection/.../IoDSA_Integrated_Report_2011.pdf. Accessed August 16, 2016.

Jia, M. and Z. Zhang. 2011. "Agency Costs and Corporate Philanthropic Disaster Response: The Moderating Role of Women on Two-tier Boards: Evidence from People's Republic of China". *International Journal of Human Resource Management* 22(9): 2011–2031.

Kakabadse, N. K., C. Figueira, K. Nicolopoulou, J. H. Yang, A. P. Kakabadse and M. F. Ozbilgin. 2015. "Gender Diversity and Board Performance: Women's Experiences and Perspectives". *Human Resource Management* 54(2): 265–281.

Kishore, K. 2016. "Representation of Women on Boards of IT Companies: An Indian Story". *Journal and Management and Public Policy* 7(2): 29–36.

Kogut, B., J. Colomer and M. Belinky. 2014. "Research Notes and Commentaries. Structural Equality at the Top of the Corporation: Mandated Quotas for Women Directors". *Strategic Management Journal* 35(6): 891–902.

Labelle, R., C. Francoeur and F. Lakhal. 2015. "To Regulate or Not to Regulate? Early Evidence on the Means Used Around the World to Promote Gender Diversity in the Boardroom". *Gender, Work and Organisation* 22(4): 339–363.

Lawrence, J. 2016. "New JSE requirements for women on boards". Grant Thornton, 17 August. Accessed February 23, 2017. www.grantthornton.co.za/insights/arti cles/new-jse-requirements-for-women-on-boards/.

Luckerath-Rovers, M. 2013. "Women on Boards and Firm Performance". *Journal of Management and Governance* 17(2): 491–509.

Mathisen, G., T. Ogaard and E. Marnburg. 2013. "Women in the Boardroom: How Do Female Directors of Corporate Boards Perceive Boardroom Dynamics?" *Journal of Business Ethics* 116(1): 87–97.

McDonald, M. L. and J. D. Westphal. 2013. "Access Denied: Low Mentoring of Women and Minority First-Time Directors and its Negative Effects on Appointments to Additional Boards". *Academy of Management Journal* 56(4): 1169–1198.

MSCI. 2015. "Women on Boards: Global Trends in Gender Diversity on Corporate Boards". *MSCI*, November. www.msci.com/documents/10199/04b6f646-d638-4878 -9c61-4eb91748a82b. Retrieved August 16, 2016.

OECD (Organisation for Economic Co-operation and Development). 2016. "Background Report: Conference on Improving Women's Access to Leadership". www. oecd.org/daf/ca/OECD-Women-Leadership-2016-Report.pdf. Retrieved August 19, 2016.

Rhode, D. and A. Packel. 2014. "Diversity on Corporate Boards: How Much Difference does Difference Make?" *Delaware Journal of Corporate Law* 39(2): 377–426.

Rowley, C., J. S. K. Lee and L.L. Lan. 2015. "Why Women Say No to Corporate Boards and What Can Be Done: Ornamental Directors in Asia". *Journal of Management Inquiry* 24(2): 205–207.

Schreiber, U. 2016. "Shaping the Future for Women in Leadership". EY Women in Leadership Summit. https://betterworkingworld.ey.com/purpose/women-in-lea dership. Retrieved August 19, 2016.

Sojo, V. E., R. E. Wood, S. A. Wood and M. A. Wheeler. 2016. "Reporting Requirements, Targets and Quotas for Women in Leadership". *Leadership Quarterly* 27(3): 519–536.

Sonnabend, S., L. Gero, B. Bakke and E. Garrity. 2016. "Boardroom Diversity: When Women Lead". *2020 Women on Boards.* www.2020wob.com/sites/default/files/2020GDI-2016Report.pdf. Accessed August 16, 2016.

Sullivan, R. 2015. "Can Gender Quotas Get More Women Into Boardrooms?" *Bloomberg,* July 1. www.bloomberg.com/news/articles/2015-07-01/can-gender-quotas-get-more-women-into-boardrooms. Retrieved August 16, 2016.

Terjesen, S. and R. Sealy. 2016. "Board Gender Quotas: Exploring Ethical Tensions from a Multi-Theoretical Perspective". *Business Ethics Quarterly* 26(1): 23–65.

Torchia, M., A. Calabro and M. Huse. 2011. "Women Directors on Corporate Boards: From Tokenism to Critical Mass". *Journal of Business Ethics* 102(2): 299–317.

Triana, M., T. Miller and T. Trzebiatowski. 2014. "The Double-edged Nature of Board Gender Diversity: Diversity, Firm Performance, and the Power of Women Directors as Predictors of Strategic Change". *Organization Science* 25(2): 609–632.

Wagana, D. M. and J. D. Nzulwa. 2016. "Corporate Governance, Board Gender Diversity and Corporate Performance: A Critical Review of Literature". *European Scientific Journal* 12(7): 1857–7881.

WEF (World Economic Forum). 2014. "Global Gender Gap Report". http://reports.weforum.org/global-gender-gap-report-2014/. Accessed August 16, 2016.

2020 Women on Boards. 2016. "Boardroom Diversity: When Women Lead". www.2020wob.com/sites/default/files/2020GDI-2016Report.pdf. Retrieved August 16, 2016.

11 Conclusion

Caren Scheepers, Shireen Chengadu and Kerry-Lee Durrant

This chapter serves as a conclusion and offers a summary of the findings, with a conceptual framework as well as specific recommendations at macro-, meso- and micro-level, as explained in Chapter 1.

Summary of findings

The whole is indeed more than the sum of its parts.

Each chapter of this book contributes something distinctive and provides unique perspectives on recurrent themes in particular contexts, collectively making for a well-rounded discourse on women's leadership in emerging markets. The synergy that developed between the authors of the different chapters enabled us to produce a volume that is much greater than any one of us.

Instead of adding to the plethora of existing leadership models, the purpose of this book was to offer themes that emerged from interviews with 46 remarkable women who live in interesting, albeit challenging, contexts. Nonetheless, by applying an inquiry approach to our transcribed interview data, we realized there were crucial decision points during certain periods of their lives and careers that we call "episodes" in Figure 11.1 below. According to Maxwell (2013), qualitative research methodology is enhanced through utilizing respondents' episodic memory. We also found common influencers (or catalysts) and strengths that enabled these women to rise above the glass ceiling. We are grateful for the level of trust that our interviewers built with the interviewees. It led to the latter sharing with us the deeply personal, intra- and interpersonal processes and internal shifts in their leadership journeys, as well as the elements in their contexts that influenced this evolutionary growth. We are privileged to discuss their accounts. Our analyses of their internal and external experiences culminated in the seven themes we list below, as well as a conceptual framework for the leadership journeys of women in emerging markets.

A question we investigated during this research was whether women leaders in emerging markets had similar or different experiences to those in developed markets. In Chapter 2 we echoed Alimo-Metcalfe and Alban-

Metcalfe's (2005) warning about relying exclusively on Western, male-oriented samples in leadership studies. Chapter 6 honed in on a comparison between published literature and media releases about the barriers facing Western women and those experienced by a number of the women from emerging markets in our sample. We found that women leaders from emerging markets confirmed the findings from the West but also expanded the barrier categories. The discussion below on specific chapters summarizes the types of barriers. In addition, a number of our chapters compared developed and emerging markets according to other criteria, such as the percentage of women represented in particular professional services (Chapter 8) or the progress and contribution of women's movements (Chapter 3).

There are a number of common themes in these chapters and this discussion does not intend to repeat what has already been covered; instead, it focuses on relevant comparisons between developed and emerging markets. We found that women in emerging markets are even more disadvantaged than women in developed markets with regard to:

1   unemployment rates;
2   second-generation bias;
3   educational levels;
4   traditional values;
5   additional dimensions of diversity;
6   slowing growth rates; and finally
7   informal relations.

These themes will be examined in more detail below.

Unemployment

Unemployment figures in emerging markets are higher than in developed markets. Also, women represent the largest category of unemployment, leading to the feminization of poverty. This is described in Chapter 3, which details the following unemployment rates: South Africa, 26.4% (Statistics South Africa 2015); India, 9.33% (BSE 2016); Brazil, 11.9% (Trading Economics 2016d); compared to the USA figure of 4.9% (Wells 2016), Great Britain, 5%, and Germany, 4.2% (Statista 2016).

The fact that a higher percentage of women are represented in top management in some emerging markets than in some developed markets (Grant Thornton 2016) conceals the more fundamental issue of the unemployment of the masses (Khalaf 2014). The demographics of emerging markets indicate a younger population than in developed nations and the fact that unemployment is concentrated amongst the youth makes both the current situation and projections into the future more serious. For example, Statistics South Africa (2015, 12) reveals the alarming rate of 40.7% unemployment for female youth (15–34 years) and 33.8% for their male counterparts, whereas India's youth unemployment was 10.1% in the same period (World Bank 2016). Chapter 7 on entrepreneurship referred to the important role small businesses can play to reduce unemployment. In Chapter 3 on women's movements and Chapter 4 on education, the authors express concern about the feminization of poverty.

Second-generation/subtle bias

A number of scholars in the West have warned that "second-generation bias" due to societal stereotyping is harder to detect and surmount, as detailed in Chapter 5 on institution-level interventions. As Grover (2015, 1) explains, "second-generation gender bias is hidden, invisible, planned, organized and has a more neutral face than visible first generation, but the underlying practices, values and beliefs remain distinctly male-oriented." Chapter 5 highlighted a number of examples of this phenomenon. We argue that the higher percentages of women on boards and executive teams suggest that at least overt discrimination has been taken care of, whereas covert discrimination is more difficult to address. Chapter 8, on professional services, provides examples of unconscious bias:

The kind of responses women's ideas get in board meetings; or clients' responses in cases where female engineers are allocated to build their refinery plants; the often condescending language used to address women; clients who assume that women in their engineering environment are there to serve them tea; or male networks that are stronger than male-female engagements. One of our interviewees declared, "The only way to overcome prejudice is by excellence."

This interviewee realizes that bias often comes from historical pre-conceptions and that only by building interpersonal connections and being outstanding can the layers of bias be dismantled. This woman leader illustrates a constructive approach to bias—that is, not taking it personally. It serves as an example of "cognitive restructuring", a technique that leads to an emotionally appropriate response and consequently to collaborative behavior, as described by Scheepers (2012). Individual women who struggle with bias could benefit from support in the form of focused mentoring and leadership coaching (Scheepers 2012).

However, the authors of this volume are not convinced that intervention at individual level is adequate to address organizational and institutional systems-level discrimination, be it overt or unconscious. As the authors of Chapter 8, on professional services, put it, "Apartheid is destroyed, the Berlin wall has fallen and there is an awareness and inclination to embrace diversity." We suggest better-coordinated efforts to address bias in the quest for gender equality. We echo Stella Nkomo's lamentation on education in Chapter 4: "My view is if you get to that table and you are not using that position of power to support others, then you are wasting an opportunity because not everyone gets to the table."

Chapter 6, on barriers, also recommended that women at the top, as representatives of all women, call attention to gender issues. Contemporary research by Derks, van Laar and Ellemers (2016), however, indicates that when women of marginalized groups bridge the gap and rise to senior roles, they may well support the status quo, only attempting to change the status quo if there is a strong alliance with their out-group. Classic social identity theory explains this phenomenon as follows: in-group characteristics are comprehended and formulated by comparing to the out-group and thereby deriving value and unity from the in-group (Turner and Tajfel 1986; Ashforth and Mael 1989). A number of women in our sample admitted that they had assumed masculine mannerisms to fit in—see particularly Chapters 9, on corporate enterprises, and 10, on women on boards. Fitzsimmons, Callan and Paulsen (2014), as well as Kolb, Williams and Frohlinger (2010), explain that masculine stereotypes involve acting agentically, with highly assertive behavior, whereas feminine stereotypes prescribe behaving communally and demonstrating relational skills. Grover (2015, 4) advises women to be authentic and create space for themselves and our interviewees also revealed that, over time, they had developed more authentic leadership styles.

Access to education

Third, women's access to education in emerging markets is currently lower than men's (Khalaf 2014). The gap between men and women in employment and promotion opportunities is expected to widen even further in future. Figure 11.1 below illustrates this "Emerging markets threshold" between the episodes of schooling and tertiary education. We argue for a preventative approach to gender inequality, focusing on the "Emerging markets threshold" rather than the "glass ceiling" (Catalyst 2016) or even "labyrinth" (Eagly and Carli 2007) found in developed markets.

For example, Chapter 8, on professional services, highlighted that in emerging markets, fewer women than men graduate as accountants (34% in 2015 in South Africa, from 27% in 2009), whereas they are on par in developed markets. In 2013, 61% of chartered accountants in the USA and 49% in Canada were female (Catalyst 2013 and SAICA 2009). We believe that addressing gender inequality should start early, consistent with Tsang's contention that "Schools should ensure stereotypes are not reinforced and girls are not deterred from making ambitious career choices at an early age" (Tsang 2014). Hiller (2014, 455) agrees that existing cultural norms entrench gender inequalities—for example, when a decision is taken early on about investment in the education of boys rather than girls. Chapter 3, on women's movements, also highlighted the phenomenon of "son-preference" in a number of emerging markets—which can even lead to parents traditionally offering more nutritious food to their sons than to their daughters.

We also observed that the "glass ceiling" effect in emerging markets (Glass and Cook 2016, 51) occurs even earlier in women's careers and resembles more a "sticky ladder" (Grover 2015) due to the masculine prototype of leadership (Elliot and Stead 2008; Heilman 2012). Given that patriarchy is more prominent in emerging markets than in developed markets (for instance, Scandinavia), women internalize the traditional patriarchal notion of male dominance to a larger degree—both in families and institutions (Eagly and Johannesen-Schmidt 2001, 781; Eagly and Karau 2002, 573). As a result, women tend to refrain from promoting themselves or developing the confidence required of demanding leadership roles. Chapters 4, on education, and 6, on barriers, quoted from interviews during which even those women who had broken through the glass ceiling expressed the self-doubt they had had to overcome during early phases of their careers: "Am I really qualified to do this? Do I really know what I am talking about? Should this be me here?"; "I came from a very poor background. I was not supposed to be sitting where I am sitting now;" "Do I even deserve to be here?"

These findings are consistent with current literature (Ibarra, Ely and Kolb 2013). Our book contributed a number of additional sub-themes. For example, in Chapter 8, on professional services, interviewees who experienced a lack of confidence when they returned to work after maternity leave were quoted. Chapter 7 reported that even entrepreneurship has a "male" image, with the assumption that for a business to be successful it needs to be owned and run by a man. The authors of Chapter 7, on entrepreneurship, identified the lack of female role models as one of the key barriers to entrepreneurship for women. Chapter 6, on barriers, confirmed the lack of representation of women at the top and explained that this may also lead to less focus on gender-related issues. "Working mom" guilt was also confirmed as an important barrier by the research in Chapter 6.

Contrary to the "glass ceiling" literature from the West, which indicates that women get stuck prior to reaching top management, we found that, especially in professional services (Chapter 8), women's lack of progress occurs quite early. It typically happens when women start to have a family, usually about five to ten years into their careers. On their return from maternity leave these women face a number of invisible obstacles (glass ceiling) and even worse stereotyping. In addition, it appears that gender stereotypes still influence the career choices of women and that gendered careers—careers perceived as feminine—are preferred by women. In the medical profession, for example, the majority of women doctors with families choose specializations with more predictable working hours such as haematology, paediatrics, psychiatry or radiology. In contrast, very few women choose to study surgery.

Another sub-theme concerns the sectors in which women tend to work. For example, 32% of chief financial officers (CFOs) were female in South

Africa in 2013 (Grant Thornton 2015). Chapter 9, on professional ser-vices, reports that the majority of enterprises headed by women tend to be found in the retail and personal service sectors and that women are under-represented in the manufacturing, extraction and business services sectors. Chapter 1 reports that the largest proportion of senior management roles held by women are in education and social science or healthcare and hospitality and the smallest in the construction and mining industries (Grant Thornton 2015).

Traditional values

Religions such as Catholicism, Confucianism and Islam are perceived by many as dictating that women should maintain their traditional caregiving roles. Women in emerging markets therefore have to deal with even more resistance to their pursuit of ambitious career goals than do women in developed markets. This was observed in all nine emerging market coun-tries discussed in Chapter 3. Similarly, Khalaf (2014) reports that although "women lead Argentina, Brazil and Chile—70% of executives in Latin America say family pressures cause women to leave their jobs".

This finding is in line with our research. For example, in Chapter 4, on education, an interviewee acknowledged that, despite India having a female prime minister, "women are so deeply conditioned that they don't even realise they can explore different identities and mark out something for themselves besides being mothers and wives". Chapter 4 also laments that, "in African, South American and Asian contexts, the patriarchal system, traditional beliefs and cultural attitudes can make it difficult to rise to positions of leadership."

Chapter 6, on barriers, also highlighted that societal role expectations dictate that women should take care of their families, while the same strictures do not apply to men. In this regard, Chapter 2 discussed the views of early feminists such as de Beauvoir (1949) that are echoed today in the scholarly work of Gherardi and Poggio (2001, 245), Fletcher (2004, 647) and others. Helgesen (1995) contends that "the challenge today is the same challenge that the suffragists faced in the 1920s". Chapter 2 offered four reasons—from a contextual view on leadership—for why gender bias still exists.

Dimensions of diversity

A great number of women interviewees across the chapters mentioned dimensions of diversity other than gender that caused them to be part of a minority group. Chapter 8, on professional services, for example, presented this theme in the following way:

In addition to often being the only woman in the room, many of the interviewed women were also part of a minority in other ways—cultural or ethnic. Being the only Asian woman round a boardroom table of white men or the one black woman on a mining site with all Afrikaans-speaking white males or the only Western woman amongst Arab men in the Middle East is challenging and requires sustained energy to manage.

Chapter 6, on barriers, also paid attention to the obstacle of simultaneous membership of multiple social groups. For example, the top women leaders interviewed for Chapter 3 reported that they experienced cultural, age and racial discrimination. These findings are consistent with studies such as that of Bernard-Powers (2008, 315), which confirms that "gender does not function in social isolation ... it is shaped by multiple identities in specific historic, political, and economic contexts". For example, the most marginalized group in South Africa is black females; white females have greater representation than all other female groups (Department of Labour 2016; Franchi 2003), despite legislation such as the 2003 Broad-Based Black Empowerment Act and the 2013 Employment Equity Act. In our sample, race was the other diversity dimension that mattered the most to female leaders, which is consistent with the seminal research of scholars such as Rosette, Koval and Livingston (2016).

Access to finance

Lack of access to finance (ATF) is getting even worse for women given the slowing growth rates in emerging markets—for example, the contraction of China's economy (Prasad 2016); the Brazilian economy that shrank 0.3% in the first three months of 2016, with an average GDP growth rate of 0.61% between 1996 and 2016; and Russia's GDP that contracted by 0.57% (Trading Economics 2016b). Scarcity of funds is increasing women's competition with men for investment in their viable business ideas. Decrease in foreign investment exacerbates the problem, particularly for countries such as South Africa, where GDP declined for two consecutive years, 2014 and 2015 (Trading Economics 2016c), causing lower credit ratings from global rating agencies and scaring off investors (Trading Economics 2016a).

Gender studies in developed markets overwhelmingly focus on large corporations, inventing the term "glass ceiling" (Ibarra, Ely and Kolb 2013). Emerging markets in contrast cannot rely on large corporations to reduce unemployment by growing the economy. As a result, small and medium-sized enterprises (SMEs) are increasing in value. The attention given in this book to women's positions in corporate enterprises has been balanced by chapters focusing on educational institutions (Chapter 4), entrepreneurial organizations (Chapter 9) and professional services firms (Chapter 8). The factor that is therefore particularly relevant for women in emerging markets is "access to finance", or ATF, with "glass ceiling" of less consequence. Tsang (2014) reports that if women's participation in the labor market was raised to the same level as that of men, Egypt's economy would grow by a third and the United Arab Emirates' GDP would expand by 12%. Estimates based on International Labour Organisation data suggest that of the 865 million women who could be contributing more to their national economies, 812 million live in emerging economies (Tsang 2014). Chapter 1 offered a detailed description of this reality, calling it "smart economics". The authors of Chapter 10 argued that, while the demand for more women board directors may be growing due to legislative requirements, the limited pool of women executives in senior leadership positions from which to draw continues to be a barrier.

Informal relations

Emerging market economies are often characterized by informal relations and ways of doing business based on patronage and affiliation, more so than in developed countries. This is described in Chapters 3, on women's movements, and 8, on professional services. Access to informal networks and meaningful connections outside of formal reporting lines is crucial in this landscape. This places women at a disadvantage, as current literature reveals (Perriton 2006) and our interviewees confirm. Chapter 6, on barriers, contended that men often have better access to, and receive more support from, their networks than women do, which negatively affects women's career advancement. Scholars such as Fitzsimmons and Callan (2016) state that women focus on completing tasks at work and are less available after work, as they are balancing family and work life. This limits their opportunity to network and develop social capital. Women thus become invisible and less likely to be considered for line management roles. Dolly Mokgatle, one of our interviewees quoted in Chapter 1, believes that "men create and access the boys' clubs easily".

Tsang (2014) emphasizes that nearly half the women in the world do not work in the formal economy. Our Chapter 7, on entrepreneurship, revealed the importance of informal trade in emerging markets. These informal exchanges are not registered or regulated and are therefore not protected by law. They rely solely on informal relations and, sometimes, fraudulent exchanges and intimidation. Gaining insight into these trading situations in emerging markets is important. At our business school (Gordon Institute of Business Science, University of Pretoria), we frequently expose our MBA and Executive Education students to these unique contexts. These immersion exercises allow them to interact with informal traders in the Johannesburg inner city area and gain understanding of prostitution and drug addiction in informal settlements to the north of the capital, Pretoria. The victimization of women is particularly evident in these informal environments and requires further scholarly research and investigation. Chapter 3, in the section about China, highlighted the dire circumstances of women in China's rural areas, as well as the plight of migrant workers, and future women's movements should focus more on these marginalized groups.

The seven themes outlined above provide an overview of key findings across the chapters. Each chapter also offered recommendations both for individual women leaders and for institution-level interventions. The next section summarizes our insights and suggests a way forward.

Conceptual framework

As authors of this volume, we support the view of current scholars of women's leadership such as Ibarra, Ely and Kolb (2013, 4) that "It's not enough to identify and instil the right skills and competencies as if in a social vacuum. The context must support a woman's motivation to lead and also increase the likelihood that others will recognise and encourage her efforts." The conceptual framework we suggest also emphasizes the context of the women leaders. Chapter 2 paid attention to "Women's leadership in context" and will not be summarized here; instead, we illustrate how both the internal (intrapersonal) and external (interpersonal and sociocultural) contexts influenced the women in our sample.

In line with Elliot and Stead's (2008) assertion, we argue that leadership is a social process rather than a particular attribute of an individual. Our analysis of the interviews revealed 523 pages of code and we grouped these into 81 code families. The data is available for further research. For the purpose of this volume and in the interest of an executive summary, we chose to focus on the developmental ecosystem, a phrase we coined during the discussion of our findings. Nyasha Mugadza, a doctoral student at our business school, was instrumental in analyzing the transcripts using ATLAS.ti, a software programme for qualitative analysis. A number of her findings revolved around the influencers that we illustrate in Figure 11.1 below. These include professional exposure and family and support structures, as well as the role of high self-awareness and deliberate self-sponsorship. According to Mugadza (2016), self-sponsorship involves taking ownership of leading the self towards the desired goal; conscious self-development and advancement; recognizing a need to outperform for recognition; and respect for and embracing self-sacrificing choices. These developmental highlights are demonstrated in the figure below. Phumzile Mlambo Ngcuka, executive director of UN Women, states that "A girl child born today will have to be 81 before she stands the same chance of being a CEO of a company and she will have to wait 50 years to have an equal chance of leading a country."

This quote refers to the life cycle of an individual leader and we chose to use life stages in our illustration of specific episodes in the lifetime of women leaders, ranging from childhood to their ascent to top management positions. The feedback loop, from women in top positions back to childhood, demonstrates an interactive pattern in which women in powerful positions in both government and commercial organizations influence society. A number of the women interviewed mentioned that they wanted to "give back" to society and had designed programs in their organizations; Wendy Ackerman, for example, had designed one to improve work–life balance for her staff and create a parent-friendly work environment. These women purposefully influence society, paving the way for future generations. The figure below also demonstrates that there are particular influences at important decision points, illustrated by the milestone symbol, over the life cycle of women leaders.

The centre of the illustration shows the importance of the inner psychological leadership journey as internal context, indicating that societal influencers are still filtered through the cognitive, emotional and spiritual processing of the individual leader. This in turn, influences the decision of a woman leader to either move up the "ladder" or opt out and take a different course in her life and career.

In terms of the specific episodes and their influencers, our findings are outlined below.

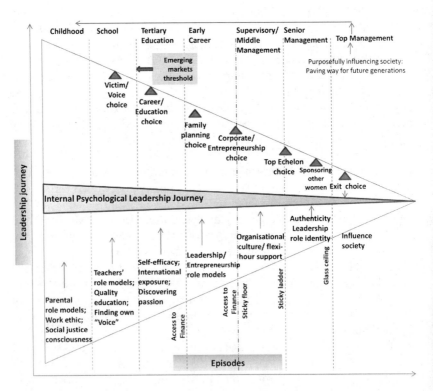

Figure 11.1 Conceptual framework of women's leadership journey in emerging markets

Note: A triangle represents a decision point.

Childhood and school episodes

During the childhood episode, parental role models play an important part in establishing a work ethic. Interestingly, specific to the emerging markets context with its tendency to have high levels of inequality, a sense of social justice and social consciousness is evident early in the women's lives. A number of interviewees in Chapter 2 show how this phenomenon played out. Both Chapter 1, which quoted various women leaders in public service, and Chapter 8, on professional services, mentioned the sense of purpose felt by, for example, Phumzile Mlambo Ngcuka, Geraldine Fraser Moleketi, Dolly Mokgatle; Barçin Yinanç, Betty Bigombe and Gill Marcus, who had been socialized in a context that instilled in them the importance of "what kind of society we are living in" and "wanting to be a part of making a contribution to change it". In her research report, Mugadza (2016) calls this phenomenon "early experiences of taking leadership of community concerns".

During the years of primary and secondary school, the women interviewed reported on the role of teachers as role models. A couple of them also considered their "all-girls school" an opportunity to find their "voice" and, of course, the quality of education provided by these single-sex institutions also had a huge influence on the progress of these women. Having become socially conscious in the previous phase, by this phase they had already taken up leadership roles by standing up for issues around fairness. A number of them experienced challenging circumstances, as described in detail in the accounts of women in education in Chapter 4. As one of the interviewees observed: "even with the death of my father when I was seven, even in all of the adversity I experienced, I have something to celebrate". They interpreted adversity as conducive to forming their character. During this period the women we interviewed took the unconscious or conscious decision to take control of their lives and not become victims; they chose to be a voice or, as one called it, "a cause rather than an effect" (in Chapter 10, on women on boards).

Emerging markets threshold: Education

As illustrated in Figure 11.1, the problem in emerging markets is the lack of access to quality tertiary education for women relative to men. We called this the "emerging markets threshold", as the episodes that follow would undoubtedly be influenced by these women's access to education. The women who had the privilege of higher education had the freedom of career choice and could afford to follow their passions and experiment with different career options until they discovered their place in society and the actual contribution they wished to make. It was interesting to discover that, for the majority of these women, exposure to developed countries and a more international environment when traveling with their families, particularly in earlier episodes of their lives, made a huge impression on them. It influenced their perspectives and their horizons. For example, Isabel Neiva from Dubai said that women's contextual appreciation is now far richer because, since they travel extensively, their experiences are no longer so localized. We therefore urge exchanges between countries in the emerging and developed markets to increase exposure for women leaders.

Early career episode

Access to finance is also a decisive factor during the early career years. Women who would like to set up entrepreneurial businesses obviously require finance. In addition, if women can build up personal funds, they have more choice in terms of where they work and what work they do. During this time, women also take decisions with regard to family planning. In a number of emerging market countries women are not allowed to use contraceptives (as discussed in Chapter 3) and this limits their decisions around family planning. Societal norms play an important role in this episode: stereotypical thinking around the work women should be doing and how much time women should take out from their careers to raise young children are both influencers. Expectations of women's leadership and available female role models also play a part.

Supervisory/Middle management episodes

For a number of women the re-entry into the work place after maternity leave had been problematic. In Chapter 8 we discussed the choice between starting small consulting businesses or staying in large professional services firms. During this phase, the organizational culture, attitude towards women leaders and unconscious second-generation bias, as described earlier, could cause a "sticky floor" for women and they might opt out of the organization or more demanding leadership roles. Flexi-hours, mobile offices and parenting-friendly work environments were some of the institution-level changes suggested in Chapter 5. The next hurdle that can be problematic for women leaders is the proverbial "sticky ladder", as described by Grover (2015).

Appropriate institution-level responses are required to bridge the gender gap during these episodes. For some organizations, creating learning opportunities solely for women would be relevant; for others, gender diverse interventions where male participants are included in the learning process would be best. (Chapter 5 described the difference between these programs.) These interventions could have a huge impact on the decisions women take at these times to opt out of corporate environments and pursue an entrepreneurial career.

Senior and executive management episodes

During these episodes, women decide whether to take up top-echelon positions. Scholars like Ibarra, Ely and Kolb (2013, 8) advise that "focusing exclusively on acquiring new skills isn't sufficient; the learning must be accompanied by a growing sense of identity as a leader". In our research we observed that there were a couple of women in top positions who had not perceived themselves as leaders: "I never saw myself as a leader"; "I just got on with it." It was as if there was disconnect between how they perceived themselves and how others perceived them. This would, of course, be an interesting topic for further research.

In addressing the proverbial "glass ceiling," we advocate a generally proactive approach rather than a quota system at board level. We require a larger pool of highly qualified, capable women with access to finance earlier in their careers to feed the leadership pipeline. Addressing gender inequality should therefore start early. In Figure 11.1, the "internal psychological leadership journey" is wider in the early years, illustrating the importance of the influence of these early life experiences for the women we interviewed. We observed interesting development in the women interviewees' sense of authenticity as leaders. As discussed above, earlier in the women's careers they exhibited masculine leadership styles but later found themselves more comfortable "in their own skin;" they "found their space" and became more authentic, exhibiting more feminine leadership styles.

It is time

We advocate for a new leadership prototype in this age of volatility, uncertainty, complexity and ambiguity (VUCA). We need to unlearn (Rautenbach, Sutherland and Scheepers 2015), our gendered notions of leadership, as we emphasized in Chapter 1,

"With increasing complexity and volatility in the strategic landscape of emerging markets, there is the awareness that calls for a new way of leading, one that is less hierarchical and traditional, characterized by a collaborative and inclusive approach."

Globally, women who occupy leadership positions and have learned masculine traits to fit the prototype are doing women a disservice. It perpetuates the stereotype of feminine versus masculine leadership qualities and negates the contribution of communal or female qualities. We call on women leaders to be authentic by exhibiting both their masculine and feminine traits, contingent on the context (as we explained in Chapter 2). We understand why women adopt agentic behavior in order to stand their ground within a male-dominated society. Nonetheless, we need more contextually intelligent leaders who exhibit "behavior flexibility" and build a dynamic balance and synergy from supposedly opposite leadership practices. Chapter 4, on women in education, also emphasized the androgynous leadership style. This might entail unlearning some particularly aggressive behaviors and relearning empathetic, collaborative behaviors. Grover (2015) advises women to establish their identity as leaders rather than female leaders.

We assert that we actually do women a disfavor by attributing either feminine or masculine stereotypical behaviors to them when they are, in fact, operating within roles where the expectation is (for example) that you hold others accountable. Instead, the pertinent question is "how can we create a fair environment for both genders?" To this end we need to unlearn our behaviors of the past.

Once equality on a societal level is achieved, there will be less bias and discrimination at the institutional level and more freedom to choose at the individual level. Individuals might still choose to be "stay-at-home mothers", but they might decide what else works for them. We envision a world where all can thrive equally; where environments are as welcoming to women as they currently are to men (as expressed in Chapter 6).

Limitations of study and suggestions for future research

Our sample included a particular set of women—that is, those who made it despite existing broad gender stereotypes. We did not interview women who had leaked out of the leadership pipeline to offer a comparison. Future studies could include different samples. In addition, the data collected for this volume is derived from interviews with women at a particular level of management and that would have influenced their viewpoint on enablers and barriers. Further studies could include women at different levels in an organization. We also interviewed women who were at a particular point in their careers and did not conduct a longitudinal study on their development. The interviewees had to rely on their memories to account for previous phases in their growth. Nevertheless, this volume, with its interview data transcripts, establishes a baseline, and longitudinal studies would be fascinating. Future researchers could track the ascent of these women and their contribution to other women's careers.

Recommendations

Creating new narratives and shifting mindsets in emerging markets. It's about time that policymakers and corporate leaders cottoned onto the fact that women are fit, proper and willing to write new narratives for their countries, their corporate institutions and themselves. They are the untapped talent pool, particularly in emerging markets where they are the potential re-visioning and re-imaging of leadership.

The "deep dive" discourse with the 46 women and eight men from emerging markets we interviewed for this book gives us the confidence to state that women are looking for new ways to tackle the intractable problems of the volatile, uncertain, complex and ambiguous world in which they live and work. They are not willing to wait on the sidelines and have traditional—and mostly patriarchal—mindsets stop them from reaching their full potential and taking the societies in which they live to a better place. They are open and willing to work with men in a complementary manner to carve a better future for all. Throughout our robust discourse with these leading women there was a palpable sense of urgency and of their fearlessness in tapping into unexplored terrain, not for personal individual gain alone but so more for macro-economic and organizational gains.

Those we interviewed often referred to history and why history teaches valuable lessons, particularly with regard to the significant role played by women in bringing about change. The dominant narratives in history are those of men and their roles in creating our present. Our respondents pointed out that women have always been active agents of change. Lerner (1997) said the same thing in *Why History Matters*. Lerner makes two particular points which history should have made clear to policymakers, leaders and practitioners who try to address gender equality. First, "the basic error [of] patriarchal thought has been to make claims of universality for descriptions of the activities of a small elite group of upper-class white males. However, by rejecting this androcentric distortion of the past, we have opened the way to new insights and challenges"; and second, "women cannot be treated as a unified category any more than men as a group can". Women's race, class, socio-economic status, geographic location, culture, traditions and religion complicate the issue of gender equality because women's issues cannot be conflated into a single basket.

This is echoed by Chant and Sweetman (2012) who point out that smart economics should not be seen as the only solution to address gender equality. Smart economics, or the practice of investing in the development of women and girl children, ignores the many nuanced complications of race, gender and class. Holvino (2010) highlights that this three-legged schema unfolds simultaneously, which further compounds the strategies we propose and embrace to secure gender equality. It becomes clearer through this perspective that the strategies for addressing gender parity or seeking gender equality are neither linear nor singularly formulaic. Holvino goes on to suggest three systematic ways in which individuals and corporates can respond to the trickiness of gender compounded by the "simultaneity" of race and class, all of which exacerbate or complicate the agendas relating to gender equality. In unpacking the stories of the 46 women we interviewed, we found their narratives at least tinged and sometimes richly colored by the impact of race and class, which acted as either enablers for or impediments to them reaching their full potential, irrespective of the markets from which they came. In this section of the chapter we adopt this three-pronged approach as a lens through which we address the complexity of gender in a more holistic manner. The strength of the approach lies in its applicability at macro-, meso- and micro-level and their intersectionality.

First, Holvino advances the argument that dominant narratives in organizations or institutions (country, corporate or home) are the result of privilege based on race, gender and class or a permutation of these attributes. It is only when the stories of others—that is, those who fall outside the dominant narratives category—start to form and take hold that the dominant narratives are diluted or even displaced. Blumberg (2015), a young architect who challenged the invisibility of hired help through her architectural designs suggests that to get to the "reform" stage one has to "deform" the "uniform" or "question the norm". Without the stories of those who fall outside the dominant narratives, the norm is uncontested and we will fail to reach the "reform" stage. Holvino suggests that the telling of these alternative narratives alters the consciousness of institutions and makes the "generalized other" become a "concrete other". The focus shifts from the dominant actors to the concrete other actors. By "researching and publishing" Holvino (2010, 264) the hidden stories, the power bases of dominant narratives are shaken. The simple act of telling the stories of "others", repeatedly and to multiple stakeholders, can produce small and immediate wins. This first recommendation creates a natural link to her second recommendation, that of "Identifying, untangling and changing the impact of everyday practices in the organizations."

The very practices that prevail in organizations need to be observed and questioned. Why do certain groups, the in-groups, enjoy more opportunities and higher remuneration than the "general other". Take a simple, seemingly innocent and well-intentioned planned weekend retreat for leadership teams. Where does it happen? Who sets the theme or agenda? And who enjoys prominence on the agenda? Who is compelled to attend but is "silenced" by how the agenda is structured? Holvino (2010, 260) advances that in observing and paying attention to the practices of organization we will find "silencing apparent in these everyday practices" and these may be "displayed in the material, discursive and symbolic practices which act as forms of power and control".

Her final recommendation concerns the need to shift traditional thinking away from returns on investment for the organization to the rewards of working at the boundary of organization and society. Given the volatility, uncertainty, complexity and ambiguity of the world in which we live, we have to "locate organizational dynamics within a broader social context and developing change interventions with a larger social justice agenda" Holvino (2010, 18).

With gender parity the desired end state, we offer recommendations that, while specifically aimed at emerging markets, do not exclude benefits they may have in developed markets. Based on our findings, these recommendations are offered at three levels.

Macro-level

Policies and legislation need to be developed for the particular context of the country where they are to be operationalized. While there are policies that work well across different markets, developed or emerging, policy-makers must move away from the practice of adopting policies from other markets for implementation in their own country. Our interviewees told us again and again how the context of a country matters and, while the gender gap is a universal problem, the context should dictate the nature of policies and strategies how they are implemented. Another of the main country-level rubbing points that emerged was the lack of female representation around the most important ministerial and political portfolios. This leads us to our first recommendation.

Recommendation 1

The leadership of ruling governments have to possess the political will to appoint women of substance to the most respected and most powerful political and governmental portfolios. Women's political leadership patterns and positioning in a few portfolios is not unique to emerging markets; it shows up equally strongly in developed markets. There is a "denial of full political participation and access to the traditional sources of power and decision making afforded to males" (Frederick 2013 and Rosser-Mims 2015). While women's political participation is diminished by relegation to a few pre-identified portfolios instead of to the portfolios in which they can shape the policy agendas that will make a material difference not only to women but also to the societies in which both women and men live, we will not start to see the real change. At this level, in line with Holvino's recommendation, leadership has to be critical of itself and question why do certain groups become the dominant narrative as the in-group, thereby enjoying more access and opportunities, higher-profile assignments and chosen opportunities as opposed to the "general other" (Holvino 2010, 263). Invariably women in political roles fall into the "general other" category (Holvino 2010). There has to be a rethinking and re-imaging of political leadership roles for women. This will require a conscious decoupling from learned behavior and unearthing of unconscious biases in order for the dominant narratives in political institutions to change.

Recommendation 2

Our second recommendation stems from the "what gets measured gets done" school of thought. There are often good intentions and solid blueprints in the form of legislation for getting us to gender parity, but the lack of financial and human resources allocated to the delivery and maintenance along with monitoring and evaluation is the missing piece. As a result, the implementation phase often lands as a tick-box activity and there are no rewards for success or punishment for ineffective application. On the other hand, if the measurement phase is in place and longitudinal monitoring and evaluation processes are applied then the results speak for themselves. Take the case of the quota system imposed on Norwegian companies. Wang and Kelan (2013, 463) found that the "gender quota has had a positive impact on the number of female board chairs and female CEOs, indicating that the gender quota in Norway has not only increased gender equality within the board-room but also had spill-over effects on top leadership positions". The stringent monitoring and evaluation phase for macro policies and legislation will translate into tangible results at the organizational level.

Recommendation 3

Finally, in our view, good and relevant leaders today are those who lead authentically and by example. If country leaders in emerging markets want to truly count as trendsetters for their country's competitive advantage, they have to create inclusive and diverse leadership agendas in which the rules of the game must be in play at the highest level. One of our identified key themes, dimensions of diversity, alludes to the importance of leader-ship diversity and how for the complex world in which we live and work leadership can no longer be one-dimensional. Men, who are currently occupying the highest offices in the land, must introduce policies that favor women's political aspirations: only then will there be more tangible results.

Meso-level

Holvino raises a burning issue that sits at the heart of practices adopted by organizations to address gender parity. She posits that "In the field of organization studies and organizational change there is little evidence that the importance of race, gender and class intersections is acknowledged" (Holvino 2010, 249). Inclusion of minority groups or those previously disadvantaged are often addressed in a silo-ed manner, yet the solutions we seek for gender parity cannot exclude considerations of race and class. What complicates this phenomenon is that these three schema unfold simultaneously. Some studies have looked at the intersection of gender and race, others at ethnicity, race and gender and far too few on the inter-sectionality of all three: race, gender and class. Diversity and inclusion practices and champions who lead this in organizations do not have an effective or sophisticated grip on this complexity.

Recommendation 1

Our first recommendation for this level is that leadership and HR practi-tioners re-think the nuances that impact human behavior. We understand that businesses exist to increase business performance, but at the heart of achieving this goal sits the workforce. And a high-performing workforce requires a high-performing leadership and HR practitioner community. Organizational leadership for the volatility, uncertainty, complexity and ambiguity of the times in which we live and work requires interventions that acknowledge the intersectionality of race, gender and class. If this eludes leadership, it will elude the HR practitioner community. We are in agreement with Deloitte's Global Human Capital Trends 2014 report, which points to the urgent need for leadership, particularly in emerging markets, to invest in the retraining and upskilling of their HR communities so that they become accomplished business consultants. This research shows a "significant gap between the urgency of the talent and leadership issues leaders face today and their organizations' readiness to respond" (Deloitte 2014, 4). The same report's top three global trends categorized by urgency are "leadership, retention and engagement and re-skilling HR". Of particular significance for us is how these three identified urgencies play a crucial role in interlink diversity and inclusion as a business strategy imperative. Our research indicated that the practice of investment in women as a generic group to address challenges relating to gender parity is outdated and ineffective. The times we are in call for diversity and inclusion strategies to focus on the intersectionality of race, gender and class, otherwise smart economics will amount to throwing good money after bad.

Recommendation 2

Our second recommendation is to create an intentional awareness at all levels of the organization to vet what is "displayed in the material, discursive and symbolic practices which act as forms of power and control" Holvino (2010, 264). But that will not happen until interventions are in place to teach the organization about identifying conscious and unconscious biases and unlearning behavior. Relating back to the key themes of patriarchy and internalization, the traditional male environment strongly entrenches gender discriminatory practices because of patriarchal mindsets. Thus, the unlearning has to be intentional and directed. Ajzen's theory of planned behavior shows the intersectionality between "intentions, behaviours and attitudes to that behaviour" Ajzen (1991, 261). The unlearning process to achieve actual new behavior is therefore not easily pursued on its own; it requires a directed intentional approach. But there has to be agency involved for the new learning to take hold. Therefore, we are fans of twinning these interventions with Bandura's (1991) self-monitoring activities. He argues that:

> People cannot influence their own motivation and actions very well if they do not pay adequate attention to their own performances, the

conditions under which they occur, and the immediate and distal effects they produce. Therefore, success in self-regulation partly depends on the fidelity, consistency, and temporal proximity of self-monitoring.

(Bandura 1991, 250)

Recommendation 3

The third recommendation at this level links back to macro-policy on gender parity targets. There must be a reporting convention in a public domain that tracks the progress of gender gap index within organizations. A transparent public reporting standard will force organizations to consistently question their achievements, or lack thereof, and force them to hold a mirror to self.

Recommendation 4

We have been made acutely aware through this research investigation that an intentional approach is required for "Identifying, untangling and changing the impact of everyday practices in the organizations" Holvino (2010, 264). This is where we advocate that employees in organizations, irrespective of their level in their organization, either individually or collectively call out these practices. To be silent will merely strengthen and entrench such practices. Whether they are about leave policies for parents, flexible working arrangements, the anywhere, anytime model of work or opportunities and rewards awarded to certain groups of people—they must be called out, repeatedly if necessary. What is silent is never on anyone's radar. Make it your business to put it on the radar.

Recommendation 5

Finally, organizations cannot operate blind to the context in which they are located. Women's narratives are most frequently located within that larger social context. Businesses can no longer succeed or compete without knowing those stories—how women got into the room and how they hope to get out. Holvino's (2010, 265) last recommendation "locates organizational dynamics within a broader social context and developing change interventions with a larger social justice agenda".

This kind of change requires a new kind of leader: the traditional, hierarchical leader is going to destroy our institutions if they do not embrace "situational adaptability which underpins inclusive leadership competence" (Bluen 2013, 234). Bluen goes on to describe the new sort of leader as one who "understands, is committed to, and communicates the business case for, diversity in the company and his/her own functions" (2013, 234).

Micro-level

Throughout our research and discourse with women and men leaders we kept coming back to the women in emerging markets themselves—their leadership aspirations, what their definition of success looks like, their dilemmas, and the pushes and pulls connected to wanting the best for themselves without losing their most prized asset, their families, or losing sight of the communities in which they live and work. Alongside their pursuit of personal success as leaders, the women want to initiate change interventions that also deliver a social justice agenda. Three themes that have been identified, access to education, traditional values and unemployment, probably account for the strong justice-based outcomes that women seek for themselves and their societies.

Our recommendations for the women themselves in their pursuit of gender parity and true inclusion are in some ways simple but they are not necessarily easy to achieve.

Recommendation 1

In achieving your professional successes remain true to yourself. Women want more than the power, package and position. They want their journey of success to be led by purpose and passion. Our women leaders suggested that where there is congruence between personal and professional success, women are more driven to achieve because their successes take others along on a journey of success.

Recommendation 2

Women in emerging markets—and particularly in markets with firmly established cultural practices—often feel a tension between professional success and cultural practices that limit their freedom of choice. They battle with the notion of adopting multiple personas, switching from power positions and roles to playing the stereotypical wife, mother and daughter roles. Our recommendation, especially to millennial women in these markets and based on frank advice from women leaders in those markets is simply this: do not feel diminished or less powerful on the occasions when you are expected to play the traditional role. In fact, recognise that these events help you to be tougher and more resilient when you have to deal with adverse situations in your professional life. If these practices are not harming you physically or scarring you emotionally then embrace them as part of what makes you a more powerful woman.

Recommendation 3

The next recommendation is that you develop a voice. Own it and use it to win the best outcomes for yourself and other women and future leaders. In advocating for yourself and others you become known for something, rather than being swallowed up in the "general other".

Recommendation 4

Embrace motherhood in your professional leadership journey. It is not a tug of war. Let people in your work environment know that you are a mother—being a mother is a significant part of your narrative, so don't make an apology for it. Smart workplaces and smart technology mean motherhood need not detract from your performance: you can achieve desirable work-related outputs as effectively at home as you can from your desk in the office.

Recommendation 5

Own your ambition! If you want a position and you have as a minimum the credentials for it and the stomach for the hard work, put your hand up for it.

Recommendation 6

Be prepared to:

- negotiate a good deal for yourself;
- disrupt yourself when you feel too comfortable;
- ask for what you want;
- question the norm!
- stand up for what is right;
- gather the tools and techniques that allow you to do more than bounce back after dealing with adversity; and
- look after yourself holistically.

We sit in a far richer place and position than when we started this journey and it is from this place that we make the following offerings.

We advocate freedom of choice and oppose value judgments being made about:

- contraception;
- whether women should work or be stay-home moms; or
- women subservient to abusive partners at home or bullies at work.

Abuse against women and children is a human rights issue, not a gender issue.

Let us create opportunities for women to have a choice by:

- building women-friendly, supportive organizational cultures and introducing practices like flexi-hours and mobile office options;
- providing access to education;
- creating access to finance for viable entrepreneurial endeavors;
- realizing that patriarchy is not serving our emerging markets;
- confronting unconscious biases; and
- changing the rigid stereotypical feminine and masculine leadership models to an androgynous, adaptive, contextually intelligent model of leadership that values authenticity in women leaders, and, ultimately, achieves workplace gender equity.

The Vice Chancellor at the University of Pretoria, Cheryl de la Rey, contends:

One thing that has not shifted is the tendency for women to get defined mostly by their sexual attractiveness, or sexuality—in a way that male leaders do not have to deal with. Women have more freedom than before, but a second thing that has not shifted sufficiently is men taking responsibility for family and domestic life. The issue of power is fundamental in those men who are abusive, and these are serious ongoing challenges that the next generation faces. There is a real absence of a gender equality movement now, and the silence is quite concerning.

In response to this call and the call of the remarkable trailblazers that we interviewed, we say, this book is a movement.

We call on women and men to stand up and be counted for gender equality.

Let us stand on the shoulders of the 46 women leaders in this book to enhance women's leadership in emerging markets.

May the generations to come enjoy the return on our investment in pioneering gender equality in the emerging markets.

Lerner (1997, 15) said, "This understanding of the problem of 'otherness' and the denial of self-definition led me to the study of women." From her mouth to our ears, we suggest that "our problem, our definition and our otherness as women" gives us no choice but to become the new "band" who writes our own present and future. Others will join the band along the way: may our collective energy and efforts be felt long after we are gone.

References

Alimo-Metcalfe, B. and J. Alban-Metcalfe. 2005. "Leadership: Time for a new direction?" *Leadership* 1(1): 51–71.

Ajzen, I. 1991. "Theories of cognitive self-regulation". *Organizational Behavior and Human Decision Processes* 50(2): 179–211.

Ashforth, B. E. and F. Mael. 1989. "Social identity theory and the organization". *Academy of Management Review* 14(1): 20–39.

Bandura, A. 1991. "Social cognitive theory of self-regulation". *Organizational Behaviour and Human Decision Processes* 50(2): 248–281.

Bernard-Powers, J. 2008. "Feminism and Gender in Education for Citizenship". In J. Arthur, I. Davies and C. Hahn (eds) *SAGE Handbook of Education for Citizenship and Democracy*. London: Sage, 314–328.

Bluen, S. 2013. *Talent Management in Emerging Markets*. Randburg: Knowres.

Blumberg, J. M. 2015. "Reconfiguring invisible labour: Dignifying domestic work and cultivating community in suburbia, Johannesburg". Faculty of Architecture, Wits School of Architecture and Planning, Johannesburg.

BSE (Bombay Stock Exchange). 2016. "Unemployment rate in India". *BSE*, August 14. Accessed August 15, 2016. http://unemploymentinindia.cmie.com/.

Carter, N. M. and H. M. Wagner. 2011. "The bottom line: Corporate performance and women's representation on boards (2004–2008)". *Catalyst*, March 1. Accessed August 13, 2016. www.catalyst.org/system/files/the_bottom_line_corp orate_performance_and_women's_representation_on_boards_(2004-2008).pdf.

Catalyst. 2016. "Pyramid: Women in S&P 500 companies". *Catalyst*, February 3. Retrieved March 23, 2016. www.catalyst.org/knowledge/women-sp-500-companies.

Catalyst. 2013. "Women in Accounting". *Catalyst*, March 28. Retrieved March 23, 2016. www.catalyst.org/knowledge/women-accounting.

Chant, S. and C. Sweetman. 2012. "Fixing women or fixing the world? 'Smart economics', efficiency approaches, and gender equality in development". *Gender and Development* 20(3): 517–529.

De Beauvoir, S. 1949. *The Second Sex*. Transl. and edited by H. M. Parsley in 1997. London: Gallimard.

Deloitte. 2014 "Global human capital trends: Engaging the 21st-century work-force." Deloitte report. Accessed February 17, 2017. www2.deloitte.com/global/ en/pages/human-capital/articles/human-capital-trends-2014.html.

Department of Labour. 2016. "16th Commission for Employment Equity annual report". Department of Labour, Pretoria.

Derks, B., C. van Laar and N. Ellemers. 2016. "The queen bee phenomenon: Why women leaders distance themselves from junior women". *Leadership Quarterly* 27(3): 456–469.

Eagly, A. H. 2013. "Why 'lean in'? Hybrid style succeeds, and women are best at it". *New York Times*, March 20. Accessed August 10, 2016, www.nytimes.com/room fordebate/2013/03/20/shery-sandberg-says-lean-in-but-is-that-really-the-way-to-lead /why-lean-in-hybrid-style-succeeds-and-women-are-best-at-it.

Eagly, A. H. and M. C. Johannesen-Schmidt. 2001. "The Leadership Styles of Women and Men". *Journal of Social Issues* 57(4): 781–797.

Eagly, A. H. and S. J. Karau. 2002. "Role congruity theory of prejudice toward female leaders". *Psychological Review* 109(3): 573.

Eagly, A. H. and L. L. Carli. 2007. "Women and the labyrinth of leadership". *Harvard Business Review* 85(9): 62.

Elliot, C. and V. Stead 2008. "Learning from leading women's experience: Towards a sociological understanding". *Leadership* 4(2): 159–180.

Fitzsimmons, T. W. and V. J. Callan. 2016. "Applying a capital perspective to explain continued gender inequality in the C-suite". *Leadership Quarterly* 27(3): 354–370.

Fitzsimmons, T. W., V. J. Callan and N. Paulsen. 2014. "Gender disparity in the C-suite: Do male and female CEOs differ in how they reached the top?" *Leadership Quarterly* 25(2): 245–266.

Fletcher, J. K. 2004. "The paradox of post-heroic leadership: An essay on gender, power and transformational change". *Leadership Quarterly* 15(5): 647–661.

Franchi, V. 2003. "The racialization of affirmative action in organizational discourses: A case study of symbolic racism in post-apartheid South Africa". *International Journal of Intercultural Relations* 27(2): 157–187.

Frederick, A. 2013. "Bringing narrative in: Race–gender, storytelling, political ambition and women's paths to political office". *Journal of Women, Politics and Policy* 34(2) 113–137.

Gherardi, S. and B. Poggio. 2001. "Creating and recreating gender order in organisations". *Journal of World Business* 36(3): 245–259.

Glass, C. and A. Cook. 2016. "Leading at the top: Understanding women's challenges above the glass ceiling". *Leadership Quarterly* 27(1): 51–63.

Grant Thornton. 2015. "Women in business: The path to leadership". Accessed August 12, 2016. www.grantthornton.be/Resources/IBR-2015-Women-in-Business.pdf.

Grant Thornton. 2016. "Women in business: Turning promise into practice". Accessed August 12, 2016. www.grantthornton.global/globalassets/wib_turning_promise_into_practice.pdf.

Grover, V. K. 2015. "Second-generation gender bias: Invisible barriers holding women back in organisations". *International Journal of Applied Research* 1(4): 1–4.

Heilman, M. E. 2012. "Gender stereotypes and workplace bias". *Research in Organizational Behavior* 32: 113–135.

Helgesen, S. 1995. *The Female Advantage: Women's Ways of Leadership*. New York: Doubleday.

Hiller, V. 2014. "Gender inequality, endogenous cultural norms, and economic development". *Scandinavian Journal of Economics* 116(2): 455–481.

Holvino, E. 2010. "Intersections: The simultaneity of race, gender and class in organization studies". *Gender, Work and Organization* 17(3): 248–277.

Ibarra, H., R. J. Ely and D. M. Kolb. 2013. "Women rising: the unseen barriers". *Harvard Business Review* 91(9): 60–61.

Khalaf, R. 2014. "Ambition and growth help narrow gender gap". *Financial Times*, March 7, Special report: Women in business: Emerging markets. Accessed August 15, 2016. http://im.ft-static.com/content/images/0724cd16-d149-11e3-bdbb-00144fea bdc0.pdf.

Kolb, D., J. Williams and C. Frohlinger. 2010. *Her Place at the Table: A Women's Guide to Negotiating Five Key Challenges to Leadership Success*. San Francisco, CA: Jossey-Bass.

Lerner, G. 1997. *Why History Matters*. New York: Oxford University Press.

Maxwell, J. A. 2013. *Qualitative Research Design: An Interactive Approach*. 3rd ed. London: Sage Publications.

Mugadza, N. 2016. "*Code families research data report for women's leadership in emerging markets project*". Unpublished research report by ACOF Consulting for the Gordon Institute of Business Science, University of Pretoria.

Perriton, L. 2006. "Does women + a network = career progression?" *Leadership* 2(1): 101–113.

Prasad, E. S. 2016. "Five myths about China's economy." *Washington Post*, 7 January. Accessed August 16, 2016. www.washingtonpost.com/opinions/five-m

yths-about-chinas-economy/2016/01/07/08a8d5e6-b4c4-11e5-a842-0feb51d1d124_
story.html?utm_term=.4fee8755aa8b.

Rautenbach, R., M. Sutherland and C. B. Scheepers. 2015. "The process by which executives unlearn their attachments in order to facilitate change". *South African Journal of Labour Relations* 39(2): 145–164.

Rosette, A. S., C. Z. Koval, A. Ma and R. Livingston. 2016. "Race matters for women leaders: Intersectional effects on agentic deficiencies and penalties". *Journal of Applied Psychology* 27: 429–445.

Rosser-Mims, D. M. 2015. "Black American women's political experiences: Leadership lessons for women globally". In S. R. Madsen, F. W. Ngunjiri, K. A. Longman and C. Cherrey (eds) *Women and Leadership Around the World*. Charlotte, NC: Information Age Publishing, 171–186.

SAICA. 2009. "Celebrating women chartered accountants [CAs(SA)] – SA's women CAs(SA) are creating a new glass ceiling mould". *Saica*, August. Accessed February 23, 2017. www.saica.co.za/tabid/695/itemid/1760/pageid/2/la nguage/en-ZA/Celebrating-women-chartered-accountants-CAsSA.aspx.

Scheepers, C.B. 2012. *Coaching Leaders: The 7 "P" Tools to Propel Change*. Randburg: Knowres.

Statista. 2016. "Unemployment rate in member states of the European Union". May. Accessed August 15, 2016. www.statista.com/statistics/268830/unemploym ent-rate-in-eu-countries/.

Statistics South Africa. 2015. "National and provincial labour market: Youth, Q1: 2008–Q1: 2015". Department of Labour, Pretoria.

World Bank. 2016. "Unemployment, youth total (% of total labor force ages 15–24)", International Labour Organization figures, 2014 and 2015. Accessed August 15, 2016. http://data.worldbank.org/indicator/SL.UEM.1524.ZS.

Trading Economics. 2016a. "South Africa credit rating". Accessed August 16, 2016. www.tradingeconomics.com/south-africa/rating.

Trading Economics. 2016b. "Russia GDP growth rate". Accessed August 12, 2016. www.tradingeconomics.com/russia/gdp-growth.

Trading Economics. 2016c. "South Africa GDP growth rate". Accessed August 12, 2016. www.tradingeconomics.com/south-africa/gdp-growth.

Trading Economics. 2016d. "Brazil unemployment rate up to record high of 11.9%". Accessed August 12, 2016. www.tradingeconomics.com/articles/12292016113256.htm

Tsang, A. 2014. "Expectations, pressures and biases drag down salaries". *Financial Times*, 7 March, Special report: Women in business: Emerging markets. Accessed 15 August, 2016. http://im.ft-static.com/content/images/0724cd16-d149-11e3-bdbb-0014 4feabdc0.pdf.

Turner, J. C. and H. Tajfel. 1986. "The social identity theory of intergroup behavior". In W. G. Austin and S. Worchel (eds) *Psychology of Intergroup Relations*. Monterey, CA: Brooks Cole, 7–24.

Von Bertalanffy, L. 1973. *General Systems Theory: Foundations, Development, Applications*. Harmondsworth: Penguin.

Wang, M. and E. Kelan. 2013. "The gender quota and female leadership: Effects of the Norwegian gender quota on board chairs and CEOs". *Journal of Business Ethics* 117(3): 449–466.

Wells, N. 2016. "Charts: What is the real unemployment rate?" *CNBC*, June 3. Accessed August 15, 2016. www.cnbc.com/2016/06/03/charts-whats-the-rea l-unemployment-rate.html.

Index